GREAT CHRISTIAN JURISTS IN AMERICAN HISTORY

From the early days of European settlement in North America, Christianity has had a profound impact on American law and culture. This volume profiles nineteen of America's most influential Christian jurists from the early colonial era to the present day. Anyone interested in American legal history and jurisprudence, the role Christianity has played throughout the nation's history, and the relationship between faith and law will enjoy this worthy and unique study. The jurists covered in this collection were pious men and women, but that does not mean they agreed on how faith should inform law. From Roger Williams and John Cotton to Antonin Scalia and Mary Ann Glendon, America's great Christian jurists have brought their faith to bear on the practice of law in different ways and to different effects.

Daniel L. Dreisbach is a professor in the School of Public Affairs at American University in Washington, DC. His research interests include the intersection of religion, law, and politics in American public life. He has authored or edited ten books, including *Thomas Jefferson and the Wall of Separation between Church and State* (2002) and *Reading the Bible with the Founding Fathers* (2017). He has published numerous book chapters, reviews, and articles in scholarly journals, including *American Journal of Legal History*, *Journal of Church and State*, *Politics and Religion*, and *William and Mary Quarterly*.

Mark David Hall is Herbert Hoover Distinguished Professor of Politics and Faculty Fellow in the William Penn Honors Program at George Fox University. Mark has written, edited, or coedited a dozen books, including *Did America Have a Christian Founding?: Separating Modern Myth from Historical Truth* (2019); *Roger Sherman and the Creation of the American Republic* (2013); and *The Sacred Rights of Conscience: Selected Readings on Religious Liberty and Church-State Relations in the American Founding* (2009).

LAW AND CHRISTIANITY

Series Editor

John Witte, Jr., Emory University

The Law and Christianity series publishes cutting-edge work on Catholic, Protestant, and Orthodox Christian contributions to public, private, penal, and procedural law and legal theory. The series aims to promote deep Christian reflection by leading scholars on the fundamentals of law and politics, to build further ecumenical legal understanding across Christian denominations, and to link and amplify the diverse and sometimes isolated Christian legal voices and visions at work in the academy. Works collected by the series include groundbreaking monographs, historical and thematic anthologies, and translations by leading scholars around the globe.

Books in the Series

Great Christian Jurists and Legal Collections in the First Millennium
Philip L. Reynolds

English Ecclesiastical Lawyers: A History of Their Life and Work
R. H. Helmholz

Law, Love, and Freedom: From the Sacred to the Secular Joshua Neoh

Great Christian Jurists in French History Olivier Descamps and Rafael Domingo

Church Law in Modernity: Toward a Theory of Canon Law between Nature and Culture Judith Hahn

Common Law and Natural Law in America: From the Puritans to the Legal Realists Andrew Forsyth

Care for the World: Laudato Si' and Catholic Social Thought in an Era of Climate Crisis edited by Frank Pasquale

Church, State, and Family: Reconciling Traditional Teachings and Modern Liberties John Witte, Jr.

Great Christian Jurists in Spanish History Rafael Domingo and Javier Martínez-Torrón

Under Caesar's Sword: How Christians Respond to Persecution edited by Daniel Philpott and Timothy Samuel Shah

God and the Illegal Alien Robert W. Heimburger

Christianity and Family Law John Witte, Jr. and Gary S. Hauk

Christianity and Natural Law Norman Doe

Great Christian Jurists in English History edited by Mark Hill, QC and R. H. Helmholz

Agape, Justice, and Law edited by Robert F. Cochran, Jr and Zachary R. Calo

Calvin's Political Theology and the Public Engagement of the Church Matthew J. Tuininga

God and the Secular Legal System Rafael Domingo

How Marriage Became One of the Sacraments Philip L. Reynolds

Christianity and Freedom (Volume I: Historical Perspectives, Volume II: Contemporary Perspectives) edited by Timothy Samuel Shah and Allen D. Hertzke

The Western Case for Monogamy over Polygamy John Witte, Jr.

The Distinctiveness of Religion in American Law Kathleen A. Brady

Pope Benedict XVI's Legal Thought Marta Cartabia and Andrea Simoncini

Great Christian Jurists in American History edited by Daniel L. Dreisbach and Mark David Hall

Great Christian Jurists in American History

Edited by

DANIEL L. DREISBACH

American University

MARK DAVID HALL

George Fox University

CAMBRIDGE
UNIVERSITY PRESS

CAMBRIDGE
UNIVERSITY PRESS

University Printing House, Cambridge CB2 8BS, United Kingdom

One Liberty Plaza, 20th Floor, New York, NY 10006, USA

477 Williamstown Road, Port Melbourne, VIC 3207, Australia

314–321, 3rd Floor, Plot 3, Splendor Forum, Jasola District Centre, New Delhi – 110025, India

79 Anson Road, #06–04/06, Singapore 079906

Cambridge University Press is part of the University of Cambridge.

It furthers the University's mission by disseminating knowledge in the pursuit of education, learning, and research at the highest international levels of excellence.

www.cambridge.org
Information on this title: www.cambridge.org/9781108475358
DOI: 10.1017/9781108609937

First published 2019

Printed and bound in Great Britain by Clays Ltd, Elcograf S.p.A.

A catalogue record for this publication is available from the British Library.

Library of Congress Cataloging-in-Publication Data
NAMES: Dreisbach, Daniel L., editor. | Hall, Mark David., 1966– editor.
TITLE: Great Christian jurists in American history / Daniel L. Dreisbach, American University, Washington DC; Mark David Hall, George Fox University.
DESCRIPTION: Cambridge, United Kingdom ; New York, NY, USA : Cambridge University Press, 2019.
IDENTIFIERS: LCCN 2018059158 | ISBN 9781108475358
SUBJECTS: LCSH: Christian lawyers – United States – Biography.
CLASSIFICATION: LCC KF353 .G74 2019 | DDC 340.092/8773–dc23
LC record available at https://lccn.loc.gov/2018059158

ISBN 978-1-108-47535-8 Hardback

This book is dedicated to the men and women in the legal profession who have devoted their time, talent, and resources to defending what many American founders called "the sacred rights of conscience."

Contents

Contributors

Thomas C. Berg is the James L. Oberstar Professor of Law and Public Policy at the University of St. Thomas School of Law (Minnesota), where he teaches religious liberty, constitutional law, intellectual property, and the religious liberty appellate clinic. He is the author of *The State and Religion in a Nutshell* (3rd edn., 2016) and coauthor, with Michael W. McConnell and Christopher C. Lund, of *Religion and the Constitution* (4th edn., 2016). He has written more than 100 scholarly and popular articles, and approximately fifty briefs in the U.S. Supreme Court and other courts on freedom of religion and expression. He codirected St. Thomas's Murphy Institute for Catholic Thought, Law, and Public Policy, and he contributes to Mirror of Justice, SCOTUS Blog, and other weblogs. He has earned degrees from the University of Chicago (law, religious studies), University of Oxford (philosophy and politics), where he studied as a Rhodes Scholar, and Northwestern University (journalism). He practiced law in Chicago and was a law clerk to a federal appellate judge.

Wendell Bird is a visiting scholar at Emory University School of Law. He earned a DPhil degree in legal history from the University of Oxford and a JD from Yale Law School. He is the author of *Press and Speech under Assault: The Early Supreme Court Justices, the Sedition Act of 1798, and the Campaign against Dissent* (2016) and *Criminal Dissent: Prosecutions Under the Alien and Sedition Acts of 1798* (forthcoming 2019).

Daniel D. Blinka is Professor of Law at Marquette University Law School. He holds JD and PhD (American History) degrees from the University of Wisconsin–Madison. In addition to books and articles on evidence law, trials, and criminal procedure, he has written articles on legal history published in the *Journal of the Early Republic* and *American Journal of Legal History*. He is currently working on the history of jury trials in the early American republic and is writing a book on the Sixth Amendment confrontation right as part of Wright & Graham, *Federal Practice and Procedure: Evidence*.

Gerard V. Bradley is Professor of Law at the University of Notre Dame, where he teaches Legal Ethics and Constitutional Law. At Notre Dame, he directs (with John Finnis) the Natural Law Institute and coedits *The American Journal of Jurisprudence*, an international forum for legal philosophy. He is a senior fellow of the Witherspoon Institute in Princeton, New Jersey, and he served for many years as President of the Fellowship of Catholic Scholars. Bradley received his BA and JD degrees from Cornell University, graduating *summa cum laude* from the law school in 1980. After serving in the Trial Division of the Manhattan District Attorney's Office, he joined the law faculty at the University of Illinois. He moved to Notre Dame in 1992. Bradley has published over 100 scholarly articles and reviews. His most recent books are an edited collection of essays titled *Challenges to Religious Liberty in the Twenty-First Century* (2012) and *Essays on Law, Religion, and Morality* (2013). In 2019, Cambridge will publish his volume (coedited with Christian Brugger) on Catholic Social Teaching.

Jane E. Calvert is Associate Professor of History at the University of Kentucky and Director/Chief Editor of the John Dickinson Writings Project. She earned a PhD degree at the University of Chicago. Her research interests are in the intersection of theology and political thought during the American founding era. Her publications include *Quaker Constitutionalism and the Political Thought of John Dickinson* (2009), *Selected Writings of Thomas Paine* (2015), and numerous articles and essays in popular and scholarly journals. She is currently working to produce *The Complete Writings and Selected Correspondence of John Dickinson*, which has received support from the National Endowment for the Humanities, the National Historic Publications and Records Commission, American Philosophical Society, the William Nelson Cromwell Foundation, and several other private institutions and foundations.

Paolo G. Carozza is Professor of Law and Concurrent Professor of Political Science and Director of the Kellogg Institute for International Studies, at the University of Notre Dame. With expertise in comparative constitutional law, human rights, law and development, and international law, he focuses his research on Latin America, Western Europe, and international themes more broadly. His most recent book is *Italian Constitutional Justice in Global Context* (2016), and his numerous articles and book chapters have concentrated primarily on foundational principles of human rights law, such as human dignity, democracy, and subsidiarity. A member of the Inter-American Commission on Human Rights (2006–2010), he served as its president in 2008–2009. He has also served the Holy See in various capacities and was appointed in 2016 to be a member of the Pontifical Academy of Social Sciences.

Nathan S. Chapman is Associate Professor of Law at the University of Georgia School of Law. He has written articles in leading law reviews about the history of due process of law, religious freedom, and Christianity and the law. Before joining the faculty at the University of Georgia, he was the Executive Director of the Constitutional Law Center at Stanford Law School, practiced law at WilmerHale in Washington, DC, and clerked for the Honorable Gerald B. Tjoflat of the U.S. Court of Appeals for the Eleventh Circuit. He studied law and theology at Duke University.

Donald L. Drakeman is Distinguished Research Professor in the Program on Constitutional Studies at the University of Notre Dame, and a fellow in Health Management at the University of Cambridge. He has taught in the Department of Politics at Princeton University and at Notre Dame Law School. A fellow of the Royal Historical Society, he has written or edited several books on religion and law, including, most recently, *Church, State, and Original Intent* (2010), which was a *Choice* Outstanding Academic Title. Several of his works have been cited by the Supreme Courts of the United States and the Philippines. He is a graduate of Dartmouth College, and he received a JD degree from Columbia University and a PhD degree from Princeton University.

Daniel L. Dreisbach is Professor of Legal Studies, and Affiliate Professor in the Department of History, at American University in Washington, DC. He earned a DPhil degree from the University of Oxford, where he studied as a Rhodes Scholar, and a JD degree from the University of Virginia. His research interests include the intersection of religion, law, and politics in American public life. He has authored, edited, or coedited ten books, including *Thomas Jefferson and the Wall of Separation between Church and State* (2002) and *Reading the Bible with the Founding Fathers* (2017). He has published numerous book chapters, reviews, and articles in scholarly journals, including *American Journal of Legal History, Constitutional Commentary, Journal of Church and State, Politics and Religion*, and *William and Mary Quarterly*.

Mark David Hall is Herbert Hoover Distinguished Professor of Politics and faculty fellow in the William Penn Honors Program at George Fox University. He is also an affiliated fellow at the Center for the Study of Law and Religion at Emory University and a senior fellow at Baylor University's Institute for Studies of Religion. He has written, edited, or co-edited a dozen books, including *The Political and Legal Philosophy of James Wilson, 1742–1798* (1997), *The Founders on God and Government* (2004), *The Forgotten Founders on Religion and Public Life* (2009), *The Sacred Rights of Conscience: Selected Readings on*

Religious Liberty and Church-State Relations in the American Founding (2009), *Roger Sherman and the Creation of the American Republic* (2013), *Faith and the Founders of the American Republic* (2014), and *Did America Have a Christian Founding?: Separating Modern Myth from Historical Truth* (2019).

Glenn A. Moots is Professor of Political Science and Philosophy at Northwood University and Director of the University's Forum for Citizenship and Enterprise. He is author of *Politics Reformed: The Anglo-American Legacy of Covenant Theology* (2007) and coeditor, with Phil Hamilton, of *Justifying Revolution: Law, Virtue, and Violence in the American War of Independence* (2018). He has also published a variety of essays and review essays in edited collections and academic journals, including *American Political Thought*, *Locke Studies*, *Perspectives on Political Science*, *Journal of Church and State*, and *Journal of Religious History*. He earned a PhD at Louisiana State University. He has also served as a William E. Simon fellow in the James Madison Program in American Ideals and Institutions at Princeton University.

Andrew R. Murphy is Professor of Political Science at Virginia Commonwealth University. His research focuses on Anglo-American political thought, particularly on the relationship between religion and politics. He is the author, most recently, of *William Penn: A Life* (2018) and *Liberty, Conscience, and Toleration: The Political Thought of William Penn* (2016). Murphy is also coauthor, with David S. Gutterman, of *Political Religion and Religious Politics: Navigating Identities in the United States* (2015). His previous books include *Prodigal Nation: Moral Decline and Divine Punishment from New England to 9/11* (2008) and *Conscience and Community: Revisiting Toleration and Religious Dissent in Early Modern England and America* (2001). He edited *The Blackwell Companion to Religion and Violence* (2011) and *The Political Writings of William Penn* (2002). Murphy has taught at Rutgers University, Valparaiso University, the University of Chicago, and Villanova University.

Linda Przybyszewski is Associate Professor of History, Concurrent Faculty at the Law School, and Affiliated Faculty with the Gender Studies program, at the University Notre Dame. Her scholarly work considers how people have used the power and authority of the state in the name of race, morality, religion, and even beauty. She is the author of the American Historical Association's guide to *Religion, Morality and the Constitutional Order* (2011), *The Republic According to John Marshall Harlan* (1999), and *The Lost Art of Dress: The Women Who Once Made America Stylish* (2014). She received a Public Scholar Award from the National Endowment for the Humanities for 2016 to finish a book on the Cincinnati Bible War of 1869.

Charles J. Reid, Jr. is Professor of Law at the University of St. Thomas (Minnesota). He has published on a broad range of topics in the fields of legal history and jurisprudence. He has published important works on the Roman law of succession and the Emperor Augustus's morals legislation. He has also written studies in the field of canon law, especially in the areas of war and peace, and marriage and sexuality. He is the author of *Power over the Body, Equality in the Family: Rights and Domestic Relations in Medieval Canon Law* (2004) and editor of *Peace in a Nuclear Age: The Bishops' Pastoral Letter in Perspective* (1987). He is currently writing in the field of historical jurisprudence. He earned a PhD at Cornell University, under the supervision of Professor Brian Tierney, and degrees in canon law and American law at the Catholic University of America.

Darren Staloff is Professor of Early American History at The City College of New York and Director of the Hertog Scholars Program, Macaulay Honors College, The City College of New York. He received his PhD from Columbia University and a postdoctoral fellowship at the Omohundro Institute of Early American History and Culture. He has been awarded scholarships from the National Endowment for the Humanities, as well as from the James Madison Program in American Ideals and Institutions at Princeton University. His scholarly interests focus on political and intellectual history in early America and the Atlantic littoral. In addition to various essays, he is the author of two books: *The Making of an American Thinking Class: Intellectuals and Intelligentsia in Puritan Massachusetts* (1998) and *Hamilton, Adams, Jefferson: The Politics of Enlightenment and the American Founding* (2005). His current research project is an overview of the Enlightenment in early America.

James R. Stoner, Jr. is Hermann Moyse, Jr., Professor and Director of the Eric Voegelin Institute in the Department of Political Science at Louisiana State University. He is the author of *Common-Law Liberty: Rethinking American Constitutionalism* (2003) and *Common Law and Liberal Theory: Coke, Hobbes, and the Origins of American Constitutionalism* (1992), as well as a number of articles and essays. A senior fellow of the Witherspoon Institute, he has coedited three books the Institute has published: *The Thriving Society* (with Harold James, 2015), *The Social Costs of Pornography* (with Donna M. Hughes, 2010), and *Rethinking Business Management* (with Samuel Gregg, 2007). He also coedited, with Alan Levine and Thomas W. Merrill, *The Political Thought of the Civil War* (2018). His current research is on the nature of the legislative power, on freedom of speech, and on the legacy of Aristotle.

John Witte, Jr., JD (Harvard), Dr. Theol. h.c. (Heidelberg), is Robert W. Woodruff University Professor of Law, McDonald Distinguished Professor, and Director of the Center for the Study of Law and Religion at

Emory University. A leading specialist in legal history, family law, religious liberty, human rights, and law and Christianity, he has published 250 articles, 16 journal symposia, and 31 books. His recent titles include *The Western Case for Monogamy over Polygamy* (2015), *Religion and the American Constitutional Experiment* (4th edn., 2016); *Christianity and Family Law: An Introduction* (2017); and *Church, State, and Family: Reconciling Traditional Teachings and Modern Liberties* (2018).

Preface

The first English settlers in British North America brought with them laws and legal traditions steeped in Christianity and its sacred text. Long before their arrival in the early seventeenth century, Christianity had infused the English legal culture, specifically the common law, that the colonists would bring to the New World. Indeed, leading jurists in both England and America claimed that the common law was rooted in Christianity and nothing in the common law is valid that is not consistent with divine revelation. Sir William Blackstone, for example, wrote in his famous *Commentaries on the Laws of England* that "Christianity is part of the laws of England."[1]

When the colonists began to establish their own political communities and frame their own legal codes, they continued to draw on Christianity and the Bible.[2] The earliest expressions of law framed in the colonies, both in Virginia and New England, bear the unmistakable influence of Christianity.[3] New England's Puritan colonies, especially, set out to establish Bible commonwealths and remake political society in conformity with biblical laws as they understood and interpreted them in their religious traditions. Christianity's

[1] William Blackstone, *Commentaries on the Laws of England* (Oxford: Clarendon Press, 1765–1769), 4:59. This view, it must be acknowledged, was not uncontested in England or America. See John Cartwright, *The English Constitution Produced and Illustrated* (London: T. Cleary, 1823), 388, and Thomas Jefferson, "Whether Christianity Is Part of the Common Law?" (1764?) in *The Sacred Rights of Conscience: Selected Readings on Religious Liberty and Church-State Relations in the American Founding*, ed. Daniel L. Dreisbach and Mark David Hall (Indianapolis: Liberty Fund, 2009), 539–543. See generally Chapter 8 in this volume.

[2] See David D. Hall, *A Reforming People: Puritanism and the Transformation of Public Life in New England* (New York: Alfred A. Knopf, 2011); Michael P. Winship, *Godly Republicanism: Puritans, Pilgrims, and a City on a Hill* (Cambridge, MA: Harvard University Press, 2012).

[3] See Daniel L. Dreisbach, "The Bible in American Law," in *Oxford Handbook on the Bible in America*, ed. Paul Gutjahr (New York: Oxford University Press, 2017), 276–288.

pervasive influence on early colonial legal culture is no surprise because it was integral to the colonists' identity, cultural traditions, and civic pursuits. This influence extended to principles of rule of law and due process, forms and role of civil government, the rights and responsibilities of righteous citizens, and the protection of religious liberty. Christianity, in short, made significant and substantive contributions to American jurisprudence. Significantly, however, Americans making arguments purportedly based on Christianity and the Bible sometimes found themselves on opposite sides of some of the most contentious debates in American society, including the right to resist political tyranny, the scope of religious liberty, and the legitimacy of slavery, illustrating, perhaps, the flexible and contested use of theology and Scripture in legal and political debates.

Christianity and the Bible were often the explicit bases of early colonial laws. Colonial statutes in both southern and northern colonies borrowed explicitly and extensively from biblical codes, especially the Ten Commandments. For instance, the "Articles, Lawes, and Orders, Divine, Politique, and Martiall for the Colony in Virginea," as enlarged in 1611, prohibited speaking "against the holy and blessed Trinitie," blaspheming God's holy name, deriding or defying God's holy word, Sabbath breaking, murdering, and committing adultery.[4] In New England, similar legal provisions were often accompanied by specific references to biblical authority supporting them. The influential "Massachusetts Body of Liberties" (1641), for example, borrowed from Mosaic law even more explicitly than Virginia's law, mandating the death penalty for "worship[ping] any other god, but the lord god"; "Blasphem[ing] the name of God, the father, Sonne, or Holie ghost"; and committing adultery or engaging in sexual sins forbidden in Mosaic law.[5]

As amply illustrated in this volume, many leading jurists in the colonies identified as Christians and unapologetically articulated a jurisprudence they believed was derived from Christian thought. Influential jurists of this age, such as the Puritans John Winthrop and Nathaniel Ward, were as learned in biblical theology as in law, and their training in one discipline was frequently used in the service of the other. More broadly, judges in the colonial era and beyond often cited the Bible as authority in their legal opinions.

4 "Articles, Lawes, and Orders, Divine, Politique, and Martiall for the Colony in Virginea" (1610, 1611), in *Sacred Rights of Conscience*, 84–86.

5 "Massachusetts Body of Liberties" (1641), in *Colonial Origins of the American Constitution: A Documentary History*, ed. Donald S. Lutz (Indianapolis: Liberty Fund, 1998), 83–84.

The framers of a distinctly American constitutional tradition that emerged in the colonial era and was refined in the founding era looked to the Bible and Christian tradition, among other sources, for political and legal concepts that they sought to incorporate into their constitutional regimes. For example, a biblical anthropology that views humankind as essentially fallen inspired a constitutional architecture characterized by the separation of government powers and checks and balances, reflecting a reluctance to vest unchecked civic power in the hands of sinful rulers. Some in the founding generation saw in the separated powers of prophet, priest, and king described in Deuteronomy 16–18 a model worthy of study and, perhaps, emulation in their own constitutions. The New England Puritans and some key figures in the founding generation believed that the Hebrew commonwealth described in the Old Testament provided a model for republican government. There were those who thought that passages chronicling the experiences of the Hebrew polity, more specifically, supported notions of consent of the governed and representative government. These are a few examples of the ways, some commentators have argued, that Christianity contributed to the American constitutional tradition. Other constitutional principles and provisions were arguably informed by biblical thought.[6]

Diverse intellectual, legal, and political traditions and perspectives have informed American law and politics. Among the influences scholars have identified and studied include British constitutionalism, Enlightenment liberalism in various forms, and republicanism (including Hebraic, classical, and civic).[7] This volume gives evidence that another, often overlooked, source of influence on the American legal system and jurisprudential thought is Christianity. While it is important to identify and examine this source of influence, its significance should not be overstated nor should other perspectives be ignored. This volume's focus on Christianity's influence on leading jurists acknowledges Christianity's impact on American law and jurisprudence, but it is not meant to discount, much less dismiss, other traditions. Even before independence and adoption of the US Constitution, influential jurists and jurisprudential perspectives more secular and at times antagonistic to Christianity began to emerge. These jurists and jurisprudential schools of thought were increasingly in tension with legal perspectives more in harmony with traditional Christian thought. Indeed, by the twentieth century,

[6] See Introduction.

[7] For an introduction to and survey of diverse schools of political thought that influenced the American founding, see Alan Gibson, *Interpreting the Founding: Guide to the Enduring Debates over the Origins and Foundations of the American Republic* (Lawrence: University Press of Kansas, 2006).

principles of nonestablishment and church–state separation were increasingly deployed to exclude from public fora legal arguments and opinions apparently informed by Christianity or the Bible.

This volume focuses on the interplay between religion and law in the American experience by examining the jurisprudence of selected influential Christian jurists representing various eras in American history, from the establishment of English settlements in the early seventeenth century to the twenty-first century. By "jurist" we mean men and women who have had an important influence on the creation, application, and/or interpretation of constitutional, case, and statutory law or the philosophy of law. This broad definition includes judges, scholars, legislators, and legal practitioners. A few of the profiled jurists are better known for their professional pursuits as political or religious leaders than for their contributions to the law, but we believe these profiles reveal why they merit inclusion in this volume.

The essays in this volume take seriously the role of religion in informing the thought and actions of the profiled jurists. Each chapter commissioned for this volume examines the life and thought of a selected jurist who not only had a significant influence on law but also clearly identified with the Christian tradition and purportedly drew on Christianity to inform their jurisprudence. Religion mattered to these jurists, and, to varying degrees, they all sought to apply their religious beliefs to their professional pursuits. Most, if not all, of these jurists worked consciously to apply their Christian faith, theology, biblical interpretations, and ethical framework to their understanding or reform of the laws of the civil state; influential treatises or constitutions, statutes, or canons they drafted; or landmark cases they decided or litigated.

Selecting just a handful of jurists from the last four centuries of American history was an extraordinarily difficult task. The jurists profiled were chosen in consultation with approximately fifty scholars from a variety of academic disciplines who assisted us in identifying and evaluating the contributions of Christian jurists in American history. (Regrettably, due to space limitations, we were unable to include in this volume an examination of some important jurists we identified in this selection process and acknowledge as worthy of scholarly attention.) We urged the contributors to examine their subjects in the manner they thought appropriate. That said, to the extent possible, each chapter includes a biographical sketch of the profiled jurist, including mention of the jurist's religious beliefs, denominational affiliations, etc.; a brief review of the scholarship on that jurist with an emphasis on whether Christianity's influence on his or her jurisprudence has been studied adequately; an examination of the influence Christianity played on various aspects of the jurist's legal philosophy and/or substantive legal positions; and a discussion of the extent to which the profiled jurist influenced or represents a larger group or tradition.

It should come as little surprise that most of the jurists profiled in this volume are white males. Women and persons of color were excluded from the practice of law for much of American history and, once they gained entry into the profession, were often marginalized. We would have liked to have included more jurists who were not white males, but space limitations forced us to make difficult choices. In so doing, we decided that, in terms of sustained influence on American jurisprudence, we would not replace John Marshall Harlan with, say, Myra Bradwell or Antonin Scalia with Clarence Thomas. We understand that some readers will disagree with these decisions, and we hope that this volume encourages scholarship on jurists we did not profile.[8]

Prior to the twentieth century, most prominent jurists were Protestants (Roger Taney is a notable exception to this rule). Since the 1950s, arguably a disproportionate percentage of distinguished Christian jurists have been Roman Catholics – a shift illustrated by the fact that from Justice John Paul Steven's retirement in 2010 until Justice Antonin Scalia's death in 2016, there were six Roman Catholics and no Protestants sitting on the US Supreme Court. This change is also reflected in the latter chapters in this volume – four of the last six essays profile influential Catholic jurists.

We find it difficult to generalize about *how* faith influenced each jurist. Some explicitly drew legal guidance from the Bible, Christian theology, and church traditions. Others did not clearly do so, and some indisputably pious jurists even contended that it is inappropriate for judges to engage in such an enterprise (see Chapter 14). It is fair to say, however, that the profiled jurists in the early colonial era reflected the religious perspectives of the communities and the times in which they lived. Many of the Christian jurists examined in this volume from the late twentieth and twenty-first centuries, by contrast, have espoused countercultural values and perspectives insofar as their jurisprudence challenges aspects of an increasingly secular and postmodern culture. It is perhaps no coincidence that many of the jurists profiled early in the volume held high political or judicial offices, whereas those considered later in the collection are more likely to be academics with less direct political or judicial involvement.

[8] In some cases, of course, scholarship already exists on the men and women we were unable to include. See, for instance, Jane M. Friedman, *America's First Woman Lawyer* (Amherst, NY: Prometheus Books, 1993) and Ralph A. Rossum, *Understanding Clarence Thomas: The Jurisprudence of Constitutional Restoration* (Lawrence: University Press of Kansas, 2014).

Professor John Witte, Jr. is the series editor of Cambridge Studies in Law and Christianity, which includes this subseries on "Great Christian Jurists in World History." We are grateful to him for his vision and able editorial guidance and honored that he invited us to edit this volume on American jurists. He provided invaluable advice regarding possible subjects for examination and contributors – and he penned an excellent chapter for the volume. We thank the Center for the Study of Law and Religion at Emory University, especially Amy Wheeler and Anita Mann, for indispensable administrative support. In addition, we are indebted to the interdisciplinary group of scholars who contributed to this volume by evaluating and recommending jurists for inclusion in the project or writing chapters. The direction of Senior Editor John Berger and his able team at Cambridge University Press, along with the recommendations of external reviewers, improved the book significantly. The Maguire Oil Company provided generous support for this project. We are deeply thankful to Mr. Cary M. Maguire, Chair and President of the Maguire Oil Company in Dallas, Texas, as well as other members of the company for their support. Both editors are grateful for institutional support from their respective universities – American University and George Fox University.

Introduction: Christianity and American Law

Daniel L. Dreisbach

Christianity and its sacred text have had a distinct and significant influence on American jurisprudence. This reflects Christianity's expansive influence on Western culture in general and legal tradition in particular. Christian influences were introduced to American legal culture and incorporated into law both directly through appeals to biblical texts and indirectly through the adoption of legal systems and practices that had long before drawn on Christian beliefs and customs. The first English colonists in British North America brought with them the common law, a system of jurisprudence they had known in England. According to authoritative common law jurists, including Sir Edward Coke, Sir Matthew Hale, Sir William Blackstone, and Lord Mansfield, Christianity is and always has been the foundation of the common law, and any expression of the common law inconsistent with divine revelation is invalid.[1] In colonies both north and south, the Bible was an important source for early colonial codes. The New England Puritans, especially, sought to establish Bible commonwealths based in part on biblical law as they understood it. A distinctly biblical influence – both Hebraic and Christian – was manifested in broad principles of law and politics and in specific laws, including provisions pertaining to Sunday or Sabbath observance, oaths, usury, blasphemy, marriage and domestic relations, various sexual practices, etc. And lest there be any doubt, written laws often included references to specific biblical authority for legal provisions contained in them. The law that emerged in the colonies was a blend of common law (adapted to local conditions), biblical law (interpreted through the lens of Protestant theology), and developing local customs.

A variety of intellectual, legal, and political traditions and perspectives informed American law and politics in the colonial and founding eras.

[1] See note 36 below.

Among the influences scholars have identified and studied are British constitutionalism, classical and civic republicanism, and Enlightenment liberalism (in a variety of forms). Christianity also contributed to American legal culture and jurisprudential thought, especially colonial and early national laws and traditions. Even before the adoption of the US Constitution, however, influential jurists and jurisprudential perspectives distinctly secular and at times antagonistic to Christianity began to emerge. These jurists and jurisprudential schools of thought were increasingly in tension with legal perspectives in harmony with traditional Christian thought. By the early nineteenth century and continuing to the present, secular and separationist perspectives increasingly challenged the propriety, legitimacy, and constitutionality of lingering Christian influences on law and politics. Thomas Jefferson, for example, disputed the ancient maxim that Christianity was the basis of common law.[2] Also, biblically inspired laws regarding Sabbath observance, blasphemy, and, in the twentieth century, the teaching of creation in public schools, were challenged through legislation and litigation.[3] Christianity's influence on law was strongest in the colonial era, but it continued to exert influence in the founding era and the centuries that followed, albeit to a diminishing extent as other, secular, jurisprudential perspectives emerged and exerted influence on the legal culture. Indeed, the vestiges of Christian influences on American law have, over the course of the last two centuries, faced increasing challenges in courts of law and public opinion.

This chapter reflects on Christianity's influence on American law, starting with a brief overview of the Bible's mark on colonial laws. Attention is then to turned to Christianity's and the Bible's contributions to an emerging constitutional tradition, culminating in the framing of the national constitution of 1787. Finally, several nineteenth-century controversies are briefly considered to illustrate challenges to Christian influences on selected laws and practices. This chapter's focus on Christianity's influence is not meant to discount, much less dismiss, other sources of influence or schools of thought that shaped American jurisprudence. Rather, highlighting Christianity's place in the legal culture provides a more complete picture of the ideas that informed American law.

[2] See note 34 below.

[3] See generally Daniel L. Dreisbach, "The Bible in American Law," in *The Oxford Handbook of the Bible in America*, ed. Paul C. Gutjahr (New York: Oxford University Press, 2017), 276–288 (portions of this work were adapted for this chapter); Patrick M. O'Neil, "Bible in American Law," in *Religion and American Law: An Encyclopedia*, ed. Paul Finkelman (New York: Garland Publishing, 2000), 30–35.

BIBLICAL INFLUENCES ON COLONIAL LEGAL CULTURE

Since the first colonists arrived and established permanent settlements in British North America, Christianity and the Bible have had a significant impact on American legal culture. The New England Puritans, in particular, set out to build Bible commonwealths based on God's law and Reformed theology; accordingly, they looked to the Bible in establishing political and legal institutions. They consulted biblical sources for their laws because they feared that reliance on the mind of man to frame their laws, given humankind's fallen nature, would unavoidably taint their legal codes. The Puritan divine John Cotton remarked that "[t]he more any Law smells of man the more unprofitable."[4] "[D]ivine ordinances, revealed in the pages of Holy Writ and administered according to deductions and rules gathered from the Word of God," were the only laws uncorrupted by a fallen, sinful world.[5] Moreover, the Bible was a "unifying force" in the law insofar as it "commanded ultimate loyalty and juridical respect" from a Bible-loving people.[6]

Early colonial laws drew extensively from biblical sources, especially Mosaic law, and colonial jurists frequently cited Scripture as legal authority. The colonists, to be sure, did not adopt all aspects of biblical law, and the Bible was not the sole source of their laws. Indeed, they sometimes departed from a literal application of biblical legal pronouncements when a biblical provision did not appear to meet the pressing concerns and values of the community or they did not believe a biblical text was binding on them in their time and place.[7] Nonetheless, the Bible was a vital, authoritative source of law in their new political communities.

The foundational expressions of law written in New England often claimed explicitly to be based on the "Word of God." When colonists convened in 1639 to frame the "Fundamental Articles for the Colony of New Haven," they unanimously affirmed that "the Scriptur[e]s doe holde forth a perfect rule for the direction and government of all men in all duet[ies] which they are to

4 John Cotton, "How Far Moses Judicialls Bind Mass[achusetts]," in Worthington Chauncey Ford, *John Cotton's Moses His Judicialls and Abstract of the Laws of New England* (Cambridge, MA: John Wilson and Son, 1902), 15; Worthington Chauncey Ford, "Cotton's 'Moses His Judicialls,'" *Massachusetts Historical Society Proceedings*, 2nd series, XVI:284 n. 121.

5 John D. Cushing, introduction to *The Laws and Liberties of Massachusetts, 1641–1691: A Facsimile Edition, Containing Also Council Orders and Executive Proclamations*, 1 (Wilmington: Scholarly Resources Inc., 1976), xvi.

6 John W. Welch, "Biblical Law in America: Historical Perspectives and Potentials for Reform," *Brigham Young University Law Review* 2002 no. 3 (2002): 635.

7 See George Lee Haskins, *Law and Authority in Early Massachusetts: A Study in Tradition and Design* (New York: Macmillan, 1960), 145–154.

performe to God and men as well in the government of famyles and commonwealths as in matters of the chur[ch]."[8] The New Haven colonists agreed "that the word of God shall be the only rule to be attended unto in ordering the affairs of government in this plantation."[9] The "Fundamental Orders of Connecticut" (1639), arguably the first written constitution in North America, declared that a governor and his council "shall have power to administer justice according to the Lawes here established, and for want thereof according to the rule of the word of God."[10] The "Massachusetts Body of Liberties" of 1641 identified "the word of god" as a standard of law.[11] It further affirmed that "No custome or prescription shall ever prevaile amongst us in any morall cause, our meaneing is maintaine anythinge that can be proved to bee morrallie sinfull by the word of god."[12]

The Puritans were not alone among early colonists in their attraction to Mosaic law. Even before the Pilgrims and Puritans arrived in New England, the Virginians wove the laws of Moses into their rules and regulations. When discipline deteriorated in Jamestown, the Virginia Company of London retained Sir Thomas Dale, a professional military man, to restore order in the troubled, fractious settlement. Shortly after arriving in the colony in May 1611, he issued military regulations, supplementing a civil code promulgated the previous year, that together was known as "Articles, Lawes, and Orders, Divine, Politique, and Martiall for the Colony in Virginea" (1610–1611). These rules and regulations have been described as "the earliest extant English-language body of laws in the western hemisphere."[13] Like the legal codes subsequently framed in Puritan commonwealths to the north, it bore the unmistakable influence of the Ten Commandments (Exodus 20:1–17), as interpreted through the lens of their religious tradition. It prohibited and harshly punished speaking "impiously or maliciously against the holy and blessed Trinitie, ... [or] the Christian faith," blaspheming God's "holy

8 "Fundamental Articles of New Haven" (1639), in *Colonial Origins of the American Constitution: A Documentary History*, ed. Donald S. Lutz (Indianapolis: Liberty Fund, 1998), 222.

9 Charles J. Hoadly, ed., *Records of the Colony and Plantation of New Haven, from 1638 to 1649* (Hartford: Case, Tiffany and Co., 1857), 21.

10 "Fundamental Orders of Connecticut" (1639), in *The Sacred Rights of Conscience: Selected Readings on Religious Liberty and Church-State Relations in the American Founding*, ed. Daniel L. Dreisbach and Mark David Hall (Indianapolis: Liberty Fund, 2009), 89.

11 "Massachusetts Body of Liberties" (1641), in Lutz, *Colonial Origins*, 71; see the same language in "Connecticut Code of Laws" (1650), in Lutz, *Colonial Origins*, 242.

12 "Massachusetts Body of Liberties" (1641), in Lutz, *Colonial Origins*, 79.

13 Brent Tarter, "Lawes Divine, Morall and Martiall," *Encyclopedia Virginia* (Virginia Foundation for the Humanities, January 20, 2012). Web. Aug. 31, 2017.

name," subjecting God's "holy word" to derision, Sabbath-breaking, murder, swearing false oaths, bearing false witness, and committing adultery, fornication, sodomy, and other sexual offenses.[14]

Biblical precepts were woven into the fabric of early New England codes even more explicitly and extensively than Virginia's law. A seminal code was the Massachusetts "Body of Liberties" (1641), which was enlarged upon in "The Laws and Liberties of Massachusetts" (1648). A decade after the Puritans arrived in Massachusetts Bay, and after several failed attempts to frame a body of laws, the Massachusetts General Court approved the "Body of Liberties" in December 1641.[15] It has been described as the first code of laws established in New England and the first colonial bill of rights. Compiled by the Reverend Nathaniel Ward, the "Body of Liberties" borrowed from a draft code known as "Moses His Judicials" framed by the Reverend John Cotton, the colony's leading clergyman, in 1636,[16] which, in turn, was based largely on Mosaic principles. Cotton wanted to demonstrate the supremacy and sufficiency of God's revealed Word for guiding a godly commonwealth in legal concerns. Ward's version drew on both the English common law and Mosaic law with which he was familiar as a barrister and clergyman. Ward was a Cambridge-educated lawyer, clergyman, and pamphleteer. The son of a Puritan minister, he, too, became a leading Puritan minister in England, following a ten year career in the law. He eventually immigrated to Massachusetts in 1634 to escape the persecution of the Puritans. Few seventeenth-century jurists in British North America were more overt than he in incorporating biblical law into the laws of their community or as successful in advancing an explicitly Christian jurisprudence.[17]

The "Body of Liberties" borrowed from Mosaic law, as interpreted within the colony's theological tradition, in mandating the death penalty for "worship[ping] any other god, but the lord god"; "Blasphem[ing] the name of God, the father, Sonne, or Holie ghost"; witchcraft; murder; man-stealing

14 "Articles, Lawes, and Orders, Divine, Politique, and Martiall for the Colony in Virginea" (1610, 1611), in Lutz, *Colonial Origins*, 315–318.

15 See generally Haskins, *Law and Authority in Early Massachusetts*, especially 113–140.

16 See Shira Wolosky, "Biblical Republicanism: John Cotton's 'Moses His Judicials' and American Hebraism," *Hebraic Political Studies* 4.2 (Spring 2009): 104–127.

17 K. Grudzien Baston, "Ward, Nathaniel (1578–1652)," in *Oxford Dictionary of National Biography*, ed. H. C. G. Matthew and Brian Harrison (Oxford: Oxford University Press, 2004), online ed., ed. David Cannadine, October 2006, www.oxforddnb.com/view/article/28700 (accessed October 20, 2017); Frederick S. Allis, Jr., *Nathaniel Ward: Constitutional Draftsman* (Ipswich, MA: Ipswich Historical Society, 1984). Ward and Cotton were among the handful of leading figures responsible for framing "The Laws and Liberties of Massachusetts," the 1648 enlargement on the "Body of Liberties" and a code that would form the colony's basic statutory law through the remainder of the seventeenth century. Haskins, *Law and Authority in Early Massachusetts*, 106, 132–134, 136.

(kidnapping); perjury with intent to secure the death of another; bestiality; homosexuality; and adultery.[18] It also contained provisions, derived from diverse jurisprudential sources, which later Americans would recognize as essential to a regime of ordered liberty. Indeed, a number of the "liberties" set forth in the document found expression in the national Bill of Rights written in 1789 and added to the US Constitution in 1791. It affirmed in the first article, for example, the rights of due process of law. It then proceeded in subsequent sections to recognize equal protection under the law (art. 2), a right to trial by jury (art. 29), a right to a speedy trial (arts. 2, 41), a right to bail (arts. 18, 41), the protection of private property from a taking for public use without fair compensation (art. 8), a privilege against self-incrimination (art. 45), a prohibition on double jeopardy (art. 42), and a prohibition on cruel and unusual punishment (arts. 43, 46). In designated sections, it specifically recognized the rights or liberties of women, children, servants, "foreigners and strangers," and "brute creatures."

Biblical influence was evident in the laws of other New England colonies. Well over 50 percent of the provisions in a 1655 code adopted in New Haven, for example, give evidence of biblical authority.[19] As one measure of that influence, every commandment in the Decalogue found expression in at least one of New England's colonial legal codes. The biblical citations that often accompanied these early statutes underscored how closely and deliberately these provisions followed biblical precepts.

Historians have debated the nature of the relationship between the colonial codes explicitly based on "the Lawes of God"[20] and the common law the colonists brought with them from England. As Daniel J. Boorstin observed: "Scholarly dispute as to whether early New England law was primarily scriptural or primarily English is beside the point. For early New Englanders these two turned out to be pretty much the same." These pious settlers believed English common law was derived from Christianity and biblical sources and, thus, biblical law and common law were thought to be in substantial harmony. The New England Puritans, to be sure, made statutory revisions to the common law, especially to the catalog of capital offenses, which aligned their laws even more closely with Mosaic law.[21] They saw a coincidence, for

18 "Massachusetts Body of Liberties" (1641), in Lutz, *Colonial Origins*, 83–84.

19 Louis Israel Newman, *Jewish Influence on Christian Reform Movements*, vol. 23 of Columbia University Oriental Studies (Columbia University Press, 1925; reprinted New York: AMS Press, 1966), 642.

20 "The Laws and Liberties of Massachusetts" (1647), in Lutz, *Colonial Origins*, 99.

21 Daniel J. Boorstin, *The Americans: The Colonial Experience* (New York: Random House, 1958), 28.

the most part, "between what the scriptures required and what English law had already provided."[22] They were clear, however, that biblical law took priority over man's laws, including the laws of England. In short, they believed that no human law should be permitted to contradict the revealed or divine law found in Scripture.

THE BIBLE AND THE AMERICAN CONSTITUTIONAL TRADITION

The founding generation, in the last third or so of the eighteenth century, contributed to an evolving constitutional tradition built on biblical, European, and American legal foundations. Many in the founding era retained a profound respect for the Bible and its relevance to their legal culture. Judge Nathaniel Freeman, in an 1802 charge to a Massachusetts grand jury, expressed the deference many in the new nation continued to accord biblical law: "The laws of that system . . . must be respected as of high authority in all our courts. And it cannot be thought improper for the officers of [our] government to acknowledge their obligation to be governed by its rules."[23]

Despite increased secular influences, Americans continued to draw on legal principles informed by Scripture in framing new constitutions at both the state and national levels. Contrary to claims that the US Constitution crafted in Philadelphia in the summer of 1787 was a strictly secular – or even "godless" – document,[24] selected constitutional provisions, in content and design, were familiar to a Bible-reading people. More important, the constitutional tradition and political vision that informed the US Constitution and the two dozen or so state constitutions framed in the wake of independence reflected biblical influences. These influences – both direct and indirect – were manifested in several ways:

First, general theological or doctrinal propositions regarding human nature, civil authority, political society, and the like informed conceptions and institutions of law and civil government.

Scholars have remarked, for example, that a biblical understanding of original sin and humankind's radical depravity (Genesis 3) inspired the framers to design a constitutional system that would guard against the concentration or abuse of government powers vested in fallen human actors. The most

22 Boorstin, *The Americans*, 24.

23 Nathaniel Freeman, *A Charge to the Grand Jury, at the Court of General Sessions of the Peace, holden at Barnstable, within and for the county of Barnstable, March term, A.D. 1802* (Boston: Manning & Loring, 1802), 7.

24 See, e.g., Isaac Kramnick and R. Laurence Moore, *The Godless Constitution: The Case against Religious Correctness* (New York: W. W. Norton, 1996).

basic, fundamental features of the American constitutional design – limited government, separation of powers, checks and balances, and representative government – are best understood in the light of this theological doctrine of radical depravity and the attendant necessity to check, in the words of Federalist # 37, "the infirmities and depravities of the human character."[25] This biblical anthropology was expressed in the Convention chambers. James Madison, for example, remarked: "The truth was that all men having power ought to be distrusted to a certain degree."[26]

Oaths of office and civic responsibility, ubiquitous in state constitutions and statutes in the founding era, were often explicitly premised on a belief in a future state of rewards and punishments – a belief in a heaven and hell. The South Carolina Constitution of 1778, for example, described a qualified elector as one who "acknowledges the being of a God, and believes in a future state of rewards and punishments."[27] The Pennsylvania Constitution of 1790 stated: "no person, who acknowledges the being of a God and a future state of rewards and punishments, shall, on account of his religious sentiments, be disqualified to hold any office or place of trust or profit under this commonwealth."[28]

The Constitution's four oath requirements found in Article 1, § 3, cl. 6; Article II, § 1, cl. 8; Article VI, cl. 3; and Amendment IV arguably mandated a profoundly religious act. Moral philosophers and constitutional framers in the founding era typically defined an oath as a solemn appeal to God for the

25 Publius, *The Federalist*, Number 37, in *The Federalist*, The Gideon Edition, ed. George W. Carey and James McClellan (Indianapolis: Liberty Fund, 2001), 185. Because men are not angels, James Madison famously counseled in *The Federalist*, Number 51, "[a]mbition must be made to counteract ambition." Ibid., 268. Although this is the most famous passage, it is certainly not the only passage in *The Federalist Papers* that addresses humankind's fallen nature. See also Publius's warning in Number 6: do not forget "that men are ambitio[u]s, vindictive, and rapacious." Ibid., 21. In Number 10, Publius lamented that "[t]he latent causes of faction are thus sown in the nature of man"; and faction, of course, reflects man's most base, selfish, oppressive, vexatious, and mischievous impulses. Ibid., 43. In Number 15, Publius wrote: "Why has government been instituted at all? Because the passions of men will not conform to the dictates of reason and justice, without constraint." A love of power and biased disregard to the "public weal" (or public good), Publius continued, "results from the constitution of man [or 'human nature,' in other editions]." Ibid., 73, 74. In Number 24, Publius lamented that "a man of calm and dispassionate feelings . . . would indulge a sigh for the frailty of human nature." Ibid., 119. It should be acknowledged that various political traditions recognize the fallibility of human actors, but the tradition that most influenced Americans of the founding era on this point was Reformed Protestantism.

26 Speech of James Madison, July 11, 1787, in *The Records of the Federal Convention of 1787*, ed. Max Farrand (New Haven: Yale University Press, 1911), 1:584.

27 South Carolina Constitution of 1778, art. XIII.

28 Pennsylvania Constitution of 1790, art. IX, sec. 4.

truth of what is said by a person who believes in the existence of a Supreme Being and in a future state of rewards and punishments.[29] The accompanying provisions permitting an "Affirmation" in the alternative to an oath were almost certainly an accommodation for Quakers, Moravians, Mennonites, and other religious sects for whom swearing oaths offended their religious scruples because they take literally the biblical injunction to "swear not at all" (Matthew 5:33–37; see also James 5:12) and, for some, they objected to references to God in oaths (fearing, perhaps, that this violated the Third Commandment).

Second, the founding generation saw in the Bible political and legal models that they sought to incorporate into their political and legal systems.

For example, in Article IV, § 4, cl. 1, the Constitution requires every state to maintain "a Republican Form of Government." Many in the founding generation believed that the Hebrew commonwealth described in the Old Testament provided a divinely inspired model for republican government (see Exodus 18:13–27; Deuteronomy 1:9–18), which was worthy of emulation in their own political experiments. In an influential 1775 Massachusetts election sermon, Samuel Langdon, the president of Harvard College and later a delegate to New Hampshire's constitutional ratifying convention, opined: "The Jewish government, according to the original constitution which was divinely established, … was a perfect Republic … The civil Polity of Israel is doubtless an excellent general model, allowing for some peculiarities; at least some principal laws and orders of it may be copied, to great advantage, in more modern establishments."[30]

[29] This standard definition of an oath was repeated in the debates on Article VI of the US Constitution in the state ratifying conventions. See, e.g., the July 30, 1788 speech of Judge James Iredell (NC), in *The Debates in the Several State Conventions on the Adoption of the Federal Constitution*, ed. Jonathan Elliot, 2nd edn., vol. 4 (Washington: Printed for the editor, 1836), 196. See also "Kentucky Constitution of 1792," art. VIII, § 5; and "Kentucky Constitution of 1799," art. VI, § 7, *Text of Kentucky Constitutions of 1792, 1799 and 1850* (Frankfort, KY: Legislative Research Commission, 1965). Virtually every late eighteenth-century moral philosopher defined oaths in similar terms. See, e.g., John Witherspoon, "Of Oaths and Vows," in *Lectures on Moral Philosophy*, ed. Varnum Lansing Collins (Princeton: Princeton University Press, 1912), 130.

[30] Samuel Langdon, *Government Corrupted by Vice, and Recovered by Righteousness. A Sermon Preached before the Honorable Congress of the Colony of the Massachusetts-Bay in New England, Assembled at Watertown, on Wednesday the 31st Day of May, 1775. Being the Anniversary Fixed by Charter for the Election of Counsellors* (Watertown: printed by Benjamin Edes, 1775), 11, 12. See also Samuel Langdon, *The Republic of the Israelites an Example to the American States. A Sermon, Preached at Concord, in the State of New-Hampshire; Before the Honorable General Court at the Annual Election.* June 5, 1788 (Exeter: printed by Lamson and Ranlet, 1788), 8–12.

Most of what the founders knew about the Hebrew commonwealth they learned from the Bible. They were well aware that ideas like republicanism found expression in traditions apart from the Hebrew experience, and, indeed, they studied these traditions both ancient and modern. The republic described in the Hebrew scriptures, however, reassured pious Americans that republicanism was a political system that enjoyed divine favor. And this was reason enough for them to embrace this form of civil government.

Third, the Bible *may* have influenced some specific provisions written into the US Constitution. To be sure, it can be difficult to establish definitively that a specific constitutional provision was taken directly from a specific biblical text; rather, a more plausible claim is that constitutional principles were indirectly influenced by biblical concepts that had long before found expression in western legal tradition, especially in the English common law and, more recently, colonial laws.[31]

Consider, for example, Article I, § 7, cl. 2, which excepts Sundays from the ten days within which a president must veto a bill. This is an implicit recognition of the Christian Sabbath, commemorating the Creator's sanctification of the seventh day for rest (Genesis 2:1–3), the fourth commandment that the Sabbath be kept free from secular defilement (Exodus 20:8–11, 31:12–17), and, in the Christian tradition, the resurrection of Jesus Christ from the dead (Matthew 28:1–8; Mark 16:1–8; Luke 24:1–10; see also John 20:1–8).

The Article III, § 3, cl. 1 requirement that convictions for treason be supported by "the testimony of two witnesses" conforms to a familiar biblical mandate for conviction and punishment (see, e.g., Deuteronomy 17:6; see also Deuteronomy 19:15; Numbers 35:30; Matthew 18:16; John 8:17; 2 Corinthians 13:1; 1 Timothy 5:19; Hebrew 10:28).

For one final example, the Fifth Amendment, crafted by the first federal Congress, prohibits double jeopardy, or trying a defendant twice for the same offense, which St. Jerome in a late fourth-century commentary, and legal scholars ever since, have said was a principle found in the book of the prophet Nahum 1:9 ("affliction shall not rise up the second time"). This doctrine was incorporated into canon law and then transferred to civil law, common law,

[31] The evidence for biblical influence on the US Constitution is not necessarily reflected in the abbreviated and arguably unreliable notes on deliberations in the Constitutional Convention of 1787. The delegates only occasionally referenced the Bible in debates on substantive provisions, which critics have said indicates that the Bible had little or no influence on the Constitution. This analysis, however, misses the multiple channels through which the Bible exerted its influence on the legal culture and constitutional tradition that informed the Constitution.

American colonial codes, early state constitutions, and eventually the US Constitution. Interestingly, in *Bartkus* v. *Illinois*, Associate Justice of the US Supreme Court, Hugo L. Black, traced this biblical lineage of the principle of double jeopardy.[32]

These examples illustrate ways in which Christianity and its sacred text are consistent with and likely influenced the content of an American constitutional tradition. (Commentators have pointed to additional examples of the Bible's influence on specific constitutional provisions, including provisions on standards of weights and measurements, cruel and unusual punishment, and corruption of blood.) There is no doubt that Christianity and the Bible informed aspects of canon law, civil law, English customary and common law, and the legal traditions crafted by early colonists. The constitutional framers of 1787 were surely aware of this influence on selected constitutional concepts they discussed and debated. They might have concluded that these ideas also found expression in traditions apart from Christianity and the Bible or, with the passage of time, that the Christian influence had become attenuated. It is true that many of these constitutional concepts can be found in sources other than Christianity and the Bible. For many Americans, however, the Bible would have been a widely accessible, authoritative source of these ideas. And the purported compatibility of these ideas with Scripture would have reassured pious Americans that these constitutional provisions enjoyed divine favor. In any case, tracing the sources of influence can be complicated, but a cursory review of the American constitutional tradition suggests that, at a minimum, Christianity and the Bible had a discernible influence on it.

CHALLENGING CHRISTIAN INFLUENCES ON AMERICAN LAW

Although Christianity remained a dominant force in the culture and the Bible's influence on law and constitutional tradition lingered, various nineteenth-century rationalists, church–state separationists, and secularists began to challenge Christianity's influences on American law.[33] Critics argued that laws lacking a legitimate secular purpose could not pass constitutional muster. These challenges, with varying degrees of success, have continued to the present, greatly diminishing Christianity's influence on the legal culture.

32 See Jay A. Sigler, "A History of Double Jeopardy," *American Journal of Legal History* 7.4 (1963): 284; *Bartkus* v. *Illinois*, 359 U.S. 121, 152 n.4 (1959) (Black, J., dissenting).

33 I discuss some of these challenges to Christianity's influence on the law and legal culture in the new nation in *Religion and Politics in the Early Republic: Jasper Adams and the Church-State Debate*, ed. Daniel L. Dreisbach (Lexington: University Press of Kentucky, 1996) (portions of this work were adapted for this chapter).

In an essay written in his youth but only published posthumously, Thomas Jefferson famously disputed Christianity's seminal contributions to common law, asserting "that Christianity neither is, nor ever was, a part of the common law."[34] In his inaugural lecture as Harvard's Dane Professor of Law, Associate Justice of the US Supreme Court Joseph Story promptly countered that "[t]here never has been a period in which the common law did not recognize Christianity as lying at its foundations."[35] All sides were keenly aware that this debate was about the extent of Christianity's influence on the fabric of the American legal tradition.[36]

Other controversies in the last two centuries illustrate secular challenges to vestiges of Christianity's influence on American law. For example, congressional enactments in 1810, and again in 1825,[37] requiring Sunday mail delivery, were described by religious traditionalists as the first congressional enactment requiring a violation of a biblical precept and Christian custom – the sacred observance of a day of rest.[38] While rationalists and separationists staunchly

34 Thomas Jefferson, "Whether Christianity Is a Part of the Common Law?," in *Reports of Cases Determined in the General Court of Virginia. from 1730, to 1740; and from 1768, to 1772* (Charlottesville: F. Carr and Co., 1829), 140, reprinted in Dreisbach and Hall, *Sacred Rights of Conscience*.

35 Joseph Story, "The Value and Importance of Legal Studies: A Discourse Pronounced at the Inauguration of the Author as Dane Professor of Law in Harvard University, August 25, 1829," in *The Miscellaneous Writings of Joseph Story*, ed. William W. Story (Boston: Charles C. Little and James Brown, 1851), 517. See also [Joseph Story], "Christianity a Part of the Common Law," *American Jurist and Law Magazine* 9 (April 1833): 346–348, reprinted in Dreisbach and Hall, *Sacred Rights of Conscience*, 551–552.

36 See generally Stuart Banner, "When Christianity Was Part of the Common Law," *Law and History Review* 16 (1998): 27–62; Bradley S. Chilton, "Cliobernetics, Christianity, and the Common Law," *Law Library Journal* 83 (1991): 355–362; Courtney Kenny, "The Evolution of the Law of Blasphemy," *Cambridge Law Journal* 1.2 (1922): 127–142; and James R. Stoner, Jr., "Christianity, the Common Law, and the Constitution," in *Vital Remnants: America's Founding and the Western Tradition*, ed. Gary L. Gregg II (Wilmington: ISI Books, 1999), 175–209.

37 "An Act regulating the Post-office Establishment," *Statutes at Large*, II, sec. 9, 592, at 595 (April 30, 1810); "An Act to reduce into one the several acts establishing and regulating the Post-office Department," *Statutes at Large*, IV, sec. 11, 102, at 105 (March 3, 1825).

38 See Jasper Adams, *The Relation of Christianity to Civil Government in the United States*, 2nd edn. (Charleston: A.E. Miller, 1833), 33–34 note D. For further discussion on the Sunday mail controversy, see Harmon Kingsbury, *The Sabbath: A Brief History of Laws, Petitions, Remonstrances and Reports, with Facts and Arguments, Relating to the Christian Sabbath* (New York, 1840); Wayne E. Fuller, *Morality and the Mail in Nineteenth-Century America* (Urbana and Chicago: University of Illinois Press, 2003); Richard R. John, "Taking Sabbatarianism Seriously: The Postal System, the Sabbath, and the Transformation of American Political Culture," *Journal of the Early Republic* 10.4 (1990): 517–567; and James R. Rohrer, "Sunday Mails and the Church-State Theme in Jacksonian America," *Journal of the Early Republic* 7.1 (1987): 53–74.

defended the legislation, religious traditionalists mobilized a potent political movement in opposition to the Sunday mail.

The Sunday mail controversy was only one skirmish in a larger conflict over the propriety and constitutionality of Sunday laws. Although religious traditionalists were unsuccessful in their campaign to end Sunday mail services in the first half of the nineteenth century, Sunday laws, also known as "blue laws," which prohibited or restricted a variety of activities on Sunday, such as commercial transactions, secular employment, and recreational pursuits, remained on the law books in many jurisdictions.[39] Beginning in the first half of the nineteenth century and continuing to the present day, these laws have been challenged by, among others, strict separationists, secularists, Christian seventh-day Sabbatarians, and Jews.[40]

Blasphemy laws have faced similar challenges since the early nineteenth century. In the western legal tradition, blasphemy laws, which typically forbid expressions exposing God, the Christian religion, or the Bible to calumny, contempt, ridicule, or vilification, are rooted in part in biblical injunctions against defiling God's name. Several high profile prosecutions for blasphemy not only upheld these laws but also affirmed the Christian origins of these laws. A blasphemy conviction for a defendant who said "Jesus Christ was a bastard, and his mother must be a whore," was affirmed by a New York court in 1811. Writing for the court in *People* v. *Ruggles*, Chief Justice James Kent opined that such words are "punishable because they strike at the root of moral obligation, and weaken the security of the social ties."[41] This was followed by similar cases in Pennsylvania, Delaware, and Massachusetts.[42] Although blasphemy laws survived well into the twentieth century, these cases served notice that laws generally viewed as rooted in biblical commands would be challenged in an increasingly secular polity committed to the separation of church and state. By the mid-twentieth century, an increasing number of state and federal courts had struck down as unconstitutional state blasphemy laws.

Numerous other controversies involving Christianity and the Bible in American law have garnered attention in the twentieth and twenty-first centuries. Although since colonial times judges have cited the Bible in their

39 See David N. Laband and Deborah Hendry Heinbuch, *Blue Laws: The History, Economics, and Politics of Sunday-Closing Laws* (Lexington: Lexington Books, 1987).

40 See, e.g., *Town Council of Columbia* v. *C.O. Duke and Alexander Marks*, 2 Strobhart 530 (S.C. 1833); *McGowan* v. *Maryland*, 366 U.S. 420, 445 (1961).

41 *People* v. *Ruggles*, 8 Johnson 290, 292, 296 (N.Y. 1811).

42 See *Updegraph* v. *Commonwealth*, 11 Sergeant & Rawle 394 (Pa. 1824); *State* v. *Chandler*, 2 Del. (2 Harrington) 553 (1837); *Commonwealth* v. *Kneeland*, 37 Mass. (20 Pickering) 206 (1838).

rulings,[43] in recent decades parties have successfully objected to judges, prosecutors, and deliberating jurors invoking the Bible as authority in judicial proceedings. In an increasing number of reported criminal cases, appellate courts have held that references to the Bible are inadmissible and have even set aside convictions when invocations of the sacred text may have affected the outcome of a case.[44] Those challenging uses of the Bible in judicial processes have expressed concern that such references will have a prejudicial impact on those in the judicial system who regard the Bible as divine authority, and such appeals to the Bible constitute an "establishment of religion" in violation of the First Amendment.

CONCLUSION

Christianity and the Bible have left a distinct and significant mark on American jurisprudence. Indeed, Christian influences were woven into the common law the colonists brought with them from England and the laws the colonists framed once they arrived in the New World. Moreover, several colonies were established as Bible commonwealths and their laws drew extensively on biblical law as the colonists understood it and adapted it to their time and place.

[43] See Daniel G. Ashburn, "Appealing to a Higher Authority?: Jewish Law in American Judicial Opinions," *University of Detroit Mercy Law Review* 71 (1994): 295–352; James Brown, "The Bench and the Bible," *Case and Comment* 29.1 (Jan.–Feb. 1923): 3–8; J. Michael Medina, "The Bible Annotated: Use of the Bible in Reported American Decisions," *Northern Illinois University Law Review* 12 (1991): 187–254; Bernard J. Meislin, "The Role of the Ten Commandments in American Judicial Decisions," in *Jewish Law and Current Legal Problems*, ed. Nahum Rakover (Jerusalem: Library of Jewish Law, 1984), 109–120; Sanja Zgonjanin, "Quoting the Bible: The Use of Religious References in Judicial Decision-Making," *New York City Law Review* 9 (2005): 31–91.

[44] See, e.g., *Roybal* v. *Davis*, 148 F. Supp. 3d 958, 1043–1052 (S.D. Cal. 2015) ("It is well settled that biblical law has no proper role in the sentencing process" and the "prosecutor's reference to biblical authority was clear misconduct"). For legal analyses of these practices, see Courtney Rachel Baron, "An Eye for an Eye Leaves Everyone Blind: *Fields* v. *Brown* and the Case for Keeping the Bible Out of Capital Sentencing Deliberations," *Northwestern University Law Review* 103 (2009): 369–399; John H. Blume and Sheri Lynn Johnson, "Don't Take His Eye, Don't Take His Tooth, and Don't Cast the First Stone: Limiting Religious Arguments in Capital Cases," *William & Mary Bill of Rights Journal* 9 (2000): 61–104; Monica K. Miller, Joseph Dimitrov, Brian H. Bornstein, and Ashley Zarker-Sorensen, "Bibles in the Jury Room: Psychological Theories Question Judicial Assumptions," *Ohio Northern University Law Review* 39 (2013): 579–625; Gary J. Simson and Stephen P. Garvey, "Knockin' on Heaven's Door: Rethinking the Role of Religion in Death Penalty Cases," *Cornell Law Review* 86 (2001): 1090–1130; and Cory Spiller, "*People* v. *Harlan*: The Colorado Supreme Court Takes a Step toward Eliminating Religious Influence on Juries," *Denver University Law Review* 83 (2005): 613–638.

Many colonial laws and regulations derived from Scripture undoubtedly strike twenty-first-century observers as harsh (even brutal), excessively restrictive, anti-libertarian, and invidiously discriminatory; and some are, by the standards of a later age. It is also worth remembering that, from early in the colonial experience, colonists also used Christian theology and the Bible to make arguments for religious liberty, nonestablishment, church–state separation, the abolition of slavery, and other causes that seem remarkably liberal and enlightened to later generations. That said, the Bible was often at the heart of arguments over these and other matters. Indeed, on some issues, such as religious liberty, resistance to civil authority, and slavery, opponents often appealed to the same Bible in support of their respective positions.

Christianity's influence on the culture and law has diminished over time. Laws informed by biblical precepts that were uncontested in the seventeenth century began to be questioned by some rationalists in the eighteenth century and politically and legally challenged in the nineteenth century and thereafter as secular and separationist perspectives in law and policy gained ascendancy. Nonetheless, vestiges of Christian influence remain a part of the legal culture in the twenty-first century. The persistence of this influence is a testament to how thoroughly Christian thought and practice once infused the culture. Many explicitly Christian influences, however, have been stripped from the law as unconstitutional establishments of religion, and only those laws that can be defended on secular terms have survived into the twenty-first century. Popular and even some scholarly accounts describe Christian influences on the law as a feature only of New England's Puritan colonies. This misses, however, how deep and sustained Christianity's influence has been on American jurists and jurisprudence.

1

John Cotton and Roger Williams

Glenn A. Moots

This chapter summarizes how Puritan ministers John Cotton (1584–1652) and Roger Williams (c. 1603–1683) used Christian scripture and theology to pioneer greater democracy and freedom of religion. While both were clergymen and significant public theologians, they were also eminent Christian jurists. John Cotton was a prominent spokesman both for the laws of Massachusetts Bay and for a particular style of congregational church government that influenced American political and legal thought. Cotton also authored a legal code adopted by the colony of New Haven that had influence in Massachusetts Bay. Cotton's code, deliberately based on both scripture and English law, serves as an example of early American constitutionalism. Roger Williams received a preeminent legal education as apprentice and recording secretary for the eminent English jurist Sir Edward Coke and founded the colony of Rhode Island. Williams not only secured the colony's charter but also served as its President. In addition, Williams was one of the most prominent advocates for religious liberty in the mid-seventeenth century. Williams's persuasive defenses of religious freedom separated citizenship from one's religious faith and provoked John Cotton to engage him in a famous debate published in London and read on both sides of the Atlantic. Each was an eloquent representative for opposing sides of a legal question contested as much in colonial America as today, namely the question of church–state relations and religious liberty.

THE ENGLISH BACKGROUND

The Puritans, those nonconforming English churchmen who settled New England, have been cast as either the authoritarian foes or noble founders of American freedom. Puritanism was a movement of diverse ideas affecting both church and state, but there are two notable Puritan ideas that are particularly relevant for early American legal and political thought. First, the Puritans who settled in New England were "congregationalists" (sometimes called "independents") in their church government.[1] Broadly defined, congregationalists believed that each congregation should rule itself and rejected the idea that any church could be in authority over another. Some congregationalists believed in direct congregational rule while others wanted rule by elected representatives. All congregationalists rejected episcopal church government (rule by bishops). They also rejected presbyterianism, wherein standing groups of churches had authority over their individual member churches and all churches were ruled by elected elders rather than by direct congregational vote. In rejecting both episcopal and presbyterian rule, congregationalists exhibited a democratic spirit that favored close accountability and local rule.

The second relevant Puritan idea, held among some congregationalists, was "separatism." Separatism emphasized self-rule as well as the sanctity of conscience. Puritan separatists not only dissented from various traditions within the Church of England (such as the use of clerical vestments or the use of the Book of Common Prayer in worship) but also demanded total separation from the English Church. Separatists discouraged attending non-separating (i.e., conforming) churches, even if only to hear sermons (the least ceremonial and most Puritan part of worship). Separatists were also expected to repent of past association with the Church of England. Separatism was controversial and did not characterize all congregationalists, however. English Puritans William Bradshaw and Henry Jacob, for example, were congregationalists but not separatists. Puritan Henry Barrow was a separatist, as was Robert Browne. Puritans and congegationalists disagreed among themselves about the appropriate extent of separation from the Church of England.

Insofar as the Church of England was essentially a state parish church, geographically organized and governed by bishops accountable to the king, congregational self-governance was not only more democratic but also implicitly seditious. James's famous aphorism, stated at the Hampton Court conference in 1604, expressed the concern pithily: "No bishop, no King." Congregationalists were sometimes prosecuted for treason however much they denied that they were subversive. Bradshaw and Jacob, for example, labored to prove that congregationalists were indeed *loyal* to the king. Both went so far as to argue that bishops actually stole ecclesiastical authority from

[1] Scholars debate the capitalization of these terms. Because of the diversity of opinion among those identified by these labels, and because I do not want to necessarily confuse them with a particular confessional tradition, I have elected to leave the titles without capitalization.

the king.[2] Protesting the demands of bishops *while* professing one's loyalty to the civil government therefore cast congregationalists (or presbyterians) as *conservative defenders* of civil magistracy over the churches.[3] Not all congregationalists were in agreement, however, and some refused to recognize *any* civil authority over ecclesiastical matters. Browne and Barrow were willing to not only reform the church without getting civil approval; they were inclined to hold magistrates accountable for their religious opinions.

John Cotton and Roger Williams, both Puritan ministers, sharply disagreed on many matters but nonetheless reflect this congregational emphasis on self-government and believed that the civil magistrate should have only limited control over church matters. In their own way, each believed in the importance of freedom of conscience. Both Massachusetts Bay and Rhode Island therefore represented a relative departure from the Erastian church–state status quo left behind in England wherein the civil authority had extensive control over ecclesiastical matters.[4]

THE EARLY CAREERS OF COTTON AND WILLIAMS

John Cotton was educated by Puritans at Emmanuel College, Cambridge. Beginning in 1612, he served as vicar of St. Botolph's in Boston (Lincolnshire) for twenty years. Cotton's preaching and lectures became enormously popular and likely drew a young Roger Williams to hear him. Cotton's wise counsel and irenic nature gained sympathy for his non-conformity. Cotton was not a separatist as such, but he did begin a practice of gathering the "elect" members of his congregation for a separate worship service.[5] Opponents found this objectionable, seeing such a separate gathering as a rejection of both the parish model and its implicit conflation of church and state.

Between 1629 and 1633, Cotton's life changed dramatically. Both Cotton and his first wife Elizabeth Horrocks were stricken with malaria; she did not survive. Shortly thereafter, Cotton married his second wife, Sarah Story (with whom he would have six children), and also learned that he would be called before the

2 Michael P. Winship, *Godly Republicanism: Puritans, Pilgrims, and a City on a Hill* (Cambridge, MA: Harvard University Press, 2012), 76–80, 83–84. This argument was especially popular after Archbishop Parker's *Advertisements* in 1566 forced conformity without an act of Parliament or the Queen.

3 Such arguments contributed to a budding Anglo-American argument lasting two centuries wherein the British constitution and rule of law had to be protected against "popish" elements intending to subvert it.

4 See, e.g., Article 37 of the Thirty Nine Articles of the Church of England, wherein the magistrate is given power over matters both civil and ecclesiastical.

5 Larzer Ziff, *The Career of John Cotton* (Princeton: Princeton University Press, 1962), 49.

High Commission Court for nonconformity. Charles I and Archbishop Laud offered no leniency for dissenting churchmen. Cotton had previously declined to go to North America, so his only choices now were to flee to Holland or go into hiding. He chose the latter. Even during this domestic exile, Cotton was a seminal voice influencing influential Puritan ministers Thomas Goodwin and John Davenport.[6] In 1633, Cotton decided to rejoin his wife and travel to the Massachusetts Bay Colony. Having already scolded the church in Salem for their separatism, Cotton knew that he was sailing toward controversy.

Williams, like Cotton and other nonconforming ministers, felt pressured by the ecclesiastical dictates of Laud and Charles and had already crossed the Atlantic in 1631. Younger than and not nearly as famous as Cotton, Williams nevertheless possessed an impressive resume. In England, Williams had been apprenticed to the famous English jurist Sir Edward Coke. Not only did Williams learn legal argumentation as Coke's assistant in proceedings before the Star Chamber court, he likely witnessed the persecution of outspoken Puritans. As a recording secretary, Williams perfected a shorthand method that became a marginalia code not cracked by scholars until four centuries later.[7] With Coke's sponsorship, Williams obtained his education at Charterhouse. He completed his ministerial studies at Pembroke College, Cambridge (a hotbed of Puritan sentiment) in 1629. Like others with Puritan inclinations, Williams declined a parish post and thereby eluded the crosshairs of persecution. He instead served as chaplain for William Masham, a Puritan sympathizer. He married Mary Barnard that same year, with whom he would have six children.

John Winthrop (subject of the following chapter) greeted Williams as a salutary addition to the new "City on a Hill." When Williams refused to teach at First Church Boston (a position that Cotton would later accept and hold for nineteen years), it became clear that Williams adhered to the more sectarian and separatist strain of Puritanism. This was the beginning of Williams's dissent, an upending of a delicate church–state relationship in New England.

THE POLITICS OF CHURCH AND STATE IN PURITAN NORTH AMERICA

Although generations of Americans have thought that Puritan colonists came for "religious freedom," that freedom was not what one might think. This first

6 Goodwin would serve as chaplain to Oliver Cromwell and facilitate the execution of Charles I. Goodwin also became an advocate for congregationalists in the mostly presbyterian Westminster Assembly. Davenport became founder of the New Haven colony in New England.

7 Linford D. Fisher, J. Stanley Lemons, Lucas Mason-Brown, *Decoding Roger Williams: The Lost Essay of Rhode Island's Founding Father* (Waco: Baylor University Press, 2014).

generation of settlers desired a strict orthodoxy and close spiritual communion on doctrinal matters. The freedom that American Puritans sought was to dissent from the Church of England (and its bishops) insofar as their conscience understood "reformed" worship. Furthermore, ministers landing in the New World considered their freedom to have apocalyptic significance. Echoing a long argument associating Protestantism with liberty, New England settlers feared "Popish tyranny" and subterfuge by Roman Catholics in Europe. They hoped to found a truly Protestant polity to make war against Satan and Rome.[8]

To Puritans, freedom to worship properly was the only freedom that mattered.[9] In his most famous exchange with Roger Williams, begun in 1644, Cotton defined freedom as the right to conform to one's conscience *rightly informed*. Persecution, according to Cotton and his colleagues, was not the punishment of *any* dissenting opinion. If one knew the truth, but persisted in error, he sinned against his own conscience.[10] Correction of an opinion judged to be erroneous was not persecution at all, Cotton argued. What migrating Puritans desired in North America was therefore freedom for their own *particular* dissent, not *any dissent whatsoever*. What modern readers might consider *genuine* religious freedom for one's conscience existed nowhere in Britain or North America until Roger Williams established it in Rhode Island.[11]

Williams's move toward religious freedom began with radical separatism, however, and Williams's separatism was very controversial. Even where

8 This theme endured. Edward Johnson in 1653 compared New England Puritans to Israelites, hoping that they would become an army raised by Christ for "freeing his people from their long servitude under usurping Prelacy." Cotton Mather announced "War with none but Hell and Rome!" during King William's War (1689–1697). The association of the Church of Rome with tyranny or anarchy continued even into the early years of the American Revolution and was especially pronounced during the French and Indian War.

9 In 1634, John Cotton told a young minister back in England, "It hath been no small inducement to us, to choose rather to remove hither than to stay there, that we might enjoy the liberty not of some ordinances of God but of all, and all in purity." Cotton to a Minister in England, December 3, 1634, in *The Correspondence of John Cotton*, ed. Sargent Bush, Jr. (Chapel Hill: University of North Carolina Press, 2001), 184. A similar sentiment is expressed by Cotton in *An Exposition of First John* (Oswestry: Quinta Press, 1656), 572. I have silently modernized spelling, some capitalization, and grammar in these quotations though not in titles if using the first edition.

10 John Cotton, "The Answer of Mr. John Cotton of Boston in New-England against the Aforesaid Arguments against Persecution for the Cause of Conscience," in Roger Williams, *The Bloudy Tenent of Persecution, for Cause of Conscience, Discussed, in a Conference between Truth and Peace* (London, 1644), 41–54.

11 I am leaving aside comparisons with Pennsylvania, Delaware, New Jersey, or Maryland, all of which had greater relative degrees of religious liberty at one time or another in colonial history.

separatism was more popular, such as in the Plymouth colony, it did not necessarily mean "religious freedom." From a political standpoint, the charters establishing Puritan colonies (and their right to some degree of *de facto* self-government) existed at the good pleasure of a king already deeply suspicious of Puritans. To the degree that the New England churches engaged in radical dissent or separatism, they threatened their own existence.[12]

Resisting radical separatism was not just a question of political prudence, however; Puritan settlers desired a church–state partnership preserved for over a millennium and approved by the magisterial Protestant reformers such as Martin Luther, Ulrich Zwingli, and John Calvin. New England colonists did advance a relatively progressive separation of church and state authority, but they still desired to preserve Christendom and a confessional state. At this time, almost all of Western Christendom still associated religious freedom with anarchy and moral collapse. Only the Anabaptist traditions, as reflected in the Schleitheim Confession (1527), had seriously questioned this close alliance of church and state. Reformed Protestants (including the Puritans) roundly condemned Anabaptist political theology, however.

John Cotton was arguably the most gifted exponent of the balance of civil and ecclesiastical power desired in the Bay colony. Roger Williams was its most articulate critic. We turn first to Cotton's political ideas and then to Williams's dissent.

JOHN COTTON AND THE "NEW ENGLAND WAY"

Two significant documents from 1636 provide insight into John Cotton's legal and political thought. Invited by the General Court of Massachusetts Bay in that year to draft a legal code, Cotton drew up a document that was part constitution and part legal code. It came to be published as *Abstract of the Laws of New England* and (as John Winthrop later called it) *Moses His Judicials*. It was not adopted by Massachusetts Bay, perhaps because it was terse to a fault. The honor of adoption by the Bay colony fell to Puritan Nathaniel Ward's *Body of Liberties*, which reflects Cotton's influence. It was adopted by the General Court in 1641, and became the first constitution in New England. Cotton's *Abstract* did become the basis of law in the New Haven colony, however. Cotton's adoption of Old Testament law (the Hebrew Torah), was also influential for basic laws adopted by both Massachusetts and Connecticut.[13]

12 This is why New England's Cambridge Platform of 1648 would repudiate separatism.

13 Edward Chauncey Baldwin, "The Permanent Elements in the Hebrew Law," *International Journal of Ethics* 25:3 (April 1915), 360–371.

Cotton drew from Deuteronomy, Exodus, and Leviticus and therefore believed his code superior to "all the municipal laws and statutes of any of the Gentile nations and corporations under the cope of Heaven." His *Abstract* reflects his belief in the contemporary legal and political relevance of the Old Testament, an idea that Williams would reject entirely. Defending the legal relevance of the Old Testament in a reply against Williams in 1647, Cotton wrote, "Though Christ abolished a national church-state, and instead thereof set up a congregational church: yet Christ never abolished, a national civil state, nor the judicial laws of Moses."[14] In short, the church and state were no longer one, but Old Testament legal ideas were no less relevant for state and society.

Cotton's *Abstract*, divided into ten sections, created civil and judicial offices reflecting the democratic nature of congregationalism and English rights and liberties. He made the office of "counselor" a lifetime appointment, however, which may also account for why colonists did not approve his *Abstract*. Cotton, like Ward, also incorporated English legal precedent without hesitation or scriptural justification. Cotton included rules governing property and made provision for defense and foreign relations. He made provision for popular election and jury trials, for example. Section nine protected English rights to due process, rules of evidence, habeas corpus, and trial by a jury of one's peers. Unlike other sections, section nine does not include biblical citation but is also implicitly drawn from scripture insofar as English law had biblical roots (e.g., the limit of forty lashes).[15] Sections seven through nine articulated a strict legal code rooted in Old Testament civil and moral law, including capital punishment for blasphemy (particularly atheism), perjury, slavery, idolatry, witchcraft, rebellion by children, rape, treason, prostitution, and "profaning of the Lord's Day."[16] Lesser penalties included corporal punishment or fines. Modern readers shocked by Cotton's strict moral code, including those who might ascribe its severity to Puritanism, must compare it with contemporary colonial documents. Though composed under somewhat different circumstances, Sir Thomas Dale's *Articles, Laws, and Orders, Divine, Politic, and Martial* written for (Anglican) Virginia (1610–1611), was equally severe. Dale similarly deployed Old Testament juridical ideas, but did *not* make comparable provision for civil rights or liberties.

14 John Cotton, *The Bloudy Tenent, Washed and Made White in the Bloud of the Lambe* (London, 1647), 126.

15 John Cotton, *Abstract of Laws and Government* (London, 1641; reprinted by Will Aspinwall, London, 1655).

16 Prohibition of Sabbath desecration, for example, was found in the laws of many other colonies as well.

Another occasion for discerning Cotton's legal and political ideas also comes from around this same time. In 1636, William Fiennes (Lord Saye and Sele) and Robert Greville (Lord Brooke), both investors in New England ventures, expressed their desire to emigrate to Massachusetts Bay. Before joining the colony, however, they hoped to secure hereditary political authority and extend voting rights in the colony to property owners (it was by then confined to church members). Cotton had the unenviable duty of replying against the charge that Massachusetts Bay was somehow both too democratic (for rejecting hereditary authority) and too undemocratic (for confining the franchise to church members). Cotton's reply is another terse expression of his fundamental political ideas.

Cotton rejected the common association of congregationalism with democracy, but on theological grounds. He argued that God did not ordain democracy as a "fit government either for church or commonwealth." Emphasizing the Puritan idea of vocation, not denying popular accountability, Cotton added, "If the people be governors, who shall be governed?"[17] This now-famous assertion was not a rejection of a democratic polity as such; accountability to the people and self-rule was, after all, the basis of all congregationalism. Cotton's argument simply reflected disagreement among congregationalists about whether parishioners should rule directly or if elected representatives should make decisions. Cotton insisted that this latter idea was not democracy but instead a *status popularis* (popular constitution). Cotton called this rule by elected officers aristocracy or monarchy – forms, Cotton argued, that were "clearly approved, and directed in scripture."[18]

Regardless of the form, however, Cotton insisted that all governments were subject to the sovereignty of God, or what Cotton called "theocracy." In defining "theocracy," Cotton articulated what he understood to be the sum of the church–state partnership. Theocracy limited the franchise and office-holding to church members. Cotton anticipated the retort: this looked too much like the subversion of civil authority by ecclesiastical leaders, similar to what the pope had attempted by excommunicating Henry VIII or Elizabeth I.[19] Cotton did not deny the possibility that a civil magistrate could come under church discipline, but rejected that such discipline constituted a reason to remove a magistrate from office. Furthermore, church officers were *not* to

17 Cotton to William Fiennes, Lord Saye and Sele (1636), in *The Correspondence of John Cotton*, 245.

18 Ibid.

19 Exercise of ecclesiastical authority, particularly the pope, was precisely what the Thirty Nine Articles had rejected as a "foreign jurisdiction" in Article 37.

serve as civil rulers. Cotton later argued that such power would make a "monster" or "beast" of the church.[20]

In his letter to Lord Saye and Sele, Cotton's justification for "theocracy" was rooted both in scripture and in traditional political theory. As he did in his *Abstract*, Cotton praised the scriptures not only as a basis for theology but also for practical legal matters (e.g., "ethics, economics, politics, and church-government").[21] Cotton ascribed Massachusetts Bay governance not to "any conceit or will of ours" but instead to "the holy counsel and will of the Lord Jesus."[22] Cotton was not implying that unbelievers necessarily lacked sound political theory altogether, only that a Christian's should be better.[23] Popular government was an essential part of a good (and biblical) polity because it served as a conduit for righteousness in both church and state. In a passage resembling John Winthrop's "Little Speech on Liberty," Cotton wrote, "Purity, preserved in the church, will preserve well-ordered liberty in the people, and both of them establish well-balanced authority in the magistrate." God, Cotton argued, was the author of all three: morality, liberty, and authority.[24]

The proper balance of liberty, morality, and authority was the whole point of this so-called theocracy of believers. In an exposition of Revelation 13, Cotton wrote, "Let all the world learn to give mortal men no greater power than they are content they shall use, for use it they will: and unless they be better taught of God, they will use it ever and anon."[25] This principle applied in both church and commonwealth, Cotton contended. Cotton was not arguing this as a proto-liberal, however. He was equally concerned with the challenge of keeping liberty within proper limits. "There is never peace," Cotton wrote, "where full liberty is not given, nor never stable peace where *more* than full liberty is granted."[26] Just as rulers will abuse *too much* power, so men and women will abuse *too much* liberty. The context for Cotton's

20 John Cotton, *An Exposition upon the Thirteenth Chapter of the Revelation* (London, 1655), 17–18.

21 Cotton was here citing William Perkins, *A Treatise of the Vocations, or Callings of Men, with the Sorts and Kinds of Them, and the Right Use Thereof* (1605). Perkins was, by this time, outselling Calvin in England. At the zenith of publishing in Elizabethan England (the 1590s), Perkins's works were twice as popular as Shakespeare's. See W. B. Patterson, *William Perkins & the Making of a Protestant England* (New York: Oxford University Press, 2014).

22 Cotton to William Fiennes, 246.

23 Perry Miller, *The New England Mind: The Seventeenth Century, Volume 1* (Cambridge, MA: Belknap Press of Harvard University Press, 1939), 197.

24 Cotton to William Fiennes, 246–247.

25 John Cotton, *An Exposition*, 71.

26 Ibid., 73.

prescription is the Beast of Revelation, a blasphemer and an enemy of the church. Cotton was concerned with political order generally, but he was especially concerned with the "soul-stealing danger of blasphemy, a liberty that men never had in the first place."[27] In short, Cotton did not conceive of a purely civil liberty, or a secular civil order separated from the church. The result of either would be political anarchy (i.e., a failed political order) or the spiritual evils associated with the Beast of Revelation.

Where Cotton did separate the civil from the ecclesiastical, the distinction was largely one of jurisdiction. Consistent with his *Abstract*, he argued that the church should be subordinate to the state in "civil matters ... as is the disposing of men's goods or lands, lives, or liberties, tributes, customs, worldly honors, and inheritances."[28] He added to this "first sort" of things, a "second sort of things which concern civil peace." Civil authorities must also concern themselves with "the establishment of pure religion, in doctrine, worship, and government, according to the word of God, as also is the reformation of all corruptions in any of these."[29] Citing Old Testament scripture, Cotton argued that even though the church had only spiritual weapons (synods, the Word, or church censure), magistrates could command or stir up the churches to deploy these spiritual weapons or use civil punishments themselves against any who opposed or disturbed the church. This theory would become practice in Williams's case, who was eventually referred to the magistrates when ministers failed to dissuade him. Cotton explained his reasoning for the partnership in a reply to Williams: civil laws concern the good of the polity, and religion was the best good of the polity. Therefore, civil laws and civil authority must protect religion. How else, Cotton argued, would laws promote and preserve the good of the people?[30]

Cotton did not confuse the civil work of ecclesiastical protection with the work of conversion, however. While Cotton charged the civil magistrate to "establish and reform religion, according to the Word of God," he did not condone civil power to "compel all men to come and sit down at the Lord's table [take communion], or to enter into the communion [membership] of the Church, before they be in some measure prepared of God for such fellowship."[31] While some civil prosecution of religious opinion or practice

27 Ibid., 71–72. Cotton also compared this to an infection. John Cotton, *The Bloudy Tenent, Washed*, 34–35.

28 Cotton, *The Keyes of the Kingdom of Heaven, and Power Thereof, according to the Word of God* (1644) (Boston: S.K. Whipple & Co., 1852), 95.

29 Ibid., 95–97.

30 Cotton, *The Bloudy Tenent, Washed*, 151.

31 Cotton, *Keyes*, 97.

was punitive in Cotton's model, it could also be corrective. Using a justification similar to that used by Augustine, Cotton argued that civil prosecution could be spiritually salutary.[32] Legal sanction might prepare the heart for a converting work of God, even if it could not bring about that work. Cotton considered "legal terrors" to be "ordinary means blessed of God to prepare hard and stout hearts to conversion."[33] Cotton considered it carnal, worldly, and ungodly to confine the work of the magistrate to bodies and goods but exclude them from the care of souls.[34] That confinement of souls to the church was precisely what Williams wanted, however.

For Cotton, the ecclesiastical also touched the civil insofar as persecution of the church became legitimate justification for resistance against civil authority. Cotton echoed the earliest British Protestants (such as Christopher Goodman, John Knox, and John Ponet) who had plotted resistance against Catholic Mary I. Like his predecessors, Cotton forbade the sword to the church and advocated patient suffering under persecution. But, in an argument echoing Calvin and Melanchthon, Cotton contended that designated legal custodians of the people's will (e.g., an elected legislative body) could engage in acts of civil resistance. Consistent with this theory, Cotton not only condoned the actions of the army in "Pride's Purge" (enabling the execution of Charles I in 1649) but also suggested that "trainbands" (militia with elected officers) in Massachusetts could resist the imposition of an English governor general. Such actions protected both English liberties *and* sound religion, Cotton argued, consistent with the civil magistrate serving as a "nursing father" for the church – the latter being an image from Isaiah 49 popular with other Reformed Protestants as well.[35]

Cotton saw all of church and state through the lens of the covenant, a mutual agreement defining the extent and limits of authority and consent. Cotton defended covenanting from both scripture and "the light of nature" (i.e., reason). In his defense of the New England churches against attacks by Westminster Assembly presbyterians in 1645, Cotton wrote, "It is evident by the light of nature that all civil relations are founded in Covenant." Excepting the relationship of parents and children or conquerors and captives, Cotton added, "there is no other way given whereby a people free from natural and

32 See, e.g., Augustine's *De Correctione Donatistarum* (c. 417).

33 Cotton, *The Bloudy Tenent, Washed*, 20.

34 Ibid., 67–68.

35 Cotton, *Keyes*, 94–100, and "Sermon upon A Day of Publique thanksgiving: By Mr. John Cotton Sr." (1651), reprinted within Francis J. Bremer, "In Defense of Regicide: John Cotton on the Execution of Charles I," *The William and Mary Quarterly*, 3rd Ser., 37.1 (Jan. 1980), 110–124.

compulsory engagements can be united or combined together into one visible body."[36] All power was therefore ultimately voluntary and accountable in both a horizontal *and* vertical direction. Men were accountable to one another *and also* to God. Cotton's contract was not a Lockean investment of preexisting natural authority, however. Cotton wrote that church elders, for example, received their authority partly from the people's choice and their voluntary subjection, but also because God invested the office with authority.[37]

Of course, since only church members consented to civil authority, where did it leave those outside of church membership? Though the numbers are unreliable, it is estimated that three quarters of people in Massachusetts Bay in 1640 were not church members. One ministerial colleague reportedly complained to Cotton in 1642, "Many [are] murmuring that we come to make heathens rather than convert heathens to Christianity."[38] Furthermore, how would dissenters be treated in Massachusetts Bay? In short, Cotton's center would not hold. Roger Williams threatened to release the anarchy that Puritans feared would come from ecclesiastical discord.

THE "SOULE LIBERTY" OF ROGER WILLIAMS

When Roger Williams declined the post later offered to Cotton, it was because he refused to have fellowship with a church that had not thoroughly renounced the Church of England. Reflecting the separatist strain, Williams insisted that members of the Boston church repent of any "communion" with the system of parish churches back home in England. Ironically, Williams's intolerance of his brethren's toleration set him on the road to establishing a colony with tolerance for all.

In defending his indictment of the Boston church, Williams engaged Cotton and began a self-appointed war on hypocrisy. Williams interrogated the consistency of geographically separating from the Church of England and its hierarchy, a *de facto* separation, *while* denying separatism. Furthermore, Williams argued, the churches in the Bay colony were *de facto* separatist churches for treating membership just as separatist churches had elsewhere – by examination of one's confession and life before acceptance into

36 John Cotton, *The Way of the Churches of Christ in New England* (London, 1645), 4.

37 Cotton, *Keyes*, 73.

38 David D. Hall, *Puritans in the New World: A Critical Anthology* (Princeton: Princeton University Press, 2004), 7. On church membership numbers, see Thomas Lechford, "Plain dealing or Newes from New England," *Mass. Hist. Soc. Coll.*, Series III, vol. iii, 143; Albert E. McKinley, *Suffrage Franchise in the Thirteen English Colonies* (Philadelphia: University of Pennsylvania Publications, 1905), 313.

membership. To refuse his demands for total renunciation of the Anglican hierarchy, Williams therefore believed, was nothing short of hypocrisy.[39]

Challenging the *corpus Christianum* begun under Constantine 1,300 years prior, blessed by Augustine, nurtured in the medieval church, sustained by magisterial reformers in the Reformation, and continued in the Church of England, Williams used a metaphor that foreshadowed Thomas Jefferson's famous 1802 letter to the Danbury Baptists. Williams asserted that there ought to be a "hedge or wall of separation between the Garden of the church and the wilderness of the world."[40] Whereas Jefferson's "wall" is open to interpretation, Williams's intentions were quite clear: the church can flourish only as a gathered body of believers *apart* from the world. This meant not simply an end to Cotton's carefully crafted synthesis, including its *de jure* lines of authority and its *de facto* parish church model. Protecting the church from worldly pollution meant the creation of a purely secular civil realm, distinct from the ecclesiastical realm, and stripped of civil authority over religion.

Like Cotton, Williams expressed his ideal in scriptural terms. To Williams, Massachusetts Bay leaders wanted a national church, and to Williams any national church resembled not only the Roman Catholic Church but also the "Great Whore of Babylon" who persecuted the true church in Revelation 17. Likewise, hypocrites were the tares that grew up among the wheat in Christ's parable of Matthew 13. Unlike Cotton, Williams was not prepared to wait until Judgment Day to separate the tares from the wheat. Williams understood the sorting to happen in the self-selecting membership of the church gathered *out* of the world. The church must be, as Williams described it, a garden separated from the wilderness (and weeds) of the world. In his response to Cotton, Williams wrote,

> When they [the Church] have opened a gap in the hedge or wall of separation between the garden of the church and the wilderness of the world, God hath ever broke down the wall itself, removed the Candlestick, etc., and made His Garden a wilderness as it is this day. And that therefore if He will ever please to restore His garden and Paradise again, it must of necessity be walled in peculiarly unto Himself from the world, and all that be saved out of the world are to be transplanted out of the wilderness of the World.[41]

39 There was inconsistency in the minds of Massachusetts Bay leaders; Cotton, for example, dismissed the separatism of Henry Barrow while John Winthrop lauded Barrow, even comparing him to Martin Luther.

40 Roger Williams, "Mr. Cotton's Letter Lately Printed, Examined and Answered," in *The Complete Writings of Roger Williams* (New York: Russell & Russell, 1963), 1:392.

41 Ibid., 1:108.

Williams did not advance this separation because he believed that only a *particular* political body was corrupt (e.g., Stuart England, or the English church under Archbishop Laud). *Any* community not distinguishing the elect from the unconverted comprised a "wilderness of the World." This included any church–state partnership in England or New England.

Whereas Cotton believed that church and state must flourish together, and therefore both obliged the care of the magistrate, Williams believed that the church's identification with the world choked off its lush spiritual greenery. For Williams, the world was always a wilderness. Only church discipline and scripture guarded against its encroaching wildness. The civil magistrate wielded the sword for civil matters alone. So, whereas Cotton feared spiritual corruption and hypocrisy in the church and state together, and was prepared to deploy civil *and* ecclesiastical censure, Williams cared only about corruption or hypocrisy in the church and was prepared to deploy only ecclesiastical censure.

When Williams's demands were refused by the Boston church, he looked to Salem's now-vacant pulpit. When Massachusetts Bay's Court of Assistants protested any such appointment, Williams moved on to the Plymouth colony. He bided his time there by farming and by trading with Native American tribes. He preached regularly in a lay capacity. In his subsequent relations with the Narragansett Indians, Williams gained profound respect for what he judged to be their superior moral conduct. His study of their language (motivated partly by a desire for evangelism) enabled his first publication, *A Key into the Language of America* (1643), and brought fame in England among those hungry for exotic knowledge about North America. Williams's relationship with the Narragansett would also pay dividends in facilitating relatively peaceful relations with the New England Confederation and later enable for Williams a free grant of property for his Providence settlement. Perhaps most importantly for his exploration of a new civil-church relationship, Williams's study of Native Americans convinced him that successful civil relationships did not require a common religious foundation – or even Christianity.

In Plymouth, Williams continued to kick against the goads. Cotton Mather relates that Williams ("obstreperous" and "leavened . . . with the humors of the rigid separation") objected to use of the customary English salutation of "Goodman" (e.g., "Hello, Goodman Smith") unless that person was evidently spiritually regenerate. John Winthrop took the occasion of a visit to Plymouth (obliging travel across forty miles that Mather describes as "a howling wilderness") to admonish Williams for confusing a *civil* custom with a *theological* classification.[42] In Williams's mind, however, even this minor pleasantry was a crack in the wall protecting the integrity of the church.

Challenging salutations was one thing, but challenging the king and charter was quite another. Williams protested the giving of Indian lands to Plymouth and Massachusetts by a "Christian" Stuart king who, Williams insisted, was not Christian at all. Before returning to Salem from Plymouth, Williams composed a manuscript in which he described Charles I (and his father James I) as horns of the Whore of Babylon's beast in Revelation. Puritans were already suspect in the eyes of Charles's privy council; they hardly needed someone spreading seditious interpretations of scripture. When confronted by Governor Winthrop, Williams insisted that he had articulated his sentiments only at the request of Plymouth's Governor Bradford. Williams pledged his loyalty and acknowledged his station as a layperson.

Soon, however, Williams became more than a layman when he was called to take Salem's pulpit in 1634. Williams considered the church in Salem the purest in New England and relished the mantle of prophet. He protested "polluted" household worship involving unconverted family members and customary civil oaths administered to unconverted persons – the latter being essential to the Massachusetts Bay polity because such oaths bound persons not bound by church covenants. Williams considered these acts corrupted worship, weeds encroaching on the garden. He would later argue that even hearing sermons, something Cotton argued as ideal for the unconverted, was a form of hypocrisy for unconverted persons.[43] Additionally, Williams condemned civil oaths administered to converted persons, the royal charter, church members attending parish churches when visiting England, and the colony's display of the banner of St. George, which included an "idolatrous" red cross. While some were sympathetic to Williams on these points, his greatest success was arguably on this last point.[44]

Williams's insistence on total separation of the "civil" from the ecclesiastical – exemplified in the Providence Agreement (1637), for example – seemed to him the perfect conclusion of congregationalist reforms begun half a century earlier. Cotton and others were not prepared to countenance such separation – especially when associated with a loose cannon like Williams. Williams refused to repent of his positions even after counseling from other ministers, so it fell to civil authorities to banish him in 1635. Almost a decade later, Williams and

42 Cotton Mather, *Magnalia Christi Americana; or, The Ecclesiastical History of New-England* (1702) (Hartford: Silas Andrus and Son, 1853), 1:128.

43 Williams, *Bloudy Tenent*, 203.

44 Howard Millar Chapin, *Roger Williams and the King's Colors: The Documentary Evidence* (Providence: E.L. Freeman Company, 1928).

Cotton would contend over the question of religious freedom, heating up presses already hot from religious disputes during the Wars of the Three Kingdoms in Britain and Ireland.

THE "BLOUDY TENENT" CONTROVERSY (1644–1652)

Although religious disputes were indeed heating up presses in London, Williams's 1644 work addressed to Parliament, *The Bloudy Tenent of Persecution for Cause of Conscience*, was hotter still: many in Parliament burned it upon reception. Williams's polemic was sparked by the publication of A *Model of Church and Civil Power* (1644), written by Massachusetts Bay ministers, and by the Westminster Assembly in England. Williams's *Bloudy Tenent* inspired a 1647 response from Cotton and subsequently a 1652 riposte from Williams. Though often wordy, repetitive, and evincing haste (in terms of pages, Williams out-produced Cotton by a factor of almost five to one), Williams displays a legal advocate's thoroughness that he probably learned as Coke's apprentice in the Star Chamber.

Williams attacked Cotton's holy commonwealth. If civil government was indeed a covenant (or contract) wherein the people delegate authority, would not even "the wildest Indians in America" then become "keepers of the Church of both Tables?"[45] Recall that Cotton argued that *God* invested rulers (e.g., church elders) with their authority (his was not a Lockean transfer of an entirely natural or original power), but Williams's point remained: how did one determine when God did or did not invest a particular government with authority over religion? Williams pressed this point further, arguing for the existence of a profane or secular civil order. Religion has little to do with civil peace, Williams asserted. "Kingdoms and governments in the world have long … enjoyed civil peace and quiet," he argued, "notwithstanding their religion is so corrupt" or at least not shared in common.[46] This point was the very inspiration for Williams's title: religious conformity (i.e., persecution) was the *enemy* of peace.[47]

Just as Cotton drew from the Old Testament, Williams deployed it in response. Williams rejected the idea that Old Testament Israel, or the covenant with Abraham, could be applied to *any* modern polity. This Old Testament "type" was instead the Christian Church, and the weapons of the

45 Williams, *Bloudy Tenent*, 249–250.

46 Ibid., 251–252; *The Bloody Tenent Yet More Bloody by Mr. Cotton's Endeavour to Wash it White in the Blood of the Lamb* (London, 1652), 238.

47 Williams, *Bloudy Tenent*, 43, 60–62, 247.

Hebrew magistrate were now the spiritual censure of the minister.[48] Furthermore, Old Testament rulers proved Williams's point. Artaxerxes's policy of toleration enabled the Jews to worship while Nebuchadnezzar's demand for conformity did not.[49] Williams drew his point forward to historical and contemporary examples, including the English upheavals from Henry VIII to Elizabeth I illustrating the perilous consequences of religious conformity.[50] All persecutors, Williams charged, marched under "the white colors of peace, civil peace, public peace."[51] Williams deployed a reverse jeremiad against Cotton. God no longer punished idolatrous nations (as Cotton feared for an apostate New England). God did, however, punish those who persecuted his people.[52]

Against the Bay colony's confining civil authority to believers, Williams cited historical and contemporary cases of pagan nations where no believers existed to either vote or hold office; yet, many of these were successful polities. Pagans, Williams argued, were perfectly capable of possessing what he called the "civil and moral duties" necessary to manage a civil state.[53] The reason that pagans could have a perfectly suitable civil order was that God did not intend for it to address men's souls. Nor should it, Williams argued, insofar as all civil polities (after Christ's first advent) were "merely civil." There was no longer any divine favor for any so-called holy commonwealth. There was no new Israel. All civil polities were now profane.[54] Williams began his *Bloudy Tenent* with this famous charge: "Next to the saving of your souls (in the lamentable shipwreck of mankind), your task (as Christians) is to save the souls, but as magistrates, the bodies and goods, of others."[55]

Against Cotton's concern against infection, Williams deployed the doctrine of predestination: "Dead men cannot be infected."[56] Let the wilderness be the wilderness, Williams insisted. The civil magistrate would enforce only the *second* table of the Ten Commandments.[57] To deny a magistrate this purely civil authority, recognized even by Jesus to Caesar in his statement "Render unto Caesar's what is Caesar's," was to deny scripture.[58] Depending

48 Ibid., 251–252.
49 Ibid., 317, 76.
50 Williams, *Bloody Tenent Yet More Bloody*, 180.
51 Ibid., 68.
52 Williams, *Bloudy Tenent*, 6; *Bloody Tenent Yet More Bloody*, 71–72, 170, 179, 189.
53 Williams, *Bloudy Tenent*, 413–415.
54 Ibid., 160, 281, 317–321.
55 Ibid., 5.
56 Ibid., 125, cf. 111–113.
57 Ibid., 45.
58 Williams, *Bloody Tenent Yet More Bloody*, 414.

on one's reckoning, Williams thereby relegated, or freed, the protection of souls to the garden only.

LEGACY

It is perhaps not surprising that the legacies of Cotton and Williams have followed contrary paths, especially over the last two centuries. Cotton's contemporaries and immediate successors such as Cotton Mather esteemed him as a godly example of scholarship and prudence.[59] By 1878, however, Moses Coit Tyler branded Cotton unoriginal and unimpressive. It wasn't until the 1960s that two full-length studies of Cotton's life and work appeared. Everett Emerson's was critical. He began by implicitly refuting Cotton's epitaph (*Cujus Ultima Laus est, Quod fuerit inter Nov-Anglos Primus*) making him "first man in New England." Across the centuries, Emerson retorted, "Of the first generation of New England writers, John Cotton is doubtless not the greatest." Progressive historian Vernon Parrington found Cotton charming but blamed him for the "sins" of "the oligarchy" of New England.[60] Only Larzer Ziff demonstrated sympathy for Cotton.

By contrast, contemporaries condemned Williams and moderns have canonized him. As the American Puritan establishment has been increasingly cast as theocratic, authoritarian, and narrow-minded, Cotton became a villain and Williams a hero. The earliest historians of New England – Nathaniel Morton, Cotton Mather, William Hubbard, and John Winthrop – were critical of Williams and even more critical of his ideas. Since the nineteenth century, however, ten times as many monographs have been devoted to the life and work of Williams and all of them are complimentary. Such prodigious study of Williams's life is surprising, given John Howland's claim in 1831 that all anyone knew of Roger Williams could not fill more than half a dozen pages.[61] Williams was even lionized in literature by Nathaniel Hawthorne's narrative history of New England, *The Whole History of Grandfather's Chair* (1851). Four Hawthorne grandchildren are told by "Grandfather" of the "good clergyman" Williams. Grandfather blames Williams's banishment on those who believed "the country could not be safe unless all the inhabitants thought and felt alike." But, Grandfather continues, "it often happens that the outcasts

[59] Mather, *Magnalia Christi Americana*, 1: 273–274.

[60] Vernon Parrington, *Liberalism, Puritanism and the Colonial Mind: Main Currents in American Thought* (1927) (New Brunswick: Transaction Publishers, 2011), 30.

[61] Bradford Fuller Swan, "Introduction" to *An Answer to a Letter Sent from Mr. Coddington* (Providence: Roger Williams Press, 1946).

of one generation are those who are reverenced as the wisest and best of men by the next."[62]

Other critics of Puritanism went even further in praising Williams, imagining (against all evidence to the contrary) Williams to be a liberal democrat or proto-progressive. Influential Progressive historian Vernon Parrington, for example, said of Williams in 1927, "The gods, it would seem, were pleased to have their jest with Roger Williams by sending him to earth before his time."[63] Historian Samuel Hugh Brockunier likewise made Williams a man out of time, titling his 1940 biographical study *Irrepressible Democrat: Roger Williams*. That title suggests how Williams became a figure existing only in a liberal American imagination; he was no longer the man who rowed thirty strenuous miles from Providence to Newport at seventy-one years of age to tell Quakers how wrong their theology was. What is heartening in Brockunier's ham-fisted title, however, and more so in the precise scholarship of Michael Winship, is a recovery of the democratic and republican nature of Puritanism, particularly in both Cotton and Williams.

Not surprisingly, Williams has also enjoyed a supporting role in decisions of the Supreme Court. In the landmark *Engel* v. *Vitale* (1962) case, extensive quotations from Williams's *Bloudy Tenent* were used in footnotes to defend the Court's decision against recitation of prayer in public schools. Of particular interest to Justice Hugo Black were Williams's assertion that Constantine's care for the church was detrimental, and that it was imprudent to allow civil magistrates authority over religious questions. Justice Black was correct in identifying Williams as "one of the earliest exponents of the doctrine of separation of church and state,"[64] but it is doubtful that Williams would have confused school prayer with the kind of authority over religion asserted by Cotton or Constantine. Rather, Williams would have argued that prayers offered by unregenerate schoolchildren were hypocritical corruptions of worship – an argument Justice Black was no doubt reluctant to deploy. When the Warren Court ruled in *Abington School District* v. *Schempp* (1963) that public school sponsorship of Bible reading was also unconstitutional, Williams was elevated by Justice Thomas Clark from the footnotes to the opinion itself. In a dubious bit of intellectual history, Clark joined Williams with Madison and Jefferson as influences "incorporated not only in the Federal Constitution but likewise in those of most of our States."[65] In *Lee* v. *Weisman* (1992), Justices

[62] Nathaniel Hawthorne, *The Whole History of Grandfather's Chair: Or, True Stories from New England, 1620–1692* (Boston: Houghton, Mifflin and Company, 1887), 27–28.

[63] Parrington, *Liberalism, Puritanism and the Colonial Mind*, 62.

[64] *Engel* v. *Vitale*, 370 U.S. 421, 434 n. 20 (1962).

[65] *Abington School District* v. *Schempp*, 374 U.S. 203, 214 (1963).

Harry Blackmun, John Paul Stevens, and Sandra Day O'Connor deployed Williams's wall and garden metaphor in their concurring opinion that public schools should not sponsor non-denominational prayer by local clergy. They quoted Mark DeWolfe Howe's study of Williams, "[W]ordly corruptions … might consume the churches if sturdy fences against the wilderness were not maintained."[66]

Advocates of separation also cited Williams in their dissents. In *Agostini et al.* v. *Felton et al.* (1997), Justices Stevens, David Souter, Ruth Bader Ginsburg, and Stephen Breyer presumed the support of Williams for their dissent, arguing that public school teachers should be prohibited from teaching in religious schools. When Justice Souter joined with Justice Stevens and Justice Ginsburg to dissent in *Mitchell et al.* v. *Helms et al.* (2000), another "Establishment" case, they likewise cited Williams to argue that separation *protected* religion.

Those who have desired to *extend* government support of religious activity have both used Williams *and* resisted his use in contrary opinions. In his dissent in *Wallace* v. *Jaffree* (1985), Justice William Rehnquist's defense of a moment of silence in public schools (implicitly appropriate for prayer) scorned the aforementioned use of Williams by the majority in the precedent of *Abington*, arguing that neither Williams nor Madison and Jefferson were fathers of the First Amendment. Rehnquist stated sharply, "Stare decisis may bind courts as to matters of law, but it cannot bind them as to matters of history."[67] In *Marsh* v. *Chambers* (1983), the Court ruled that government funding of chaplains was not unconstitutional. In this case, Williams was cited as an advocate of religious liberty whose colony of Rhode Island still began its ratification convention sessions with prayer. Hence, one of America's primary apologists for separation would have approved of government-funded chaplains. Of course, Williams was dead for many years by the time of the Constitution's ratification and could not have approved of decisions made by Rhode Island political leaders over a century later. And though *Minersville School District* v. *Gobitis* (1940), a decision against exemption for Jehovah's Witnesses, was quickly overturned, Williams was cited by the majority. Justice Felix Frankfurter cited two secondary studies of Williams to defend the mandatory recitation of the Pledge of Allegiance as "general law" not aimed at the promotion or restriction of particular religious beliefs.

66 Mark DeWolfe Howe, *The Garden and the Wilderness: Religion and Government in American Constitutional History* (Chicago: University of Chicago Press, 1967), 6.

67 *Wallace* v. *Jaffree*, 472 U.S. 38, 99 (1984) (Rehnquist, J., dissenting).

What Williams would have thought about his appropriation by the United States Supreme Court is debatable. It is certain, however, that no line of *direct* influence is traceable from him into subsequent centuries apart perhaps from the favorable reappraisal of him first launched in the nineteenth century. "As for any direct influence of his thought on the ultimate achievement of religious liberty in America," Perry Miller bluntly concluded, "he had none."[68] The greatest enemy of Williams's legacy was Williams himself. Chris Beneke rightly concluded, "Williams probably exercised very little influence on the development of colonial religious discourse. He simply lived too early and separated too regularly."[69] If America now looks more like what Williams desired, that is owed to an organic and historical consequence of events in England and America that overwhelmed religious establishment and forced religious liberty.

Although Cotton has never been deployed in a Supreme Court opinion, he should not be presumed irrelevant. Cotton's legacy is discerned in those who support religious activity for the health of the polity and its members. While Justices Scalia, Thomas, or Rehnquist would not consider the civil magistrate a "nursing father," they have questioned with good reason the aggressive separation that began in the mid-twentieth century. While Williams provides a solution for our pluralistic age and challenges the limitations of religious establishment, Cotton reminds us to protect the spiritual needs of human nature in the legal and political order.

68 Perry Miller, "Roger Williams: An Essay in Interpretation," in *The Complete Writings of Roger Williams*, 7:10.

69 Chris Beneke, *Beyond Toleration: The Religious Origins of American Pluralism* (New York: Oxford University Press, 2006), 33.

2

John Winthrop and the Covenantal Ideal

Darren Staloff

No figure had a larger impact on the legal, jurisprudential, constitutional, and political life of Puritan Massachusetts than John Winthrop. From the colony's inception in 1629 to his death in early 1649, Winthrop was a permanent fixture in the Bay government, serving twelve terms as governor, three as deputy governor, and four as an Assistant (a magistrate and member of the upper chamber of the General Court). Winthrop was the most critical figure in establishing the interlocking institutions of state and church that would characterize the New England Way, and was at the center of both the establishment of the judicial institutions of Massachusetts and its legal debates. More than that, his statesmanship established a pattern that served as an exemplar of civic-minded leadership for the generations that succeeded him. As one historian has argued, if Massachusetts had a founding father, that person was certainly John Winthrop.[1]

Born in 1588, Winthrop hailed from a family known for its "precise" or Puritan Protestantism. Avowed Calvinists who championed plain style sermons and simplified church services, Puritans were the vanguard of the reformation in Elizabethan and early Stuart England. The Puritan movement at the time was most famed for opposing priestly vestments and ceremonies as well as pushing the church in a more vigorously reformed direction. The Winthrops achieved their gentry status when John's grandfather Adam, a successful clothier, purchased part of a monastic estate (Groton Manor in Suffolk) that had been confiscated during the Henrican reformation. In contemporary denominational terms, John was a non-separating Congregationalist. As such, he favored a gathered church of visible saints but, unlike the more radical Brownists, refused to break communion with

[1] Francis J. Bremer, *John Winthrop: America's Forgotten Founder* (New York: Oxford University Press, 2003).

the established English church. Winthrop's Puritan convictions were central to his identity, both as a Christian and as a statesman, but his inherent irenicism made him one of the more moderate figures within that movement.

Winthrop's Puritan piety prompted him to enroll at Trinity College, Cambridge, at the age of fourteen to study for the ministry. His wedding to Mary Forth in 1605 (the first of three marriages) led him to drop out and secure an immediate income. John's father, Adam, purchased Groton Manor from his elder brother and in 1609 he installed his son as the head of the manorial court. To facilitate his service in this function, John entered the Inns of Court where he received the legal training that would be so important in his subsequent career. Despite never being admitted to the bar, John was made a member of the Commission of the Peace for Suffolk in 1615, and would serve as a Justice of the Peace until his departure from England. After a failed campaign for Parliament in 1626, Winthrop was appointed to the office of attorney at the Court of Wards in 1627.

Despite these advancements, Winthrop's career had reached a crossroads. The personal rule of Charles I in the latter half of the 1620s had resulted in the promotion of persons hostile to Puritanism to the Suffolk and metropolitan benches, and he became increasingly disenchanted with the political and religious climate of his motherland. As one historian has noted, he "realized that his puritan values" precluded "his achieving a greater role in county or national government."[2] The final blow came with the advancement of the implacably anti-Puritan William Laud as the Bishop of London and the ensuing harrying of Puritans. Winthrop resigned his position in the Court of Wards and looked for an avenue of escape. After briefly considering the Protestant settlements of Ireland, he finally decided on Massachusetts and never looked back.

CONSTITUTING THE NEW ENGLAND WAY

The central tenet of Winthrop's political thought was the notion of the covenant, a mutually binding voluntary agreement. As he reminded his fellow emigrants aboard the *Arabella*, they had entered into a covenant with God "by a mutuall consent" the immediate purpose of which was to establish "a due forme of Government both civill and eccelesiasticall" in the new world.[3] The

2 Francis J. Bremer, *John Winthrop: Biography as History* (New York: Continuum International, 2009), 21.

3 "A Modell of Christian Charity," *The Winthrop Papers* (Boston: Massachusetts Historical Society, 1929–), 2:293.

covenant was obviously central to the ecclesiastical order of New England. It was voluntary consent to a written covenant by believing Christians who pledged to follow all ordinances and doctrines authorized by the Word that gave being to the various churches that comprised the Congregational establishment in Massachusetts. But covenantal rituals were equally important for its political institutions. Winthrop, like his fellow Puritans, held that only God had the "prerogative" to rule over men without their consent and fixed rules. To "usurpe such Aut[horit]ye, is Tiranye, and impietye," Winthrop insisted, and the very marrow of "Arbitrary Government."[4] A truly legitimate government or "common weale," by contrast, "can be founded but by free consent."[5]

Winthrop's central constitutional task, then, was to establish just such a covenantal commonwealth in Massachusetts, a task largely completed within the first decade of settlement. When Winthrop and his fellow Assistants arrived in the Bay colony, they had not only all been previously elected to their offices by the Massachusetts Bay Company, a joint stock trading firm, they were also the only shareholders among the residents, giving them a legal monopoly on political power. Yet among the first acts they took in the autumn of 1630 was to request the consent of the new settlers to be governed by them. They also invited them to apply for the status of "freemen" of the corporation, and on May 18, 1631, 116 men took an oath of loyalty to the regime and were duly empowered to elect any additional Assistants that might be needed in the future.[6] The following spring Winthrop announced to his fellow Assistants that the freemen desired the right to elect the governor and deputy governor (both had been chosen by the Assistants previously) as well as all the Assistants on an annual basis. At least one of his colleagues "grew into passion," but Winthrop had his way at the next General Court and further established that each town would be entitled to send two "deputies" to confer with the Assistants on matters of taxation.[7] On May 14, 1634, a scant two years later, the deputies requested and were granted a full incorporation in the General Court of Massachusetts, the colony's supreme legislative and judicial body.[8] Although a full bicameral separation would not occur for another

4 "John Winthrop's Discourse on Arbitrary Government," *The Winthrop Papers*, 4:468.

5 "A Declaration in Defense of an Order of Court Made in May, 1637," *The Winthrop Papers*, 3:423.

6 Over 1,200 more freemen took the oath in the following decade, quite likely comprising close to half the adult male householders. They are listed in Nathaniel B. Shurtleff, ed., *Records of the Governor and Company of the Massachusetts Bay in New England* (Boston, 1853), 1:366–379.

7 James Savage, ed., *The History of New England from 1630 to 1649. By John Winthrop, Esq. First Governour of the colony of the Massachusetts Bay. From Original Manuscripts*, vol. I (Boston: Phelps and Farnham, 1825), 74. Hereafter referred to as *Winthrop Journal* 1.

8 Ibid., 1:132.

decade, the civil government of Massachusetts had been transformed from a trading company into a covenantal commonwealth, all of whose members were annually elected.

Despite the Bay government's grounding in popular consent, John Winthrop ensured that it was never purely popular or majoritarian. Unlike the deputies who represented the views of their electorate, Winthrop insisted that the Assistants, once elected, held their authority "from God, in way of an ordinance, such as hath the image of God eminently stamped upon it."[9] What set the Assistants apart was their embodiment of particular "gifts of God, as wisdom, learning, etc." Winthrop did not deny that some of the deputies were men of learning, but he rightly insisted that both in fact and "in common repute" the Assistants were among the most educated laymen in the colony.[10] Given their "natural aristocratic" qualities, Winthrop and his fellow Assistants demanded and received a great deal of deference and titular respect. In the spring of 1634, John Cotton delivered an election sermon that argued that no Assistant ought ever be voted out of office barring serious malfeasance or heresy, a doctrine that was embraced throughout Winthrop's career and thereafter.[11] When Israel Stoughton, one of the leaders of the deputies, argued the following year that the power of the governor was merely ministerial rather than magisterial, the General Court barred him "for three years from bearing any publick office."[12] The deputies might serve as the bulwark of the liberties of the freemen they represented, but all authority, properly understood, was reserved for the Assistants, and questioning that authority was met with condign justice.

Winthrop had in fact been reticent to allow the deputies a full and equal seat in the General Court, preferring that they merely consult with the Assistants "to revise all laws, etc. and to reform what they found amiss" without any power "to make any new laws," but he reluctantly acquiesced in the interest of unity and concord.[13] But when, at their very first session, they insisted on the right to set policy as a majority of the General Court, Winthrop flatly refused, demanding that the Assistants enjoy a "negative voice" on all legislative and judicial decisions.[14] To overrule the collective

9 Commonly known as Winthrop's "Little Speech on Liberty," delivered to the General Court in July 1645, it can be found in James Savage, ed., *The History of New England from 1630 to 1649. By John Winthrop, Esq. First Governour of the colony of the Massachusetts Bay. From Original Manuscripts*, vol. II, 228–230. Hereafter referred to as *Winthrop Journal* 2.

10 "John Winthrop's Defense of the Negative Vote," *Winthrop Papers*, 4:382

11 *Winthrop Journal*, 1:132.

12 Ibid., 1:155–156.

13 Ibid., 1:128–129.

14 Ibid., 1:140–142.

judgment of the Assistants, he argued, would "incurre Scandall, by undervaluing the gifts of God" represented by their godly wisdom and learning as "men precedinge in gifts and experience." Even worse, "if the Neg[ative] vo[te] were taken away our Government would be a mere Democratie," and, as Winthrop reminded his fellow settlers, "a Democratie is, among most Civill nations, accounted the meanest and worst of all formes of Government."[15]

The problem with democratic regimes was not only their inherent instability, but their tendency to promote licentiousness. In such regimes, a spirit of liberty arose whereby each person was free "to do what he lists," a freedom "to evil as well as to good." Such a purely natural or fallen liberty was "incompatible and inconsistent with authority, and cannot endure the least restraints of the most just authority." A truly Christian and "civil" liberty, by contrast, was "a liberty to that only which is good, just, and honest." This latter liberty was covenantal, resting on both "the covenant between God and man, in the moral law" as well as "the politic covenants and constitutions, amongst men themselves." Winthrop did not deny the liberties of the freemen or the role of the deputies as their spokesmen, but he insisted that such liberties must be "maintained and exercised in a way of subjection to authority," and that authority was exclusive to the Assistants.[16] This was no violation of the freemen's liberty or power because it was grounded in their electoral consent and thus established "accordinge to their will, and Covenant."[17] Moreover, because this authority required the additional consent within the General Court of the deputies, Winthrop considered the Bay government one of the ideal forms, namely "a mixed aristocracy" that was consensual in its covenanting and, as a true commonwealth, in "no waye Arbitrary."[18]

The regime Winthrop created then was a mixed republic led by an educated and godly natural aristocracy. But as a Puritan commonwealth, Winthrop was equally influential in arranging the extensive imbrication of the churches and the state as in establishing the latter. To be sure, the Bay regime was never a mere theocracy. The very being of the congregational churches of Massachusetts was distinct from civil government. As independent bodies, each church was a self-governing ecclesiastical institution whose powers and discipline were restricted to fully covenanting members. The civil authority, by contrast, exercised it power over all residents. To ensure that

15 "Defense of Negative Vote," *Winthrop Papers*, 4:382–383.
16 "Speech on Liberty," *Winthrop Journal*, 2:280–281.
17 "Defense of Negative Vote," *Winthrop Papers*, 4:385.
18 "Arbitrary Government," *Winthrop Papers*, 4: 482.

church and state were kept in their proper spheres, the Assistants were forbidden to exercise ecclesiastical powers and church officers were barred from political office.

Despite these demarcations, the congregational churches exercised immense influence over the political life of the colony. Indeed, Winthrop assured this influence in early 1631. After admitting the first cadre of freemen, he passed an order restricting the franchise to church members to ensure that "the body of the commons may be preserved of honest and good men."[19] Since these men had explicitly agreed to a congregational discipline based on the duly authorized ministerial interpretation of the Word, Winthrop had helped institute a Puritan one-party state in Massachusetts.[20] Although banned from elective office, the clergy had immense political sway. As the duly authorized interpreters of Scripture, they were uniquely positioned to mold public opinion among the covenanted electorate, especially in their election sermons and in their mid-week lectures. In fact, outside of the General Court they enjoyed something of a monopoly on public political discourse. Nor did they lack direct influence over the regime, as they were routinely placed on most committees created by the General Court, often taking the leading role in drafting laws and formulating policy. They also enjoyed a robust role as arbiters of almost all disputes within the regime. Thus, when the deputies once again attacked the "negative vote" in 1643, the Assistants requested the judgment of the clerics. Not only did they support the Assistants fully, one of them "wrote a small treatise" that almost directly restated Winthrop's warning of "the unavoidable change into a democracy, if the negative voice were taken away." Suffice it to say that the Assistants veto was upheld and those agitating against it "appeared no further in it."[21] Many of these ministerial consultations were initiated by the clerics themselves, and they were far from infrequent; one historian has chronicled at least seventy between 1633 and Winthrop's death in 1649.[22] Altogether, the Bay churches had profound political power.

Perhaps even more remarkable was the intrusion of the state into the religious life of the colony. To be sure, all Calvinists acknowledged that the civil magistrate had, in addition to his secular role, a duty to suppress "idolatry,

[19] Shurtleff, *Colony Records*, 1:87.

[20] This argument is more fully fleshed out in Darren Staloff, *The Making of an American Thinking Class: Intellectuals and Intelligentsia in Puritan Massachusetts* (New York: Oxford University Press, 1998).

[21] *Winthrop Journal*, 2:115–119.

[22] David D. Hall, *The Faithful Shepherd: A History of the New England Ministry in the Seventeenth Century* (Chapel Hill: University of North Carolina Press for the Institute of Early American History and Culture, 1972), 130.

sacrilege against God's name, blasphemies against his truth, and other offenses against religion" so that "a public manifestation of religion may exist among Christians."[23] That the Bay authorities certainly did, from suppressing Antinomians and Separatists on one side to Arminians and Presbyterians on the other. But they went further than simply curtailing heresy. Although church membership was entirely voluntary and covenantal, church attendance was mandatory for all, and in 1635 the General Court passed a law mandating fines and imprisonment for violators.[24] More than that, the Assistants exercised a restraining hand over the churches themselves. Precisely because the Congregationalists lacked an ecclesiastical hierarchy, whenever a church was either hopelessly divided or unable to suppress heresies, it was Winthrop and his fellow Assistants who interceded, either mediating or directly suppressing dissent. Indeed, the General Court forbade any laymen from gathering into a church without the "approbation" of the Assistants and "the elders of the greater part of the churches."[25] Although each congregation was free to establish any mode of compensation for its ministers it chose, the General Court ordered in 1638 that those expenses must be shared by "every inhabitant in any towne" whether full members or not.[26] Even disruptive or disrespectful acts toward clerical authority were subject to fines and public humiliation, including wearing a paper affixed to the perpetrator's chest reading "A WANTON GOSPELLER."[27] Finally, it was the General Court that summoned the clerics to Synods (some five were held during Winthrop's tenure) and then enforced their edicts. The congregational churches constituted the political nation that comprised the Puritan regime in Massachusetts, and Winthrop and his fellow Assistants were their "nursing fathers."

JUDICIAL AND LEGAL FOUNDING

John Winthrop's impact on the judicial life of Puritan Massachusetts was every bit as profound as its constitutional forms. With his fellow Assistants, he forged the basic legal institutions and procedures of the Bay colony, combining traditional English forms with covenantal religious imperatives. He also sought to control the legal mores of the settlement by forestalling the

23 John Calvin, *Institutes of the Christian Religion, 1536 Edition*, trans. Ford Lewis Battles (Grand Rapids: Wm. B. Eerdmans, 1975; revised, 1986), 208 (4.20.3).

24 Shurtleff, *Colony Records*, 1:140.

25 Ibid., 1:168.

26 Ibid., 1:240–241.

27 Ibid., 2:179.

formulation of a fixed legal code. Here too they combined traditional practices with the needs of a godly community. Although this latter effort was ultimately unsuccessful, Winthrop's leadership in it and his arguments in defense of a common law approach to Massachusetts' laws reveals both his own understanding of the purposes of the law as well as his deeper covenantal commitments.

The legal institutions that Winthrop helped establish appear, at first glance, largely traditional. At their very first meeting in Massachusetts, the Assistants proclaimed themselves and a select group of prominent settlers empowered with all the "power that justices of [the] peace hath in England for reformation of abuses and punishing offenders" within their respective settlements.[28] Like their English counterparts, they could only inflict corporal punishments and minor fines, and more serious offenses required the presence of several Assistants while the most heinous cases were reserved for the entire Court of Assistants. As such, each Bay magistrate occupied the same status as the traditional justice of the peace, while the Assistants collectively served the role of the English county commission of the Peace and its select quorum members.[29] They also adopted English forms for civil and criminal pleadings and procedures.[30] Like the English commission of the Peace, the Court of Assistants assumed broad administrative functions like licensing taverns, enforcing sumptuary codes, establishing poor rates, and maintaining infrastructure.[31]

On closer inspection, however, the legal powers and modes of the Bay magistrates were far from traditional. Unlike their English counterparts, Bay magistrates exercised broad powers over matters of religion, enforcing church attendance and mandating fast and thanksgiving observances. Even more striking was their treatment of religious dissent. As one historian has noted, whatever leniency was offered to "ordinary offenders" was withheld from "political and religious offenders."[32] While generally imposing acts of public exposure and ridicule, punishments were generally prompt and occasionally brutal. Indeed, one scholar of the Bay's legal procedures has characterized them as inquisitorial; "the magistrates themselves compiled evidence,

[28] Ibid., 1:74.

[29] Francis J. Bremer, "The County of Massachusetts: The Governance of John Winthrop's Suffolk and the Shaping of the Massachusetts Bay Colony," in *The World of John Winthrop: Essays on England and New England, 1588–1649*, ed. Francis J. Bremer and Lynn A. Botelho (Boston: Massachusetts Historical Society, 2005), 212.

[30] Bremer, *Biography*, 29.

[31] Bremer, "County of Massachusetts," 214 & 212.

[32] Edgar J. McManus, *Law and Liberty in Early New England: Criminal Justice and Due Process, 1620–1692* (Amherst.: University of Massachusetts, 1993), 117.

prosecuted, questioned witnesses and the accused, judged, and passed sentence." Given the rarity of juries in non-capital crimes (perhaps four were empaneled before 1660), it is not surprising that the magistrates enjoyed a conviction rate of near ninety percent.[33] Despite their use of some traditional forms, the magistrates vigorously enforced religious and political orthodoxy, supplying vital cohesion for the covenanted community of the godly.

Although several of those outside the congregational order did object to the legal procedures of Winthrop and his colleagues, most church members and their representatives had little problem with them. What they resented, and resisted, was the absence of a fixed legal code. This left each magistrate with an immense deal of discretion. The Reverend Thomas Hooker frankly told Winthrop that he considered such latitude "a way which leads directly to tyranny," adding that "if it was in my liberty I should choose neither to live nor leave my posterity to such a government."[34] In fact, Puritans in England had been in the forefront of the struggle for legal codification, and much of the laity brought that struggle with them to New England.[35]

The drive to curtail this discretion began in 1635 when the deputies insisted on the establishment of a committee to draft a code of fixed laws.[36] As a member of the committee, Winthrop was able to check the effort, but the very next year the deputies empaneled a fresh committee that resulted in John Cotton's code popularly known as "Moses His Judicialls" that was presented in October 1636.[37] Cotton's code, however, was primarily a set of constitutional and biblical principles, and was therefore passed over without comment. Undeterred, the deputies commissioned yet another committee in March 1638 to solicit from the towns the "heads of such necessary & fundamentall lawes" as seemed requisite to ensure their liberties and "make a compendious abri[d]gment of the same."[38] After further prompting in 1640, Nathaniel Ward's *Body of Liberties* was finally adopted in December 1641.[39] Winthrop resisted this effort, as he had all its predecessors and successors, and for that resistance was charged with supporting arbitrary

33 John M. Murrin, "Magistrates, Sinners, and a Precarious Liberty: Trial by Jury in Seventeenth-Century New England," in *Saints and Revolutionaries: Essays on Early American History*, ed. David D. Hall, John M. Murrin, and Thad W. Tate (New York: W. W. Norton & Co., 1984), 163–164.

34 Quoted in Bremer, *Biography*, 54–55.

35 Bremer, "County of Massachusetts," 222.

36 Shurtleff, *Colony Records*, 1:147.

37 Ibid., 1:174–175; and *Winthrop Journal*, 1:202.

38 Shurtleff, *Colony Records*, 1:222.

39 *Winthrop Journal*, 2:52–56. On the further "prompting" of this codification in 1640, see Shurtleff, *Colony Records*, 1:292–293.

government (a charge which he defended on October 30, 1644). Even so, the *Body of Liberties* fell far short of a full codification and "in many key respects more resembled a bill of rights than a law code."[40] It would not be until 1648, shortly before Winthrop's death, that the Bay freemen finally adopted a fixed code of laws and penalties.

Winthrop's reasons for resisting the codification of Massachusetts' laws reveal the same combination of traditional mores and covenantal ideal found in his design of legal institutions and procedures. To begin with, Winthrop reminded his fellow freemen that they were bound by their charter to "make no laws repugnant to the laws of England." But the charter was silent on mere "orders" and discretionary acts, so that enforcing civil marriages and congregational discipline did not violate the charter provided these were done "by practice and custom."[41] Winthrop also held that such a codification would violate the pattern that God had established in his Word "where so few penalties are prescribed" and many punishments were "referred to the judges." Indeed, even "God himself varies the punishments of the same offences, as the offences vary in their circumstances." It was for this reason that he insisted that "all punishments, except such as are made certain in the law of God," should be "left arbitrary to the wisdom of judges."[42] Such arbitrary discretion would be limited, in Winthrop's account, by the growing body of customary or common law that had been emerging gradually in the first decade of settlement.

Winthrop's defense of a common law position was hardly surprising given his own immersion in that tradition in England. Given the variety of English regions from which settlers hailed, and the concomitant variety of customary laws they established in their townships, Winthrop believed that any uniform code of law would be more arbitrary than none at all.[43] As he reminded the General Court, "God hath not confined all wisdom, etc., to any one generation, that they should set rules for all others to walk by."[44] It was far wiser, as in England, to allow the "fundamental laws" to emerge "*pro re nata*" as "occasions" and circumstances demanded.[45] Even biblical codes, like that of John Cotton, ignored the reality of varied circumstances and changing needs. In

40 McManus, *Law*, 9.

41 Quoted in Bremer, "County of Massachusetts," 223.

42 Quoted in Bremer, *Biography*, 86.

43 On customary laws in the Bay townships, see David Grayson Allen, *In English Ways: The Movement of Societies and the Transferal of English Local Law and Custom to Massachusetts Bay in the Seventeenth Century* (New York: W. W. Norton & Co., 1982), 208–209.

44 Quoted in Bremer, *Biography*, 86

45 Quoted in Bremer, "County of Massachusetts," 223.

fact, Calvin himself had insisted that "the law of God which we call the moral law" was not a fixed and final code so much as a commitment to equity arising from "that conscience which God has engraved upon men's hearts." It was for that reason that he, like Winthrop, defended common and customary laws, and as long as those "laws shall be framed to that rule" of equity, he insisted that "there is no reason why we should disapprove of them, howsoever they may differ from the Jewish law, or among themselves."[46]

Underlying Winthrop's defense of a common law stance in the Bay colony was another of his covenantal ideals, that of Christian charity. Winthrop feared that the set penalties and fines entailed by a fixed code would weigh unduly on the least advantaged. "All punishments ought to be just," he noted, and yet each offense varied by "occasion of circumstances." Given that variety, he believed "it would be unjust to inflict the same punishment upon the least as upon the greatest."[47] In fact, the unstated but widely acknowledged reason that Winthrop favored judicial discretion was that it allowed him to show far more leniency toward godly violators than his fellow Assistants or the deputies approved of. He believed that fines should be light and second and third chances frequent, a practice his far stricter colleague Thomas Dudley thought a ploy for personal popularity. It was just such leniency toward Roger Williams that resulted in a rebuke from the ministers in early 1636. "Strict discipline" rather than covenantal compassion, they insisted, "was more needful in plantations than in a settled state." Winthrop duly acknowledged his error and pledged "to take a more strict course hereafter."[48]

STATESMANSHIP AND CHRISTIAN CHARITY

John Winthrop was not merely the most influential constitutional and legal theorist in early Massachusetts, he was also its most important statesman. His

46 Calvin, *Institutes of the Christian Religion*, 216 (4.20.16). Calvin had specifically rejected criticisms of the "common laws of nations" as "perilous and seditious," as well as "false and foolish." Ibid., 215 (4.20.14).

47 Quoted in Bremer, *Biography*, 86.

48 *Winthrop Journal*, 1:178. Despite this rebuke, Winthrop received some small measure of vindication from the clerics in the following decade. In reply to several interrogatories from the deputies, they concluded that, although the laws and their penalties ought to be fixed, "where the law may seem to the conscience of the judge to inflict a greater penalty than the offence deserveth" the judge might suspend sentence until the next meeting of the General Court which might decide to "inflict the sentence or to mitigate it." See " Answers of the Reverend Elders to Certaine Questions Propounded to Them," *A Collection of Original Papers Relative to the History of the Colony of Massachusetts-Bay*, ed. Thomas Hutchinson (Boston, 1769; reprint, Albany, 1865), 1:210–211.

constitutional and legal doctrines informed that statesmanship, but so too did his Puritan covenantalism, especially his commitment to Christian charity, the purported title of his lay *Arabella* sermon. As he reminded his fellow emigrants, God had placed them in a variety of social roles, some eminent and others humble. The purpose of this unequal status was not to exalt the more prominent but that "every man might have need of other[s]." The covenant Winthrop and his fellow settlers were entering was not only with God but also with each other to the end that "they may be knitt together more nearly in the Bond of brotherly affeccion."[49] This bond of Christian charity required a willingness to sacrifice for the public good of the larger covenanted community. "The welfare of the whole," he urged when defending immigration restrictions passed in the aftermath of the Antinomian controversy, must never "be put to apparent hazard for the advantage of any particular members."[50] It was "not onely conscience" that demanded that "the care of the publique must oversway all private respects," he insisted, it was required to uphold "mere Civill pollicy."[51] The communitarian bent of Winthrop's covenantalism required deference and obedience from the common citizens, but it also demanded that those of higher status sacrifice for their less exalted brethren and the common good. God had not made anyone "more honourable than another or more wealthy, etc., out of any perticular and singuler respect" to that person, Winthrop informed his auditors, "but for the glory of his Creator and the Common good of the Creature, Man."[52] The pursuit of that common good, and the willingness to sacrifice for it, characterized much of the statesmanship of John Winthrop.

Perhaps Winthrop's greatest act of statesmanship, one that occurred before he set foot upon the *Arabella*, exemplified this commitment to charity and sacrifice. As is well known, in the summer of 1629 Winthrop and eleven other "planters" mutually pledged to emigrate to Massachusetts under the sole condition that the charter and control of the colonial government travel with them. This condition was accepted by the stockholding "adventurers," and John Winthrop was duly elected governor on October 20. Winthrop had thus eliminated the crippling government-at-a-distance that had proved so disastrous for previous corporate colonies in Virginia and Plymouth. But what is less known is that he also alleviated the bigger burden that had hampered those settlements,

49 "Modell of Christian Charity," *Winthrop Papers*, 2:283.
50 "Defense of an Order," *Winthrop Papers*, 3:423.
51 "Modell of Christian Charity," *Winthrop Papers*, 2:293.
52 Ibid., 283.

namely their crushing debt and consequent lack of financial and fiscal resources.

On the very day Winthrop was elected, the company agreed to establish a series of committees staffed with planters and adventurers to determine what to do with the company's assets and debts. Winthrop reported to the General Court the following month that the committees had not yet been able to agree, but nonetheless he urged the adventurers to double their investment (not surprisingly, they demurred). On December 1, he proposed that the current stock be devalued by two-thirds and that the planters be given seven years to repay that sum. In exchange, fresh investments would be unencumbered and solely devoted to commerce. Understandably, many investors were none too pleased, but Winthrop appealed to their covenantal consciences. As in his subsequent *Arabella* sermon, he reminded them that "the eyes of all the godly are upon you" and "what can you doe more honorable" than to "denye your own profit, that we may say Londoners can be willing to lose that the Gospell" might gain. The adventurers were the fathers of this new project, and a loving father "will not send forth a Childe without a blessing and a portion." "Consider the difficulty of plantations," he urged, and how even the settlement of Israel had required God's miraculous aids. But most importantly, he reminded them of the covenantal promises that underlay their willingness to sacrifice their investments. "You have given it to God," he insisted, "and made such protestation, as if Godes gloiye and the welfare of the plantation should require it, you would not onely lende it, but lose it."[53] The adventurers ultimately agreed to his terms only to discover at the next, and final, meeting of the General Court in London that Winthrop intended to devalue all of the stock by two-thirds, both the original and the subsequent issue, and would secure it all from repayment for a full seven years. Predictably "some exceptions was taken" by those adventurers who had disbursed fresh funds, but Winthrop held his ground, stating forcefully that "the undertakers would not continue their said undertaking but upon the same conditions."[54] If the planters were to risk their lives, so too should the adventurers their funds. Winthrop's victory ensured that, with adequate funds and clear control of future revenues, the Puritan settlement of Massachusetts would never face the brutal starving time of the Virginia or Plymouth plantations.

Winthrop's fiscal charity, especially with other people's money, earned him more than a few opponents. One of the original adventurers who travelled to

53 "Address of John Winthrop to the Company of the Massachusetts Bay," *Winthrop Papers*, 2:175–177.

54 Shurtleff, *Colony Records*, 1:67.

Massachusetts with him, William Vassall, spent much of the following decades trying to undermine Winthrop and the regime he established. Even his colleague and occasional rival, Thomas Dudley, bristled when Winthrop dared question him "about some bargains he made with some poor men" that he "held to be oppressing usury, and within compass of the statute."[55] But Winthrop practiced what he preached as Dudley was to learn some two years later. When Dudley first succeeded Winthrop as governor in 1634, he spitefully initiated an investigation of Winthrop "for such commodityes as hee hath receaved of the common stocke."[56] The reported account must have shocked the new governor: his predecessor had expended over £1,200 of his own wealth during his tenure, and had received in compensation roughly £250.[57] Winthrop had been secretly subsidizing the new colony, and in fact it so wrecked his finances that in the following decade some of the deputies suggested he lacked the necessary means to uphold the dignity of the office of magistrate.[58] Winthrop's commitment to covenantal charity decidedly began at home.

It was this charitable devotion to "brotherly affection" that gave rise to Winthrop's notorious leniency. As previously noted, he simply thought it unjust to impose the same fines on the poor as the rich. But it also informed his leniency toward some forms of religious heterodoxy. To be sure, Winthrop could be every bit as draconian as his colleagues when faced with dissidents who denied the legitimacy of the New England Way or refused to respect its authorities. But for those sincere dissenters who were part of the covenanted communities of the Bay churches and accepted the legitimacy of its civil institutions, Winthrop was remarkably patient if not indulgent. As he told one interlocutor, his preferred strategy when facing differences among the godly was to "improve that which is profitable, and cover the rest with love."[59] It was in that spirit that Winthrop dealt, often with great success, with recalcitrant and errant church members. To cite just one example, in late November 1631, the church of Watertown fell into divisions over doctrines espoused by their lay ruling elder, Richard Brown. Among other errors, Brown "persisted in his opinion of the truth of the Romish church." Upon learning of this heresy (no small one for a Protestant), Winthrop and his colleagues wrote to the congregation suggesting that they consider removing Brown from his office. Brown's faction responded that they might consider it if he was proven to be

55 *Winthrop Journal*, 1:73.
56 Shurtleff, *Colony Records*, 1:120.
57 Ibid., 1:131. A full statement of the accounting can be found in *Winthrop Papers*, 3:172–174.
58 *Winthrop Journal*, 2:55–56.
59 Quoted in Bremer, *Biography*, 29.

in error. Winthrop did not summon Brown to court or reprove his supporters. Instead, in early December he visited their church with two other Assistants and made the following statement:

> . . . the governour told them, that being come to settle peace, &c. they might proceed in three distinct respects: 1. As the magistrates, (their assistance being desired). 2. As members of a neighbouring congregation. 3. Upon the answer which we received of our letter, which did no way satisfy us.

Winthrop's combination of irenic opening and veiled threat worked to perfection. The congregation chose the second option. Winthrop, after hearing both sides, reconciled them to "seek God in a day of humiliation" with "each party promising to reform what hath been amiss, &c.; and the pastor gave thanks to God, and the assembly brake up."[60] Once the congregants of Watertown acknowledged the authority of the Assistants, Winthrop eschewed all coercion and sought godly reconciliation. Less than one year later, the church of Watertown removed Brown from his office "in regard passion and distemper in speech," and even Brown acknowledged the legitimacy of their decision and "declared his repentance."[61] Winthrop had covered the discord in Watertown with love.

This same combination of patience and firmness characterized Winthrop's treatment of the errant divine Roger Williams. Williams arrived in Boston in early 1631 and promptly refused to join its church because it refused to embrace his separatist principles. From there he went to Salem, whose congregation sought to ordain him despite his continued separatism and principled stand against the magistrates' interference in religious matters. Rather than punish or censure Williams, Winthrop simply wrote to the church of Salem to express his surprise that "they would choose him without advising with the council" and requesting they "forbear to proceed till they had conferred about it."[62] The congregation promptly withdrew their offer and Williams, after being made a freeman of the colony, obligingly decamped for the friendlier confines of Plymouth Plantation.

When Williams returned to Salem in late 1633, he once again roiled its political waters by writing a letter to the governor of Plymouth questioning the validity of the Massachusetts charter. Just as before, Winthrop wrote to the church of Salem and Williams appeared penitently before the General Court,

60 *Winthrop Journal*, 1:67–68.
61 Ibid., 1:93–96.
62 Ibid., 1:53.

explaining that the letter had been meant only "for the private satisfaction of the governour" of Plymouth, and professing his loyalty to the regime and the king.[63] Once more, Winthrop had avoided a pointed confrontation and breach.

Williams's fate only became dire when, in the following year, Winthrop was replaced as governor with the implacable Thomas Dudley. In November, Williams resumed his public criticism of the colony's charter. No letter was sent this time. Instead, Dudley summoned him before the General Court and censured him. Williams and his fellow congregants in Salem responded in kind. Williams refused to recant his critique of the charter and began urging a complete religious disestablishment, while the congregants of Salem, without any clerical or political sanction, ordained him as their teacher. When Williams remained intractable before a conference of his fellow ministers, on May 6, 1635 the electors of the Bay removed John Endecott, Salem's magistrate, from the Court of Assistants. The church of Salem responded by sending angry letters to the other churches, decrying their narrow and persecuting spirit. Williams was summoned again before the General Court on July 8, and he and his fellow congregants were warned that those who persisted in their protest "were to be removed."[64] In early September, Dudley and the court dropped the proverbial hammer, ejecting all representatives from Salem until its church disowned its letters and demanded that Williams recant his various errors. Although the congregants of Salem finally relented, Williams, with his back against the wall, refused. For his persistent dissent he was banished, although the sentence was suspended until the following spring. When Dudley and the Assistants learned that Williams continued to preach in his home in early January 1636, they finally decided to ship him back to England lest he and his followers "erect a plantation about the Narragansett Bay, from whence the infection would easily spread into these churches."[65] It was at this point that Winthrop broke from his colleagues and secretly warned Williams of his fate, allowing him the opportunity to escape and make his perilous winter passage to what would become Rhode Island. It was this singular act of lenity more than any other that brought the previously mentioned clerical rebuke on Winthrop some few weeks later. Winthrop had defied the collective judgment of the constituted authorities and undermined their attempt to uphold orthodoxy and the discipline of

63 Ibid., 1:122–123.
64 Ibid., 1:162–163.
65 Ibid., 1:175–176.

the godly community. But given the decidedly harsh treatment that Williams would undoubtedly have faced from the ecclesiastical authorities under the Laudian regime upon his arrival in England, it is hard not to see Winthrop's act as one of kindness extended to an errant but sincere fellow-traveler in the faith. Indeed, it was a model of Christian charity.[66]

66 For a brief synopsis of the political dimension of Williams's sojourn in Massachusetts, see Staloff, *Thinking Class*, 21–22, 31–32, and 36–39.

3

Friendly Laws: William Penn's Christian Jurisprudence

Andrew R. Murphy

To many seventeenth-century observers, including a Quaker in a volume devoted to "Christian jurists" would have been anathema, since orthodox early modern Christians considered it plainly evident that Quakers were anything but Christian. Jonathan Clapham's 1668 *Guide to the True Religion*, for example, described Quakers as not "properly . . . a sect of Christians, but rather . . . a total apostacy from Christianity" – devoid of learning, elevating the Light Within to a standard sufficient for salvation – and charged them with "plainly overthrow[ing] the foundations of Christianity."[1] Quakers, on the other hand, just as fervently believed that they were the true Christians and authentic heirs of the Protestant Reformation. William Penn and fellow Quaker George Whitehead referred to themselves as "your greatly traduced, but truly Christian Friends" in *The Christian-Quaker*, their 1674 defense of Quakerism against its many critics.[2]

BIOGRAPHY

William Penn was born in London in 1644. His father, Admiral (later, Sir) William Penn, served as an officer in the parliamentary navy during the Civil Wars (1642–1649), and later – showing a political adroitness his son would never quite match – supported the Restoration of King Charles II in 1660. Educated at the Chigwell School in Essex and by private tutors on the family's estates in England and Ireland, William entered Christ Church, Oxford, in

1 Jonathan Clapham, *A Guide to the True Religion, or, A Discourse Directing to Make a Wise Choice of That Religion Men Venture Their Salvation Upon* (London, 1668), 62, 63–64. Penn's response was *The Guide Mistaken, and Temporizing Rebuked, or, A Brief Reply to Jonathan Clapham's book* (London, 1668).

2 William Penn and George Whitehead, *The Christian-Quaker and his Divine Testimony Vindicated* (London, 1674), Epistle Dedicatory.

1660, and was expelled (apparently for religious nonconformity) just two years later. Following his expulsion, Penn traveled to the Continent, where he studied with noted theologian Moses Amyraut at the Protestant Academy in Saumur, France. We do not know his specific course of study at either of these institutions, but do know the general shape of the curriculum to which students were exposed. The undergraduate course of study at seventeenth-century Christ Church, for example, "embraced in theory if not always in practice, logic, mathematics, natural and moral philosophy, the elements of religion, and prescribed classical authors."[3] The standard curriculum leading to the Master's degree at Saumur generally took two years, with first-year logic and ethics and second-year physics and metaphysics, in addition to Greek, Hebrew, theology, rhetoric, and mathematics. Theology students tended to spend an additional year focusing on Scripture and rhetoric. The institutional backdrop of Penn's time at Saumur would likely have been similar to that in Oxford: attending worship, hearing sermons, and engaging in disputations on philosophical and theological topics.[4] His study of the law ended almost as soon as it began, when plague broke out just as Penn enrolled at Lincoln's Inn, London, in February 1665.

After exiting Lincoln's Inn, Penn was sent to Ireland by his father and charged with settling Sir William's land claims and negotiating leases with his Irish tenants. He became a convinced Quaker in 1667, after attending a Meeting in Cork. Over the next few years, Penn spent time in prison (both in England and Ireland) for his Quakerism.[5]

Penn's career as a public religious controversialist began in earnest with the 1670 publication of *The People's Ancient and Just Liberties Asserted*, a purported transcript of his trial, along with fellow Quaker William Mead, for disturbing the peace by preaching in a London street. He spent much of the 1670s traveling, writing, and speaking on behalf of fellow Quakers in England and Europe, arguing for toleration as a general principle as well as for the rights of Quakers more specifically. As prospects for toleration in

3 E. G. W. Bill, *Education at Christ Church, Oxford, 1660–1800* (Oxford: Oxford University Press, 1988), 245. See also *The History of the University of Oxford*. Volume IV: *Seventeenth-Century Oxford*, ed. Nicholas Tyacke (Oxford: Clarendon Press, 1997), and Judith Curthoys, *The Cardinal's College: Christ Church, Chapter and Verse* (London: Profile, 2012).

4 Betty Haglund, "Guest Editor's Introduction," *Quaker Studies* 16:2 (2012), 147–156; René Fillet, "Les relations entre la Touraine et la Pennsylvanie au XVIIe siècle: Moyse Amyraut et William Penn," *Bulletin de la société d'études anglo-américaines des XVIIe et XVIIIe siècles* 37:1 (1993), 121–140.

5 See Andrew R. Murphy, "From Practice to Theory to Practice: William Penn from Prison to the Founding of Pennsylvania," *History of European Ideas* (2016), http://dx.doi.org/10.1080/01916599.2016.1203592.

England dimmed in the late 1670s, Penn became increasingly interested in obtaining land in America, to instantiate the principles of religious liberty for which he had been advocating – largely unsuccessfully – for more than a decade. In 1681, King Charles II granted Penn a charter for Pennsylvania, and the following year Penn crossed the Atlantic to take up the governorship.

Although shortly after his arrival in 1682 he told a correspondent that "I am like to be an adopted American," Penn returned to England just two years later to pursue a border dispute with his southern neighbor, Lord Baltimore. While there, Penn was swept back up into English politics. He was instrumental in James II's campaign for toleration, and has been called the "intellectual architect of the king's toleration project and one of its leading exponents."[6] That effort came crashing down around James (and Penn) in 1688. After the "Glorious Revolution," his close relationship with the ejected king occasioned widespread suspicion: he was questioned and arrested by the new regime several times, and spent much of the next several years out of the public eye. In the meantime, American affairs brought Penn no shortage of troubles: a bitter schism divided Pennsylvania Quakers in 1692 and 1693, and the Crown took control of the colony between 1692 and 1694. Political and economic relations between Quakers and non-Quakers were notoriously uneasy. The Quaker "peace testimony" complicated issues of colonial defense and law enforcement, and many settlers perceived Penn as a demanding absentee landlord.

The mid-1690s saw Penn emerge once again into his former role as advocate for Quaker causes and for liberty of conscience more generally. His 1693 *Essay Toward the Present and Future Peace of Europe* proposed a European diet of states in an effort to stem the flow of war and conflict that had engulfed Europe throughout the seventeenth century. Penn continued to play an active role in religious debates in both England and Ireland, defending Friends from their critics and pushing for the right to make affirmations, rather than oaths, in English legal settings, an effort that yielded the Affirmation Act of 1696.

Penn finally returned to Pennsylvania late in 1699, but it would be another short visit. He sailed for England less than two years later to oppose renewed efforts to centralize royal control over the American colonies, and never returned. Disputes with the family of his longtime agent Philip Ford landed Penn briefly in debtors' prison during 1708, a humiliating come-down for one who had once dined with monarchs. Strokes paralyzed and enfeebled him during the final six years of his life. He died in 1718, and was buried in the

6 Scott Sowerby, "Of Different Complexions: Religious Diversity and National Identity in James II's Toleration Campaign," *English Historical Review* 124 (2009), 41.

cemetery of the Friends Meeting House in Jordans, Buckinghamshire. Although late in life Penn despaired about the fate of his "holy experiment," his colony thrived, and its capital city grew into the "richest, fastest-growing, and most cultivated of American cities" by the middle of the next century, a "major center of modernity."[7]

PENN'S TREATMENT BY SCHOLARS

For an individual who played such a crucial role in the history of religious toleration, the scholarly literature on William Penn's social, political, and legal thought is surprisingly sparse. Mary Maples Dunn's *William Penn: Politics and Conscience*, which explored the important role that liberty of conscience played in Penn's political thought over the course of his long public career, long stood as the most extensive treatment. Dunn saw in liberty of conscience "the key to the young Penn's politics," and concluded that he was "always constant to that great principle," from which he derived "a political theory which dictated his American settlement." That said: "In America and in England he was, in the end, unable to translate his vision into political terms which were immediately successful."[8] In *Quaker Constitutionalism and the Political Thought of John Dickinson*, Jane Calvert emphasized Penn's role in the broader development of what she calls "Quaker constitutionalism." Originating in early Quakerism's commitment to "peaceful resistance to government to effect constitutional change," the tradition came to embody "a twin emphasis on constitutional unity and perpetuity and a peaceful process of rights advocacy and reform." Although Penn differed in some particulars from the broader Quaker tradition – he balanced Quaker reliance on the inner Light with a healthy respect for the powers of human reason, for example – Calvert calls the 1701 Pennsylvania Charter of Privileges "a quintessentially Quaker document." "In pushing for a constitution that effectively placed power in the hands of the people and alienated their leader, Quakers were repeating a pattern of behavior learned and practiced in the earliest years of their existence in England."[9] She traced the influence of Quaker constitutionalism down to the American Revolution, and more specifically in the political career of eighteenth-century American founder John

7 Henry F. May, *The Enlightenment in America* (New York: Oxford University Press, 1976), 80, 197. See also, generally, my *William Penn: A Life* (New York: Oxford University Press, 2019).

8 Mary Maples Dunn, *William Penn: Politics and Conscience* (Princeton: Princeton University Press, 1967), vii, 193.

9 Jane E. Calvert, *Quaker Constitutionalism and the Political Thought of John Dickinson* (New York: Cambridge University Press, 2009), 6, 11, 134–135.

Dickinson. Most recently, my book *Liberty, Conscience, and Toleration* traced the emergence and development of Penn's political thought by focusing on the major political episodes that attracted his attention as a political thinker and engaged political actor: the controversy over the Second Conventicle Act, the Popish Plot and Exclusion Crisis, the founding and settlement of Pennsylvania, and the contentious reign of James II. Through an examination of writings published in the midst of the religious and political conflicts of Restoration and Revolutionary England, I contextualized Penn's career in England and America, illuminating the mutual interconnections between Penn's political thought and his colonizing venture in America and arguing that studying Penn provides an unparalleled opportunity to explore the relationship between political theory and practice.[10]

Yet William Penn remains, in many ways, a little-known figure. Edward C. O. Beatty's *William Penn as Social Philosopher* presents a wide-ranging treatment of Penn's views on a number of topics, but reads more like a series of set pieces than a coherent treatment of its topic.[11] *The World of William Penn*, an influential collection of essays that appeared in the mid-1980s, contains just one chapter on Penn's political thought, and that essay focuses narrowly on Quaker debates over oaths in legal settings.[12] Penn's role in the Society of Friends has been explored by historians of Quakerism H. Larry Ingle, Hugh Barbour, and William C. Braithwaite.[13] Melvin Endy's focus in his sophisticated account of Penn's thought, *William Penn and Early Quakerism*, is largely restricted to Penn's attempt to harmonize reason and the Inner Light.[14] Penn's role in Quakers' engagement with the English legal system has been chronicled by Craig Horle.[15] Edwin Bronner, J. William Frost, John

10 Andrew R. Murphy, *Liberty, Conscience, and Toleration: The Political Thought of William Penn* (New York: Oxford University Press, 2016).

11 Edward C. O. Beatty, *William Penn as Social Philosopher* (New York: Columbia University Press, 1939). Penn as "crusader for religious toleration," for example, appears after Penn as "builder of a new utopia" and "founder and governor," when in fact Penn advocated for toleration long before he founded and governed.

12 J. William Frost, "The Affirmation Controversy and Religious Liberty," in *The World of William Penn*, ed. Richard S. Dunn and Mary Maples Dunn (Philadelphia: University of Pennsylvania Press, 1986).

13 H. Larry Ingle, *First among Friends: George Fox and the Creation of Quakerism* (New York: Oxford University Press, 1994); Hugh Barbour, ed., *William Penn on Religion and Ethics: The Emergence of Liberal Quakerism* (Lewiston, NY: E. Mellen Press, 1991); William C. Braithwaite, *The Second Period of Quakerism* (London: Macmillan, 1919).

14 Melvin B. Endy, Jr., *William Penn and Early Quakerism* (Princeton: Princeton University Press, 1973).

15 Craig W. Horle, *The Quakers and the English Legal System, 1660–1688* (Philadelphia: University of Pennsylvania Press, 1988).

Smolenski, and Sally Schwartz have analyzed the founding of Pennsylvania and its unique brand of religious and cultural politics.[16] Nor has all the scholarly attention paid to Penn been laudatory: Mary Geiter sharply criticized Penn's conduct as colonial proprietor and courtier, and Ethan Shagan has emphasized the limited nature of Penn's "moderate" Protestant toleration.[17] Other scholarly treatments of Penn have focused on those with whom he associated, or on broader contexts in which he was active. Penn's relationship with English republican Algernon Sidney has been subtly examined by Jonathan Scott, and Penn also figures in Nicholas P. Miller's interpretation of American religious liberty.[18] Despite the recent publication of *The Worlds of William Penn*, with an interdisciplinary roster of scholars exploring Penn's multifaceted life and legacy, William Penn has hardly attracted sustained scholarly analysis in recent years, notwithstanding the explosion of interest in early modern Britain, the Atlantic world, and the history of religious toleration.[19]

TOLERATION AND LIBERTY OF CONSCIENCE

The defining aspiration of Penn's public career lay in his advocacy of religious toleration and liberty of conscience. Toleration generally refers to the political protection of dissenting individuals and groups from the exercise of punitive state power and popular hostility, a basic level of social acceptance and coexistence for people who had long faced fines, corporal punishment, and jail time for attempting to follow the dictates of their consciences. Toleration is also closely connected to "liberty of conscience," a term that sought to

[16] Joseph E. Illick, *William Penn, the Politician: His Relations with the English Government* (Ithaca, NY: Cornell University Press, 1965); Edwin B. Bronner, *William Penn's "Holy Experiment": The Founding of Pennsylvania, 1681–1701* (New York: Temple University/ Columbia University Press, 1962); J. William Frost, A *Perfect Freedom: Religious Liberty in Pennsylvania* (Cambridge: Cambridge University Press, 1990); John Smolenski, *Friends and Strangers: The Making of a Creole Culture in Colonial Pennsylvania* (Philadelphia: University of Pennsylvania Press, 2010); Sally Schwartz, *A Mixed Multitude: The Struggle for Toleration in Colonial Pennsylvania* (New York: New York University Press, 1988).

[17] Mary Geiter, *William Penn* (New York: Longman, 2000); Ethan H. Shagan, *The Rule of Moderation: Violence, Religion and the Politics of Restraint in Early Modern England* (New York: Cambridge University Press, 2011), esp. 306–310.

[18] Jonathan Scott, *Algernon Sidney and the Restoration Crisis, 1677–1683* (New York, Cambridge University Press, 1991), esp. 128–134; Nicholas P. Miller, *The Religious Roots of the First Amendment: Dissenting Protestants and the Separation of Church and State* (New York: Oxford University Press, 2012).

[19] *The Worlds of William Penn*, ed. Andrew R. Murphy and John Smolenski (New Brunswick, NJ: Rutgers University Press, 2019).

ground such protections on a natural rights footing. That said, the seventeenth-century sense of these terms was hardly a model of consistency: Penn himself often used the two terms interchangeably, and the extended title of his *Great Case of Liberty of Conscience* proclaimed the work to be "a general reply to such late discourses as have opposed a toleration."[20] (Worth noting in this regard is the fact that religious toleration proved to be compatible with a range of moral restrictions: Penn's 1679 *Address to Protestants* called on the civil magistrate to act against "drunkenness, whoredoms and fornication ... [and] profuse gaming," which threatened to bring God's judgment on the land.[21])

In recent years, scholars have devoted a great deal of attention to the growth of tolerationist ideas during the Restoration. Of course the period culminated with the passage of the Toleration Act of 1689 and the publication of Locke's well-known *Letter Concerning Toleration* in English that same year. But Locke's *Letter* did not advance entirely new arguments; rather, it synthesized the leading defenses of toleration circulating at the time. Restoration tolerationist arguments came in several forms, and built on parallel arguments that had been offered during the 1640s and 1650s. *Christian arguments* (often appearing, in England, as self-consciously Protestant in nature) emphasized the sanctity of individual conscience, incorporating Scriptural references from the Gospels and letters of Paul or more general reflections on the noncoercive example of the early church. *Epistemological arguments* were grounded on a particular understanding of human belief, which held that true religion requires inner conviction, and that belief resides in the understanding and not the will and was thus impervious to physical coercion. (Governments, on this view, were charged with controlling their subjects' bodies and regulating their property for the common good, but not with compelling belief.) *Historical and political arguments* drew on foundational English concepts and documents – the ancient constitution, Magna Carta – and often involved the presentation of lists of statesmen who endorsed principles of religious liberty, thus providing an historical pedigree for tolerationist claims and fending off criticisms of toleration as novel or an unwarranted "innovation." Finally, *prudential arguments* insisted that toleration produced economic prosperity and civil peace, pointing to the example of tolerating polities like the Netherlands. These arguments often made the sociological point that Dissenters in

20 William Penn, *The Great Case of Liberty of Conscience* (London, 1670).

21 William Penn, *An Address to Protestants* (London, 1679), 7. See also Shagan, *The Rule of Moderation*.

England made up an "industrious" component of the British economy, whose persecution would wreak havoc on the nation's economic health.[22]

FUNDAMENTAL LAW

A key component in the movement for toleration lay in the notion of fundamental law. Penn consistently claimed that legitimate government was founded on two types of laws, fundamental and superficial. Failure to make the important distinction between the two had led, he claimed, to parliamentary overreach and the unjust persecution of peaceful Dissenters.

Fundamental law (in the English case, Magna Carta), as the name suggests, must not to be abrogated under any circumstances, and exists to preserve essential liberties like liberty, property, and representation. Superficial laws, on the other hand – passed by specific parliaments in response to the needs of their day – must change with the times. More importantly, they must not conflict with fundamental law. Fundamental laws form the bedrock of society, and must be maintained at all times, whereas superficial ones may (and indeed must) be adjusted due to specific contingencies and circumstances.[23] Fundamental law secured Englishmen from the exercise of arbitrary power; it was like "stars or compass for [rulers] to steer the vessel of this kingdom by."[24] Furthermore, the rights guaranteed by fundamental law could only be forfeited by clear violations of fundamental law and by established procedures for deciding when this had occurred (the classic case being the right to jury trial, and hence the significance that the Penn-Mead trial held in establishing his public profile). Penn's distinction between fundamental and superficial law enabled him to balance continuity with the need for change and evolution, and to argue that the changes he sought were not reckless innovations but rather a return to time-honored traditional constitutional values.

Penn grounded his argument for liberty of conscience squarely in his English heritage, and aimed it at English audiences, drawing on the notion of fundamental law to establish his claims. To find clear and compelling arguments against persecution, he wrote, we do not need to "scour the Corpus Civile of Justinian"; instead, we need only recommit to the "good,

22 These arguments are canvassed in *Liberty, Conscience, and Toleration*, passim; see also Andrew R. Murphy, *Conscience and Community: Revisiting Toleration and Religious Dissent in Early Modern England and America* (University Park: Penn State University Press, 2001), esp. Chapters 3 and 4.

23 Penn, *England's Present Interest Considered* (London, 1675), in *The Political Writings of William Penn*, ed. Andrew R. Murphy (Indianapolis: Liberty Fund Press, 2002), 26.

24 Ibid., 52.

old, and admirable laws of England" which, were they faithfully implemented, would be more than adequate to safeguard liberty and property. English liberty and property were guaranteed by fundamental law, which predated Protestantism in England (after all, "civil society was in the world before the Protestant profession"). On this understanding, the 1670 Conventicle Act, which punished gatherings for worship outside the established Church of England, was a superficial law that was deeply incompatible with fundamental law. In this regard, the movement for religious toleration took issue with the persecutory framework of Restoration England itself. An anonymous contemporary of Penn's cautioned magistrates to "look, not so much whether they act regularly according to the late Act against Conventicles, as whether the Act itself be regular and according to the fundamental laws."[25] Simply passing legislation through Parliament was no guarantee of that legislation's legitimacy; certainly Catholics had passed anti-Protestant legislation in the past, legislation long denounced by Protestants as illegitimate.[26]

JUDGES, JURIES, AND THE LAW

One of the most extensive meditations on English law that William Penn ever engaged in appeared early in his career: *The Peoples Ancient and Just Liberties asserted*, a "transcript" of his 1670 trial with William Mead for disturbing the peace. ("Transcript" appears in quotation marks here since no true record of the trial's proceedings exists. Though presented in a dialogue format, purporting to recount what happened in the courtroom, *Peoples* presents a stylized and heroic construction, aimed at presenting the two as railroaded by a persecuting state-church system.[27]) In the trial, Penn and Mead gave voice to a tradition of political and legal argument deeply committed to the idea that juries were legitimate judges of both law *and* fact, empowered to protect individuals from the tendency of governments to exceed the just limits of their powers and trample on individual liberty.

In an especially important passage at the trial's conclusion, Penn cited Coke's *Institutes*, the touchstone for understandings of English common law. He

25 Anonymous, *The Englishman* (London, 1670), 12.

26 Penn, *The Great Case*, 35.

27 For a more extensive account of the trial, the transcript, and the light it sheds on Penn's political and legal thought, see Andrew R. Murphy, "Trial Transcript as Political Theory: Principles and Performance in the *Penn-Mead* Case," *Political Theory* 41:6 (2013), 775–808; and *Liberty, Conscience, and Toleration*, Chapter 3.

> [a]ppeal[ed] to the jury, who are my judges, and this great assembly, whether the proceedings of the court are not most arbitrary, and void of all law, in offering to give the jury their charge in the absence of the prisoners: I say, it is directly opposite to, and destructive of the undoubted right of every *English* prisoner, as *Cook* [sic] in the 2. *Inst.* 29. on the Chapter of *Magna Charta* speaks.[28]

Collapsing the distinction between juries and judges, as Penn did here – "the jury, who are my judges" – in effect makes judges virtually irrelevant to the finding of guilt and innocence and elevates juries to supreme judicial function. Penn frames the jury as the guardian of English liberties against the arbitrary proceedings of the bench. And in making these claims, Penn appeals to authoritative proof-texts (here, Coke's commentary on Magna Carta in Volume 2 of the *Institutes*).[29]

The position advanced by Penn and Mead in their trial closely resembles what Lois Schwoerer has called a "jury ideology," which defended the jury as protector of "subjects and their rights, liberties, and laws from arbitrary and lawless government."[30] Such a view had deep roots in early modern English law. As Thomas Green has put it, "the coercion of jurors meant more than the deprivation of the defendant's right to trial by jury. Coercion of jurors also meant the loss by Englishmen of control over the law."[31] This commitment to the importance of juries reflected earlier Leveller critiques of the English legal system, and continued to animate Anglo-American law and politics, as Shannon Stimson and Jason Frank, among others, have noted.[32]

Part of the reason that juries were so important to Penn had to do with his suspicion about the susceptibility of common law to abuse by politically motivated prosecutors. The common law was another deeply rooted element of English political and legal culture; the judge in the Penn-Mead case, London mayor Sir Samuel Starling, referred to it as "lex non scripta,"

28 Penn, *The Peoples Ancient and Just Liberties Asserted* (London, 1670), in *Political Writings of William Penn*, 13.

29 See Coke, *The Second Part of the Institutes*, Chapter 29. The most accessible recent version can be found in *The Selected Writings of Sir Edward Coke*, ed. Steve Sheppard (Indianapolis: Liberty Fund, 2003), 2:848–873.

30 Lois Schwoerer, "Law, Liberty, and Jury 'Ideology,'" in *Revolutionary Currents: Nation Building in the Transatlantic World*, ed. Michael A. Morrison and Melinda Zook (Lanham, MD: Rowman and Littlefield, 2004), 36.

31 Thomas Andrew Green, *Verdict according to Conscience: Perspectives on the English Criminal Trial Jury, 1200–1800* (Chicago: University of Chicago Press, 1985), 154.

32 Shannon Stimson, *The American Revolution in the Law: Anglo-American Jurisprudence before John Marshall* (Princeton: Princeton University Press, 1990); Jason Frank, *Constituent Moments: Enacting the People in Postrevolutionary America* (Durham, NC: Duke University Press, 2010), Introduction and Chapter 1.

or unwritten law, growing organically out of English historical experience from time immemorial.[33] But Penn found common law as used in his case to be arbitrary and vague. When he asked the Court to specify which law he had broken, he was told that he had violated the common law, to which he replied:

> It is too general and imperfect an answer to say it is the common law, unless we knew both where and what it is. For where there is no law there is no transgression, and that law which is not in being is so far from being common that it is no law at all.

Leveller spokesman John Lilburne had claimed during his own trial, in 1646, that "I think no man in the world fully and truly knows" the common law, and Penn and Mead implied the same sort of disbelief.[34] Combine a vague standard like common law with the widespread persecuting impulses of the Restoration state-church regime, *Peoples* suggests, and one finds situations like that faced by Penn and Mead, to which the language of the ancient constitution and of "ancient" and fundamental law offered a means for resistance and opposition.[35]

CIVIL INTEREST

In *One Project for the Good of England*, published in the midst of the Popish Plot crisis of the late 1670s, Penn argued that although one might hope for a religiously-unified society, a more realistic prospect would be to "recur to some lower but true principle for the present."[36] He named that "lower but true principle" civil interest, describing it as "the foundation and end of civil government . . . a legal endeavour to keep rights, or augment honest profits, whether it be in a private

[33] Elsewhere Starling identified it as "common right," something that was "imprinted in every man's mind" (Starling, *An Answer* [London, 1671], 18).

[34] John Lilburne, *The Just Mans Justification: or A Letter by Way of Plea in Barre* (London, 1646), 5.

[35] See Janelle Greenberg, *The Radical Face of the Ancient Constitution: St. Edward's "Laws" in Early Modern Political Thought* (New York: Cambridge University Press, 2001). On Penn's distrust of common law, see Calvert, *Quaker Constitutionalism*, 91–94. The scholarly literature on the period often links the common law with discussions of the "ancient constitution" so definitively laid out by J. G. A. Pocock, Glenn Burgess, and others. See J. G. A. Pocock, *The Ancient Constitution and the Feudal Law: A Study of English Historical Thought in the Seventeenth Century* (New York: Cambridge University Press, 1957); and Glenn Burgess, *The Politics of the Ancient Constitution: An Introduction to English Political Thought, 1603–1642* (University Park: Penn State University Press, 1992).

[36] Penn, *One Project for the Good of England*, 1, in *Political Writings*, 120. For details of the Plot and exclusion controversies, see J. P. Kenyon, *The Popish Plot* (London: Heinemann, 1972), and J. R. Jones, *The First Whigs: The Politics of the Exclusion Crisis, 1678–1683* (New York: Oxford University Press, 1961).

person or a society."[37] Having witnessed his country in the throes of religio-political strife for as long as he could remember, Penn emphasized the civil bonds uniting English Protestants and the political threat posed by Catholics:

> ENGLAND is a country populous and Protestant, and though under some dissents within it self, yet the Civil Interest is the same, and in some sense the religious too. For, first, all English Protestants, whether conformists or non-conformists agree ... that they only owe allegiance and subjection unto the civil government of England .... And in the next place, they do not only consequentially disclaim the pope's supremacy, and all adhesion to foreign authority ... but therewith deny and oppose the Romish religion, as it stands degenerated from Scripture, and the first and purest ages of the church; which makes up a great negative union .... In short, it is the interest of the ruling, or Church-Protestants of England, that the pope should have no claim or power in England. It is also the interest of the Dissenting Protestants, that the pope should have no claim or power here in England. ...[38]

The religious issues dividing English Protestants were real, but not fundamental; they did not implicate core doctrines. Penn sought to boil down articles of faith to an absolute minimum: "I say then, that the belief of Jesus of Nazareth to be the promised Messiah, the Son and Christ of God, sent to restore and save mankind, is the first and was then the only requisite article of faith... ."[39] Far more important, politically speaking, was the common Protestant rejection of Catholic claims like papal supremacy and the subordination of individual conscience to ecclesiastical hierarchies.

A commitment to civil interest, then, represents a key element of legitimate government and contributes to social peace, economic prosperity, and the political community's territorial integrity. Civil interest can be threatened by two different sets of actors: a government that legislates on things not properly civil (e.g., the persecuting Restoration state); or an external enemy that seeks to undermine the civil government and substitute its own interests for those of the political community (e.g., the French King, or the Pope). By virtue of its claims to political dominion, Penn argued, Catholicism constitutes not only a religion "degenerated from the Scriptures" but also an existential political threat to English liberties.[40] The religious error was sincerely felt by English Protestants, but what really raised political concerns were the *political*

37 Penn, *One Project*, in *Political Writings*, 121.
38 Penn, *One Project*, in *Political Writings*, 122–123.
39 Penn, *An Address*, in *Political Writings*, 163.
40 Penn, *One Project*, in *Political Writings*, 122; Penn, *An Address to Protestants*, in *Political Writings*, 171–181.

implications of "popery," the real or perceived intentions of the French king's armies and the pope's claims with regard to the political allegiance of English (or Irish) Catholics.

This "negative union" that Penn invoked, the rejection of Catholic religious and political pretensions, was nonetheless a substantive concept. Even though real theological issues divide them, he argued, English Protestants should not blind themselves to their shared interest in the preservation of English liberties and the defense of Protestantism at home and abroad. The preservation of England's limited monarchy from the absolutist tendencies of Catholicism was of obvious interest to all citizens of the realm, and would require them to look past their internal divisions in order to face a much more serious external threat.

What all these discussions led to was Penn's diagnosis of a fundamental misunderstanding at the heart of Restoration policy, a "twofold mistake, First, that the difference betwixt Protestants and their Dissenters is generally managed as if it were civil. Secondly, the difference betwixt papist and Protestant is carried on, as if it were chiefly religious."[41] Such a view was echoed by other Protestants during these years: In describing the miseries that would attend the establishment of Catholicism in England, the author of *Europe a Slave* insisted that "the dispute is not here about religion: that's but the mantle which covers the design of the popishly affected party and their leaders, to keep off the sitting of Parliaments."[42] The experience of other European nations demonstrated, on this view, that Catholic theology was more compatible with hierarchical and absolutist governments than with any form of political representation. The preservation of British liberties thus required the rejection of Catholicism in the most emphatic terms.

Protestant unity, civil interest, and antipopery, then, were all prongs of the same political strategy.[43] Toleration for Protestant Dissenters was therefore an essential element of the political agenda that sought to prevent Catholic tyranny.[44] Divisions among England's Protestants, Penn argued, played into the hands of Catholics by dissolving the bonds of civil interest which ought to strengthen the nation. The very title of Penn's *Address to Protestants of all Persuasions* announced the idea of Protestant unity, an ongoing theme in the

41 Penn, *One Project*, in *Political Writings*, 128.

42 [Jean-Paul Cerdan], *Europe a Slave, Unless England Break her Chains* (London, 1681), 64–65.

43 See Richard Ashcraft, *Revolutionary Politics and Locke's Two Treatises of Government* (Princeton: Princeton University Press, 1986), 327–329.

44 "The Case of the People, Called Quakers . . . ," in *To the King, Lords, and Commons, in Parliament Assembled* (London, 1680), 56ff. See also Penn, *One Project*, in *Political Writings*, 132.

tolerationist campaigns in seventeenth-century England.[45] Much of Penn's *Address* dwelt on the moral sins of the nation – drunkenness; whoredom and fornication; gaming; oath-swearing, cursing, and blasphemy; and profaneness – that threatened to bring God's judgment upon the land, and called on the civil magistrate to act swiftly to cut them off.[46] But more to the point of this chapter, the *Address* also took aim at the propensity of people to persecute. Penn's political project involved fusing the shared *civil* interest of all English Protestants with the additional *religious* emphasis provided by their shared renunciation of any doctrine that would undermine that integrity: "Their interests must needs be one against pope and foreign authority."[47]

Not only did this understanding of government and its appropriate limitations respect the religious and political liberties of the English people, Penn argued, but it also redounded to rulers' own advantage. He reminded his readers that "more custom comes ... to the King, and more trade to the kingdom, by encouraging the labour and traffick of an Episcopalian, Presbyterian, Independent, Quaker and Anabaptist, than by an Episcopalian only."[48] Civil interest, then, was *interest* in the best sense of the word (i.e., not the pursuit of one's own advantage to the exclusion of all else), "a legal endeavour" to protect the rights and property of all. The preservation of liberty was not only required by principle, but was advantageous as well.

Penn viewed England as a *civil commonwealth*, with a generic Protestant ethos and a balanced governing relationship between Crown and Parliament. The fact that tolerating polities like the Netherlands prospered economically did not escape Penn's notice either, and his arguments for toleration had always emphasized its material advantages. When King James II promulgated his Declaration of Indulgence in 1687, it was viewed with great suspicion by many English Dissenters, not least because of their distrust of the Catholic king's

45 As Blair Worden has contended, Cromwell's tolerationist policies were driven in large part by a desire for Protestant unity against the Catholic threat. See Worden, "Toleration and the Cromwellian Protectorate," in *Persecution and Toleration: Studies in Church History*, ed. W. J. Sheils (Oxford: Blackwell, 1984), 21.

46 In *The Rule of Moderation*, Ethan Shagan emphasizes the repressive nature of this sort of toleration, which eschews doctrinal niceties but just as surely turns the full force of state power on certain marginalized segments of the populace. Shagan focuses more specifically on *Penn's Address*: "When we look more deeply at Penn's discussion of state sins ... we see how thoroughly his vision of toleration was dependent on a coequal prosecution of vice" (308).

47 Penn, *One Project*, in *Political Writings*, 123. See also *Europe a Slave*: religion is "but the mantle which covers the design of the popishly affected party and their leaders, to keep off the sitting of Parliaments" (64).

48 Penn, *One Project*, in *Political Writings*, 126.

intent to promote a liberty of conscience that encompassed England's Catholics. Penn was one of the few, and certainly the most prominent, Dissenter who took the king's side, and he urged his fellow Dissenters to support the king's efforts. Such a position was a radical political miscalculation on Penn's part, as mentioned above. It does, however, show just how crucially important the issues of toleration and liberty of conscience were for Penn throughout his career. Through many twists and turns over the course of his nearly five decades in British public life, he never retreated from the powerful argument that he had sketched out in his 1670 treatise *The Great Case of Liberty of Conscience*: that religious toleration is natural, reasonable, and Christian, and reflects the practice of enlightened rulers throughout history.

AMERICA

Of course the theater in which Penn was able to exercise the most influence was not England itself: the campaigns for toleration in which he participated during the 1670s were largely unsuccessful. America was both a longstanding interest of Penn's – he had been involved in mediating disputes between the proprietors of East and West Jersey during the 1670s, and signed the *West Jersey Concessions and Agreements* of 1677 – and a potentially lucrative business proposition.[49] The English had been settling the North American coast, with varying degrees of success, for nearly a century: from Jamestown in 1607 through Massachusetts and Maryland during the 1630s; from Carolina in the 1660s through New Netherland, which the English finally took from the Dutch in the 1670s. The scope of religious toleration Penn envisioned for his colony was broad and expansive: no established church, no religious tests for office holding, and no swearing of oaths in legal settings. In correspondence, he referred to his colony as a "holy experiment" and voiced his hope that it would form "the seed of a nation."[50] That he was constantly in debt, shunted to the side by the very Quakers whom he had labored to set up in positions of power in his colony, adds a poignant note to considerations of Penn's role in the broader context of Britain's early empire.

49 Richard S. Dunn, "Penny Wise and Pound Foolish: Penn as a Businessman," in *The World of William Penn*, 37–54.

50 The phrase "holy experiment" is from Penn's letter to James Harrison, Aug. 25, 1681, in *The Papers of William Penn*, ed. Mary Maples Dunn and Richard S. Dunn (Philadelphia: University of Pennsylvania Press, 1981–1987), II:108 (hereafter *PWP*). The phrase "seed of a nation" is from Penn's letter to Robert Turner, March 5, 1681, *PWP* II:83.

Penn's attempt to create a governing document for his colony went through a series of phases leading up to his first voyage to America in 1682. His first attempt, *The Fundamental Constitutions of Pennsylvania*, was drafted shortly after he received the charter; he never published it, and it is unclear whether Penn ever intended it as a serious proposal for governance.[51] It was a fairly radical document, with an annually elected lower house, whose members were to receive written instructions from their electors, granted the authority to "consult, debate, and resolve, and . . . to consent, to the enacting or abolishing of laws, and whatever is the privilege of an English House of Commons."[52] *The Fundamental Constitutions* explicitly endorsed habeas corpus, the rule of law, Magna Carta, and the Petition of Right; ensured a jury system, "that we may, in whatever we can, resemble the ancient constitution of England";[53] and emphasized the importance of a written constitution as a fundamental law over and against the will of any particular political actor. There were also some specifically Quaker elements, including a provision that no oaths be sworn in legal proceedings.

By the time that Penn published his *Frame of Government* shortly before departing for America in spring 1682, the constitutional foundations he envisioned for his colony had undergone some important revisions. The *Frame* contains a far more elaborate theoretical preamble than the *Fundamental Constitutions*. It endorsed the principle of consent as a necessary requirement of governmental legitimacy.[54] That said, the government now derived much of its political momentum from the Governor and a small, directly elected Council, who were to initiate legislation and make the weightiest political decisions. The *Frame* relegated the Assembly to the distinctly secondary role of providing affirmation or negation of laws proposed by the Governor and Council. It also provided a mechanism for its own amendment, though with a steep threshold (agreement of the governor and six-sevenths of the colony's legislators).[55]

51 For a more detailed exploration of the *Fundamental Constitutions*, see Murphy, *Liberty, Conscience, and Toleration*, Chapter 5.

52 Penn, *Fundamental Constitutions*, *PWP*, II:144; *William Penn and the Founding of Pennsylvania, 1680–1684: A Documentary History*, ed. Jean R. Soderlund (Philadelphia: University of Pennsylvania Press, 1983), 99. For the more specifically Harringtonian elements of Penn's theorizing of Pennsylvania, see Mary Maples, "William Penn, Classical Republican," *Pennsylvania Magazine of History and Biography* 81 (1957), 139–143, and Smolenski, *Friends and Strangers*, 67–70; though both focus much more on the *Frame of Government* and *Laws Agreed upon in England* than on the *Fundamental Constitutions*.

53 Penn, *Fundamental Constitutions*, *PWP*, II:149; *William Penn and the Founding of Pennsylvania*, 104.

54 Penn, *Frame* of Government (London 1682), 2.

55 Penn, *Frame*, 11.

The first two decades of Pennsylvania history are replete with examples of the Assembly's dogged struggle to play a substantive role in the colony's political life and to contest Penn's (and the Council's) attempts to relegate them to a "yea or nay" function. These political struggles would continue for years: "[T]he popular Assembly [sought] to co-opt the legislative powers of both Penn … and the Provincial Council, while Penn and his supporters tried to curb the Assembly in its grasping for power."[56] With Penn out of the picture (he returned to England in 1684 to pursue a border dispute with Lord Baltimore, and would not return for fifteen years), conflicts between Pennsylvania Friends and the colony's Anglicans over the status of oaths in legal proceedings (Quakers objected to them; Anglicans insisted on them) and the provision of a militia for colonial defense (Quakers' peace testimony forbade it; Anglicans insisted on it) characterized much of the early history of the province. Conflict between the Assembly and Penn himself was also frequent and bitter, as Friends, who dominated the Assembly, proved far less compliant than Penn had hoped for, and he took their independence and failure to remit funds owed to him as a personal affront and a monstrous expression of ingratitude.

By the time Penn agreed to the Charter of Privileges in 1701, he had endured two turbulent decades in his personal and public life, and was weakened politically in both England and America.[57] The Charter enshrined liberty of conscience for all who confessed belief in God and would "live quietly under the civil government," while restricting office holding to Christians. Government was to be entrusted to an "Assembly yearly chosen," which was to – at long last, to Assembly partisans – "prepare bills in order to pass into laws," determine its own adjournment, and "impeach criminals, and redress grievances."[58] Although six-sevenths of the Assembly could petition the Governor for changes to the government, in an implicit nod to his earlier search for a "new Magna Charta" for liberty of conscience in England, Penn insisted in the 1701 Charter of Privileges that

> Because the happiness of mankind depends so much upon the enjoying of liberty of their consciences as aforesaid … the first article of this charter relating to liberty of conscience … according to the true intent and meaning of, shall be kept and remain, without any alteration, inviolably for ever.[59]

Penn's grant of legislative initiative to the Assembly in the Charter of Privileges represented both a major advance in popular politics in one of the most

56 Calvert, *Quaker Constitutionalism*, 103.

57 "Charter of Privileges," *PWP*, IV: 105.

58 Ibid., IV: 106–107.

59 Ibid., IV: 108.

vibrant colonies in British America *and* his own renunciation of one of the central elements of his fundamental vision for the colony. It was, as Jane Calvert has put it – with Penn's control of Pennsylvania threatened by hostile English forces and a unified Assembly making a concerted pitch for political power – a "peaceful coup d'état."[60]

Pennsylvania's legacy in the history of Anglo-American religious liberty hinges on its persistent commitment to liberty of conscience (present since the founding) and the popular control of the legislative process since 1701.[61] It was hardly the only colony that embraced the former or that politically enshrined the latter; but it did turn out to be the most prosperous and vibrant of them all, thanks in large part to Penn's ability to draw on his European networks and to attract industrious individuals and their capital on a grand scale.[62]

CONCLUSION

Although John Locke's 1689 *Letter Concerning Toleration* has often been accorded primacy in the story of liberal toleration, Locke's *Letter* actually distills a much longer-running discourse that reached back to the first half of the seventeenth century. This tolerationist discourse was shaped by the experience of religious and political dissent on both sides of the Atlantic, generating substantive principles of spiritual and political liberty that ultimately gave rise to one of the hallmarks of liberal thought: the idea that individuals and groups ought to be free to follow the dictates of their conscience not only in the narrow essentials of religious worship but across the spectrum of ways in which issues of conscience arise in public life (including the refusal to swear oaths, show deference to social "superiors," support armed forces with public funds, and so on). In the achievement of this principle, and the legal and political practices necessary to secure it, William Penn's career at the heart of English and American political life from the late 1660s through the early 1700s – a crucial time period for both the theory of religious liberty and its instantiation across the British Atlantic – grants his political thought a signal importance in the emergence of toleration as both a philosophical principle and a political reality.

60 Calvert, *Quaker Constitutionalism*, 133.

61 Ibid.

62 Evan Haefeli, "Pennsylvania's Religious Freedom in Comparative Colonial Context," in *The Worlds of William*.

4

The Friendly Jurisprudence and Early Feminism of John Dickinson

Jane E. Calvert

John Dickinson (1732–1808), of Delaware and Pennsylvania, had one of the most illustrious legal and political careers of the American founding era. Known today as the "Penman of the Revolution," he wrote more for the cause than any other figure, becoming the leader of the resistance to Britain and an international celebrity before independence. His reputation suffered when he abstained from the vote on independence and refused to sign the Declaration. Yet he continued to serve at the state and national levels of government, offering his considerable legal expertise as Americans wrote and implemented their new constitutions, and bringing a unique perspective to all his work. Although he never became a formal member of the Religious Society of Friends (Quakers), he was a devout fellow traveler. Faith was always important to Dickinson, but he rejected organized religion. Over the course of his life, however, the constant influence of Quaker relatives and colleagues in Pennsylvania worked on him, and he gradually adopted many of the Friends' theological beliefs and accompanying social concerns while steadfastly refusing formal membership in the Society. He likewise adhered to their brand of Friendly jurisprudence.

That there are so few surviving documents from Dickinson's childhood and youth means we know little about his upbringing and early education. He was born to Quaker parents in Talbot County, Maryland. His father, Samuel, was a planter and the first judge in the Court of Common Pleas in Kent County, Pennsylvania (one of the three lower counties that are now Delaware), where the family moved in 1740. Although Dickinson's father moved away from Quakerism, his mother remained a devout Friend. Dickinson's early education was typical of a boy in an elite family of his day. He was schooled by tutors who resided with the family. His first, while still in Maryland, may have been Francis Alison, student of the Scottish Enlightenment and later a prominent "Old Side" Presbyterian minister, who resided with the family to tutor Henry,

John's older half-brother. In these early years, it is likely his mother, an unusually learned woman for the day, played some role in his education. We know that she read law with her husband and son.[1] His primary tutor, however, was Irish-born William Killen, who became chief justice of Delaware and first chancellor of that state in 1792. Dickinson's subsequent education was more elevated than that of most young American men. At the age of eighteen, he read law in Philadelphia with former King's Attorney John Moland. Then, from ages twenty-one to twenty-four, he studied law in the Middle Temple at London's Inns of Court.[2]

Upon returning to America in 1757, he established a law practice in Quaker-dominated Philadelphia and, in 1759, embarked on a career in politics that lasted over forty years. After beginning in the legislature of the three Lower Counties of Pennsylvania, he entered the Pennsylvania Assembly, where he served frequently until independence from Britain and briefly afterwards. His rise to prominence began when he wrote against the Stamp Act and served in the Stamp Act Congress (1765), where he was the lead draftsman of the *Declaration of Rights* and the Petition to the King. In 1768, his *Letters from a Farmer in Pennsylvania*, written in response to the Townshend Acts, made him renowned throughout the Atlantic world as the spokesman for the American cause. He served in the First and Second Continental Congresses (1774–1776, 1779) and drafted most of the publications of those bodies, including the first and second Petitions to the King (1774, 1775), *Letter to the Inhabitants of the Province of Quebec* (1774), the *Bill of Rights* and *List of Grievances* (1774), the *Declaration on Taking up Arms* (1775), and the first draft of the Article of Confederation (1776). During the war, he served as a colonel in the Pennsylvania militia and a private in the Delaware militia before he was elected president of Delaware (1781–1782), then Pennsylvania (1782–1785). In 1786, he served as president of the Annapolis Convention and called for Congress to convene the Constitutional Convention (1787), which he attended as a delegate from Delaware. His seminal contributions at the Convention were offering the initial proposal for what became known as the Connecticut Compromise on representation and pressing for the abolition of the Atlantic slave trade. In 1788, he published the *Fabius Letters* promoting ratification of the Constitution. His final office was president of the Delaware constitutional convention in 1791–1792. During these decades, even while he

[1] JD to Samuel Dickinson, February 19, 1755. John Dickinson Family Papers, Library Company of Philadelphia (hereafter JDFP/LCP).

[2] There is no satisfactory biography of Dickinson. The most recent by a scholar is Milton E. Flower's *John Dickinson: Conservative Revolutionary* (Charlottesville: University of Virginia Press, 1983). The erratic citation of sources, however, makes it unreliable.

held other offices, he continued his law practice and frequently served as a judge in Pennsylvania and Delaware courts. When he finally retired from public service, he continued to act as informal advisor to Democratic-Republican politicians, advocate of peace with France and for the education of youth, and philanthropist for social reform and education.

Despite Dickinson's unmatched political celebrity before the Revolution and his extensive contribution to the founding, his activities and thought have received only minimal scholarly treatment. The only monograph to analyze his political and constitutional thought in depth and treat his religion seriously is my *Quaker Constitutionalism and the Political Thought of John Dickinson* (Cambridge, 2009). Elsewhere I have explained some political and historiographical reasons for this dearth.[3] Dickinson's jurisprudence has received even less attention. Eric Stockdale and Randy J. Holland discuss his time in law school and some of his political achievements in *Middle Temple Lawyers of the American Revolution* (2007), arguing that "Dickinson has a strong claim to be considered the foremost American member of the Middle Temple."[4] But this brief account treats neither his jurisprudence nor his religion. Aside from the historiographical and political reasons for his obscurity, his complete papers have never been collected in a scholarly edition. Work is currently underway to transcribe, edit, and publish these records, which will open this area of his life to scholarly inquiry.[5] What follows, therefore, is necessarily a preliminary assessment of what can be known so far.

By Dickinson's time, Quakers already had a long history with the Anglo-American legal system and can rightly be said to have originated their own distinctive brand of jurisprudence in the process of resisting religious persecution. Their main theological tenet, the doctrine of the Light within, informed their understanding of the law and its application. God's Light in the conscience was both how man knew the fundamental law and what made all men and women spiritually equal before God. Quakers strived to enact these beliefs in the public sphere and reform the civil law accordingly. Believing that individuals could not experience the Light within if they were oppressed by external circumstances, such as unjust human laws or poverty, they sought to free all people to find God in their consciences. Although they eschewed litigation among members of their own Society in favor of mediation, from

[3] Jane E. Calvert, "Myth-Making and Myth-Breaking in the Historiography of John Dickinson," *Journal of the Early Republic* 34.3 (2014), 467–480.

[4] Eric Stockdale and Randy J. Holland, *Middle Temple Lawyers of the American Revolution* (Eagan, MN: Thomson West, 2007), 68.

[5] The John Dickinson Writings Project (JDP) is undertaking this work. For more information, visit the JDP information page: www.uky.edu/DickinsonWritingsProject/.

their earliest years they challenged the British legal system by dissenting against persecutory civil laws and effectively using the machinery of the system against itself.[6] They also pioneered the theory and practice of civil disobedience, as an alternative to violent revolution, for peaceful and incremental constitutional change.[7] Once in America, in colonies with Quaker constitutions such as West Jersey and Pennsylvania, Friends were able to put their legal ideals into practice, including religious liberty, a broadened franchise, and limited use of the death penalty.[8] They then moved from resisting from outside the political and legal systems to promoting Friendly concerns as leading politicians and lawyers from within.

Toward the middle of the eighteenth century, in order to liberate individuals to find the Light, Quakers engaged increasingly in efforts to improve the lives of subordinated peoples and vulnerable populations. Although Quakers had always taken care of their own sick-poor, as governors of Pennsylvania, they expanded this mission to the entire population, founding the Friends Almshouse and the Pennsylvania Hospital. Similarly, Native American rights had always been a key concern, and in 1756 they founded the Society for Preserving the Peace with the Indians by Pacific Measures. They also began an abolition movement within their Society, which resulted in the foundation of the Pennsylvania Abolition Society in 1776. Never having forgotten their own experiences in British prisons, in 1787 they founded the Philadelphia Society for Alleviating the Miseries of Public Prisons.

John Dickinson shared all of these concerns as well as the Quaker understanding of the law. His legal career was defined by his efforts to secure unenfranchised individuals and groups equal protection for their rights under the law. The most significant example of Dickinson's Quaker leanings was in his leadership of the resistance to Britain, in which he attempted to secure American rights under the British constitution. A detailed analysis of these efforts can be found in *Quaker Constitutionalism*. It argues that Dickinson followed Quaker constitutional theory – a secularized version of their theology – which held that the civil constitution was amendable through peaceful means by raising public awareness of injustices, achieving a repeal of

6 Craig W. Horle, *The Quakers and the English Legal System, 1660–1688* (Philadelphia: University of Pennsylvania Press, 1988).

7 Jane E. Calvert, *Quaker Constitutionalism and the Political Thought of John Dickinson* (New York: Cambridge University Press, 2009).

8 See the "Frame of Government [of Pennsylvania]," 1682, in *The Papers of William Penn: Volume 2: 1680–1684*, ed. Mary Maples Dunn and Richard S. Dunn (Philadelphia: University of Pennsylvania Press), 211–220; and the West Jersey Concessions and Agreements, (1676/77), *The Papers of William Penn: Volume 1: 1644–1679*, ed. Mary Maples Dunn and Richard S. Dunn (Philadelphia: University of Pennsylvania Press), 387–410.

unconstitutional positive laws (in this case, the British taxation statutes), and replacing them with new, just laws. His unwillingness to declare independence reflected his belief in the sacred bonds of the civil constitution. Yet, his willingness – after he had spoken his piece and removed his obstruction to the Declaration – to join with his countrymen who had declared independence, demonstrates a Quakerly desire for civil unity, and also his rejection of strict Quaker pacifism.[9]

The Quaker influence on Dickinson is apparent in the earliest years for which we have records of his thought, during his legal training at the Middle Temple. In the first place, he believed that law and religion were related and that both were required to create a happy society. Observing the recent widespread corruption in British elections, he wrote, "We have a Maxim in the Law that 'The People is unhappy – when the Laws are unsettled' But I think with much more Truth it may be said – 'When Religion is unsettled.'"[10] In other words, good laws were not enough for public happiness; a people must also have religion. Expressing a sentiment he repeated at the founding of the United States, he explained, "People are grown too Polite to have an old fashioned Religion, & are too weak to find out a new – from whence follows the most unbounded Licentiousness, & utter Disregard of Virtue which is the unfailing Cause of the Destruction of all Empires for it is as impossible for Publick Dignity & Security to exist w[ith]out private Virtue & Honesty."[11] Dickinson carried these private virtues with him into his public service and practice of the law.

In letters to his mother and father from London, and in his earliest writings afterwards, he laid out the basic principles that would guide his approach to the law, explaining that "when I reflect on the End & Intent of my Profession, & my particular Designs in it . . . I find no Consideration of equal Weight with defending the Innocent & redressing the injurd – That seems to Me the Noblest Aim of Human Abilities & Industry."[12] He was concerned with equality under the law, and, like his Quaker relatives, did not have faith that the common law could ultimately protect everyone. He and they were ultimately concerned with the fact it was unwritten, and thus its enforcers were unaccountable to the rights of the people. By contrast, written statutes,

9 He explained that "I am on all proper occasions an advocate for the lawfulness of defensive war. This principle has prevented me from union with Friends." JD to Tench Coxe, January 24, 1807. Tench Coxe Papers, Historical Society of Pennsylvania (hereafter HSP).

10 JD to Samuel Dickinson, January 21, 1755. JDFP/LCP.

11 Ibid.

12 JD to Mary Cadwalader Dickinson, January 22, 1755. JDFP/LCP.

explained Dickinson, "may be calld 'Political Revelations'. They contain Truth, Certainty, and Safety. Crimes declard by them are plain, & not left to the Invention of Judges." He justified his position with a biblical argument: "Saint Paul says, 'Where there is no Law', that is, no revealed Law, 'there is no Transgression.'" "It may be fairly deducd from these Words of the Great Apostle," he explained, "that without a positive Law, or the Conviction of a Man's own Conscience by the Light of Nature, none ought to be accounted guilty of any Crime."[13] Because of this risk with the common law, Quakers preferred not just written statutes, but also written constitutions. They also looked to the courts.

At first, they entered the English courts as adversaries of the system. But by Dickinson's time, and in Pennsylvania where they controlled the legal system, the courts were where they enacted their faith. "The most fond Admirer of our Common Law," he explained, "must allow, that there are some Cases in which the Severity of its Rules, requires some little softening." Quakers believed in progressive revelation, an idea that demanded that man must always be ready to adapt as he learned more about God's will, especially when it came to the oppressed in society. Accordingly, Dickinson believed that "the Necessities of Human Nature are greater than our Foresight, & that the most excellent Institutions may be extremely just & reasonable in the Ninety nine Instances, & quite defective or improper in the hundredth."[14] Dickinson was concerned with that hundredth case. And he looked to the legal system of Pennsylvania to achieve his ends. Rather than lament that the colony did not have a Court of Chancery as in England, he viewed it another way. "I think," he explained, "it woud be much properer to say, Every Court [in Pennsylvania] is a Court of Equity, for both Judges & Juries think it hard to deny a Man that Relief which he can obtain no where else."[15] Most significantly, for Dickinson, like Quakers, there was a higher power that determined the law, and it was man's obligation to remain open in his conscience for what God might convey about equity and rights. As Dickinson expressed it, "Rights may exist before they are acknowl[edge]d by Laws."[16] He spent his career seeking to reveal these unacknowledged rights, making him one of the most legally progressive of the American founders.

Once he began practicing, conscience was paramount to Dickinson, and he was as far from being the unscrupulous lawyer as can be. He did not succumb

[13] JD, "Reflections on the Flag of the Truce Trade," [c. 1760]. JDFP/LCP.

[14] JD to Samuel Dickinson, August 2, 1756. JDFP/LCP.

[15] Ibid.

[16] JD, Set Two of Notes for an Essay on the Constitutional Power of Great Britain, [1774]. R. R. Logan Collection, Historical Society of Pennsylvania (hereafter RRL/HSP).

to the temptation to take any case, regardless of the moral or ethical cost. In preparing his notes for a murder trial, he confirmed his belief that the innocence of his client was all important. "If I thought Death intended" by the defendant, "No Consid[eration] shoud tempt me to speak on this Occasion."[17] Elsewhere he clarified, "if at any Time, I am engaged in a Cause by being misinformed, and on Enquiry find it unjust, no Offers however extravagant shall tempt Me to undertake the sordid Employment of acquiring gain, by violating my conscience."[18] Later in his career, after he had fully adopted Quakers' social testimonies, he took a firmer stance than even they did on legal ethics. In 1791, he sold a lot in Philadelphia to William Geisse with the understanding that the property was not to be used for theatrical productions, which Quakers opposed. Geisse immediately violated the agreement. With the encouragement of the leading Quakers in Philadelphia, Dickinson brought suit against Geisse. But, after a protracted battle, it became clear that he would lose the case. At this point, the Quakers urged Dickinson to win by "resorting to the 'usual Course of Law,' that is, trying to tire out the other Party by Delays." Although Dickinson was pained at having inadvertently facilitated play-acting in the city, he rejected that approach, saying, "This Mode I will not pursue." He would not be one of those men who "endeavour to evade the Laws, and to distress his Opponent, by the weight of his purse. I have never acted, and I will never act in this Manner."[19]

It was Dickinson's adherence to conscience that first made him famous among his contemporaries and then infamous to historians. As the conflict with Britain increased during the 1760s, Dickinson stepped to the forefront of national affairs to become an international celebrity and spokesman for the American cause. From the beginning, he advocated resistance to Britain and the defense of American rights and liberties in the firmest but most peaceable manner. Drawing on his Quaker heritage and culture, he became the first American to propose a national campaign of civil disobedience. This mode of resistance was unlike anything most Anglo-Americans had seen before, unless they were aware of Quaker history. Whereas Whigs condoned violent riots and eventually endorsed armed revolution, and whereas Tories denied the legitimacy of any resistance, Quakers trod a middle ground. Civil disobedience is properly understood as the public, non-violent breaking of unjust laws with the intent to raise public awareness of the injustice and promote constitutional reform from the bottom up. Dickinson advocated this method from

17 JD, "Three Questions [on a Murder]," [n.d.]. Logan Family Papers, HSP.

18 JD to unknown, [1770]. Logan Family Papers, HSP.

19 JD to George Logan, December 15, 1791. RRL/HSP.

a conviction that bloodshed was unnecessary to resolve the conflict with Britain. Arguably, it worked (though it was not the sole method the colonists used); the offending legislation was repealed. Eventually, however, the colonists grew restive under Dickinson's leadership and turned toward revolution. Yet Dickinson maintained his stance for peace through the debate on whether to issue a declaration of independence. His decision to lead the Pennsylvania battalion he had raised and then enlist in the Delaware militia as a private to defend his country seems contradictory, but it is very Quakerly in a particular way, reflecting his and their belief in constitutional unity.

Although his countrymen rejected Dickinson's leadership at that moment, and some even turned on him, calling him a traitor for refusing to sign the Declaration, they eventually sought his moderate leadership again, in both Delaware and Pennsylvania. And although at the moment of independence, Americans rejected peaceful protest, with the ratification of the Constitution, they would be compelled to recognize civil disobedience as the most extreme form of protest in which a democratic people can engage if they want to honor and preserve their constitutional order.[20]

On the matter of rights for the people, Dickinson's actions with regard to Britain were only the most visible expression of his Friendly jurisprudence. Quaker priorities permeated his legal thinking at every level, from his personal interests, to his private practice, to his prescriptions for new national laws. Most notably, we see his priorities in his attitudes toward and prescriptions for the treatment of the most vulnerable members of society – free and enslaved blacks, Native Americans, the poor, and women. Elsewhere I have detailed his abolition activity and treatment of his former slaves.[21] Of the leading founding figures, Dickinson was the only one to free his slaves and work for abolition at the state and national levels. Although he had always been concerned with the humane treatment of the family slaves, which he had inherited from his father, by 1776, he was beginning to question the ethics of slavery publicly. In 1777, he freed his slaves conditionally, but soon that was not sufficient to quiet his conscience. In 1781 and 1786, he manumitted them completely. At the same time, he was helping Quakers who were attempting to pass abolition legislation in Delaware. It was unsuccessful, as was his attempt to have slavery abolished in the new 1792 Delaware Constitution, which he helped create.

20 See Calvert, *Quaker Constititionalism.*

21 Jane E. Calvert, "An Expansive Conception of Rights: The Abolitionism of John Dickinson," in *When in the Course of Human Events: 1776 at Home, Abroad, and in American Memory*, ed. William R. Jordan (Macon: Mercer University Press, 2018), 21–54.

At the national level, Dickinson had a bit more success when his motion in the Federal Convention to have the slave trade abolished as early as 1808 passed.

The following pages will explore his ideas of women's rights and how he tried to secure them. Because Dickinson left no systematic account of his legal philosophy, nor did he write explicitly about his attitudes toward women and other subordinated people, we must resort to circumstantial evidence. An examination of Dickinson's closest relationships, which were with Quaker women, allows us to understand his legal philosophy and its practical expression at the lowest and highest levels, in criminal and constitutional law.

Legal historian John Phillip Reid has argued that "the rights of women ... were unknown during the revolutionary era."[22] This is true only if one does not consider the Quaker community. Most of the leading founders had no thought of attempting to promote women's voices or acknowledge – let alone secure – their rights. Yet Dickinson, by contrast, submerged as he was in the Quaker culture, was arguably an early feminist. Like his Quaker relatives, he saw women as spiritually equal to men, deserving of equal religious rights and being equally capable of exemplifying virtue and piety. The evidence shows further that he extended this trust to women's ability to express sound political sentiments worthy of dissemination to male audiences. Moreover, evidence also suggests he approved of women possessing financial agency and trusted their management of money and business matters, which likely translated into a belief that women were entitled to one of the basic rights of men – that of owning property. He evinced an understanding of problems, legal and otherwise, particular to women, and he sought to protect and advance their rights in various ways.

In his family and personal life, Dickinson was surrounded by strong Quaker women who actively helped shape his theology, which, in turn, informed his jurisprudence as well as his politics. His closest relationships, which the record suggests were very harmonious, were with his wife, Mary (Polly) Norris, his mother, Mary Cadwalader, his two daughters, Sally and Maria, and his aunt by marriage, Mary Parker Norris.[23] When he began courting his future wife, he insinuated himself into a circle of single, financially independent women living at Fairhill, the Isaac Norris estate, which, not insignificantly, possessed one of the largest libraries in the colony. Polly and her sister Sarah (Sally) lived there with their aunt, Elizabeth Norris, and cousins Mary and Hannah

[22] John Phillip Reid, *Constitutional History of the American Revolution: The Authority of Rights* (Madison: University of Wisconsin Press, 1986), 4.

[23] Another relative by marriage, Deborah Norris Logan, wife of Senator George Logan, also became a trusted friend. See Deborah Norris Logan Diary, 1808–1814. Manuscript 14720.Q (uncatalogued), LCP.

Griffitts, the Quaker poet. In addition to being a poet herself, Polly owned and managed, with little male interference, the vast estate, its finances, and tenant properties. Dickinson must have been impressed with Cousin Hannah's business acumen because she helped manage his tenant properties for decades thereafter. Historian Karin Wulf suggests that Polly, content in this close-knit group of women, likely would not have married at the age of thirty had her beloved Sally, whom Dickinson professed to love like a sister, not died the year before.[24]

Mary was a more devout Quaker than her future mother-in-law, and her husband-to-be was not yet ready to conform entirely to the ways of Friends. Mary wanted a wedding "under the care of Friends," but Dickinson would not consent. He objected that Mary was "brought up . . . with such a Veneration for the Society of Friends, as teaches one to revere all its Rules as {equally} inviolable." He urged her instead "to distinguish between those essential to Virtue & Piety, and those merely arbitrary & derived only from ~~private~~ Rules of ~~a certain Sett of~~ {private} Men" and tried to convince her "that it must be more pleasing to Heaven, to communicate Happiness by a virtuous Act, than to spread Affliction by the Obedience to Rules, which neither the {divine} Laws nor those of our Country command Us to observe."[25] Mary agreed to John's terms, marrying him in a civil ceremony on July 19, 1770. For her transgression of marrying out of the discipline, she was reprimanded by the Religious Society of Friends.[26] Once married, Dickinson joined the sorority at Fairhill, where the newlyweds spent their first three years of marriage.[27] It is hard to imagine any other founder in such a situation, surrounded by outspoken Quaker women whose demonstrated skills were both literary and financial.

Lest we doubt the strong and unusual influence these women exerted on Dickinson, we need only look to the commentary left by his colleagues in Congress as tensions with Britain escalated. It vexed them that Dickinson accepted political counsel from his mother and wife, whose Quakerism was more strident than his.[28] One documented example is revealing. In 1774, as Philadelphians were deliberating about how to respond to increasing British

24 Karin Wulf, "A Marginal Independence: Unmarried Women in Colonial Philadelphia," (PhD diss., Johns Hopkins University, 1993), 319.

25 JD to Sarah Norris, [1768], RRL/HSP. Words in curly braces indicate an authorial insertion; struck-through words were cancelled by Dickinson.

26 *Encyclopedia of American Quaker Genealogy*, vol. 2 (Ann Arbor: Edwards Brothers, Inc., 1938), 505.

27 Wulf, "A Marginal Independence," 319.

28 "Copy of a paper drawn up by Joseph Reed for W. Henry Drayton," [n.d.]. Maria Dickinson Logan Collection, HSP.

aggression, sentiments were tending toward violence. But the leaders in favor of such resistance knew that because of Dickinson's "vast influence not only over the public at large but among the Quakers in particular," they would need his approval. The problem was that not only was he reluctant, "Mr. Dickinson's lady, & Mother," were present, and the latter being "extremely sensible cautious, & had a great influence over him." After much persuasion, aided by "circulating the glass briskly," they finally convinced Dickinson to attend their meeting at City Tavern. But until the meeting, the group "resolved he should not be left alone in the interval, lest his wife, or Mother should speak with [him], & overthrow at once, all that had been done." Ultimately, Dickinson attended the meeting and calmly dissuaded the group away from violent actions and toward peaceful protest.[29]

John Adams reinforced this picture with observations of his own. Adams, who ridiculed his own wife's pleas for women's rights, comparing her to a disobedient child and an insolent negro, was appalled at the liberties Dickinson allowed his womenfolk, exclaiming that similar behavior on the part of his own female relatives would "wholly unman" him.[30] "[T]he Quakers," as Adams recorded the concerns of Charles Thomson, "had intimidated Mr. Dickinson's mother and his wife, who were continually distressing him with their remonstrances."[31] Reflecting in later years, he recalled, "[Dickinson] had a wife and a mother who were both Quakers, and they tormented him exceedingly, telling him that he was ruining himself and his country by the course he was pursuing. If I had such a wife, and such a mother, I believe I should have shot myself. If they had opposed me, it would have made me so very unhappy." Adams assumed, of course, that Dickinson also wanted independence and was simply too timid to resist their harangues.[32]

Of course, when we strip away the veneer of disdain Adams displayed for women, Dickinson, and Quakerism, we see a very different picture of John and Mary's relationship. Rather than being "intimidated" by Quakers, Dickinson's wife and mother were deeply convinced of peaceful principles. Rather than "tormenting" Dickinson, they voiced their opinions, which, evidence suggests, Dickinson was already inclined to share. When we

29 Ibid.

30 John Adams, *Diary and Autobiography of John Adams*, ed. Lyman H. Butterfield, vol. 3 (Cambridge, MA: Harvard University Press, 1961), 316; John Adams to Abigail Adams, April 14, 1776, *The Adams Papers*, Adams Family Correspondence, vol. 1, *December 1761–May 1776*, ed. Lyman H. Butterfield (Cambridge, MA: Harvard University Press, 1963), 381–383.

31 Adams, *Diary and Autobiography*, 316.

32 Josiah Quincy, *Figures of the Past: From the Leaves of Old Journals* (Boston: Roberts Brothers, 1888), 80.

understand that Dickinson, unlike Adams, already viewed women as equal to men, we can see that not only was he not horrified at women expressing their opinions, he was receptive to their counsel.

Because the couple's daughters destroyed most of their letters, we hear little from Mary directly. But her poetry gives us a tantalizing insight into the sort of Quakerly advice – in tone and substance – she gave to her husband. Although not naming him, "To the Young Gentleman," bears too striking a resemblance to Dickinson to be about anyone else. Written in 1768 or after, when Dickinson's *Farmer's Letters* launched him to international renown, the poem expresses Mary's concern about the gentleman's rise to fame in advocating "liberty and laws" and that his vanity may thwart his efforts if he does not find religion and marry it to his extensive education. She counsels piety, humility, moderation, and using his powers to help those less fortunate, concerns that we see exemplified in Dickinson's writings throughout his career.

> ffor one a moment to advice attend
> and mark the prudent council of a friend
> the love of Pennsylvania fires my breast
> to wish the merits of her sons confest
> justly admired by all the wise & good
> and for their bright resplendant worth belovd
> ffirst fire Religions Empire in your Soul
> put ev'ry passion under her control
> and when Religion laid the perfect plan
> join education to compleat the man
> let strict Politeness make the diamond glow
> And brave Humanity that melts at woe
> teach you to aid the poor mans fr[ien]dless cause
> defend your Countrys liberty & laws
> that so your virtues may like stars arise
> Shine in your life & fit for [th]e skies
> And to posterity transmit your fame
> the shining Honours of a virtuous name
> And Oh beware of Pride & self conciet
> ffor if you've these you'l n'ere be good or great[33]

We can only speculate about the extent the women in his life influenced Dickinson's decision not to sign the Declaration of Independence. He left no record of their conversations; but he was very much aware of the perception of

[33] Mary Norris Dickinson, "To the Young Gentleman," [1768]. Poems, 1764–1768. JDFP/LCP.

the influence of the Society of Friends, and he did not deny it.[34] He did, however, account for his increasing turn toward Quakerism. It was not the "remonstrances" of his wife or mother, but rather the pious example of his young daughter who moved him in that direction. Late in life, he reminisced that it was Sally who, when she proclaimed she would rather be a Friend than take dancing lessons, inspired him to embrace Quakerism more fully.[35] Clearly, unlike Adams, Dickinson did not fear any "Despotism of the Peticoat."[36]

It was not merely the close familial relationships with women that made Dickinson receptive to their ideas. He valued the contribution of women to causes dear to him and encouraged the publication of works by and about women to further political, civic, and religious ends. Before independence, he corresponded with Catharine Macaulay, writing that her works would be instrumental in "rendering Justice" and, he doubted not, they would "facilitate the Endeavors of future Patriots throughout the British Dominion in every age."[37] For her part, Macaulay was "elated" to receive a present of American-made silk "from {a Man of} the most Dignified Character on the other side of the Atlantick."[38] He had a varied relationship with Philadelphia literary figure Elizabeth Graeme Fergusson, who wrote a poem based on his *Farmer's Letters* called "Dream of the Patriotic Philosophic Farmer."[39] She sent him other poetry, and he acted as her attorney, being one of the few privy to her secret marriage to Hugh Henry Fergusson. Dickinson was also good friends with Susanna Wright, the Quaker feminist, ferry operator, landowner, physician, and author, whom he visited on occasion and referred to as "the Susquehannah Muse."[40] Little is known yet about their relationship, except that it was primarily a friendship, and it was conducted in person rather than by post. In 1772, she began a letter without salutation, writing, "As this is the first time I have done my Self the honour of writing one line to thee, my Very Good and Obliging ffriend, I am at a loss for an Address; But as mine is to be

34 JD to unknown, August 25, 1776. RRL/HSP.

35 James Bringhurst to Elizabeth Coggeshall, October 8, 1799. James Bringhurst Letters, Friends Historical Library, Swarthmore College.

36 John Adams to Abigail Adams, *Adams Papers*, 1:383.

37 JD to Catharine Macaulay, 1770, Correspondence of Catherine Macaulay, Gilder-Lehrman Collection. http://gilderlehrman.pastperfect-online.com/33267cgi/mweb.exe?request=ks (accessed March 2011).

38 Catharine Macaulay to JD, July 18, 1771. RRL/HSP.

39 Little is yet known about the extent of their relationship or whether he attended her famous salons. Anne M. Ousterhout, *The Most Learned Woman in America: A Life of Elizabeth Graeme Fergusson* (College Park: The Pennsylvania State University Press, 2004), 133–134.

40 JD to Mary Cadwalader Dickinson, July 15, 1765. RRL/HSP; *The Complete Writings and Selected Correspondence of John Dickinson*, ed. Jane E. Calvert (Newark, DE: University of Delaware Press, forthcoming), 2:229.

a letter of Business, I will imediatly advert to it."[41] Before independence, he corresponded on political matters with sculptor Patience Lovell Wright in London, who had created a wax statue of him in 1771.[42] In retirement, he was an enthusiastic correspondent and supporter of Mercy Otis Warren, a Democratic-Republican whose history of the Revolution put Dickinson in a sympathetic light without eliding his position on independence.[43] He considered her good opinion of him a "real Honor" and took great pleasure in their "Communion of Minds" despite their lack of "personal Acquaintance."[44] Like with Macaulay, he encouraged her, writing, "Thy generous Exertions to inform thy fellow citizens, and to present thy Country before the World in a justly favorable Light, will be, I firmly believe, attended with the desired Success."[45]

Dickinson eagerly purchased books about the lives of strong women. Although he certainly had their piety in mind, unlike earlier admirers of Quaker women, he did not attribute their strength wholly to God; rather, he gave them credit for it and urged the reprinting of works on women – and not particularly Quaker women – "who have been eminently distinguished by Talents or Strength of Mind, where these Qualities have been dedicated to laudable purposes."[46] Significantly, he seems to give them credit for their own strength. He wrote to Philadelphia printers Birch and Small that he valued "women worthies" for what they could contribute as moral human beings.[47] He therefore trusted that the printers would publish *Female Biography, or Memoirs of Illustrious Women of all Ages and Countries* (1803) out of

41 Susannah Wright to John Dickinson, November 3, 1772. JDFP/LCP.

42 Patience Lovell Wright to JD, March 10, 1775 and April 6, 1775. HSP. See the announcement of the wax figure in *The Censor*, September 5, 1771.

43 Mercy Otis Warren, *History of the Rise, Progress and Termination of the American Revolution*, 3 vols. (Boston: Manning and Loring, 1805), 1:307–308.

44 JD to Mercy Otis Warren, September 25, 1805, in *Adams-Warren Letters: Being Chiefly a Correspondence between John Adams, Samuel Adams, and John Warren*, 2 vols. (Boston: The Massachusetts Historical Society), 2:347; and December 22, 1806, ibid., 2:348–349, 348.

45 JD to Mercy Otis Warren, September 25, 1805, ibid., 2:347.

46 JD to William Y. Birch and Abraham Small, January 7, 1807. JDFP/LCP. For a discussion of early Quaker writers on women and attributing their strength to God, see Amanda Herbert, "Companions in Preaching and Suffering: Itinerate Female Quakers in the Seventeenth- and Eighteenth-Century British Atlantic World," *Early American Studies* 9.1 (2011), 73–113.

47 In 1975, Gerda Lerner identified the study of "women worthies," a term coined by Natalie Zemon Davis, as "[t]he first level at which historians, trained in traditional history, approached women's history." But, as can be seen from Dickinson's explanation, he took his interest to the next level identified by Lerner, valuing these women expressly not for their exceptionalism, but rather for their contribution to society, albeit a male-dominated one. See "Placing Women in History: Definitions and Challenges," *Feminist Studies* 3.1/2 (1975), 5–14, 5.

a "Desire . . . to promote a Love of Virtue and Religion" rather than "to gratify the Curiosity" of an audience unused to reading about extraordinary women. He recommended it especially because the genre of biography allows the accounts to be "adorned with {some} Points of the ~~su~~ persons {described} which, is a pleasing addition to such kind of Writing, as it forms a sort of Acquaintance between the Reader and the subject." It thus appears that Dickinson also appreciated something like what feminist scholars would later value in women's biographies, a "relationship between the personal and political."[48] He even offered to lend the printers his volumes of Daniel Dana's *Memoirs of Eminently Pious Women* (1803), "tho, such is my Estimation {of [those]} that on no other Consideration {would} [I] let them go out of my Hands."[49]

Dickinson realized his law school goal to defend the innocent and injured and brought his concern for female equity and justice under the law to bear in multiple ways. A glimpse into his legal practice suggests that he frequently accepted poor female clients in situations that were unique to women. Although little remains except for cryptic notes on which exhaustive research remains to be completed, we know that among his clients were "a poor Widow" in *Manlove* v. *Prior*, an impoverished woman and her two infant children in *Overseers of Marple Township* v. *Overseers of Newtown Township*, and, perhaps the most intriguing, Rachel Francisco.

We know very little about the case of *Dominus Rex* v. *Rachel Francisco* (1767).[50] Francisco was a "free mollato" servant woman who was charged with infanticide after her newborn infant was discovered dead.[51] Dickinson's case notes reveal that he constructed a plausible defense for Francisco against both the charges of infanticide and concealment. But rather than adhering strictly to the facts in crafting his argument, he sought to humanize her. A few words at the top of the page set a surprisingly sympathetic tone: "Women have suff[ere]d no doubt," he wrote, "for the Conc[ea]l[men]t of a dead Child." It was a "Harsh Statute" – the concealment statute – under which Francisco was being tried, and would have meant the death penalty

48 Leila J. Rupp, "Women Worthies and Women's History," *Reviews in American History* 12.3 (1984), 409–413, 409.

49 JD to William Y. Birch and Abraham Small, January 7, 1807. JDFP/LCP.

50 Laura T. Keenan conducted as much research as one can on this document without the court records, which are difficult to come by, if they exist at all. See "Reconstructing Rachel: A Case of Infanticide in the Eighteenth Century Mid-Atlantic and the Vagaries of Historical Research," *Pennsylvania Magazine of History and Biography* 130.4 (2006), 361–385.

51 John Vining to Benjamin Chew, April 13, 1767, Supreme Court of Pennsylvania, Gratz Collection/HSP

had she been convicted.[52] It should be noted that this statute applied only to unmarried women; the law assumed that respectable married women did not have bastards.[53] But his mention of Francisco's "Sense of Honour" challenges this basic assumption of her disrespectability and suggests that even a woman "Very ignorant & brout up in very low Life" possessed dignity she wished to preserve.[54] Even when research is completed on these notes, we will probably not know all the details, such as how Dickinson came to represent the defendant or whether he took the case pro bono. But we can safely assume that he was not obliged to help this woman. It is also probable that not all elite men in Pennsylvania would have such compassion for the plight of a woman of the lower sort who engaged in fornication and possibly infanticide. Historian Susan E. Klepp notes that colonial men were generally "reluctant to interfere in childbirth and fertility as legislators and judges."[55] Considering Dickinson's status as a leading legal and political figure in the colony, his acceptance of the case is telling. He at least took pity on Francisco; he may also have hoped to destigmatize her situation.

Although Dickinson's work as an attorney certainly evinces his sympathy for misfortunate women and a Quakerly concern for their well-being, it is in constitutional law that Dickinson's Quaker priorities come through most clearly. Seventy years before the women's rights movement, he took the Quaker law of spiritual equality of the genders and attempted to advance it in an unprecedented way in his draft of the Articles of Confederation, three weeks before the Declaration of Independence. Significantly, not only did he encourage women to voice their opinions and serve as examples of virtue, he proposed a fundamental law to protect their right to do so. Functioning in the Quaker tradition, the only religion at the time that allowed women to preach publicly, Dickinson attempted to codify this practice in a truly innovative step.[56] He wrote the first gender-inclusive language in an American constitution.[57] In his religious liberty clause (itself a significant indicator of Dickinson's Quaker jurisprudence), we see Dickinson's thought process at

52 JD, Notes for *Dominus Rex* v. *Rachel Francisco*, [1767], Logan Family Papers, HSP.

53 Susan E. Klepp, *Revolutionary Conceptions: Women, Fertility, and Family Limitation in America, 1760–1820* (Chapel Hill: University of North Carolina Press, 2009), 226.

54 JD, *Francisco* notes.

55 Klepp, *Revolutionary Conceptions*, 226.

56 On Quaker women preaching, see Rebecca Larson, *Daughters of Light: Preaching and Prophesying in the Colonies and Abroad, 1700–1775* (Chapel Hill: University of North Carolina Press, 1999).

57 William Penn may have been the first to use gender inclusive language in a colonial charter. A provision in the 1682 Pennsylvania Frame of Government indicated that women could be summoned to court for a complaint against them.

work, as he first subsumed women under the plural possessive pronoun, then reconsidered:

> No person ~~or persons~~ in any Colony living peaceably under the Civil Government shall be molested or prejudiced in ~~his or their~~ {his or her} persons or Estate for his or her religious persuasion or Practise, nor be compelled to frequent or maintain or contribute to maintain any religious Worship, Place of Worship, or Ministry, contrary to his or her Mind.[58]

Though not, some may object, as momentous as a law for female suffrage, we must not underestimate the novelty either of the language or the clause. For Quakers, religious liberty meant the freedom to speak publicly about religion to convince non-Quakers of the truth in God's Light, so for Dickinson, this clause, particularly the word "Practise," signified not just a negative liberty, but a positive one. At a time when women were prohibited by social norms, if not law, from speaking publicly, this was a significant step protecting a right that most women themselves did not recognize – not only a right to liberty of conscience, but the right to freedom of speech. But Americans were not yet ready to implement religious liberty, let alone recognize a woman's right to free speech. The gendered language remained in his first full draft of the Articles of Confederation, but the entire clause was rejected by his colleagues. It took over two centuries before gender-inclusive language began appearing in state constitutions.

Dickinson's jurisprudence fits squarely into the tradition of peaceful dissent and rights advocacy exemplified by Quakers and their followers throughout American history, including, most notably, that of Martin Luther King, Jr. Where women's rights in particular are concerned, Dickinson's actions were the forerunner of the women's rights and suffrage movements of the nineteenth and twentieth centuries, undertaken by Quakers and fellow travelers such as Lucretia Mott, Susan B. Anthony, Elizabeth Cady Stanton, and Alice Paul.

Although Dickinson had an unusually liberal view of women's activities and spheres of influence, we should not make the mistake of thinking of him as a modern feminist who imagined women shattering a "glass ceiling." When Benjamin Rush pleaded with him to write the "Memoirs of [his] Life relating to [his] political Opinions and Conduct," as many politicians did, to serve as a model for their sons coming up in the world, he demurred, saying, "my Children are Daughters."[59] He could not imagine them following in his

58 JD, "Hints of a Confederation," RRL/HSP.

59 JD to Benjamin Rush, April 27, 1797. Benjamin Rush Correspondence, Historical Society of Delaware.

footsteps; the ceiling was not yet glass. Yet it bears remembering that at the same time, the spring of 1776, as John Adams was literally laughing at his wife for requesting security of her basic rights, John Dickinson was attempting to secure his wife hers.

Dickinson's lasting contributions to American jurisprudence are not specifically to women's rights but rather to American rights broadly considered. They are woven into the fabric of our national political culture and the institutions he helped craft through his many writings in the nation's first assemblies – the Stamp Act Congress, the First and Second Continental Congresses, the Annapolis Convention, and the Federal Convention – where he took active part and, in most cases, produced the majority of writings from those bodies. Although his colleagues were not yet ready to include protections for women and other subordinated populations in writing, Dickinson was there to nudge them in that direction while securing basic rights that would eventually, as Dickinson clearly wished, be extended to all Americans.

5

Roger Sherman, Oliver Ellsworth, and the Formation of America's Constitutional Order

Mark David Hall

In 1822, former President John Adams wrote to the biographer John Sanderson that Roger Sherman was "one of the most cordial friends which I ever had in my life. Destitute of all literary and scientific education, but such as he acquired by his own exertions, he was one of the most sensible men in the world. The clearest head and steadiest heart. It is praise enough to say that the late Chief Justice Ellsworth told me that he had made Mr. Sherman his model in his youth. ... [He] was one of the soundest and strongest pillars of the revolution."[1] Among the important participants in the War for Independence, the Constitutional Convention, and the First Federal Congress, few had as much influence on the creation of America's constitutional order as Sherman and Ellsworth. And none of the more famous founders regularly referenced by students of the era represent as well the 50–75 percent of Americans in this era who were Calvinists.[2]

BIOGRAPHIES

Sherman was born in Massachusetts in 1721 to Mehetabel and William Sherman. William was a farmer and cobbler and, like most residents of the

[1] John Adams to John Sanderson, November 19, 1822, in *Biography of the Signers to the Declaration of Independence*, ed. Robert Waln and John Sanderson (Philadelphia: R. W. Pomeroy, 1822), 3:298.

[2] Studies on religion in the American founding routinely focus on some combination of the following leaders: Benjamin Franklin, George Washington, Thomas Jefferson, James Madison, Alexander Hamilton, and John Adams. Of these men only Adams was a member of a Reformed church at the end of his life, but he came to embrace non-Calvinist (and even heterodox) theological views. For profiles of each of these men and other founders (including Sherman and Ellsworth), see Daniel L. Dreisbach, Mark D. Hall, and Jeffry H. Morrison, eds., *The Founders on God and Government* (Lanham: Rowman and Littlefield, 2004); Dreisbach, Hall, and Morrison, eds., *The Forgotten Founders on Religion and Public Life* (Notre Dame: University of Notre Dame Press, 2009); and Dreisbach and Hall, eds., *Faith and the Founders of the American Republic* (New York: Oxford University Press, 2014).

state, a Congregationalist. William died in 1741, and shortly thereafter Roger moved to New Milford, Connecticut, where he worked as a cobbler, surveyor, and store owner. Sherman never went to college, but he was a voracious reader. He taught himself advanced mathematics and, in 1750, he began publishing a popular almanac that was issued annually or biannually until 1761. Sherman also studied law and was admitted to the Litchfield bar in 1754.[3]

As Sherman prospered professionally, he was elected to several six-month terms in the lower house of Connecticut's General Assembly. In 1760, after the death of his first wife (with whom he had seven children), Sherman moved to New Haven. There he opened a store next to Yale College and sold general merchandise, provisions, and books. Sherman married Rebecca Prescott three years later, and the two had eight children. In 1766, Connecticut voters chose him to be one of the twelve members of the upper house, or Council of Assistants. Traditionally, four Assistants were selected by the General Assembly to serve with the deputy governor as judges on Connecticut's Superior Court – the colony's highest judicial body. Sherman was appointed to this court in 1766, and he held both offices until 1785, when he resigned as an Assistant. He remained a Superior Court judge until he became a member of the US House of Representatives in 1789.

We know little about Sherman's and Ellsworth's service on the Superior Court because judicial decisions were not formally reported until the end of their careers. From the manuscript records and unofficial accounts that are available, it appears that most cases adjudicated by Sherman and Ellsworth involved mundane criminal, civil, and procedural issues. Some of them reflect the political culture of late eighteenth-century Connecticut. For instance, divorces were granted only for causes like desertion and cruelty, and an ecclesiastical society was denied the ability to fire a minister who had not violated the "covenant" between him and the society. One case involved "a Presentment of Grandjury against Drake for Defaming Mr. P. a Clergyman viz. for charging him for being an Arminian, unfit to be a Minister of the Gospel." None of the judges who heard the case denied that such an accusation was slander, but the lower court decision was overturned on a procedural issue.[4]

3 Biographical details are drawn from Christopher Collier, *Roger Sherman's Connecticut: Yankee Politics and the American Revolution* (Middletown: Wesleyan University Press, 1971); William R. Casto, *Oliver Ellsworth and the Creation of the Federal Republic* (New York: Second Circuit Committee on History and Commemorative Events, 1997); and Michael Toth, *Founding Federalist: The Life of Oliver Ellsworth* (Wilmington: ISI Books, 2011).

4 John T. Farrell, ed., *The Superior Court Diary of William Samuel Johnson, 1772–1773* (Washington, DC: American Historical Association, 1942), 105, 231, 60–61; *Ecclesiastical Society* v. *Beckwith*, 1 Kirby 91 (1786). The handwritten opinion for the last case is available in the Connecticut State Library.

Beginning in 1774, Sherman accepted multiple appointments to the Continental Congress. Collectively, he served 1,543 days in that body, and he helped draft and signed virtually every significant document produced by it. He served on numerous committees, including those charged with drafting the Declaration of Independence and the Articles of Confederation. In 1783, Sherman and Richard Law accepted the task of revising *all* of Connecticut's statutes. Notably, Sherman penned a law guaranteeing religious liberty to all Christians in the state.[5]

In 1787, Sherman was appointed to the Federal Constitutional Convention where he was an active participant. He was also a leader in Connecticut's ratification convention, and he wrote six "Letters" for the *New Haven Gazette* responding to anti-Federalist objections. Under the new Constitution, Sherman was elected first to the House of Representatives (1789–1791) and then appointed to the US Senate to fill the unexpired term of William Samuel Johnson. Sherman served in the Senate until his death on July 23, 1793.

Oliver Ellsworth was born in 1745 to David and Jemima Ellsworth. Tutored as a young man by the influential New Divinity minister Joseph Bellamy, he began his college education at Congregationalist Yale College and finished it at the Presbyterian College of New Jersey (now Princeton). Upon graduation, he studied law under Jesse Root and was admitted to the Connecticut bar in 1771. The following year he married Abigail Wolcott, a member of a prominent Connecticut family, with whom he had nine children.

From 1773 onward, Ellsworth served his state in a variety of offices including as a member of the lower and upper houses of the General Assembly, Committee on the Pay Table (responsible for ensuring that Connecticut's troops in the War for Independence were paid), Council of Safety (Connecticut's Board of War), and as Superior Court Judge. From 1778 to 1783, he was a delegate to the Continental Congress. He was one of the five members of Congress to serve on the Committee of Appeals, a tribunal responsible for reviewing admiralty cases from state courts.

At the Constitutional Convention of 1787, Ellsworth joined Sherman in advocating for a stronger but limited national government. He served on the important five-person Committee of Detail, which convened in late July to translate the numerous proposals and motions into a coherent document. Ellsworth left the Convention three weeks before its conclusion, so he did not have an opportunity to sign the Constitution. But he was an active promoter of

5 Protecting only Christians may seem illiberal (with good reason!), but there is no record of any citizen living in the state at that time who would not have identified himself or herself as a Christian.

it in his home state, publishing thirteen pro-ratification essays under the pseudonym of "A Landholder." Connecticut was the only state where each of its delegates to the Constitutional Convention also served in its ratification convention. According to the *Connecticut Courant*, in this convention "all the objects to the Constitution vanished before the learning and eloquence of a Johnson, the genuine good sense and discernment of a Sherman, and the Demosthenian energy of an Ellsworth." The reporter was biased, but the sense of Federalist domination conveyed in this account was accurate as evidenced by the January 9, 1788 vote of 128–40 to ratify the Constitution.[6]

Following the ratification of the Constitution, Connecticut's General Assembly selected Ellsworth and Johnson to be the state's first two Senators. His major contribution in this body was to serve as the chief draftsman of the Judiciary Act of 1789. Article III of the US Constitution states that "The judicial power of the United States, shall be vested in one Supreme Court, and in such inferior courts as the Congress may from time to time ordain and establish." Many delegates at the Federal Convention and First Federal Congress (including Sherman) believed that it was only necessary, prudent, and cost-efficient to create one federal court, the Supreme Court, and to let state courts serve as trial and lower appellate courts. Ellsworth argued, to the contrary, that it was important to have lower federal trial and appellate courts to help establish the authority of the new national government. Section 25 of the act also made it clear that the Supreme Court could overturn state court decisions involving federal laws or the US Constitution.[7]

Institutionally, the act created a Supreme Court consisting of one Chief Justice and five Associate Justices, thirteen district courts, and three circuit courts (each consisting of two Supreme Court Justices riding circuit and a district court judge). Although a portion of this law was declared unconstitutional in *Marbury* v. *Madison* (1803) and the federal court system was altered as America expanded and grew in population, it is no exaggeration to say that this act is one of the single most important pieces of legislation ever passed by Congress.

In 1796, President George Washington nominated Ellsworth to be the third Chief Justice of the United States Supreme Court. He was unanimously confirmed by the Senate and served until illness forced him to resign in

6 *The Documentary History of the Ratification of the Constitution, vol. 3: Ratification of the Constitution by the States: Delaware, New Jersey, Georgia, Connecticut*, ed. Merrill Jensen et al. (Madison: State Historical Society of Wisconsin, 1978), 554.

7 Fergus Bordewich, *The First Congress: How James Madison, George Washington, and a Group of Extraordinary Men Invented the Government* (New York: Simon & Schuster, 2016), 105–112; Toth, *Founding Federalist*, 136–137; Casto, *Oliver Ellsworth*, 59–76.

1800. The Court heard few cases during his tenure, and Ellsworth joined too late or missed the opportunity to participate in the few relatively important cases such as *Ware* v. *Hylton* (1796), *Hylton* v. *United States* (1796), and *Calder* v. *Bull* (1798). He did issue a noteworthy opinion in *United States* v. *La Vengeance* (1796), which helped flesh out the application of the Judiciary Act to admiralty cases. Although the practice is often credited to John Marshall, Ellsworth strongly discouraged the use of seriatim opinions and successfully encouraged his fellow Justices to write single, unified opinions.[8]

An important public duty of federal judges in the eighteenth century was to provide charges to Grand Juries. These were regularly published, and they were intended to help cultivate a spirit of affection for the new national government and laws. These charges were sometimes idealistic rather than descriptive, but even so they reveal the vision Justices like Ellsworth had for his nation. A 1796 charge by Chief Justice Ellsworth is particularly telling:

> Happily for our laws they are not written in blood, that we should blush to read, or hesitate to execute them. They breath the spirit of a parent; and expect the benefits of correction, not from severity, but from certainty. Reformation is never lost sight of, till depravity becomes, or is presumed to be incorrigible. Imposed as restraints, here are, not by the jealousy of usurpation, nor by the capriciousness of insensibility; but as aids to virtue and guards to rights, they have a high claim to be rendered efficient . . . . Let there be vigilance – constant vigilance and fidelity for the execution of laws – of laws made by all, and having for their object, the good of all. So let us rear an empire sacred to the rights of man; and commend a government of reason to the nations of the earth.[9]

These passages capture well Ellsworth's beliefs that laws should encourage virtue and punish vice, but with the end of reformation in mind. They reveal both a realistic view of human nature and an optimistic view of what good laws can help accomplish.

As a Senator and Justice, Ellsworth was an important advocate for peaceful co-existence with other nations. He successfully encouraged President Washington to send then-Supreme Court Chief Justice John Jay to Great Britain in 1794 to negotiate "The Treaty of Amity, Commerce, and

8 Casto, *Oliver Ellsworth*, 109–113; *The Documentary History of the Supreme Court of the United States, 1789–1800*, ed. Maeva Marcus et al. (New York: Columbia University Press, 2003), 7:8.

9 *The Documentary History of the Supreme Court of the United States, 1789–1800*, ed. Maeva Marcus et al. (New York: Columbia University Press, 1990), 3:119–120.

Navigation, between His Britannic Majesty and the United States of America," commonly known as the Jay Treaty. In response to strong opposition to the treaty in the House of Representative, in 1796 Ellsworth, now serving as Chief Justice, issued an advisory opinion stating that the House has no role in the Treaty making process. The Treaty was ratified later that year. Although unpopular with some Americans, it helped keep the peace between Great Britain and the fledgling republic.

In 1799, in the midst of an undeclared war with France, President Adams appointed Ellsworth to be one of three commissioners to America's old ally. The commissioners were unable to resolve all outstanding controversies, but did succeed in negotiating a treaty that ended the undeclared war and guaranteed freedom of commerce between the two nations. Unfortunately, the international travel was ruinous for Ellsworth's health, and upon returning home he promptly resigned from the Supreme Court. However, he was elected to the upper house of the Connecticut legislature in 1802, and was reelected every year until his death in 1807.

RELIGIOUS COMMITMENTS

Sherman and Ellsworth were exemplary Calvinists from a region dominated by members of that tradition. John Calvin (1509–1564), whose followers comprise what is commonly referred to as the Reformed tradition, embraced the quintessential Protestant doctrines of *sola fide, sola scriptura*, and the priesthood of all believers. These beliefs encouraged widespread literacy and a commitment to translating and printing the Bible in the vernacular.[10] Although ecclesiastical structures varied, Reformed churches leaned toward democratic forms of government, and nowhere was this truer than among the Calvinists who immigrated to America. Reformed Christians also emphasized the Christian doctrine of human depravity, which inclined them to avoid concentrated political power and to support the rule of law and checks on political actors.

Sherman and Ellsworth were raised and educated in this tradition, and both became members and leaders in their local Congregational churches. It is important to recognize that even *joining* a Congregational church in the eighteenth century was not a simple formality. Someone desiring to become

10 For instance, Christopher Collier estimates that "virtually every" Connecticut voter in 1787 could read. Collier, *All Politics Is Local: Family, Friends, and Provincial Interests in the Creation of the Constitution* (Hanover and London: University Press of New England, 2003), 83.

a member had to convince the congregation that he or she had a conversion experience and was committed to living a pious life. As well, church members made every effort to elect only pious men to be church leaders (unlike Anglican churches in the South, where local gentry were routinely appointed to be church leaders regardless of their devotion to the faith). Both Sherman and Ellsworth were members of such churches, and Sherman was chosen "Deacon upon trial" in 1755 and "was established Deacon" in 1757. He was regularly elected clerk of his local ecclesiastical society, and he served on the school and other committees.[11] Ellsworth's biographers do not mention if he was a leader in his local church, but later in life he was a trustee of the Missionary Society of Connecticut, so it is likely that he was.[12]

Ellsworth was by all accounts a serious Calvinist. A pious man, when he arrived in New York City to begin his service in the Senate, he was pleasantly surprised to find the "great decence [sic] & appearance of devotion with which divine service is attended. Instead of gazing, whispering & laughing, most of the Ladies, & many of the Gentlemen kneel at prayers on ... benches in their seats with their heads inclined so as to conceal their faces."[13] Later in life he, Judge John Treadwell, and the Reverends Strong and Perkins, were appointed by the Missionary Society of Connecticut to prepare a "Summary of Christian Doctrine" for use in new settlements. Their 63-page theological primer covered doctrines such as the Trinity, the Holy Scriptures ("the word of God and the only perfect rule of faith and manners"), Providence, and "total depravity."[14] Six thousand copies of this thoroughly Calvinist work were printed in 1804.[15]

Academics hoping to find an "enlightened" founding regularly question the orthodoxy of America's prominent founders, but few have contended that Sherman and Ellsworth were anything other than pious Calvinists. For instance, Sydney Ahlstrom, in his magisterial *A Religious History of the American People*, points to Sherman as evidence that "theological maturity abounds" in the founding era.[16] Similarly, Mark Noll, Nathan Hatch, and

11 Records of New Milford/First Congregational Church, Connecticut Church Records, reel #582, 5, Connecticut State Library.

12 *The Connecticut Evangelical Magazine* IV (August 1803), 80.

13 Bordewich, *First Congress*, 24.

14 Trustees of the Missionary Society of Connecticut, *A Summary of Christian Doctrine and Practice: Designed Especially, for the Use of the people in the New Settlements of the United States of America* (Hartford: Hudson & Goodwin, 1804), 5, 7, 16–19, 23.

15 N.A., *Contributions to the Ecclesiastical History of Connecticut* (New Haven: William L. Kingsley, 1861), 168.

16 Sydney E. Ahlstrom, *A Religious History of the American People* (Garden City: Doubleday, 1975), 1:492.

George Marsden refer to him as one of the founders who "made lifelong efforts to base their personal lives on biblical teaching."[17] More recently, James H. Hutson, after noting that "many of the Founders were recognized as religious specialists," comments that "[n]o one, perhaps, eclipsed Roger Sherman."[18] Yet none of these scholars consider in detail the connection between Sherman's faith and his political views/actions. My monograph, *Roger Sherman and the Creation of the American Republic*, attempts to fill this gap in the literature.[19]

A few scholars have deemphasized the importance of Sherman's faith. For instance, in his excellent biography of Sherman, Christopher Collier mentions his religious views in passing but does not consider them in detail until a brief section in the last chapter where he writes, "one of Roger Sherman's most prominent characteristics was his compromising temper. Indeed, expedience is a hallmark of his political career. His lapses from flexibility were few. Perhaps, however, it is to be expected that a man over seventy would develop some rigidities, especially in religion, and Sherman's part in the New Divinity fracas that rumbled through Connecticut in the late eighties and nineties is most uncharacteristic."[20] Likewise, historians James D. German and Richard Bushman underestimate the significance of Sherman's commitment to Calvinist theology and practices.[21]

Students of the founding era regularly mention Ellsworth in passing, especially in works on the Federal Constitutional Convention and the pre-Marshall federal courts. However, prior to the early 1990s little scholarship focused specifically on Ellsworth, and there was virtually no discussion of his religious commitments.[22] Since that time, William Casto and Michael Toth have argued persuasively that Ellsworth's Calvinist convictions regarding human nature and Christian morality had an important influence on both his political/legal theory and his contributions to the creation of the American republic.[23]

17 Mark Noll, Nathan Hatch, and George Marsden, *The Search for Christian America* (Westchester, IL: Crossway Books, 1983), 74.

18 James H. Hutson, ed., *The Founders on Religion: A Book of Quotations* (Princeton: Princeton University Press, 2005), xiv.

19 Mark David Hall, *Roger Sherman and the Creation of the American Republic* (New York: Oxford University Press, 2013).

20 Collier, *Roger Sherman's Connecticut*, 75, 323–324, 31–37.

21 James D. German, "The Social Utility of Wicked Self-Love: Calvinism, Capitalism, and Public Policy in Revolutionary New England," *Journal of American History* 82 (Dec. 1995): 966, and Richard L. Bushman, *From Puritan to Yankee: Character and the Social Order in Connecticut, 1690–1765* (Cambridge, MA: Harvard University Press, 1967), 255.

22 A partial exception to this generalization is William Garrott Brown's uncritical biography, *The Life of Oliver Ellsworth* (New York: Macmillan, 1905).

23 See especially, Casto, *Oliver Ellsworth*; Toth, *Founding Federalist*.

Sherman and Ellsworth are worthy of study in their own right, but they are also representatives of a theological tradition that retained a significant influence among Americans in this era. Sydney Ahlstrom estimates that the Reformed tradition was "the religious heritage of three-fourths of the American people in 1776."[24] Similarly, Yale historian Harry Stout states that prior to the War for Independence "the vast majority of colonists were Reformed or Calvinist."[25] Finally, William R. Hutchinson calculates that "[a]t least 90 percent of the colonists . . . had come out of the Calvinist rather than the Lutheran side of the Protestant Reformation."[26] These figures may be high, but a plethora of studies make it clear that Calvinist churches dominated New England and were well represented throughout the rest of the nation. In 1776, 63 percent of New England churches were Congregationalist, 15.3 percent were Baptist, and 5.5 percent were Presbyterian.[27] Thus approximately 84 percent of the region's churches were in the Reformed tradition, and these tended to have larger and more influential congregations.

Calvinists differed among themselves on many issues, but a long tradition of political reflection led to a remarkable unity with respect to three late-eighteenth century controversies: the War for Independence, the Creation of the Constitution, and the Drafting of the First Amendment's religion clauses. Sherman and Ellsworth were central players in each of these controversies.

RESISTANCE TO TYRANTS IS OBEDIENCE TO GOD

The idea that tyrants may be justly overthrown is regularly attributed to John Locke, but long before he wrote the *Second Treatise* Reformed Christians had fully embraced this doctrine. In his *Institutes*, Calvin encouraged inferior magistrates to actively resist tyranny. After the publication of the final edition of this work, he may have embraced the more radical idea that the people themselves may justly revolt against a tyrant, but even if he did not, later Calvinists – particularly those in the Anglo-American tradition – clearly did.[28] The reaction of Sherman, Ellsworth, and many of their fellow Calvinists in

24 Ahlstrom, *Religious History*, 1:426

25 Harry S. Stout, "Preaching the Insurrection," *Christian History* 15 (1996), 17.

26 William R. Hutchinson, *Religious Pluralism in America: The Contentious History of a Founding Ideal* (New Haven: Yale University Press, 2003), 20–21.

27 Roger Finke and Rodney Stark, *The Churching of America, 1776–1990: Winners and Losers in Our Religious Economy* (New Brunswick: Rutgers University Press, 1992), 29. Most but not all Baptists in this era were Calvinists.

28 The development of Protestant resistance theory is told in concise form by Quentin Skinner in *The Foundations of Modern Political Thought*, vol. 2: *The Age of Reformation* (Cambridge:

America to perceived abuse by Parliament and the Crown is best understood in light of the Reformed tradition's commitment to opposing tyrants.

In 1765, Parliament's Stamp Act attempted, for the first time, to raise revenue by directly taxing American colonists. Although the taxes were not high, in the minds of many Americans they were clearly unconstitutional and to pay them would encourage arbitrary government. As the conflict with Great Britain escalated, American patriots produced a host of pamphlets, essays, and resolutions attacking perceived abuses. Many of their legal, constitutional, or political complaints were not based on Reformed theology per se, although general Calvinist concerns about tyrannical rulers seem to have heightened their wariness compared to their non-Reformed colleagues. Recognizing that many Americans were committed Calvinists helps explain why in some cases, such as the possible appointment of an Anglican bishop and the Quebec Act, Americans were alarmed by these seemingly innocuous policies.[29] Parliament eventually repealed the Stamp Act, but in a move seemingly designed to stoke Calvinist fears of tyrannical government, it passed the Declaratory Act in 1766 which asserted that Parliament had the authority to make laws binding colonists "in all cases whatsoever."

Later in the same year, Sherman wrote a letter to his friend William Samuel Johnson, then serving as Connecticut's agent in London, in which he asked:

> If the Succession according to the present Establishment Should cease for want of an Heir or if the Parliament should alter it and admit a Papist to the Crown, would not the Colonies be at Liberty to joyn with Brittain or not [?]
>
> These questions may serve for speculation but it is not likely they will need to be Resolved in our Day, and I hope not till the time comes when the Nations shall learn war no more [Isaiah 2:4].[30]

In posing this hypothetical question, Sherman could have chosen a variety of constitutional violations or immoral actions. It is telling that the nightmare scenario that came to mind was Parliament permitting a "Papist" to become king. Revealing as well is his clear understanding that situations could arise wherein the colonies would be justified in breaking away from the British empire.

Cambridge University Press, 1978), especially Chapters 7–9. See also Hall, *Roger Sherman*, 12–62.

29 On these controversies, see Hall, *Roger Sherman*, 20–27, 48–62.

30 Mark David Hall, ed., *Collected Works of Roger Sherman* (Indianapolis: Liberty Fund Press, 2016), 147.

In a personal letter written to Johnson in 1768, Sherman emphasized no "Colonial Assembly on this continent will ever concede that the Parliament has authority to Tax the colonies."[31] Well before calls for the formation of a continental congress, Sherman was an ardent defender of American rights and he indicated that using force to protect these rights was justified. When the Continental Congress convened in 1774, Sherman was among Connecticut's delegates. He served in the body throughout the War for Independence and was involved in crafting a host of significant documents including the Declaration of Rights, Articles of Association, and Declaration of the Causes and Necessity of Taking up Arms. When it came time to appoint a committee to write a declaration of independence, Sherman was a logical candidate to be a member. On June 11, 1776, Congress appointed Sherman, Benjamin Franklin, John Adams, Thomas Jefferson, and Robert Livingston to such a committee. Unfortunately for Sherman's future fame, the next day he was also appointed to the committee to draft what became the Articles of Confederation (Livingston was the only other delegate to serve on both committees). Two days later, he was appointed to the Board of War. He was the only member of Congress to serve on all three of these committees. Jefferson, of course, took the lead in drafting the Declaration, but there is no reason to suspect that Sherman did not wholeheartedly support the Declaration, including its famous assertions that

> all men are created equal; that they are endowed by their Creator with certain unalienable rights; that among these are life, liberty, and the pursuit of happiness; that, to secure these rights, governments are instituted among men, deriving their just powers from the consent of the governed; that whenever any form of government becomes destructive of these ends, it is the right of the people to alter or to abolish it, and to institute new government, laying its foundation on such principles, and organizing its powers in such form, as to them shall seem most likely to effect their safety and happiness.[32]

These words reflect arguments long made by patriots in New England. Reformed Americans were almost universally patriots, a fact recognized by many contemporaries. In a 1775 speech urging reconciliation between Great Britain and the colonies, Edmund Burke warned his fellow members of Parliament that Americans "are Protestants; and of that kind which is the most adverse to all implicit submission of mind and opinion. This is

[31] Roger Sherman to William Samuel Johnson, June 25, 1768, in Collier, *Roger Sherman's Connecticut*, 70.

[32] Hall, *Collected Works*, 193.

a persuasion not only favorable to liberty, but built upon it."[33] A few months later, British Major Harry Rooke confiscated a presumably Calvinist book from prisoners taken at Bunker Hill and remarked, "It is your G-d Damned Religion of this Country that ruins the Country; Damn your religion."[34] Similarly, the Loyalist Peter Oliver railed against "Mr. *Otis's* black Regiment, *the dissenting Clergy*, who took so active a part in the Rebellion."[35] King George III himself reportedly referred to the War for Independence as "a Presbyterian Rebellion," a sentiment echoed by a Hessian soldier who described it as "an Irish-Scotch Presbyterian rebellion."[36] Finally, and many similar observations could be given, in 1780 Anglican clergy in New York wrote that "[d]issenters in general, and particularly Presbyterians and Congregationalists were the active Promoters of the Rebellion" because "from their infancy [they] imbibe Republican, levelling Principles."[37]

Connecticut's General Assembly was not in session when the Continental Congress voted to adopt the Declaration of Independence, but when it reconvened in October 1776 its first act was to unanimously approve the document. Ellsworth was not a member of this body at the time, but through his service on Connecticut's Committee on the Pay Table, the Council of Safety, and, from 1778 to 1783, the Continental Congress, he demonstrated his commitment to American Independence.

American patriots had a variety of motives and were influenced by different intellectual traditions. But the almost unanimous support of Reformed Christians for the patriot cause at least suggests that they were drawing from a long and rich history of Calvinist resistance literature. This literature encouraged them to be ever-vigilant for those who might attack their rights. Sherman and Ellsworth indisputably shared these views.

33 Edmund Burke, "On Moving His Resolutions for Conciliation with the Colonies," in Edmund Burke, *Conciliation with the Colonies*, ed. Cornelius Beach Bradley (Boston: Allyn and Bacon, 1895), 20.

34 John Leach, "A Journal Kept by John Leach, During His Confinement by the British, in Boston Gaol, in 1775," *New England Historical and Genealogical Register* 19 (1865): 256; Douglass Adair and John A. Schutz, eds., *Peter Oliver's Origin and Progress of the American Rebellion* (Stanford: Stanford University Press, 1961), 41.

35 Johnson, *History of the American People*, 173.

36 Johann Heinrichs to Herr H., January 18, 1778, in "Extracts from the Letter Book of Captain Johann Heinrichs of the Hessian Jäger Corps," *Pennsylvania Magazine of History and Biography* 22.2 (1898): 137.

37 Clergy of New York, October 28, 1780, quoted in Patricia Bonomi, "'Hippocrates' Twins': Religion and Politics in the American Revolution," *History Teacher* 29.2 (Feb. 1996): 142.

BUILDING A CONSTITUTIONAL TRADITION

Literally millions of eighteenth-century Americans learned to read using the explicitly Calvinist *The New England Primer*. More than two million copies were printed during that century alone and, in spite of its name, the text was used throughout America.[38] Many editions included a version of the alphabet where every letter is illustrated by a brief phrase – the most famous of which is "In Adam's Fall, we sinned all." Most Christians agree that humans are sinful, but Calvinists, with their doctrine of total depravity, place particular emphasis on the idea. Politically, this often led them to support constitutional restraints on governments and to oppose concentrated power. Sherman and Ellsworth shared these convictions.[39]

On May 16, 1787, Sherman, Ellsworth, and William Samuel Johnson were appointed to be Connecticut's representatives to the Constitutional Convention. Sherman did not arrive until May 30, the day after Madison presented his famous Virginia Plan. Madison, and a few other leading lights – notably James Wilson and Alexander Hamilton – had become convinced that the United States needed a powerful national government that could act independently of the states. Madison's plan included a legislature where members of the lower house would be elected by the people from proportionately sized districts. There would be an upper house, but its members would be chosen by the lower house from candidates nominated by state legislatures. An executive and judges would be appointed by the legislature, and acting together they might negate legislation. The national legislature would have a general grant of power and the ability to veto state laws.[40]

Madison's plan would have created a national government with effectively unlimited power and where states-qua-states would be completely unrepresented. Small states would have significantly less power under Madison's proposal than they did under the Articles of Confederation, and *all* state governments would be at the mercy of the new national government's ability to pass laws and veto state legislation. Nationalists like Madison, Wilson, and Hamilton thought that a powerful national government was necessary for prosperity and the protection of liberty, and that the state governments and

38 *The New-England Primer*, ed. Paul Leicester Ford (1727; reprint, New York: Dodd, Mead, 1897).

39 Michael Toth reports that after Count de Volney "shared his plans for restructuring the French government," Ellsworth observed that "there is one thing for which you have made no provision – the selfishness of man." Toth, *Founding Federalist*, 10–11.

40 Max Farrand, ed., *The Records of the Federal Convention of 1787* (New Haven: Yale University Press, 1911), 1:20–23.

local attachments were detrimental to these ends. For many Americans, particularly Reformed Americans, such concentrated power was a threat to liberty.

Sherman may have been tempted to dismiss Madison's proposals as utopian speculation if not for the convention's May 31 votes for electing members of the first branch by the people (rather than appointment by the state legislatures, as preferred by Sherman), and, more significantly, the 9–0–1 vote to grant the new national legislature the power to legislate "in cases to which the States are not competent" – i.e., in any area it sees fit. Surprisingly, even Ellsworth voted for the plan, and Sherman cast the *only* recorded vote dissenting from this general grant of power.[41]

Throughout the summer Sherman, and eventually Ellsworth, fought tenaciously for the creation of a stronger national government; but one with limited, strictly defined powers. Early in the summer Sherman listed what he thought the national government should do:

> The objects of the Union, he thought were few. 1. defence agst. foreign danger. 2. agst. internal disputes & a resort to force. 3. Treaties with foreign nations 4. regulating foreign commerce, & drawing revenue from it . . . . All other matters civil & criminal would be much better in the hands of the States.[42]

He offered a more detailed list of powers on July 17, less than a week before the issue was sent to the Committee of Detail.[43] Ellsworth was appointed to this important committee, and the committee's draft constitution contained an early version of what became Article I, Section 8.[44] The enumeration of Congress' powers, rather than a plenary grant as desired by Madison, Wilson, and Hamilton, is one of the most significant contributions Sherman, Ellsworth, and their allies made in Philadelphia. And it is a contribution informed by their Calvinist view of human nature.

From Sherman and Ellsworth's perspective, Madison, Wilson, and other nationalists wanted to concentrate far too much power in the national government. One of the ways in which they sought to do so was by grounding it immediately on the authority of the people. Wilson, for instance, openly

> contended strenuously for drawing the most numerous branch of the Legislature immediately from the people. He was for raising the federal

41 Ibid., 1:48–50, 53–54. Sherman also wanted state legislatures to pay national representatives to increase their accountability to the states. Ibid., 1:373.

42 Ibid., 1:133.

43 Ibid., 2:25–26.

44 Ibid., 2:25–26, 181–183.

> pyramid to a considerable altitude, and for that reason wished to give it as broad a basis as possible.[45]

Because Sherman wanted to keep the "federal pyramid" as shallow as possible, and because of his commitment to states' rights, he vigorously opposed Wilson's proposal. He responded to Wilson's argument by noting that "[i]f it were in view to abolish the State Govts. the elections ought to be by the people."[46] Similarly, Ellsworth contended that "the only chance we have to support a general government is to graft it on the state governments," and that selection of senators by state legislatures would protect the states and result in better qualified senators.[47] Two years later, Sherman elaborated on the significance of having state legislatures select members of Congress when he wrote to John Adams that "senators being eligible by the legislatures of the several states, and dependent on them for reelection, will be vigilant in supporting their rights against infringement by the legislature or executive of the United States."[48]

On June 6, John Dickinson, George Read, and other small-state delegates insisted that states be represented equally in at least one house of the legislature. The next day, Dickinson proposed and Sherman seconded a motion requiring senators to be chosen by state legislatures.[49] Discussion about the composition and power of the Senate led to Sherman and Ellsworth's most famous contribution to the Constitution. On June 11, Sherman proposed

> that the proportion of suffrage in the 1st branch should be according to the respective numbers of free inhabitants; and that in the second branch or Senate, each State should have one vote and no more. He said as the States would remain possessed of certain individual rights, each State ought to be able to protect itself: otherwise a few large States will rule the rest.[50]

Ellsworth immediately seconded the proposal, but the motion was defeated. However, Sherman's observation that the "smaller States would never agree to the plan on any other principle" eventually convinced a majority of delegates to support their compromise.[51] Sherman's plea was reinforced a few days later by William Paterson's New Jersey Plan. The plan contained many of

45 Ibid., 1:44.
46 Ibid., 1:132–133
47 Ibid., 1:414–415.
48 *The Works of John Adams*, ed. Charles Francis Adams (Boston: Charles C. Little and James Brown, 1850), 6:440.
49 Farrand, *Records*, 1:136–137, 150.
50 Ibid., 1:196.
51 Ibid., 1:201; see also 1:468–469, 484–485.

Sherman's ideals, notably a strengthened national government dependent immediately on the states and the state legislatures. At a minimum, the New Jersey Plan helped delegates from the larger states to see that delegates from smaller ones would not simply surrender the power they possessed under the Articles.[52]

After weeks of debate and a multitude of proposals, the delegates agreed to form a committee consisting of one member per state to "devise & report some compromise" on the issue of representation. Ellsworth was appointed to represent Connecticut, but he was unable to serve and so was replaced by Sherman. On July 5, the committee proposed that "in the 1st branch of the Legislature each of the States now in the Union shall be allowed 1 member for every 40,000 inhabitants" and "that in the 2d branch each State shall have an equal vote."[53] After weeks of debate, the Convention agreed to Sherman and Ellsworth's "Connecticut Compromise" by a vote of 5–4–1.[54]

Sherman had proposed something akin to the Connecticut Compromise in the Continental Congress, and by any measure he and Ellsworth were its primary advocates in the Convention. The compromise provided the small states and all state governments with an important measure of protection. Extreme nationalists like Madison, Wilson, and Hamilton remained displeased with it, but they should have recognized that without this compromise the Constitution would not have been ratified by more than a handful of states.

Sherman and Ellsworth opposed concentrated power at almost every turn. Among their major victories were an enumeration of Congress' powers and the Connecticut Compromise. By empowering state legislatures to select senators, the states as states retained significant power in the new national government. The Seventeenth Amendment, ratified in 1913, removed the power of selecting senators from the state legislatures, and new interpretations of the commerce and necessary and proper clauses in the twentieth century lay the groundwork for the significant expansion of the national government's power in the 1930s. But Sherman and Ellsworth helped to create a constitution that kept the national government largely within the bounds of its enumerated powers for a century-and-a-half, and their understanding of the proper balance between state and national power serve as a useful guide for those who believe that the national government has become too large, powerful, and unwieldy.

52 Ibid., 1:282–293.

53 Ibid., 1:11, 516, 526; 2:3.

54 Ibid., 2:5, 13–15.

THE FIRST AMENDMENT'S RELIGION CLAUSES

Connecticut was the only state to send each of its Federal Convention delegates to serve in the first federal Congress. Johnson and Ellsworth, Sherman's legal mentor and his protégé respectively, were selected by the General Assembly to be Connecticut's first United States Senators. Sherman was elected to the House of Representatives. The Senate's deliberations were closed to the public, so details of Ellsworth's contributions are sketchy. But multiple newspapers covered the proceedings in the House, so reports of debates in this chamber were more widely available. They both made contributions to debates over executive power, the national debt, and the proper scope of the federal government, but perhaps most relevant for contemporary debates are their contributions to drafting the First Amendment's religion clauses.

In the 1947 case of *Everson* v. *Board of Education*, Justice Wiley Rutledge observed that "no provision of the Constitution is more closely tied to or given content by its generating history than the religious clause of the First Amendment. It is at once the refined product and the terse summation of that history."[55] To understand this history, Justice Rutledge, like many Justices after him, turned primarily to the views of Thomas Jefferson and James Madison. These two founders desired a stricter separation between church and state than virtually any of their colleagues. By way of contrast, Calvinist founders such as Sherman and Ellsworth were far more comfortable with close cooperation between church and state.[56]

Sherman and Ellsworth, like other Federalists, initially opposed a bill of rights. Sherman, taking a conservative approach, wrote in December of 1788 that he

> hoped that all the states will consent to make a fair trial of the constitution before they attempt to alter it; experience will best show whether it is deficient or not, on trial it may appear that the alterations that have been proposed are not necessary, or that others not yet thought of may be necessary; everything that tends to disunion ought to be avoided. Instability in government and laws tends to weaken a state and render the rights of the people precarious.[57]

55 *Everson* v. *Board of Education*, 330 U.S. 1, 33 (1947) (Rutledge, J., dissenting); Mark David Hall, "Jeffersonian Walls and Madisonian Lines: The Supreme Court's Use of History in Religion Clause Cases," *Oregon Law Review* 85 (2006): 563–614.

56 See Casto, *Oliver Ellsworth*; and Hall, *Roger Sherman*.

57 "Observations on the Alterations Proposed as Amendments to the New Federal Constitution," December 4, 1788, in Hall, *Collected Works of Roger Sherman*, 498.

At Madison's insistence, the House eventually approved a motion by Fisher Ames to form a select committee composed of one member from each state to consider amendments. Madison and Sherman were both appointed to it. There are no records of the committee's deliberations, but it did produce the only handwritten draft of the Bill of Rights known to exist. The draft is in Sherman's handwriting, which suggests that he played an active role in the committee's deliberations.[58]

Madison's proposed bill of rights contained nine amendments that would have been interspersed throughout the Constitution. His first proposal was to insert the words "Government being intended for the benefit of the people, and the rightful establishment thereof being derived from their authority alone" before the words "We the people" in the Constitution's preamble.[59] Sherman immediately rose to object both to the wording of the amendment and its placement. He argued that

> we cannot incorporate these amendments in the body of the Constitution. It would be mixing brass, iron, and clay . . . . I conceive that we have no right to do this, as the Constitution is an act of the people, and ought to remain entire – whereas the amendments will be the act of the several legislatures.[60]

Sherman eventually won on both points. Significantly, amendments, it was decided, would be placed at the end of the Constitution.

On August 15, the House turned to Madison's proposal to insert the phrase "no religion shall be established by law, nor shall the equal rights of conscience be infringed" into Article I, Section 9. Sherman objected that he "[t]hought the amendment altogether unnecessary, insomuch as congress has no authority whatever delegated to them by the constitution, to make religious establishments, he would therefore move to have it struck out."[61] After a short discussion, the House agreed to Samuel Livermore's substitute: "congress shall make no laws touching religion, or infringing the rights of conscience."[62]

There is no record that Sherman joined the brief debate over the remainder of what became the First Amendment. He did contribute to discussions over the second provision concerning religion to come before the House; Madison's

58 Ibid., 643–644.

59 Charlene Bangs Bickford et al., eds., *Documentary History of the First Federal Congress* (Baltimore: The Johns Hopkins University Press, 1992), 11:1208 (hereafter *DHFFC*).

60 Ibid., 11:1212, 1233; 4:27–31. Sherman's reference to "brass, iron, and clay" is an allusion to Daniel 2:31–35.

61 Ibid., 11:1260–1262.

62 Ibid., 3:149–150. In the Constitutional Convention, Sherman argued that Article VI's prohibition on religious tests was "unnecessary, the prevailing liberality being a sufficient security agst. such tests." Farrand, *Records*, 2:468.

proposal attached to what is now the Second Amendment providing that "no person religiously scrupulous, shall be compelled to bear arms."[63] Although largely forgotten today, this provision provoked almost as much recorded debate as the First Amendment's religion provisions. Sherman's most significant objection was to James Jackson's proposal that persons exempted from military service should be forced to pay for a substitute. He contended:

> It is well-known that those who are religiously scrupulous of bearing arms, are equally scrupulous of getting substitutes or paying an equivalent; many of them would rather die than do either one or the other – but he did not see an absolute necessity for a clause of this kind. We do not live under an arbitrary government, said he, and the states respectively will have the government of the militia, unless when called into actual service.[64]

Sherman was sympathetic to the plight of pacifists, but he preferred to rely on state and federal legislatures to protect them. Madison's proposal was eventually rejected by the Senate, but Madison and Sherman were able to include a similar provision in the nation's first militia bill.[65]

Unlike Sherman, Madison did not trust states to protect rights, so he proposed an amendment stipulating that "no state shall infringe the equal rights of conscience, nor the freedom of speech, or of the press, nor of the right to trial by jury in criminal cases." This restriction on the states, which Madison conceived "to be the most valuable amendment on the whole list," occasioned little debate and with minor revisions was passed by the House on August 17. However, the Senate rejected the proposed amendment and Madison was unable to save it.[66]

On August 22, the House appointed Egbert Benson, Theodore Sedgwick, and Sherman to "prepare an introduction to and arrangement of Articles of Amendment."[67] The House approved the report, which consisted of seventeen articles, and it was sent to the Senate. There are few records of the Senate's debates, but Ellsworth was clearly an active participant. After a week of debate, Ellsworth produced a record of the amendments the Senate accepted, rejected, or altered.[68] Indeed, William Casto goes so far as to call Ellsworth "the Senate floor leader for the Bill of Rights."[69]

63 *DHFFC*, 11:1285.
64 Ibid., 11:1286.
65 Ibid., 11:1285–1288.
66 Ibid., 11:1292; 4:39.
67 Hall, *Roger Sherman*, 144–145.
68 *DHFFC*, 1:168.
69 Casto, *Oliver Ellsworth*, 78.

On September 21, the House agreed to some of the Senate's amendments, disagreed to others, and appointed Madison, Sherman, and John Vining to a conference committee to reconcile the differences. Ellsworth headed the Senate's delegation to this committee. He was joined by Maryland's Charles Carroll and New Jersey's William Paterson. The conference committee eventually approved twelve amendments, and a final report, written in Ellsworth's hand, was returned to both bodies.[70] The House approved the proposed amendments with a few minor changes, the Senate consented to the amendments passed by the House, and they were sent to the states where the ten that we now know as the Bill of Rights were ratified.[71]

America's founders differed with respect to whether and/or how civic authorities should support Christianity. On balance, Reformed Christians were more sympathetic to significant state support for religion, as suggested by the survival of establishments in Vermont (1807), Connecticut (1819), New Hampshire (1819), Maine (1820), and Massachusetts (1833). Yet when Supreme Court justices have turned to founding era history to shine light on the meaning of the religion clauses, they have overwhelmingly relied on the views of two southern Anglicans – Thomas Jefferson and James Madison. This approach is particularly ahistorical because Jefferson was not even involved in crafting or ratifying the First Amendment.[72]

James Madison is often called the father of the Bill of Rights, and there is no doubt that he deserves much credit for the final product. He initially proposed it, he pushed for it, and he was heavily involved in debates and committee work surrounding it. However, even the brief treatment provided here makes it evident that he did not dominate the process. Sherman was on the important committee of eleven that reported amendments to the House (a committee chaired by John Vining, not Madison), and the draft Bill of Rights in Sherman's hand shows that he was an active participant. The text of every amendment put forward by Madison was ultimately changed, and some of his suggestions were rejected altogether. Notably, his proposal to prohibit states from restricting certain rights, which he considered "the most valuable

70 *DHFFC*, 11:1292, 19:1430, 1827; William R. Casto, "Oliver Ellsworth's Calvinist Vision of Church and State in the Early Republic," in Dreisbach, Hall, and Morrison, eds., *The Forgotten Founders on Religion and Public Life*, 65–100.

71 *DHFFC*, 4:6–9, 35–48; 3:216–218, 228–229; Robert A. Rutland, *The Birth of the Bill of Rights* (New York: Collier Books, 1962), 194–221.

72 It is sometimes asserted that Jefferson's Virginia Statute for Religious Liberty influenced the authors and ratifiers of the First Amendment. I argue that there is little evidence to support this proposition. See Hall, "Madison's Memorial and Remonstrance, Jefferson's Statute for Religious Liberty, and the Creation of the First Amendment," *American Political Thought* 3 (Spring 2014): 32–63.

amendment on the whole list," was not adopted. It was not a critical committee, yet it is worth noting that Sherman, not Madison, sat on the three-person House committee charged with arranging the amendments proposed by the House. It seems likely that Ellsworth was Madison's counterpart in the Senate, and he was clearly his equal on the conference committee.

It is understandable that scholars and jurists favoring the strict separation of church and state are drawn to Madison and Jefferson. Although even those founders did not consistently act on this principle, Madison's *Memorial and Remonstrance* (1785) and his "Detached Memoranda" (c. 1817), and Jefferson's *Bill for Establishing Religious Liberty* (1779) and his letter to the Danbury Baptists (1802) offer support for this position.[73] Yet Jefferson did not help draft the Bill of Rights, and if Madison was a driving force behind the First Amendment, the document was ultimately a product of a community – a community that included the following members of Reformed churches: Roger Sherman, Oliver Ellsworth, John Langdon, Caleb Strong, Paine Wingate, Philip Schuyler, Abraham Baldwin, Elias Boudinot, Jonathan Elmer, William Paterson, Fisher Ames, Abiel Foster, Benjamin Huntington, James Jackson, Jeremiah Wadsworth, Nicholas Gilman, Egbert Benson, James Schureman, Henry Wynkoop, Daniel Hiester Jr., Daniel Huger, Benjamin Bourne, William Smith, and Hugh Williamson. Certainly these men were not all equally influential, but at least Sherman, Ellsworth, Huntington, Baldwin, Boudinot, Paterson, and Ames played important roles in key committees and/or debates. None of these seven men advocated anything like a wall of separation between church and state, and there is little reason to believe that many of their colleagues did either.

One way to illustrate this point is to look at other actions of the First Congress that concern religion. To give just one example, *on the day after* the House approved the final wording of the Bill of Rights, Elias Boudinot proposed that the president recommend a public day of thanksgiving and prayer. In response to objections by Aedenus Burke and Thomas Tucker that those practices mimicked European customs and that such calls were properly issued by states, Sherman:

> Justified the practice of thanksgiving, on any signal event, not only as a laudable one in itself, but as warranted by a number of precedents in holy writ: For instance, the solemn thanksgivings and rejoicings which took place

73 For discussion of the founders' views on church–state relations, see Mark David Hall, "Did America Have a Christian Founding?" *First Principles Series*, The Heritage Foundation, June 7, 2011. Available at: www.heritage.org/research/lecture/2011/06/did-america-have-a-christian-founding (accessed September 18, 2017).

> in the time of Solomon, after the building of the temple, was a case in point. This example he thought, worthy of christian imitation on the present occasion; and he would agree with the gentleman who moved the resolution.[74]

The House approved the motion and appointed Boudinot, Sherman, and Sylvester to a committee to meet with senators on the matter. The Senate concurred with the House's motion, and Congress requested that President Washington issue what became his famous 1789 Thanksgiving Day Proclamation.[75] It is noteworthy that both Burke and Tucker worked *against* the Bill of Rights and that Boudinot and Sherman almost certainly supported it. There is no record of the House vote in favor of asking the president to declare a day of public prayer and thanksgiving, but the September 26 *New York Daily Advertiser* noted that it passed by "a great majority."[76]

CONCLUSION

Roger Sherman and Oliver Ellsworth represent well the many civic leaders in the founding era who were influenced by the Reformed tradition. Their convictions led them to play significant roles in securing American independence and creating a new constitutional regime. Their religious tradition taught them to be watchful of tyrannical rulers and to be suspicious of concentrated power. Their contributions, individually and collectively, to the creation of a limited national government with separated powers and checks and balances has served America well. Both initially opposed the creation of a bill of rights, but they nevertheless were important participants in debates over these constitutional amendments. Neither desired to establish a national church, but both were comfortable with a minimal cooperation between church and state at the national level, and closer cooperation between these entities at the state level. Their views on these matters may seem old-fashioned to some, but anyone interested in an accurate account for the founders' political and legal ideas cannot afford to ignore them.

74 *DHFFC*, 11:1500–1501.

75 In Daniel L. Dreisbach and Mark David Hall, eds., *The Sacred Rights of Conscience* (Indianapolis: Liberty Fund Press, 2009), 453–454.

76 *DHFFC*, 11:1501.

6

John Jay: The First Chief Justice

Wendell Bird

John Jay (1745–1829) was the first chief justice of the United States Supreme Court, and immediately prior to his appointment coauthored *The Federalist* with Alexander Hamilton and James Madison. Earlier, he had been the critical negotiator of the Treaty of Paris that ended the American Revolution on favorable terms, and in 1794 he was the negotiator of the Jay Treaty that averted a new war with Britain.

A LEADING FOUNDER

Jay, though a young lawyer, served in the Continental Congresses of 1774–1776, led drafting of the New York constitution of 1777, and became the state's first chief justice during 1777–1779. He was president of Congress from December 1778 to late September 1779, when he became the country's minister to Spain, and then joined Benjamin Franklin and John Adams in France to negotiate the Treaty of Paris. Jay returned to serve as America's secretary for foreign affairs from 1784 to 1789, and supported the Constitution with *The Federalist* and other essays. President George Washington nominated him as the first chief justice in 1789, and Jay held that office even as he traveled to Britain in 1794 to negotiate the famous Jay Treaty. Upon returning to America in 1795, Jay found that he had been elected governor of New York. Accordingly, he resigned from the Court and served as governor from 1795 to 1801. Until he concluded the controversial Jay Treaty, he was widely viewed as one of "three persons prominent in the public eye, as the successor of the actual President of the United States" (then Washington), as Hamilton put it.[1]

[1] Camillus [Alexander Hamilton], "The Defence No. 1 (July 22, 1795)," in *Papers of Alexander Hamilton*, ed. Harold C. Syrett (New York: Columbia University Press, 1961–1987), 18:479, 482.

As first chief justice of the United States Supreme Court, Jay sought to establish the new Court as "the keystone of our political fabric," as Washington charged him to do. Jay announced the Court's significant decisions denying effect to state confiscation laws after the war ended, and rejecting the power of foreign governments to establish courts in America to approve captures of ships, and wrote an individual opinion in the controversial decision denying states any sovereign immunity against lawsuits. Sitting on circuit courts, Jay issued decisions (all of which exercised judicial review) questioning the validity of a federal law that violated separation of powers, invalidating a state law that contravened the federal Constitution, and supporting the supremacy of treaties over inconsistent state legislation.[2] These reflected his commitments to strengthening the new federal government, insisting on conformity to the Constitution, and enforcing treaties in order to promote peace.

Jay's paternal ancestors were Huguenots, who fled France after the Edict of Nantes was revoked in 1685. His grandfather left the French Reformed Church in New York for Trinity Church, an Anglican church, where John Jay was baptized. His family soon moved to an Anglican church in New Rochelle. Jay graduated from the colony's Anglican college, King's College (now Columbia University), and was a member (and long-time warden) of Trinity Church until his retirement to Bedford, when he joined the local Episcopal church (after attending a Presbyterian church until the Episcopal building was constructed). There was a wide range of beliefs within his denomination, and Jay rejected "high church doctrines." Those scholars who mention Jay's faith generally identify him, on an increasingly complex religious spectrum of the time, as an orthodox Christian.[3]

SCHOLARLY TREATMENT OF JOHN JAY AND HIS RELIGIOUS FAITH

The six book-length biographies of Jay refer to him as a committed Christian, and describe his Huguenot ancestry and Anglican upbringing, but they say

Biographies are cited in n.4. Throughout, capitalization in quotations is modified to current standards, without indication.

2 *Georgia* v. *Brailsford*, 3 U.S. (3 Dall.) 1, 3–5 (1794); *Glass* v. *The Sloop Betsey*, 3 U.S. (3 Dall.) 6, 16 (1794); *Chisholm* v. *Georgia*, 2 U.S. (2 Dall.) 419, 469–79, 471 (1793) (overturned by the Eleventh Amendment); *Hayburn's Case*, 2 U.S. (2 Dall.) 409, 410n. (1792) (reprinting Jay's circuit decision); *Champion & Dickison* v. *Carey* (1791) (summarized in *The Documentary History of the Supreme Court of the United States*, 1789–1800, ed. Maeva Marcus (New York: Columbia University Press, 1988), 2:236 & n.8); *Jones* v. *Walker*, 13 F.Cas. 1059, 1067–69 (C.C. D. Va. 1793) (No. 7,507), affirmed sub nom. *Ware* v. *Hylton*, 3 U.S. (3 Dall.) 199 (1796).

3 Walter Stahr, *John Jay: Founding Father* (New York: Hambledon, 2005), 4–9, 233; John Jay to the Corporation of Trinity Church (n.d.), in *Correspondence and Public Papers of John Jay*, ed. Henry P. Johnson (New York: Burt Franklin, 1890), 4:505, 513 (hereinafter *Correspondence*).

little about his faith during his adult years (except pious language in the biography by Jay's son) and still less about its impact on his public life. The two older publications of selected papers contain many references to God but only some of Jay's private discussions of religious beliefs and their consequences in the world.[4]

There have been only three substantial discussions of Jay's religious beliefs, each article-length; all characterize Jay as an orthodox Christian. However, the first did not identify any political or public actions influenced by his faith, except irresolution about independence, anti-Catholicism in the 1770s, opposition to Tory vestiges in the Episcopal Church, and opposition to France, while the second did not discuss any public ramifications of faith at all; neither connected Jay's faith even to antislavery activities or peace negotiations. The most recent, by Jonathan Den Hartog, splendidly summarizes Jay's belief in the "great plan of Providence" for the nation as well as for his individual life, which the author connects to Jay's efforts to establish the new nation by support of the Revolution, the Constitution, the Federalist Party, and voluntarist societies; those aspects of Jay's thought will not be repeated here.[5]

Discussions of Jay in histories of the early republic, and in biographies of other founders, occasionally acknowledge his faith. For example, Gordon Wood described him as a "Christian enthusiast" (in contrast to Jefferson and Adams), Sandra VanBurkleo as a "devoted Anglican" who often used biblical imagery, James Hutson as extolled for "fervor, of his religious convictions,"

4 Stahr, *Jay*, 4–8, 82, 233; Frank Monaghan, *John Jay* (New York: Bobbs-Merrill, 1935), 218–219; George Pellew, *John Jay* (Boston: Houghton Mifflin, 1890), 2–3; William Whitelock, *Life and Times of John Jay* (New York: Dodd, Mead, 1887); Henry B. Renwick, *Lives of John Jay and Alexander Hamilton* (New York: Harper, 1841), 14–22; William Jay, *Life of John Jay* (New York: Harper, 1833), 1:463. Old biographies on chief justices, by Henry Flanders (1855) and George Van Santvoord (1854), also included Jay; short biographies were written by Richard B. Morris (1967), Donald L. Smith (1968), and Herbert A. Johnson (1970). For older editions of selected papers, Richard B. Morris, ed., *John Jay* (New York: Harper & Row, 1975–1980), 2:14 (vol. 1 is subtitled *The Making of a Revolutionary*, and vol. 2 *The Winning of the Peace*); Johnson, *Correspondence*. For correspondence in this chapter, *The Papers of John Jay* are used (n.7), and citations to Morris or Johnson are added for the reader's convenience, when documents also appear there. (Exceptions are letters dated Oct. 25, 1779, Sept. 17, 1780, June 1788, Feb. 27, 1792, July/August 1792, and May 12, 1794.)

5 Patricia U. Bonomi, "John Jay, Religion, and the State," *New York History* 81 (2000): 8, 15–18; David L. Holmes, *The Faiths of the Founding Fathers* (New York: Oxford University Press, 2006), 154; Jonathan Den Hartog, "John Jay and the 'Great Plan of Providence'," in *The Forgotten Founders on Religion and Public Life*, ed. Daniel L. Dreisbach, Mark David Hall, and Jeffry H. Morrison (Notre Dame: University of Notre Dame Press, 2009), 145, 146, 150 (and he very briefly mentions Jay's antislavery activities and thanksgiving proclamation as ramifications, ibid., 163, 164).

and Daniel Dreisbach as among "the most orthodox Christians." But these are the exceptions, and typically there is no mention of Jay's faith or its influence.[6]

Jay's unpublished papers became generally available in 2002, when Columbia University placed most online as *The Papers of John Jay* (13,000 documents containing 30,000 pages in total). Only a portion of those relevant to his beliefs is summarized here, and further research is warranted. A new seven-volume edition of selected papers of John Jay with scholarly commentary is now over half complete, and is a superb help to research.[7]

JOHN JAY'S DISCUSSION OF HIS RELIGIOUS BELIEFS

Jay's religious beliefs, as he himself discussed them, were very much the orthodox Christian faith that Wood and Dreisbach described. This summary is mostly in Jay's own words, beginning with his fullest descriptions of his beliefs in annual addresses as president of the American Bible Society late in his life. Those are quite consistent with his beliefs expressed in letters to family members and friends throughout his life.[8]

A typical passage gives a sense of Jay's views of creation and fall, atonement and salvation, and of his Calvinist perspective:

> man was originally created and placed in a state of happiness, but becoming disobedient, was subjected to the degradation and evils which he and his posterity have since experienced. The Bible will also inform them, that our gracious Creator has provided for us a Redeemer in whom all the nations of the earth should be blessed – that this Redeemer has made atonement "for the sins of the whole world," and thereby reconciling the Divine justice with the Divine mercy, has opened a way for our redemption and salvation – and that these inestimable benefits are of the free gift and grace of God – not of our deserving, nor in our power to deserve.

As the references to the Redeemer showed, Jay did not follow some founders in avoiding mention of Jesus Christ, but frequently alluded to "the great Captain

6 Gordon S. Wood, *The Radicalism of the American Revolution* (New York: Knopf, 1992), 366; Sandra F. VanBurkleo, "'Honour, Justice, and Interest': John Jay's Republican Politics and Statesmanship on the Federal Bench," in *Seriatim: The Supreme Court before John Marshall*, ed. Scott D. Gerber (New York: New York University Press, 1998), 26, 33; James H. Hutson, *Church and State in America* (New York: Cambridge University Press, 2008), 96; Daniel L. Dreisbach, "Famous Founders and Forgotten Founders," in *Forgotten Founders*, 1, 18.

7 *The Papers of John Jay* currently are at https://dlc.library.columbia.edu/jay and www.upress.virginia.edu/rotunda/collections; the seven-volume edition is *The Selected Papers of John Jay*, ed. Elizabeth M. Nuxoll et al. (Charlottesville: University of Virginia Press, 2010–).

8 The American Bible Society addresses appear in *The Papers of John Jay* (dated May 9, 1822, May 8, 1823, n.d. May 1824, and n.d. May 1825), and in *Correspondence*, 4:478–504.

of our salvation," the "Saviour" who "commanded his apostles to preach the Gospel."[9]

Jay ended that American Bible Society message with his Calvinist faith in the sovereignty of God, "who made and governs the world," who "has blessed us" with "our civil and religious rights." This was "an overruling Providence" who could change the course of history, who "in due season" would cause that "His will should be done on earth as it is done in heaven," and who "appointed and ordained" the means of salvation.[10]

Jay's view of the Bible was that Providence "cause[d] every material event and occurrence respecting our Redeemer, together with the gospel he proclaimed, and the miracles and predictions to which it gave occasion, to be faithfully recorded and preserved." Thus, "the Holy Scriptures" have God as their "Divine and merciful Author," the gospel is of "Divine origin," and the Bible is "a connected series of the Divine revelations." Jay believed the "truth of these facts" to be "unquestionable," "biblical critics" and skeptics to be mistaken, and the "inability of *mere* human reason" to be evident.[11]

He regarded the Bible as an accurate history of Noah, of Noah's "longevity" and the subsequent "diminution of longevity," of the "catastrophe at Babel" and the resulting formation of "distinct nations," and of Abraham and the "promise that the Redeemer should be of his family." He accepted that the apostles "prove[d] the truth of their doctrine" by "supernatural signs and miracles," and that their preaching was "witnessed from on high" by "divers miracles."[12]

He also saw the Bible as accurate in prophecy, such as the "Old Testament. . .prophecies respecting the Messiah" that had been fulfilled, and the prophecies of a future "conversion of the great residue of the Gentiles" and of the Jews. At that time, "the Redeemer is preparing to take possession of the great remainder of his heritage," by an earthly rule where "righteousness and felicity shall dwell."[13] Jay mixed those postmillennial views with some premillennial views, trusting that the preservation of the Jews as a separate people "fulfill[s] the prophecies" and "is a living witness to their truth," and that those Bible "prophecies declare that a time will come when all the twelve tribes shall be restored to their country," Palestine, at an unspecified time, and when the Jews again will control Jerusalem. He noted that the

9 *Correspondence*, 4:494, 498, 503. Throughout, quotations in correspondence follow the original *Papers of John Jay*, and not Morris or Johnson.

10 Ibid., 4:497, 483, 488, 499.

11 Ibid., 4:480, 492, 503, 504, 494, 501–502, 480.

12 Ibid., 4:479–480, 504, 488.

13 Ibid., 4:503, 481, 490, 486, 488.

Redeemer was of Abraham's family and that "the Divine oracles and revelations were committed" to the Jews, and he welcomed the "strange and general alteration in the feelings of Christians... towards the *Jews*," so that they "are now experiencing less oppression" and "more compassion than formerly."[14]

Jay believed in "life of endless duration" in "a state of bliss," heaven, and that a person's entrance into heaven "depends on his acceptance and use of the means for obtaining it, which his merciful Creator has for that purpose appointed and ordained." Because of that faith, coupled with human depravity and biblical prophecy, he saw a need to "preach the *gospel* to *all* people," as the "Redeemer" had directed – including to the Jews, the Indians, and "the heathen" – by missionary efforts "to diffuse the light of the gospel." He had a strongly positive view of what became known as the Second Great Awakening, and sent his younger son to Yale because it was awash in the Awakening.[15]

Jay's convictions throughout his life were consistent with these end-of-life affirmations of faith. He did not join the Deist and Unitarian rejection of the deity of Jesus Christ. Instead, Jay listed Bible verses on the "Divinity of Christ," and elsewhere said he accepted that "grace and favor did come by Jesus Christ," the "Savior," who performed miracles and who provided the "only" adequate plan of salvation. Jay believed in Christ's redemption and resurrection, and that "the Trinity was a fact fully revealed and substantiated," though he concluded that creeds failed adequately to describe the mode of the Trinity. Jay trusted that "the evidence of the truth of Christianity" would convict "candid minds." He taught his daughters that "virtue and religion must be the corner stones" of life, and that eternal life was the reward.[16]

His Calvinism, inherited from both his paternal Huguenot and maternal Dutch Reformed ancestors, appeared frequently not only in references to human depravity, but in statements about divine sovereignty over public and private affairs. "God governs the world, and we have only to do our duty wisely, and leave the issue to him," or that we must "resign to the will of God, without whose appointment or permission, nothing comes to pass."[17] "He who governs

[14] Ibid., 4:490, 481, 480, 489–490.

[15] Ibid., 4:481, 499, 487, 488, 490–491, 493, 485, 482, 497; Timothy Dwight to John Jay (Jan. 4, 1803).

[16] John Jay, Divinity of Christ from the Revelation of St. John (n.d. 1813); John Jay to John Murray, Jr. (Apr. 15, 1818), *Correspondence*, 4:403, 405, 409–410; John Jay to Lindley Murray (Aug. 22, 1794), ibid., 4:50, 52; John Jay to Jedidiah Morse (Oct. 25, 1813); John Jay to Maria Banyer (Dec. 29, 1805); John Jay to Samuel Miller (Feb. 18, 1822); John Jay to Uzal Ogden (Feb. 14, 1796), *Correspondence*, 4:203; John Jay to Maria and Nancy Jay (June 1, 1792).

[17] John Jay to Timothy Pickering (Aug. 17, 1795), *Correspondence*, 4:183, 185; John Jay to Maria Banyer (Nov. 2, 1804), ibid., 4:299; see John Jay to Frederick Jay (Nov. 2, 1791); John Jay to Sarah Jay (Mar. 13, 1795).

all nations, sometimes corrects national misrule by making it instrumental to national chastisement," as Jay often restated, and "can restrain the wrath of man" or send "delusion." There was a "great plan of Providence" that "caus[ed] this extensive part of our world to be discovered" and populated, and that "created such a nation" as America. In these references to Providence, Jay's concept was the Reformed one and not the Deistic one.[18]

Jay instructed his son that "[t]he Bible is the best of all books, for it is the word of God, and teaches us the way" to live "in this world and in the next." He wrote to a close friend, Gouverneur Morris, that the Bible is the "*one* history free from error," being written "by holy men of God . . . as they were moved by the Holy Spirit."[19] The Bible was authoritative whether in teaching doctrine or in teaching about "our first parents before their Maker breathed into them the breath of life" and about "the flood."[20]

Did these Christian beliefs affect Jay's actions as a jurist and public official?

INFLUENCE OF JOHN JAY'S FAITH ON LAW AND PUBLIC AFFAIRS

Among the influences on his values and actions, Jay's faith appears to have been the greatest. It visibly guided his selection of views and public activities. It led to his commitments to oppose slavery and to work for peace, along with other endeavors that today are less favored.[21] The remainder of this chapter will summarize ten policy activities that dominated much of Jay's public life and that he indicated were guided by his faith. It may be more accurate to say that most of Jay's beliefs and actions were informed if not governed by his faith.

[18] John Jay to William Miller (Sept. 20, 1814); John Jay to Jedidiah Morse (Jan. 1, 1813), *Correspondence*, 4:365, 367; John Jay to Jedidiah Morse (Aug. 16, 1809), ibid., 4:322; John Jay to Marquis of Lansdowne (Apr. 16, 1786), ibid., 3:188, 190; see also John Jay to Benjamin Rush (Mar. 22, 1797), ibid., 4:225, 226; John Jay to Timothy Pickering (Nov. 1, 1814), ibid., 4:378; John Jay to Richard Peters (Mar. 14, 1815), ibid., 4:386, 387; John Jay to John Murray, Jr. (Apr. 15, 1818), ibid., 4:403, 418. In private life as well, "Providence will so order events." John Jay to Sarah Jay (May 12, 1794), ibid., 4:21, 22. Jay wrote an essay on the Calvinistic doctrine of election. John Jay, [uncaptioned essay] (May 9, 1814).

[19] John Jay to Peter Jay (Apr. 8, 1784), Morris, *Jay*, 2:709; John Jay to Gouverneur Morris (Oct. 28, 1816), *Correspondence*, 4:393, 394; John Jay to John Murray, Jr. (Feb. 27, 1819), ibid., 4:428, 429; see John Jay to Jedidiah Morse (Feb. 28, 1797), ibid., 4:223, 225.

[20] Jay's Charge to the Grand Jury of Ulster County (Sept. 9, 1777), ibid., 1:158, 163; John Jay to John Murray, Jr. (Apr. 15, 1818), ibid., 4:403, 404.

[21] Controversially, he believed it was the duty and privilege "of our Christian nation to select and prefer Christians for their rulers," and that Christians should not "vote for *infidel* rulers." John Jay to John Murray, Jr. (Oct. 12, 1816), *Correspondence*, 4:391, 393; John Jay to Jedidiah Morse (Jan. 1, 1813), ibid., 4:365.

Antislavery. Early in his career, in 1780, Jay summarized his tenets about slavery in a letter to a friend:

> An excellent law might be made out of the Pennsylvania one for the gradual abolition of slavery. Till America comes into this measure her prayers to Heaven for liberty will be impious. This is a strong expression but it is just. Were I in your legislature I would prepare a bill for the purpose with great care, and I would never cease moving it till it became a law or I ceased to be a member. I believe God governs this world, and...those who ask for equity ought to do it.

In this, Jay indicated not only that religious faith led to his antislavery stance, but that it should impel a legislator to fight against that wrong. Late in his life, in 1822, Jay praised a religiously informed legislator, William Wilberforce, for doing exactly that, in leading the parliamentary fight that "abolished that detestable trade." Wilberforce was "that excellent and celebrated member of it [Parliament], whose pious zeal and unwearied perseverance were greatly and conspicuously instrumental" in winning the fight. In praising a legislator's "pious zeal" in opposing the slave trade, Jay reiterated that a legislator's faith should inform belief and guide action on a significant moral and humanitarian issue. Jay followed that principle in office as president of the American Bible Society by prominently raising the slavery issue in his first annual address, despite a large minority of its vice presidents and managers being slaveholders, despite the continued warm debate over the Missouri Compromise, and despite slaveholders' "territorial and personal concerns" – their desire to keep slaves and to add slave states – which Jay declared he "hoped that an overruling Providence will render ... unsuccessful."[22]

Jay showed pious zeal on the slavery issue in governmental offices, as well. In drafting New York's first constitution during 1776–1777, Jay sought to insert a clause calling "for abolishing domestic slavery." As president of Congress in 1779, he supported the unsuccessful proposal to free blacks who joined the continental army. As an envoy negotiating a commercial treaty with Britain in 1783, Jay proposed a provision that British subjects may not "carry or import into the [United] States any slaves," in order "[e]ntirely to prohibit the importation thereof." While serving as the secretary for foreign affairs in 1785, Jay accepted the presidency of one of the first antislavery societies, the New York Society for Promoting the Manumission of Slaves. All of that was politically daring, because New York City was the second-largest slave-trading

[22] John Jay to Egbert Benson (Sept. 18, 1780), Morris, *Jay*, 1:822, 823; American Bible Society Address (May 9, 1822), *Correspondence*, 4:478, 484, 483; see Daniel C. Littlefield, "John Jay, the Revolutionary Generation, and Slavery," *New York History* 81 (2000): 91, 107–132.

port in the nation and the state had over 21,000 enslaved persons. Jay's role was not merely honorary; among other things, he drafted the society's petition for a law prohibiting exportation of slaves (an "inhuman commerce" of persons who were "free by the laws of God"). The society succeeded in obtaining New York laws barring importation of slaves and facilitating manumission, and in establishing a school and assisting free blacks. Jay long supported, and gladly signed as governor, a New York law for gradual emancipation in 1799, though his role in passing it is unclear.[23]

The quotation above was not the only one showing that Jay's opposition to slavery grew out of his religious faith. When he was asked his views on slavery after being nominated for the governorship of New York, Jay said that "every man of every color and description has a natural right to freedom," and paraphrased a number of Bible verses. During his retirement, he told Wilberforce that it "is pleasing to behold a nation," Britain, "kindly extending the blessings of Christianity and civilization to distant countries" by prohibiting the slave trade and using its naval supremacy to intercept slaving ships. As his reference to natural rights shows, Jay offered other arguments besides religious ones, repeating that it "is very inconsistent with their [United States'] declarations on the subject of human rights to permit a single slave," and that it is "repugnant to the following positions in the Declaration of Independence, … 'that all men are created equal – that they are endowed by their Creator with certain unalienable rights.'"[24]

Despite these things, there is much room for criticizing Jay on the slavery issue. During the Missouri controversy he said slavery "ought not to be introduced nor permitted in any of the new states," but he only thought it "ought to be gradually diminished and finally abolished in all of them," and a quarter century earlier he similarly had said "the abolition of slavery must necessarily be gradual." Even as his principles seemed to forbid it, Jay had

[23] John Jay to Robert R. Livingston and Gouverneur Morris (Apr. 29, 1777), Morris, *Jay*, 1:397, 401, 402 n.4; *Journals of the Provincial Congress, Provincial Convention, Committee of Safety and Council of Safety of the State of New-York, 1775–1776–1777* (Albany: T. Weed, 1842), 1:887, 889 (because Jay was called away, Gouverneur Morris introduced the antislavery provision); Worthington C. Ford, ed., *Journals of the Continental Congress* (Washington, DC: Government Printing Office, 1909), 13:386 (proposal edited in Jay's handwriting); "Draft Treaty of Commerce with England" (June 1, 1783), Morris, *Jay*, 2:540; John Jay to English Anti-Slavery Society (June 1788), *Correspondence*, 3:341, 343–344; "Jay's 'Draft of a Memorial to the Legislature To Prohibit Exportation of Slaves'" (Feb. 1786), in Frank Monaghan, "Anti-Slavery Papers of John Jay," *Journal of Negro History* 17 (Oct. 1932): 481, 489–490; Stahr, *Jay*, 237–239.

[24] John Jay to J. C. Dongan (Feb. 27, 1792), *Correspondence*, 3:413, 414, 415; John Jay to William Wilberforce (Nov. 8, 1809), ibid., 4:324; John Jay to English Anti-Slavery Society (June 1788), ibid., 3:340, 341; John Jay to Elias Boudinot (Nov. 17, 1819), ibid., 4:430, 431.

enslaved persons throughout his life; his explanation was that "I purchase slaves and manumit them at proper ages, and when their faithful services shall have afforded a reasonable return." The federal censuses listed his household as including five slaves in 1790, five in 1800, and four in 1810; his papers showed various manumissions.[25]

While Jay did less than some, he did much more than most. Too few of the founders of the republic took any tangible steps toward emancipation, or articulated a vision of a restructured society with equal treatment and without discrimination. Jay wrote in 1785, a month after his stance became very public by accepting the presidency of the Manumission Society,

> I wish to see all unjust and unnecessary discriminations every where abolished; and that the time may soon come when all our inhabitants of every color and denomination shall be free and equal partakers of our political liberty.[26]

His sons pursued that vision by cooperating with William Lloyd Garrison.

Concern about Native Americans. Jay expressed his concern about treatment of Native Americans to John Adams, six months after he expressed similar concerns to Thomas Jefferson:

> The western Indians are uneasy and seem inclined to be hostile–it is not to be wondered at. Injustice is too often done them, and the aggressors escape with impunity–In short our governments both particular [states] and general [federal] are either so impotent, or so very gently administered, as neither to give much terror to evil doers, nor much support and encouragement to those who do well.

The last phrase shows that Jay's concern arose from his religious tenets, for it paraphrased Bible verses (Romans 13:3–4) and said that government failed to fulfill its responsibilities stated in those verses. In his 1777 state constitution, he acknowledged "the frauds too often practised towards the said Indians," and voided individual purchases of land from Native Americans after late 1775. During treaty negotiations, Jay was one of too few whose consciences were troubled by nations' claims of "equal rights, or equally unjust claims," to "Indian land" (as Conde de Aranda described Jay's conversation). Otherwise, Jay failed to take much action

[25] John Jay to Elias Boudinot (Nov. 17, 1819), *Correspondence*, 4:430; John Jay to J. C. Dongan (Feb. 27, 1792), ibid., 3:413, 414; ibid., 3:185 n.2; Manumission of Benoit (Mar. 21, 1784), Morris, *Jay*, 2:705.

[26] John Jay to Benjamin Rush (Mar. 24, 1785), *Correspondence*, 3:139, 140.

to right the treatment of Native Americans, and missed some opportunities.[27]

Pursuing Peace. Jay's fame rests primarily on his two treaties: the Treaty of Paris of 1783, where his role was pivotal; and the Jay Treaty negotiated in 1794 and ratified in 1795. The first wrested favorable terms for ending the Revolutionary War, and the second averted a renewed war with Britain. These two most important treaties of the 1780s and 1790s involved difficult crossings of the Atlantic and long stays in Europe (nearly five years, and then over one year respectively). Jay's willingness to undertake those peace missions, and his relentless pursuit of completed treaties, was motivated by his faith.

The chief justice wrote to his wife, when he was nominated as envoy in 1794, "[i]f it should please God to make me instrumental to the continuance of peace and in preventing the effusion of blood and other evils and miseries incident to war – we shall both have reason to rejoice. Whatever may be the event, the endeavour will be virtuous," and they should "repose unlimited trust in our Maker." Jay did not undertake the mission in quest of fame or popularity; he realized that any treaty would be widely opposed, as the emerging political parties were divided over Britain and France, and would doom his chances for the presidency. A decade earlier, he similarly ascribed his success with the Treaty of Paris "to the supreme author of all the good that ever was."[28]

Supporting Only Just Wars. Related to his efforts for peace, Jay was committed to national involvement only in just wars, and avoidance of other wars, and that commitment was strongly informed by his faith and its Christian just war tradition. "In my opinion there have been just and lawfull wars, as well as unjust and unlawful wars. It certainly is desireable that wars should become less frequent," and should not be waged unjustly or be provoked by aggression. That was a matter of religious principle: "*Real* Christians will abstain from violating the rights of others, and therefore will not provoke war." By contrast, "Divine ordinances did authorize just

[27] John Jay to John Adams (July 4, 1787), *Correspondence*, 3:248, 249; John Jay to Thomas Jefferson (Dec. 14, 1786), ibid., 3:222, 224; New York Constitution, art.37 (1777); "Boundary Discussions between Jay and Aranda" (Aug. 3, 1782), Morris, *Jay*, 2:270, 272; Stahr, *Jay*, 348 (omissions); John Jay to George Clinton (Oct. 25, 1779), Morris, *Jay*, 1:659 (obliviousness); see John Jay to James Duane (May 29, 1776), ibid., 1:269, 270 n.2 (honoring agreement).

[28] John Jay to Sarah Jay (Apr. 15, 1794), *Correspondence*, 4:3, 4; John Jay to Margaret Livingston (July 12, 1783).

war," and so "the right to wage *just* and *necessary* war is admitted and not abolished by the gospel."[29]

For example, when the colonies found their freedom threatened and declared independence, Jay argued that "the means of defence" must be used or America would be without excuse to "our Creator" who gave that freedom. However, when the French Revolution brought war between France and Britain and interference with American ships, Jay supported neutrality and provided the first draft of Washington's neutrality proclamation, including that "we have abundant reason to give thanks unto Almighty God that the United States are not involved in that calamity," though it is better "to prefer war to injustice."[30]

Natural Law. Jay, like most of his contemporaries, believed in natural law. "The moral or natural law was given by the Sovereign of the universe to all mankind." His reason for that conviction was his religious faith. "[T]he gospel not only recognizes the whole moral law, ... but also enjoins on *all* mankind the observance of it." Natural law took precedence over contrary human law, so that a country's "acts, in order to be valid must consist with justice, and be in no respect fraudulent." Natural law had a place in the legal system, as Jay showed by relying on it in a grand jury charge (saying that government had "no right to command what is contrary to the Law of Nature"),[31] and by supporting the "natural right to freedom" that was mentioned earlier.

Indeed, a prominent part of that natural law was the "rights bestowed by the Almighty." Jay believed God "gave to men the rights we claimed" in the Revolution, and was "the source" from which "civil and religious liberties" flow. "God hath given us freedom."[32]

29 John Jay to Eleazar Lord (Feb. 7, 1817); John Jay to John Murray, Jr. (Oct. 12, 1816), *Correspondence*, 4:391, 392; John Jay to John Murray, Jr. (Apr. 15, 1818), ibid., 4:403, 408.

30 [John Jay], Address of the Convention of the Representatives of the State of New York (Dec. 23, 1776), *Correspondence*, 1:102, 118; Draft of Proclamation of Neutrality, by John Jay (Apr. 1793), ibid., 3:474, 475–476; Francis X. J. Coleman, "John Jay on War," *Journal of the History of Ideas* 43 (1982): 145.

31 John Jay to John Murray, Jr. (Apr. 15, 1818), *Correspondence*, 4:403; John Jay to John Murray, Jr. (Oct. 12, 1816), ibid., 4:391; John Jay to William Wilberforce (Apr. 14, 1806), ibid., 4:306, 307; John Jay's Charge to the Grand Jury (C.C.D. Va. May 22, 1793), in Marcus, *Documentary History*, 2:380, 387; R. H. Helmholz, *Natural Law in Court* (Cambridge, MA: Harvard University Press, 2015), 130.

32 [John Jay], Letter from Congress to the "Oppressed Inhabitants of Canada" (May 29, 1775), *Correspondence*, 1:32, 34; Jay's Reply to the New York Committee (July–August 1792), ibid., 3:442, 443; John Jay to Committee (June 29, 1826), ibid., 4:476, 477; [John Jay], Address of the Convention, ibid., 1:118.

Religious Freedom. Foremost among those God-given and natural rights, in Jay's thinking, was freedom of conscience. The "rights of conscience and private judgment" were unalienable, "by nature subject to no control but that of the Deity." Jay praised New York's constitution of 1777, which he had principally drafted, for securing "those great and equal rights of human nature, which should forever remain inviolate in every society," and he summarized its protection of religious freedom. "Every man is permitted to consider, to adore, and to worship his Creator in the manner most agreeable to his conscience. No opinions are dictated, no rules of faith prescribed, no preference given to one sect to the prejudice of others. The constitution, however, has wisely declared, that the 'liberty of conscience thereby granted shall not be so construed as to excuse acts of licentiousness, or justify practices inconsistent with the peace or safety of the state.'" Religion was able to prosper "though unsupported by the arm of flesh" (the state), and "happy would it be for mankind if that opinion prevailed more generally." "That opinion" was relatively new to the history of nations.[33]

What Jay omitted was his unsuccessful attempts in 1777 to amend the religious freedom language of the state constitution in ways unfriendly to Roman Catholics. First, he proposed to except religious faiths holding "principles inconsistent with the safety of civil society," along the lines of a limitation in the colony's Charter of Liberties and Privileges of 1683. Second, when that faced defeat, Jay substituted an amendment excluding adherents of "the Church of Rome" from toleration until they swore "that no pope, priest or foreign authority" can "absolve the subjects of this state from their allegiance," paralleling English test oaths and the colony's Charter of Liberties of 1691. Third, when that was rejected, he proposed to exclude religious practices that "disturb or endanger the safety of the state," following the exclusion in the colony's first charter. Finally, Jay proposed to amend the naturalization provision to require prospective citizens to "renounce all allegiance" to any "foreign king, prince, potentate and state, in all matters ecclesiastical as well as civil." Three years before this, Jay's "Address to the People of Great Britain," written for the first Continental Congress, had denounced the Quebec Act because it would officially "establish a religion fraught with sanguinary and impious tenets" there, and described Catholicism as "a religion that has deluged your island in blood, and dispersed impiety, bigotry, persecution, murder, and rebellion." He was doubtless influenced by a common Protestant version of English history, and by knowledge of Catholic

33 Jay's Charge to the Grand Jury of Ulster County (Sept. 9, 1777), *Correspondence*, 1:158, 162–163; N.Y. Const., art.38 (1777).

persecution of his Huguenot ancestors. But he was not equally allowing every Catholic citizen "to worship his Creator in the manner most agreeable to his conscience."[34]

This was one of the "former prejudices [that] have worn off," which Jay mentioned in 1779. In that year, he added to a congressional thanksgiving resolution the prayer to God "that he will bestow on our great ally [the Catholic King of France] all those blessings which may enable him to be gloriously instrumental" in protecting the United States and human rights generally. In 1783, Jay criticized "the annals of religious rage in times of bigotry," and it was two years later when he looked forward to "all our inhabitants of every color and denomination" being "free and equal partakers of our political liberty" and free of all unjust discriminations. In 1796, he asked the New York legislature to provide funds for French Catholic refugees, and in 1800 his gubernatorial address said that "all religious denominations" should be placed "on an equal footing." The change was doubtless influenced by Jay's lifelong friendships with Lafayette, his "political aide de camp," and with other Catholics such as Charles Carroll, and by Jay coming to appreciate Catholic support for the Revolution. Similarly, in his American Bible Society addresses, Jay acknowledged that "both cathedrals and meetinghouses have heretofore exhibited individuals" who were "real and useful Christians," and that different Christian faiths now should "love one another" and hereafter would have no "separate apartments in the mansions of bliss" in heaven. He equally censured pre-Reformation Catholicism that had "regard[ed] toleration as pernicious" and taught "that the people had no right to think and judge for themselves respecting religious tenets and modes of worship," and early Protestantism that had inflicted "culpable acts of oppression" on other sects, though he continued to maintain typical Protestant theological disagreements with Catholicism.[35]

34 *Journals of the Provincial Congress*, 1:844, 845–846, 846; Charles Z. Lincoln, ed., *Constitutional History of New York* (Rochester: Lawyers Co-Operative, 1906), 1:95, 105–106, 107, 440, 542–543; [John Jay], Address to the People of Great Britain (Sept. 5, 1774), *Correspondence*, 1:17, 19, 28. Jay was aware that his Huguenot ancestors were persecuted. John Jay to Gouverneur Morris (Apr. 29, 1778), Morris, *Jay*, 1:475, 476.

35 [John Jay], Circular-Letter from Congress to Their Constituents (Sept. 13, 1779), *Correspondence*, 1:218, 230; John Jay, Proclamation (Mar. 20, 1779), *Journals of the Continental Congress* (Washington: Government Printing Office, 1909), 13:343; John Jay to Benjamin Rush (Mar. 24, 1785), *Correspondence*, 3:139, 140; John Jay, "Opening Speech" (Nov. 1, 1796), Charles Z. Lincoln, ed., *Messages from the Governors: Comprising Executive Communications to the Legislature* (Albany: J. B. Lyon Co., 1909), 2:379, 383–384; John Jay, "Opening Speech" (Nov. 4, 1800), ibid., 2:463, 467; Lafayette to John Jay (Feb. 15, 1783), Morris, *Jay*, 2:517, 518; American Bible Society Addresses (n.d. May 1824, May 8, 1823), *Correspondence*, 4:496–497, 491, 495.

Criminal Law Liberalization. In his first message as governor of New York, Jay suggested mitigating "the severe penalties prescribed in our laws," and replacing capital punishment for a multitude of crimes with new prisons "for confining, employing and reforming criminals." Two months later, the legislature responded by ending the death penalty for all crimes but four (treason, murder, aiding and abetting murder, and, curiously, theft from churches), and also by ending whipping as a criminal punishment; it also authorized two new state prisons. Jay's reason for concern about draconian punishments was not stated, but was likely his faith.[36]

Thanksgiving Proclamations. As a president of the Continental Congress during the American Revolution, Jay edited and issued a thanksgiving proclamation that recommended that the states appoint a specified day "to be a day of fasting, humiliation and prayer to Almighty God." Jay added to its list of petitions to God "[t]hat he will cause union, harmony, and mutual confidence to prevail throughout these states," and will enable France to be "instrumental in protecting the rights of mankind." A half-year after becoming governor of New York in 1795, Jay wrote and issued a thanksgiving proclamation recommending that the citizens "render unto him [the Deity] their sincere and humble thanks for all these his great and unmerited mercies and blessings." The proclamation began with the words, "Whereas the great Creator and Preserver of the universe is the Supreme Sovereign of Nations, and does, when and as he pleases, reward or punish them by temporal blessings or calamities, according as their national conduct recommends." Jay believed that issuing thanksgiving proclamations was "proper," and paralleled that with his conviction that government could not "be rightfully restrained from providing for the observance of the *Sabbath*," because it was part of the moral law in the Ten Commandments. Writing to a committee planning celebrations for the fiftieth anniversary of independence, Jay urged it "to *recommend* a general and public return of praise and thanksgiving to Him, from whose goodness these blessings descend." He underscored the word "*recommend*" to stress his conviction that each individual had the right to decide whether to respond by thanking God, following the pattern of his own proclamations.[37]

36 John Jay, "Opening Speech" (Jan. 5, 1796), Lincoln, *Messages from the Governors*, 2:358, 363 (using customary circumspect language); ibid., 2:363–364 n.6.

37 John Jay, Proclamation (Mar. 20, 1779), *Journals of the Continental Congress*, 13:343, 344 n.1; "By His Excellency John Jay," *American Minerva* (New York), Nov. 12, 1795, 1; John Jay to Edward Livingston (July 28, 1822), *Correspondence*, 4:464, 465; John Jay to Committee (June 29, 1826), ibid., 4:476, 477.

Religious References in Public Documents. Jay, like many other founders, included references to the Deity and to providential events in public documents, though in less denominationally specific language than in his private correspondence. He included those references, not as meaningless ornamentation, but because he accepted, as Washington famously said in his Farewell Address (which Jay joined Hamilton in editing), that "national morality" cannot "prevail in exclusion of religious principle." For example, Jay's first essay in *The Federalist* said,

> Providence has in a particular manner blessed it [America] with a variety of soils and productions, and watered it with innumerable streams . . . .
>
> . . . Providence has been pleased to give this one connected country, to one united people . . . .
>
> . . . [I]t appears as if it was the design of Providence, that an inheritance so proper and convenient for a band of brethren, united to each other by the strongest ties, should never be split . . . .

Madison used similar language in one of the later *Federalist* essays.[38]

There were similar references in public documents throughout Jay's career: his addresses for Congress during the Revolutionary War, his grand jury charges as chief justice of the New York Supreme Court and of the United States Supreme Court, his draft of Washington's neutrality proclamation, and his opinion in his best known Supreme Court decision. The same was true of his semiannual messages as governor of New York. In planning the first session of the federal Circuit Court in Connecticut (two weeks after New York ratified the Bill of Rights and in the midst of the other states' ratification), in answer to the question whether a clergy member should "attend as chaplain" to open the court with prayer, Jay wrote that "[t]he custom in New England of a clergyman's attending, should in my opinion be observed and continued."[39]

The reason Jay included these exhortations (though never commands) in public documents and official speeches was that he trusted there truly is

[38] John Jay, "Federalist No. 2," in *The Federalist*, ed. Jacob E. Cooke (Middletown: Wesleyan University Press, 1961), 8, 9; James Madison, "Federalist No. 37," ibid., 231, 236–237, 238.

[39] [John Jay], Letter from Congress to the "Oppressed Inhabitants of Canada" (May 29, 1775), *Correspondence*, 1:32, 33, 34; [John Jay], Address of the Convention (Dec. 23, 1776), ibid., 1:102, 103, 104, 109, 110; [John Jay], Circular-Letter from Congress (Sept. 13, 1779), ibid., 1:218, 223; Jay's Charge to the Grand Jury of Ulster County (Sept. 9, 1777), ibid., 1:158, 159, 161, 162; Jay's Charge to the Grand Jury of the Circuit Court (Apr. 12, 1790), in Marcus, *Documentary History*, 2:25, 26; ibid., 2:284, 382, 388, 389; [John Jay], Draft of Neutrality Proclamation (Apr. 1793), *Correspondence*, 3:474, 475; *Chisholm* v. *Georgia*, 2 U.S. at 475; Lincoln, *Messages from the Governors*, 2:359, 366, 380, 384, 397, 400, 421, 423, 451, 452, 464, 470; Richard Law to John Jay (Feb. 24, 1790), Marcus, *Documentary History*, 2:11; John Jay to Richard Law (Mar. 10, 1790), ibid., 2:13.

a "great Sovereign of Nations" who has provided the gift of "liberty and prosperity" and who, if citizens "forget" and incur the Deity's "displeasure," will not continue to provide those gifts. Similarly, Jefferson, while not sharing Jay's orthodox Christian faith, was impelled by his faith to state in the Declaration of Independence that people "are endowed by their Creator with certain unalienable rights."[40]

Integrity. A final public ramification of Jay's faith was integrity. Its supreme test came with Hamilton's proposal that Jay, as governor, manipulate the 1800 election against Jefferson, "an *atheist* in religion and a *fanatic* in politics," by recalling the state's outgoing Federalist-dominated legislature to change the method of selecting presidential electors, rather than leaving the existing method in place in view of the incoming Republican-dominated legislature. Jay, in his final major public action, recognized this proposed recall as being "for party purposes," and declined. In this, Jay's integrity was not a minor private matter; it determined the outcome of the epochal election of 1800. Hamilton was right in his electoral vote prediction, and his proposal would have stolen the election for Adams; rejecting it ensured success for Thomas Jefferson and Aaron Burr, which Jay personally opposed. In less polarized times, Jefferson himself had acknowledged Jay's integrity, saying in 1786 that Jay had served in "the highest stations with universal approbation, and with a purity of conduct which has silenced even party opprobrium," while "never permit[ting] himself to make a shilling in the public employ" beyond his salary. Jefferson's statement remained true of Jay throughout his career: he never sought employment for family members, and rebuked them for asking; he never invested in war-related or government-driven activities; he never made appointments on a partisan basis.[41]

A FINAL COMMENT

Did Jay's faith hurt or help his public service? It does not appear to have hindered it, once he abandoned his misconceptions about Catholicism. Jay's faith led him to undertake much public service and many stances that helped people – opposing slavery and enlisting others in public opposition, negotiating treaties for peace and opposing unwarranted wars, supporting natural rights, securing religious freedom, eliminating the death penalty for numerous

[40] John Jay, To the Senate (Nov. 8, 1800), Lincoln, *Messages from the Governors*, 2:469, 470.

[41] Alexander Hamilton to John Jay (May 7, 1800), *Correspondence*, 4:270, 271, 272 n.1; Thomas Jefferson to James Currie (Jan. 28, 1786), *Papers of Thomas Jefferson*, ed. Julian P. Boyd et al. (Princeton: Princeton University Press, 1950–), 9:239; Stahr, *Jay*, 351, 378.

crimes, and letting the popular will stand in the election of 1800 and otherwise exhibiting integrity in public office. Even his public activities that are out of fashion today – thanksgiving proclamations and public references to religion – left compliance on entirely voluntary grounds.

Gouverneur Morris explained why he wished Jay to be one of his newborn son's godfathers: "he shall learn from the history of your life that a man must be truly pious to be truly great." Benjamin Franklin, though not sharing Jay's religious beliefs, named Jay as one of the four executors of his enormous estate, because he trusted Jay.[42]

Jay was not only truly pious but truly great in many ways – as one of the leading founders of the republic and coauthor of *The Federalist*, as the first chief justice of the United States Supreme Court who guided establishing the Court, as an antislavery voice though with inconsistencies, as a negotiator of two critical peace treaties, as a potential president who foreclosed his chances by negotiating the Jay Treaty and by opposing slavery, as a governor who called for making criminal law more just, and as the statesman who refused the Faustian proposal that would have reversed the election of 1800. Most of these followed from his pious faith, and all benefited his country.

[42] Gouverneur Morris to John Jay (Feb. 15, 1813), *Correspondence*, 4:369.

7

James Wilson

Donald L. Drakeman

Born and raised in rural Scotland, James Wilson immigrated to America as an adult and rapidly became one of the most influential lawyers, judges, and statesmen of the founding era. Wilson signed the Declaration of Independence, played a leading role at the Constitutional Convention, and became, by appointment of President George Washington, a justice of the first Supreme Court of the United States. His October 6, 1787, "State House Yard Speech" advocating the adoption of the Constitution was, in the words of Bernard Bailyn, "the most famous, to some the most notorious, federalist statement of the time."[1] Robert McCloskey has observed that "the ideas of James Wilson more nearly foreshadowed the national future than any of his well-remembered contemporaries. No one of them – not Hamilton, or Jefferson, or Madison, or Adams, or Marshall – came so close to representing in his views what the United States was to become."[2] If it were not for some unsuccessful real estate investments, followed by a fairly early death under inauspicious circumstances, Wilson would almost certainly be recognized today as far more than "the most neglected of the major American founders."[3] That neglect cannot, however, diminish his profound importance in the formation of American law and government, and, with good reason,

[1] James Wilson, "State House Yard Speech," October 6, 1987, in James Wilson, *Collected Works of James Wilson*, ed. Kermit L. Hall and Mark David Hall (Indianapolis: Liberty Fund, 2007), 1:171–177. See Mark D. Hall, "James Wilson: Presbyterian, Anglican, Theist, or Deist? Does It Matter?" in *The Founders on God and Government*, ed. Daniel L. Dreisbach, Mark D. Hall, and Jeffry H. Morrison (Lanham: Rowman & Littlefield, 2004), 182–183. Bernard Bailyn, *Faces of Revolution: Personalities and Themes in the Struggle for American Independence* (New York: Alfred A. Knopf, 1990), 230.

[2] Robert Green McCloskey, introduction to *The Works of James Wilson*, ed. Robert Green McCloskey (Cambridge, MA: Harvard University Press, 1967), 2.

[3] William Ewald, "James Wilson and the Drafting of the Constitution," *University of Pennsylvania Journal of Constitutional Law* 10.5 (2008): 902.

Wilson has been called the "constitutional colossus from the Revolutionary Era."[4]

BIOGRAPHICAL NOTE[5]

Unlike many of the prominent Framers, James Wilson lived until his twenties outside North America. The bookish son of a Scottish farmer, Wilson won a scholarship to the University of St. Andrews, where he likely stayed two years, and then began an apprenticeship for another two years with a lawyer in Cupar, which was near his family's home. He then continued his university education at the University of Glasgow, where he was a student of theology and natural philosophy, when the faculty included both Adam Smith and Thomas Reid, the founder of the Scottish Common Sense school of philosophy.[6] After two years at the University of Glasgow, he returned briefly to his apprenticeship in Scots law, which, unlike much of the law he would encounter in America, was based primarily on civil and Roman law rather than the common law of eighteenth-century England. In the mid-1760s, Wilson set sail for America.

Wilson came with letters attesting to his scholarship, and he initially obtained a position tutoring students at what is now the University of Pennsylvania in Latin, Greek, the Scottish Enlightenment, and "the natural law doctrines of Hugo Grotius."[7] He quickly tired of teaching and set out to become an American lawyer, which would require another apprenticeship.

4 Nicholas Pedersen, "The Lost Founder: James Wilson in American Memory," *Yale Journal of Law and the Humanities* 22.2 (2010): 260.

5 See Martin Clagett, "James Wilson – His Scottish Background: Corrections and Additions," *Pennsylvania History* 79.2 (2012): 154–176, and, except as revised by Clagett, Charles Page Smith, *James Wilson: Founding Father, 1742–1798* (Chapel Hill: University of North Carolina Press, 1956); Mark David Hall, *The Political and Legal Philosophy of James Wilson, 1742–1798* (Columbia: University of Missouri Press, 1997); Andrew Bennett, *James Wilson of St. Andrews: An American Statesman, 1742–1798* (St. Andrews: J. F. Innis, 1928); Geoffrey Seed, *James Wilson* (Millwood: KTO Press, 1978). Clagett's corrections point out that the conventional stories of Wilson's early life – as the son of a church leader who initially prepared for a career as a minister in the Calvinist Church of Scotland during five years of study at the University of St. Andrews – are not supported by the documentary record in Scotland.

6 Clagett traces Wilson's attendance at the University of Glasgow in part via comparing signatures on university library lending lists with "the signatures on the Declaration of Independence and the Constitution." Clagett, *James Wilson*, 164. On Wilson's relationship with the Scottish Enlightenment, see especially William Ewald, "James Wilson and the Scottish Enlightenment," *University of Pennsylvania Journal of Constitutional Law* 12.4 (2010): 1065, 1101–1114.

7 Smith, *James Wilson*, 22, quoted in Hall, *Political and Legal Philosophy*, 10.

To afford the necessary fees, he purchased some land on credit from a relative and then sold it to leading Pennsylvania lawyer John Dickinson, with whom he began his legal training. His apprenticeship included not only learning practical lawyering skills, but also reading "the great jurists of the past, including, 'Pufendorf, Burlamaqui, and Coke,'" as well as Cicero, Montesquieu, Blackstone, Sidney, Locke, and other philosophers.[8] Wilson's broad exposure to ancient and contemporary works of political and legal philosophy while in Scotland and America, as well as to both civil law and common law legal systems, became important preparation for his leading role at the Constitutional Convention. It has also provided much-debated fodder for scholars who have wrestled over the intellectual and theological influences on Wilson's jurisprudence.

Following his training with Dickinson, Wilson built a substantial law practice in Pennsylvania, became active in politics, and in 1774 published an essay, "Considerations on the Nature and Extent of the Legislative Authority of the British Parliament," which argued for the revolutionary notion that Parliament had no authority over the American colonies. A year later, he became a member of the Continental Congress. Afterwards, when the original Articles of Confederation proved to be inadequate to the nation's need for a stronger central government, Wilson served as a delegate from Pennsylvania to the Constitutional Convention, where he spoke nearly as often as the "Father of the Constitution," James Madison. Fellow delegate William Pierce of Georgia described Wilson as "rank[ing] among the foremost in legal and political knowledge .... Government seems to have been his peculiar study, all the political institutions of the World he knows in detail . . . ." Evidently, Wilson was willing to convey that detailed knowledge at some length, as Pierce recorded, "No man is more clear, copious, and comprehensive than Mr. Wilson."[9] The results were considerable, for much of what we know today as the text of the United States Constitution was due to Madison's and Wilson's joint and several efforts in the Philadelphia conclave and in the states' political battles over ratification. In fact, recent scholarship has shown that Wilson's influence on the Constitution was considerably greater than can be seen in Madison's notes, which have been one of our major sources for information about the Convention's proceedings.[10]

8 Hall, *Political and Legal Philosophy*, 10–11.

9 William Pierce, "Character Sketches of Delegates to the Federal Constitution," in *The Records of the Federal Convention of 1787*, ed. Max Farrand, rev. edn. (New Haven: Yale University Press, 1911 [1966]), 3:92.

10 Ewald, "James Wilson and the Drafting," 983.

Throughout the Convention, Wilson's primary theme was: "If we are to establish a national Government, that Government ought to flow from the people at large."[11] He was in favor of direct election by the people of both the House and the Senate, contrary to the proposal of his fellow Pennsylvanian and one-time mentor, John Dickinson, who wanted the states to choose senators to ensure that the Senate was composed of "wealth, family or talents."[12] Dickinson was hopeful that "by combining the families and wealth of the aristocracy, you establish a balance that will check the Democracy," whereas Wilson believed that "an election by the people in large districts ... w[ould] be most likely to obtain men of intelligence & uprightness . . . ."[13]

When the Constitution was presented to the states for ratification, Wilson was the only member of the Pennsylvania ratifying convention who had attended the Constitutional Convention. His widely read State House Yard speech, together with his leadership role in the Convention, not only led to Pennsylvania becoming the first large state to vote for ratification (and the second overall), but also proved highly influential in the subsequent ratification debates. His speech was printed in numerous newspapers and was circulated widely as a pamphlet. After ratification was complete, Wilson was named one of the first Associate Justices of the newly created Supreme Court. For Wilson, this was something of a disappointment, as he had lobbied (perhaps too hard) to become Chief Justice. He served on the Court until his death, while also becoming the first professor of law at the College of Philadelphia (now the University of Pennsylvania). There, Wilson gave a series of lectures on the foundations of the law that provide considerable insight into the influence of ancient philosophy, Enlightenment thinking, and Christian theology on his jurisprudence.[14]

Alongside his dedication to law and government, Wilson desired the accumulation of wealth, first as a prosperous lawyer and then as an active investor. Real estate investing, especially in Western lands, was an arena where fortunes could be made quickly, and fellow large-scale land speculators included many prominent Americans, such as George Washington, Benjamin Franklin, Robert Morris, to name but a few. As Bernard Bailyn has written, "Everyone with any ambition or capacity, it seems, on both sides of the Atlantic, sought

11 Quoted in ibid., 956.

12 Quoted in ibid., 955, 957. Ewald notes that Wilson's statement "that as all authority was derived from the people, equal numbers of people ought to have an equal n[umber] of representatives" makes him "the only member of the Convention to endorse unequivocally the principle of one-person-one-vote." Ibid., 960.

13 Ibid.

14 James Wilson, "Lectures on Law," in Wilson, *Collected Works*, ed. Hall and Hall, 427–1204.

some profit from what promised to be the greatest land boom in history."[15] As tends to be the case in such booming markets, those same fortunes can be lost quickly as well. Eventually, the land "bubble" crashed in the mid-1790s. Wilson's creditors, who had provided the funds for these real estate endeavors, demanded repayment and had him imprisoned twice when he was unable to do so. Ultimately, Wilson, while still a justice of the Supreme Court, died of malaria at the age of 55 in Edenton, North Carolina, where he was hiding from the creditors. His career as an American lawyer ended essentially as it had begun, with land purchased on credit. He was buried in Edenton until 1906, when his remains were moved to the Episcopal Christ Church in Philadelphia, where his longtime friend, William White, had been the first bishop.

THE LITERATURE

The nature of Wilson's Christian faith and its relationship to his jurisprudence is a source of controversy in the scholarly literature. Beyond scholars' natural penchant for disagreement lies a broader, multi-century debate over whether the United States is a Christian nation, and whether the founders were devoted to building a nation on Christian principles. These arguments have been employed in lively political disputes over everything from Sunday mail service to prayer in public schools. It can therefore be challenging not to read Wilson's works in light of the fact that our views of him – and his fellow Framers – can have an effect on contemporary social and political issues.

In addressing these debates, it quickly becomes clear that even the basic facts are open to dispute. For instance, we do not know whether Wilson was a lifelong Presbyterian, an Episcopalian convert, or perhaps both. He was brought up in the Presbyterian Church of Scotland; he was a board member of a Presbyterian church during his legal studies in America; and he rented a pew at Philadelphia's First Presbyterian Church for twenty years, until his death. Yet, during his last four years, he simultaneously rented a pew at Philadelphia's Episcopalian Christ Church, where one of his sons was baptized, and another of his sons became an Episcopal priest.[16]

Like Wilson's multiple church affiliations, the relatively few statements that may reflect his religious beliefs resonate strongly in the Christian tradition, but

15 Bernard Bailyn, *Voyagers to the West: A Passage in the Peopling of America on the Eve of the Revolution* (New York: Random House, 1988), 23.

16 Mark David Hall has described the documentary record in Hall, "Presbyterian, Anglican, Theist, or Deist?," 187–188.

his precise theological and doctrinal commitments are difficult to pin down. Scholars have labeled him variously as a Deist, a "theistic rationalist," "a serious Christian thinker," and the early American heir of the natural law philosophy articulated by St. Thomas Aquinas.[17] Evidence supporting all of these conclusions can be found, and much depends on scholars' views of what it means to be a Christian, a theist, a Thomist, and so on.

In an effort to identify the Framers' religious views with even more precision than earlier debates about whether they were Christians, Deists, or, perhaps, freethinkers, Gregg Frazer has coined the term "theistic rationalist" to describe Wilson and a number of other Framers, including John Adams, Thomas Jefferson, and George Washington. In commenting on a statement by Wilson about the importance of revelation – that "our natural knowledge is greatly improved, refined, and exalted by that which is revealed" – Frazer concludes, "Unlike orthodox Christianity, revelation [for Wilson] was in service of natural knowledge; unlike deism, natural knowledge was not all there was."[18] Wilson, on this account, was neither an orthodox Christian nor a Deist.[19] Irrespective of whether he fits neatly into the "theistic rationalist" category, Wilson's description of the relationship of reason and revelation certainly shows how hard it is to determine with certainty whether one or the other was more important to his jurisprudence.

Meanwhile, some theological taxonomists (especially those who are more inclined toward lumping than splitting) point to Wilson's visible reliance on revelation in his law lectures, together with his church membership(s), to place him decidedly on the Christian side of the Christian–Deist divide.[20] There are still others who prefer to see Wilson as drawing on religious terminology only occasionally in order to bolster an essentially secular, rationalistic approach to a natural law philosophy that he derived from European philosophers and ultimately from the ancients.[21] In the end, based on his

17 Gregg L. Frazer, *The Religious Beliefs of America's Founders: Reason, Revelation, and Revolution* (Lawrence: University Press of Kansas, 2012), 187–188; Hall, "Presbyterian, Anglican, Theist, or Deist?," 184–187, 197.

18 Frazer, *Religious Beliefs of America's Founders*, 187–188.

19 Frazer notes, however, that although "Wilson never mentioned Jesus by name . . . he referred unmistakably to Jesus as 'him, by whom our nature was both made and assumed . . . '. If he did believe in the deity of Jesus, then he differed from theistic rationalists in general on that point." Ibid., 185–186.

20 Hall, "Presbyterian, Anglican, Theist, or Deist?," 197.

21 Roderick M. Hills, Jr., "The Reconciliation of Law and Liberty in James Wilson," *Harvard Journal of Law and Public Policy* 12.3 (1989): 891. Compare Daniel N. Robinson, "Do the People of the United States Form a Nation? James Wilson's Theory of Rights," *International Journal of Constitutional Law* 8.2 (2010): 287–297 at 289: "a Christianized version of Cicero's presuppositions."

Protestant religious affiliations and his approach to revelation and the law, there is certainly ample reason to include Wilson in this volume of Christian jurists, even as scholars will continue to dispute just how orthodox his Christian beliefs were and how central they were to his thinking about the law and the Constitution.

JURISPRUDENCE

Alexander Hamilton famously dubbed the judiciary the "least dangerous" branch of the government, which is a reasonably accurate description of the very early Supreme Court on which Wilson sat for a decade.[22] Compared to the modern era, the Court heard relatively few cases, and no official reporter recorded the justices' opinions. Additionally, following the British tradition, each justice gave his own judgment, delivered seriatim, with no official "opinion of the court."[23]

As a result of these various historical circumstances, our best perspective on Wilson's jurisprudence comes from his law lectures at the University of Pennsylvania. They are learned, comprehensive, and abounding in historical citations to laws, philosophers, and jurists from Greece, Rome, the Druids, the Saxons, Britain, and colonial America. After Wilson's death, the lecture notes were compiled by one of his sons and published in 1804. Numerous themes from those lectures are manifest not only in his efforts at the Constitutional Convention, but also in his most prominent Supreme Court opinion, which appeared in *Chisholm* v. *Georgia*. This 1793 case addressed the question of whether a citizen of one state could sue another state in the federal courts. But, first, we need to go back, with Wilson, to first principles, namely, the nature of law itself.

In setting out the "general principles of law" in his lectures, Wilson started with the universality of the law, enthusiastically quoting the sixteenth-century Anglican theologian, Richard Hooker: "Her seat ... is the bosom of God; her voice, the harmony of the world; all things in heaven and earth do her homage ... ."[24] Wilson's warm embrace here and elsewhere of the writings of "the excellent Hooker," whose work owed substantial intellectual debts to the writings of St. Thomas Aquinas, have encouraged some scholars to position the justice's

22 Alexander Hamilton, "Federalist 78," in Alexander Hamilton, James Madison, and John Jay, *The Federalist Papers*, ed. Lawrence Goldman (Oxford: Oxford University Press, 2008), 380.

23 See Morris L. Cohen and Sharon Hamby O'Connor, *A Guide to the Early Reports of the Supreme Court of the United States* (Littleton: Rothman, 1995); *Seriatim: The Supreme Court before John Marshall*, ed. Scott Douglas Gerber (New York: New York University Press, 1998).

24 Wilson, *Lectures on Law*, in Wilson, *Collected Works*, ed. Hall and Hall, 1:464.

jurisprudence in the tradition of Roman Catholic scholastic theology.[25] Yet, while much of the natural law discussion explicitly relies on Hooker, Wilson was unusually well read, and his lectures abound with references to Aristotle, Cicero, and others from classical literature, as well as the influential European legal theorists, Grotius and Pufendorf. But perhaps most of all, Wilson often quoted and even more frequently paraphrased a fellow Scot, the seventeenth-century philosopher and one-time Calvinist minister, Thomas Reid.[26]

As Mark David Hall has pointed out, Wilson followed Hooker and Aquinas to divide "divine law" into four types: eternal law, which relates to "God's eternal plan for the universe," "celestial law," the physical laws, and the natural law governing mankind, including both individuals and nations. Wilson's blend of reason and revelation is evident in his comment on how we know the content and contours of that natural law: it "is communicated to us by reason and conscience," which Wilson calls "the divine monitors within us," as well as "by the sacred oracles," which are the "divine monitors without [outside of] us." Wilson observed that law is "called natural" when "promulgated by reason and the moral sense," or is "revealed law" when discovered in "the holy scriptures," but whether from reason or revelation, it "flows from the same divine source: it is the law of God."[27] Accordingly, "the scriptures support, confirm, and corroborate, but do not supersede the operations of reason and the moral sense."[28]

Central to Wilson's many views on law and government is that the people are sovereign. As Wilson wrote in his opinion in the *Chisholm* case, "A state ... is the noblest work of Man. But, Man himself, free and honest, is ... the

25 See William F. Obering, *The Philosophy of Law of James Wilson: A Study in Comparative Jurisprudence* (Washington, DC: American Catholic Philosophical Association, 1938), 12: "Justice Wilson takes the doctrine of the Eternal Law, the Natural Law, the necessity of Positive Civil Law, and its dependence on the Natural Law from Hooker, who took the same doctrine ... from the *Summa Theologica* of Aquinas."

26 Shannon C. Stimson, "'A Jury of the Country': Common Sense Philosophy and the Jurisprudence of James Wilson," in *Scotland and America in the Age of the Enlightenment*, ed. Richard Sher and Jeffrey Smitten (Princeton: Princeton University Press, 1990), 199–208 at 198: "Indeed, what is evident is less accurately termed the 'influence' of Reid's thought than it is, in many instances, the verbatim transposition of text (or nearly so) from Reid's work into Wilson's discussions ... ." According to Clagett, when Wilson was attending the University of Glasgow, he "may have even attended Reid's lectures on moral philosophy and jurisprudence in the fall of 1764 and winter of 1765 and later used his notes from the class for his own lectures on law at the University of Pennsylvania." Clagett, *James Wilson*, 163.

27 Wilson, *Lectures on Law*, in Wilson, *Collected Works*, ed. Hall and Hall, 1:498. See also Hall, *Political and Legal Philosophy*.

28 Velasquez notes that Wilson here follows Frances Hutcheson. Eduardo A. Velasquez, "Rethinking America's Modernity: Natural Law, Natural Rights and the Character of James Wilson's Liberal Republicanism," *Polity* 29.2 (1996): 196–201.

noblest work of God."[29] In a pamphlet penned in 1768 but not published until 1774, Wilson denied Parliament authority over America, arguing, "All men are, by nature, equal and free: no one has a right to any authority over another without his consent." Because "such consent [is] given with a view to ensure and to increase the happiness of the governed," therefore, "the happiness of society is the *first* law of every government." Such a rule is "founded on the law of nature," and "it must regulate [even] the legislature itself."[30]

The same notion of power resting in the people can be seen in his comments at the Constitutional Convention where he, according to James Madison's notes, "contended strenuously for drawing the most numerous branch of the legislature immediately from the people."[31] As Madison recorded, Wilson "was for raising the federal pyramid to a considerable altitude, and for that reason wished to give it as broad a basis as possible . . . ."[32] In defending the Constitution's lack of a bill of rights, Wilson argued that "it would have been superfluous and absurd to have stipulated with a federal body of our own creation, that we should enjoy those privileges of which we are not divested . . . ."[33]

In specifically addressing the rights of the people, Wilson asked, "What was the primary and the principal object in the institution of government?" More precisely, "Was it . . . to acquire new rights by human establishment? Or was it, by a human establishment, to acquire a new security for the possession or the recovery of those rights, to the enjoyment or acquisition of which we were previously entitled by the immediate gift, or by the unerring law, of our all-wise and all-beneficent Creator?"[34] This was one of Wilson's relatively few formal invocations of God throughout the main body of the law lectures, but it arrived at a vital time in his narrative of human institutions. Is it the purpose of government to provide security for our rights? If so, we must know whether those rights are created by those same institutions, or whether instead they come from God. Wilson answered that "the latter . . . was the case," a clear statement rendered somewhat cloudy, at least for theological purposes, by Wilson's addition of the words, "I presume."[35] Setting his views apart from

29 *Chisholm* v. *Georgia*, 2 U.S. 419, 462–463 (1793).

30 James Wilson, "Considerations on the Nature and Extent of the Legislative Authority of the British Parliament," 1774, in Wilson, *Collected Works*, ed. Hall and Hall, 1:4–5.

31 James Wilson's Speech, May 31, 1787, in *The Records of the Federal Convention of* 1787, ed. Farrand, 2:44.

32 Ibid.

33 Wilson, "State House Yard Speech," in Wilson, *Collected Works*, ed. Hall and Hall, 1:172. See also James R. Zink, "James Wilson versus the Bill of Rights: Progress, Popular Sovereignty, and the Idea of the U.S. Constitution," *Political Research Quarterly* 67.2 (2014): 253–265.

34 Wilson, *Lectures on Law*, in Wilson, *Collected Works*, ed. Hall and Hall, 2:1053–1054.

35 Ibid., 1054.

those of Edmund Burke and William Blackstone, whom Wilson saw as locating the rights of citizens solely in the political community, Wilson wrote, "If this view be [taken], then the consequence ... is, that, under civil government, the right of individuals ... flow from a human establishment ...." In that case, people can "claim nothing but what society provides."[36] For Wilson, however, it is society that exists to serve the people, all in accord with the "law of nature."

What are the rights that are established by that natural law? Where John Locke had written of "Life, Health, Liberty, or Possessions" as foundational to the law of nature, the Declaration of Independence had spoken of "Life, Liberty and the pursuit of Happiness," and numerous founding era writers had added the rights of conscience, including several of the state constitutions,[37] Wilson focused on a person's "natural right to his property, to his character, to liberty, and to safety."[38] This is not to diminish Wilson's enthusiasm for religious freedom, but, especially for someone who frequently relies on insights from ancient authors, it may have been important for Wilson to observe in a separate lecture that the "doctrine of toleration in matters of religion, reasonable though it certainly is, has not been long known or acknowledged."[39] Moreover, while he joined others in giving Locke considerable credit for the concept of toleration, he proclaimed, "Let it be known, that, before the doctrine of toleration was published in Europe, the practice of it was established in America" in Maryland by Cecil Calvert and in Pennsylvania by William Penn.[40]

Although Wilson did not list liberty of conscience as one of the core fundamental rights of the people under the natural law, religious freedom nevertheless has a very important instrumental value for the crucial task of nation building. In his lecture on the law of nations, he pointed to the "duty of a nation to augment its members," and identified three methods of "peculiar efficacy": "The first is ... to receive all strangers of good character," the second

36 Ibid., 1057–1058. See generally Robinson, "People of the United States."

37 John Locke, *Two Treatises of Government*, ed. Peter Laslett (Cambridge: Cambridge University Press, 1988), 271; "Declaration of Independence," 1776, in *Documents Illustrative of the Formation of the Union of the American States*, ed. Charles C. Tansill (Washington, DC: Government Printing Office, 1927), 22. See, e.g., [Theophilus Parsons], "The Essex Result," 1778, in *American Political Writing during the Founding Era*, ed. Charles S. Hyneman and Donald S. Lutz (Indianapolis: Liberty Fund, 1983), 1:480–522. For an analysis of state constitutions, see Vincent Phillip Muñoz, "Church and State in the Founding-Era State Constitutions," *American Political Thought* 4.1 (2015): 1–38.

38 Wilson, *Lectures on Law*, in Wilson, *Collected Works*, ed. Hall and Hall, 2:1062.

39 Ibid., 1:433.

40 Ibid.

is "to encourage marriages," which will lead to population growth, and the third is to "preserve the rights of conscience inviolate," as the "right of private judgment is one of the greatest advantages of mankind . . . ."[41] There are limits on the extent to which those private judgments should be publicly expressed, however, and Wilson held the view not only that "Christianity is a part of the common law," but also that "[p]rofaneness and blasphemy are offenses, punishable by fine and by imprisonment."[42]

Chisolm v. *Georgia* provided Justice Wilson with the opportunity to showcase his philosophy of law in a Supreme Court case involving the question of whether a state could be sued in federal court by a citizen of another state. Where his friend and colleague Justice James Iredell looked to the common law of England to reach a negative answer, Wilson began his opinion with "the principles of general jurisprudence" in order to address what he called a very basic question: "[D]o the people of the United States form a Nation?" Citing Cicero, he argued that "Man . . . is the workmanship of his all perfect Creator," whereas the "state . . . is the inferior contrivance of man, and from his native dignity derives all its acquired importance." The state may be the "most transcendently excellent" of human creations, but it is inferior to the "divine." Accordingly, the "state [is] subordinate to the people," while "everything else [is] subordinate to the state."[43]

For too long in human history, argued Wilson, "there has . . . been a strong current against the natural order of things . . . ." In fact, when "the state has claimed precedence of the people, so, in the same inverted course of things, the government has often claimed precedence of the state, and to this perversion in the second degree, many of the volumes of confusion concerning sovereignty owe their existence."[44] But, in reality, according to Wilson, a state is a "body of free persons united together for their common benefit . . . . It is an artificial person . . . . [I]t has rights; and it has its obligations." In considering those rights and obligations of this "artificial person, we should never forget that . . . those who think and speak and act are men."[45] Such an entity must do its duty and fulfill its obligations. Since "a free man," whom Wilson called "an original sovereign," "is bound by human laws [because] he binds himself,"

41 Ibid., 1:539. In his lecture on natural rights, Wilson says that "[w]hether we consult the soundest deductions of reason, or resort to the best information conveyed to us by history, or listen to the undoubted intelligence communicated in holy writ, we shall find, that to the institution of marriage the true origin of society must be traced." Ibid., 1068.

42 Ibid., 1159.

43 *Chisholm* v. *Georgia*, 2 U.S. 453, 455 (1793).

44 Ibid., 455.

45 Ibid., 455–456.

and thus "becomes amenable to the courts," so must the state, which is simply "a collection of original sovereigns."[46]

Wilson continued this theme at considerable length until he turned to his second main line of inquiry, "the laws and practice of different states and kingdoms."[47] He invoked Isocrates, Christopher Columbus's son Don Diego, the Ephori of Sparta, "the famous Hottoman," Henry de Bracton, Frederick of Prussia, and others, all in support of finding the "jurisdiction of this court over the State of Georgia."[48] Finally focusing on the Constitution itself, Wilson argued that the language that "certain laws of the states are declared to be 'subject to the revision and controul of the Congress,'" meant that "it cannot . . . be contended that the legislative power of the national government was meant to have no operation on the several states."[49] This power extends to the executive branch as well, and, when "the application [of the laws] is doubtful or intricate ... judicial authority becomes necessary."[50] The Supreme Court, therefore, has "jurisdiction over the State of Georgia."[51] Then, alluding to the concept of judicial review, that is, the power by which justices can strike down unconstitutional laws, Wilson argued that the Constitution's goals of creating a more perfect union and establishing justice point to the need for a "superintending judicial authority" and a "controuling judiciary power."[52]

Wilson's jurisprudence, based on the political notion that "the people of the United States intended to form themselves into a nation for national purposes," and, ultimately, on the theological concept that "man himself, free and honest, is ... the noblest work of God," requires the oversight of a "superintending" judiciary.[53] As these arguments applied to the specifics of the *Chisholm* case, Wilson's conclusion won (4–1) in the Supreme Court, but turned out to be out of step with his political peers. As David Currie has noted, "Madison and Marshall flatly told the Virginia ratifying convention that [the Constitution] would not subject unwilling states to suits by individuals, and Alexander Hamilton said the same thing in *The Federalist*."[54] Five years after

46 Ibid., 456.
47 Ibid., 459.
48 Ibid., 461.
49 Ibid., 464.
50 Ibid., 465.
51 Ibid.
52 Ibid.
53 Ibid., 465, 463.
54 David P. Currie, *The Constitution in the Supreme Court: The First Hundred* Years, *1789–1888* (Chicago: University of Chicago Press, 1985), 18. Nevertheless, Currie quotes Wilson contemporary William Davie's letter as follows: "[P]erhaps, notwithstanding the tawdry ornament

Chisholm was decided, the Eleventh Amendment essentially reversed its holding. Yet, Wilson's vision of a powerful federal judiciary enforcing constitutional rights and obligations was ultimately vindicated by history. In the twenty-first century, the concept of judicial review has expanded to the point where "[a]lmost every day a judge in the United States holds a statute unconstitutional."[55] And so, in the case of judicial review, as with a number of Wilson's other positions in support of a strong national government based on the will of the people, Americans today find themselves living in a constitutional environment that James Wilson, more than any other influential Framer, sought to create.

CONCLUSION

James Wilson, who rented prominent pews at both Presbyterian and Episcopal churches, met his second wife at a Congregational church service.[56] His lectures on law embraced the importance and, indeed, the truth of revelation, but he hardly mentioned the Scriptures. Wilson was eager to accumulate great wealth and to live like an aristocrat, while being much more willing than most of his fellow Framers to grant direct political power to the people. He appealed to the Greeks, the Romans, English lawmakers and jurists, Scottish theologians and philosophers, the Druids and *Hamlet*, all without any signs that these sources may have contained inconsistent premises or contrary conclusions. These various complexities in his personal and intellectual life have not always endeared Wilson to his readers. When one scholar, writing in the 1990s, labeled Wilson's "political thought a pastiche," and dubbed the jurist a "Donald Trump-like speculator," he probably did not have in mind to call Wilson "presidential."[57]

To understand James Wilson on his own terms and in his own time requires an openness to the possibility that he would likely not have considered any of his beliefs and practices to be inconsistent with one another. He came to America in pursuit of what he saw as his God-given natural rights: property, reputation, liberty, and safety. All of these he initially found in abundance, and

and poetical imagery with which it is loaded and bedizened, it may still be very 'profound.'" Quoted in Ibid., 16 n. 79.

55 Philip Hamburger, *Law and Judicial Duty* (Cambridge, MA: Harvard University Press, 2008), 1.

56 Smith, *James Wilson*, 367.

57 Richard Sinopoli, review of *The Political Philosophy of Thomas Jefferson* by Garrett Ward Sheldon and *The Political Ideas of James Wilson* by Jean-Marc Pascal, *The William and Mary Quarterly*, 50.2 (1993): 449–452.

ultimately lost in despair. Above all, despite a relatively short three decades in America, he became one of our most influential – and, ultimately, prescient – Framers. Wilson thus provides us with a classic example of a scholar, jurist, and statesman-as-synthesizer, weaving together diverse strands of independent thought, ranging throughout nearly all of recorded human history into one powerful bond of reason and revelation, all pointing, as Wilson wrote, to "the same divine source . . . the law of God."[58]

[58] Wilson, *Lectures on Law*, in Wilson, *Collected Works*, ed. Hall and Hall, 1:498.

8

Was Justice Joseph Story a Christian Constitutionalist?

James R. Stoner, Jr.

Was Justice Joseph Story a Christian constitutionalist? In one sense, this is an easy question to answer in the affirmative: No one doubts that Story, author of the multi-volume, 1,400-page *Commentaries on the Constitution*, was an informed and ardent constitutionalist, and it is uncontroverted that he was baptized a Christian and throughout his life personally adhered to his faith, though he moved from the Congregationalism of his minister uncle to the Unitarianism that swept Harvard in his days there in the 1790s and in the decades after.[1] But my question is not biographical in that way. I mean to ask whether Story considered his Christian faith integral to his life's work as a justice on the United States Supreme Court and, for that matter, as Dane Professor of Law at Harvard, positions that he held simultaneously for many years. Indeed, even that puts the matter too personally: I want to consider whether Story considered Christianity integral to American constitutionalism, and if so, in what way? Whatever might be answered to the question of whether America is a Christian nation, I want to ask, does America have a Christian Constitution?, or rather, did Justice Story think that it did?

Justice Story surely thought himself faithful to the original meaning of the Constitution and knew (or sat with) men who made or ratified the Constitution, but no originalist in our own time would call himself a Christian constitutionalist. Instead, the originalist's aim is to arrive at an objective account of the Constitution's meaning, uncorrupted by an individual judge's (or professor's) personal religious faith. The original Constitution's prohibition of religious tests for office might seem to command such a strict separation of faith and jurisprudence, as might the prohibition of

[1] I am relying for biographical details on Kent Newmyer, *Supreme Court Justice Joseph Story: Statesman of the Old Republic* (Chapel Hill: University of North Carolina Press, 1985), esp. Chapter 1.

religious establishment in the First Amendment. When originalist justices dissent in a case like *Roe* v. *Wade* or *Obergefell* v. *Hodges*, they do not base their opinion on the incompatibility of abortion or same-sex marriage with Christian doctrine or even natural law, but instead they deny that the Constitution or its amendments as understood by those who wrote or ratified them entrench these practices as rights; typically they do not deny that these practices might be permitted or endorsed by positive legislation, only that, in the absence of legislation, they might be imposed by the Court. Similarly, although his or her faith might call into question the morality of the death penalty, the originalist does not think himself or herself entitled to find its abolition constitutionally commanded, since the practice was clearly condoned when the relevant clauses were written. Being a Christian and being a constitutionalist, in short, are to a modern originalist unrelated; if one is both, it is a mere coincidence.

Joseph Story, however, would not have denied being a Christian constitutionalist in the sense that a modern originalist would. Whether as an orator or an author or a judge, Story emphasized the continuity between Christianity as he understood it and the Constitution he was sworn to administer and uphold. Born to a patriot family during the Revolution, on September 10, 1779, in Marblehead, Massachusetts, Story graduated from Harvard in 1798 and returned home to study law in the offices of Samuel Sewall, then a member of Congress, and later in Salem. He quickly acquired a brilliant reputation as an attorney and became active in Republican (i.e., Jeffersonian) politics, serving in the Massachusetts legislature from 1805, attending Congress briefly in 1808–1809, and becoming speaker of the Massachusetts House in 1811. Later that year James Madison appointed him to the United States Supreme Court, where, at thirty-two, he became the youngest person ever to sit on the Court and where he served until shortly before his death in 1845. In addition to fulfilling his duties on the Court, which included spending half the year as federal circuit judge for New England, Story in 1829 was appointed Dane Professor of Law at Harvard, where he found time to publish numerous academic treatises, including *Commentaries on the Constitution*, a three-volume work also issued in an abridged, popular form.

In the essay that follows, I will look first at Story's published orations and related writings, then at his legal textbooks, and finally at his judicial opinions to elucidate his understanding of the relation between Christianity and the law. In conclusion, I will return to the question of the modern originalist and consider whether that approach or Story's better suits Christianity and constitutionalism in our own day.

THE COMMON LAW AND THE PURITAN LEGACY

In retirement in 1824, Thomas Jefferson wrote a letter, quickly published, to the English Radical John Cartwright in which he disputed the adage attributed to the seventeenth-century English Chief Justice Matthew Hale and reiterated by the late eighteenth-century commentator William Blackstone that "Christianity is a part of the common law."[2] Joseph Story rejected Jefferson's thesis and defended the authenticity of the maxim, first in private correspondence, later in a published article. In his inaugural discourse as Dane Professor of Law at Harvard, he alluded to this dispute and proclaimed his conclusion:

> One of the beautiful boasts of our municipal jurisprudence is, that Christianity is a part of the common law, from which it seeks the sanction of its rights, and by which it endeavors to regulate its doctrines. And, notwithstanding the specious objection of one of our distinguished statesmen, the boast is as true as it is beautiful. There never has been a period, in which the common law did not recognize Christianity as lying at its foundations.[3]

What did Story mean by saying "Christianity is a part of the common law," and how does it affect our question about Christian constitutionalism? First, it is important to note right away that for Story, common law is what gives the law as a whole its form and character; it comprises "a system of jurisprudence." In contradistinction to civil law, derived from the Roman Code, common law is English, carried over to North America by the colonists as an inheritance. In contrast to statute law, it is unwritten, anchored in the custom of the people, though modified by statute from time to time. Common law, to Story, is a science, a vast body of knowledge developed over time, memorialized in the records of cases and in legal treatises and commentaries. Moreover, since it is practical, it is changeable: "it must forever be in a state of progress, or

[2] Jefferson's letter reiterated an argument he had developed in his common-place book as a young man some sixty years before and had shared a decade previously with two other correspondents. For Jefferson's early essay and later correspondence, see Daniel L. Dreisbach and Mark David Hall, eds., *The Sacred Rights of Conscience* (Indianapolis: Liberty Fund, 2009), 539–550.

[3] Joseph Story, *Discourse Pronounced upon the Inauguration of the Author as Dane Professor of Law in Harvard University* (Boston: Hilliard, Grey, Little, Wilkins, 1829), 20–21; republished in William W. Story, ed., *The Miscellaneous Writings of Joseph Story* (Boston: Little, Brown, 1852), 517. Story's response to Jefferson is discussed at some length in James McClellan, *Joseph Story and the American Constitution* (Norman: University of Oklahoma Press, 1971), ch. 3; also in my essay, "Christianity, the Common Law, and the Constitution," in Gary L. Gregg II, ed., *Vital Remnants: America's Founding and the Western Tradition* (Wilmington, Del.: ISI Books, 1999).

change, to adapt itself to the exigencies and changes of society."[4] It is "the law of liberty, and the watchful and inflexible guardian of private property and public rights."[5] And its jurisprudence encompasses in its ambit all the topics assigned to the Dane Professorship: "the Law of Nature, the Law of Nations, Maritime and Commercial Law, Equity Law, and, lastly, the Constitutional Law of the United States," on many of which he was to publish treatises over the course of the next fifteen years.

Second, Story attributes to Christianity not only historical or traditional influence on the law – its clergy once serving as legal scholars or officials, its Sabbath and holidays being days the courts are closed – but also moral influence on the law and its administration. The whole discussion of Christianity related above arises in the context of Story's exhortation concerning the moral character of lawyers and judges, and he notes that rules of law sometimes still reflect the presumption that Christian morals underlie the legal order, for example by voiding contracts that go against such morals or by privileging the testimony of witnesses who swear upon the Bible. In his discussion of natural law, he links natural law and Christianity in terms that resemble those of Thomas Aquinas:

> Christianity, while with many minds it acquires authority from its coincidences with the law of nature, as deduced from nature, has added strength and dignity to the latter by its positive declarations. It goes farther. It unfolds our duties with far more clearness and perfection than had been known before its promulgation; and has given a commanding force to those of imperfect obligation .... It points out the original equality of all mankind in the eyes of the Supreme Being, and brings down the monarch to the level of his subjects ... and becomes the teacher, as well as the advocate of rational liberty .... Above all, by unfolding in a more authoritative manner the doctrine of the immortality of the soul, it connects all the motives and actions of man in his present state with his future interminable destiny .... Thus Christianity becomes, not merely an auxiliary, but a guide to the law of nature, establishing its conclusions, removing its doubts, and elevating its precepts.[6]

Story never wrote a treatise on natural law, nor would he condone using natural law on its own to void statutes, but it seems clear that he considers Christianity incorporated into natural law, or at least to be its harmonious and authoritative interpreter. Although he recognizes the difference in principle

4 *Miscellaneous Writings*, 508.
5 Ibid., 506.
6 Ibid., 534–535. Cf. Aquinas, *Summa Theologica*, I-II, q. 91, a. 4.

between what can be known by unassisted human reason and what is only known through revelation, he sees no ongoing conflict between the one and the other, perhaps because he would have thought both were subsumed in practice in the common law.

But if these passages seem to indicate that Story was quite comfortably a Christian jurist, it must also be noted that Story also distances himself from past Christian practice, even in the common law. In the first place, the law used to admit in court only the testimony of those who would swear on the Christian Bible, barring the testimony of "infidels and pagans," something Story thinks unwarranted. But this is nothing compared with the "error of the common law" in punishing heresy:

> [The common law] tolerated nothing but Christianity, as taught by its own established church, either Protestant or Catholic; and with unrelenting severity consigned the conscientious heretic to the stake, regarding his very scruples as proofs of incorrigible wickedness. Thus, justice was debased, and religion itself made the minister of crimes, by calling in the aid of the secular power to enforce that conformity of belief, whose rewards and punishments belong exclusively to God.[7]

The Christianity that remains a part of the common law, then, is Christianity as it has been purified over time with the growth of toleration and enlightenment. The ability of the common law to change, or progress, or adapt, is shared even by the ancient faith at its root, in Story's mind. By a different route than Jefferson – call it Burkean, perhaps, for he cites that British statesman throughout – Story seems to arrive at a similar toleration.

Before arranging his professorship, Story was widely recognized as an orator, and in that capacity he had delivered an interesting discourse the previous year that bears upon our topic. Speaking to the Essex Historical Society on the occasion of the 200th anniversary of the original settlement in Salem of the colony that became Massachusetts Bay, Story addressed the "History and Influence of the Puritans," which at sixty-six printed pages must have taken several hours to deliver. He sets a romantic scene and tells for the most part a heroic tale, praising "the resolute spirit, the manly virtues, the intelligence and piety, which pervade New England" still in his day; the deeds of the colony's founders are not in "marble domes or triumphal arches" but "in the enduring institutions which they created, in the principles which they taught, and by which they sought to live, and for which they were ready to die."[8]

7 *Miscellaneous Writings*, 517.

8 Joseph Story, "History and Influence of the Puritans," in ibid., 413, 415.

Unlike all the other North American colonies, "the offspring of private adventure and enterprise, and … of the spirit of commerce," Massachusetts was founded out of "love of religion," in particular of course of Christianity. In contrast with paganism, which "was indulgent in its general policy," Christianity

> develops one complete system of duties, fit for all times and all stations …. It humbles in the dust the proud and the arrogant …. It exalts the lowly virtues, the love of peace, charity, humility, forgiveness, resignation, patience, purity, holiness. It teaches a moral and final accountability for every action. It proposes sanctions of no earthly reach; but such as are infinite, unchangeable, and eternal.[9]

Though the warmth of a believer is evident in his rhetoric, there is also a certain detachment in the larger history of Christianity and Puritanism that he recounts, noting the irony that the Reformation, which he praises for its "restlessness for knowledge," came to England thanks to "the passions of a sanguinary and sensual monarch." He cites Hume for his account of the English Civil War and Revolution of 1688, though he berates his "philosophical indifference" as belonging to "the scoffer, or the skeptic." Of the Puritan founders, he concedes their errors, prejudices, and sternness, but on balance celebrates their real dignity: "In simplicity of life, in godly sincerity, in temperance, in humility, and in patience, as well as in zeal, they seemed to belong to the apostolic age …. They possessed a moral courage which looked present dangers in the face, as though they were distant or doubtful, seeking no escape and indulging no terror."[10] As an example of ceremonial (epideictic) rhetoric, the first half of Story's address is a masterpiece.

In the middle, however, Story's discourse pivots to confront the charges of intolerance and persecution brought upon the Puritans, again citing Hume. Story acknowledges the facts, noting however that, except for a brief moment when the Reformation began, all Christian denominations had been intolerant of what they perceived to be error, noting the situation in England and on the Continent of Europe in the same age. Still, he writes, "the fundamental error of our ancestors, an error which began with the very settlement of the colony, was a doctrine which has since been happily exploded; I mean the necessity of a union between church and state. To this they clung, as the ark of their safety. They thought it the only way of founding a Christian commonwealth." Without supposing the necessity of progress – proposing instead "a

9 Ibid., 429–431.
10 Ibid., 432, 435.

lesson of humility from which spiritual pride may learn meekness, and spiritual zeal a moderating wisdom" – Story writes:

> Let us not be untrue to the lights of our own days, to the religious privileges which we enjoy, to those constitutions of government which proclaim Christian equality to all sects, and deny the power of persecution to all. Our fathers had not arrived at the great truth, that *action*, not *opinion*, is the proper object of human legislation; that religious freedom is the birth-right of man; that governments have no authority to inflict punishment for conscientious difference of opinion; and that to worship God according to our own belief is not only our privilege, but our duty, our absolute duty, from which no human tribunal can absolve us. We should be unworthy of our fathers, if we should persist in error, when it is known to us. Their precept, like their example, speaking, as it were, from their sepulchers, is, to follow truth, not as they saw it, but as we see it, fearlessly and faithfully.[11]

He does not hesitate to pay tribute to Roger Williams, who first preached religious liberty at Salem, before being driven to found on that principle a colony of his own.

Story soon moves from the religious to the staunchly republican civil institutions of his forefathers, but not before quoting Milton on making Scripture, not tradition, the final rule in matters of religion – a clear endorsement of Protestantism against Catholicism, by the way. Concerning the native population, he defends the settlers as acting always in good faith – "Their aim was peace; their object was the propagation of Christianity"[12] – though he describes the withdrawal of the Indians as a result of pestilence and of the disappearance of their native wilderness as "tragic." Discussing the Salem witch trials, he notes again the error of the times, but makes no other apology. With regard to the role of New England in the Revolution, he is brief but celebratory.

In these several speeches, then, and throughout his occasional writings,[13] Story unfolds a consistent account of the Christian religion as formative of

[11] Ibid., 441–442.

[12] Ibid., 465.

[13] In private correspondence, Story was more emphatic about the role of Christianity in American society and its precarious situation in his day, writing to Jasper Adams that "My own private judgement has long been, (& every day's experience more & more confirms me in it,) that government can not long exist without an alliance with religion *to some extent*; & that Christianity is indispensable to the true interests & solid foundations of all free governments . . . . I look with no small dismay upon the rashness and indifference with which the American People seem in our day to be disposed to cut adrift from old principles, & to trust themselves to the theories of every wild projector in to religion & politics." In Daniel L. Dreisbach, ed., *Religion and Politics in the Early Republic: Jasper Adams and the Church–State Debate* (Lexington: University Press of Kentucky, 1996), 115.

moral virtue, both of its own peculiar charity and spiritual inquiry and of a republican virtue that stresses honesty, simplicity, equality, and courage – and of a Christianity that learns from itself and its experience to overcome its own prejudices and shortcomings. Call it Whig history,[14] if you will, although Story came to the Court a Republican from a Federalist enclave and preserved his commitment to the natural law tradition, as we saw above. His biographer Kent Newmyer concludes that he was "shamelessly eclectic," but Story himself sought practical balance, not theoretical purity, and a staunch legal adherence to constitutional compromise.[15] Whether he achieves this in his scholarly and judicial work is the topic to which I now turn.

THE CONSTITUTIONAL LAW OF RELIGIOUS LIBERTY

However important religion was to the founding of Massachusetts and religious liberty to the founding of the United States, it should be no surprise that the subject of religion gets scant attention in Story's *Commentaries on the Constitution of the United States*, for religion gets scant mention in the Constitution's text. Story begins the work reviewing the history of the Revolution and the constitutional theory that underlay the break with England, then refutes the compact theory of the Constitution, insisting that all American constitutions, state and federal, were made by the sovereign people, who were themselves constituted by social compacts before legislating constitutions to settle the powers of their governments. Providence plays no role in this tale for Story, nor do churches; constitutions are apparently human things.

Nevertheless, the Constitution of the United States does mention religion twice, first in the prohibition of religious tests for office, then of course in the First Amendment. The ban on religious tests occurs in the clause that prescribes an oath, itself an acknowledgment of divine authority – although the Constitution allows an "affirmation" in lieu of an oath, perhaps considering private conscience an adequate proxy for the divine. Story notes that affirmation was allowed in consideration of "that pure and distinguished sect of Christians, commonly called Friends or Quakers," saying of oaths that they "have a solemn obligation upon the minds of all reflecting men, and especially upon those who feel a deep sense of accountability to a Supreme Being." Most of his attention in commenting on the Oath Clause concerns the requirement

14 See James Ceaser, *Nature and History in American Political Development* (Cambridge: Harvard University Press, 2006), Ch. 1.

15 Newmyer, *Supreme Court Justice Joseph Story*, 246.

that oaths be taken by officials in the states, not only the federal government. Concerning the prohibition of religious tests, he writes as follows:

> This clause is not introduced merely for the purpose of satisfying the scruples of many respectable persons, who feel an invincible repugnance to any religious test or affirmation. It had a higher object; to cut off forever every pretence of any alliance between church and state in the national government. The framers of the constitution were fully sensible of the dangers from this source, marked out in the history of other ages and countries, and not wholly unknown to our own. They knew that bigotry was unceasingly vigilant in its stratagems to secure to itself an exclusive ascendency over the human mind; and that intolerance was ever ready to arm itself with all the terrors of the civil power to exterminate those who doubted its dogmas, or resisted its infallibility.[16]

He then proceeds to quote at length Blackstone's description of, and half-hearted apology for, the corporation and test oaths in England that prohibited any but communicating members of the Church of England from holding office there, dismissing his apology with scorn.

After this strong affirmation of religious liberty and the threat from government establishment, Story's discussion of the First Amendment to the Constitution is more accommodating to Christianity, we would now say, indeed seems to go further than any modern accommodationist:

> Indeed, the right of a society or government to interfere in matters of religion will hardly be contested by any persons who believe that piety, religion, and morality are intimately connected with the well-being of the state, and indispensable to the administration of civil justice. The promulgation of the great doctrines of religion, the being, and attributes, and providence of one Almighty God; the responsibility to him for all our actions, founded upon moral freedom and accountability; a future state of rewards and punishments; the cultivation of all the personal, social, and benevolent virtues; – these never can be a matter of indifference in any well ordered community. It is, indeed difficult to conceive how any civilized society can well exist without them. And at all events, it is impossible for those who believe in the truth of Christianity, as a divine revelation, to doubt, that it is the especial duty of government to foster and encourage it among all the citizens and subjects.[17]

For authority on this point, Story cites Grotius, Vattel, Hooker, Bynkershoek, Woodeson, Burlemaqui, and even Blackstone, whom he had earlier

[16] Joseph Story, *Commentaries on the Constitution of the United States*, 3rd edn. (Boston: Little, Brown, 1858; orig. 1833), book 3, ch. 43, sect. 1847 (vol. 2, p. 648).

[17] Ibid., book 3, ch. 44, sect. 1871 (vol. 2, p. 661).

dismissed. On the one hand, there is to be no alliance between church and state and no role for intolerance in government; on the other hand, Christian doctrines can be encouraged and Christian morals inculcated, for this, Story insists, "is a point wholly distinct from that of the right of private judgment in matters of religion, and of the freedom of public worship according to the dictates of one's conscience." How can both of these points be true?

In the first place, Story suggests that lines can be drawn by the law: "the real difficulty lies in ascertaining the limits to which government may rightfully go in fostering and encouraging religion," the outer limit being that government may not "force the consciences of other men, or . . . punish them for worshipping God in the manner which they believe their accountability to him requires."[18] States can and do choose different approaches within this range, from those that simply declare a religious establishment, to those that require a religious test for office, on one extreme, like the British, and to those on the other extreme that do not support or sustain Christianity by law, like Rhode Island. Story does not work through the catalogue of the states at the time, mentioning only Rhode Island as an outlier, without praising it as in his earlier oration and without noting, even in later editions, that Massachusetts had amended its constitution in the same year the *Commentaries* appeared to remove the old requirement that the citizens of each town be taxed for the support of the local church, with permission to divert one's payment to a congregation of one's choice. He hints that the Rhode Island system – he does not call it, as we might, the Virginia system – might indeed be the wave of the future, while reserving his endorsement:

> It yet remains a problem to be solved in human affairs, whether any free government can be permanent, where the public worship of God, and the support of religion, constitute no part of the policy or duty of the state in any assignable shape. The future experience of Christendom, and chiefly of the American states, must settle this problem, as yet new in the history of the world, abundant as it has been in the experiments in the theory of government.[19]

He does not exactly begrudge the experiment its trial, but his own position seems evident in this passage: "in a republic, there would seem to be a peculiar propriety in viewing the Christian religion as the great basis, on which it must rest for its support and permanence, if it be what it has ever been deemed by its truest friends to be, the religion of liberty."[20]

18 Ibid., sect. 1876 (p. 664).
19 Ibid., sect. 1875 (pp. 663–664).
20 Ibid., sect. 1873 (p. 662).

Fortunately, Professor Story is spared the choice, for in the second place, he holds that the Bill of Rights applies only to the federal government and the prohibition on establishment in the First Amendment had as its "real object" "not to countenance, much less to advance Mahometanism, or Judaism, or infidelity, by prostrating Christianity; but to exclude all rivalry among Christian sects, and to prevent any national ecclesiastical establishment, which should give to a hierarchy the exclusive patronage of the national government."[21] Because different denominations predominated in different states – Story mentions Episcopalians, Presbyterians, Congregationalists, and Quakers – while in some states there was a balance or a standoff, the only safe route for prudence was to prevent there being any national establishment to fight over, while in addition protecting free exercise and forbidding religious tests, as noted above. "Thus, the whole power over the subject of religion is left exclusively to the state governments, to be acted upon according to their own sense of justice, and the state constitutions" – some of which established religion, some of which forbad establishment. At any rate, "the Catholic and the Protestant, the Calvinist and the Arminian, the Jew and the Infidel, may sit down at the common table of the national councils, without any inquisition into their faith, or mode of worship."[22]

If Story celebrates religious equality at the federal level, why is he skeptical about its efficacy in the states? Since Story's *Commentaries* are on the US Constitution, unlike his friend James Kent's on American law generally, the answer is not in the text. Turning to his other books, however, not to mention back to his addresses, one finds a clue in his recognition of the comprehensive character of common law underlying the American order. In his *Conflict of Laws*, for example, generally thought his most original work, indeed inventive of a whole field of legal study, when Story turns to his chapters on marriage, he cannot avoid discussing the religion of different countries when discussing their laws on marriage, or for that matter, on divorce.[23] In his *Equity Jurisprudence*, when the subject is charities, Christianity appears on the very first page.[24] The law that pervades the life of a religious people could not avoid dealing with questions that touch upon religion, and if it is really their law, confirmed in their legislatures and applied in their juries, it could not be purged of religion even were that desirable. That it is not desirable Story makes

21 Ibid., sect. 1877 (p. 664).

22 Ibid., sect. 1879 (p. 667).

23 Joseph Story, *Commentaries on the Conflict of Laws, Foreign and Domestic*, 3rd edn. (Boston: Little, Brown, 1846), ch. 5, sect. 114 ff. (p. 198 ff.).

24 Joseph Story, *Commentaries on Equity Jurisprudence* (Boston: Hilliard, Gray, & Co., 1836), ch. 31, sect. 1137 (vol. 2, p. 389 ff.) [reprint edn. New York: Arno Press, 1972].

clear in his encomiums upon religion and its formative effect on character. In fact, however, it is striking how rarely Christianity comes up in the commentaries he wrote in the course of training lawyers at Harvard Law School. No doubt it would have had he written on education, but then, unlike now, that was not an issue thought amenable to lawyerly superintendence.

CHRISTIANITY, THE CONSTITUTION, AND THE JUDGE

Story's role on the Supreme Court is generally thought second only to Marshall's in forming American law, including American constitutional law. He had enormous respect for John Marshall, who was Chief Justice for two-thirds of his tenure, and he seems to have earned the Chief's respect for his scholarship as well as his friendship. Story's jurisprudence is usually noted for its resolute nationalism, its promotion of commercial exchange, and its support for the emerging law of the corporation. If there was nothing specifically Christian about these aims, it also seems clear that Justice Story thought there was nothing in them that was in tension with Christian duty; on the contrary, he seems to have supposed they provided a theater for virtue. The Religion Clauses were not prominent in the jurisprudence of the early Court, but Story did write two of the most important cases that involved religion, and both deserve some consideration here, albeit briefly. Then I will turn even more briefly to his dealings with the Devil, that is, with slavery and its law.

Terrett v. *Taylor* began as a bill in equity brought by Taylor and other vestrymen of the Episcopal Church in Alexandria, Virginia, seeking to establish the title of the church and thus their right to sell certain lands which the church had acquired before the Revolution as glebe lands, meant for the relief of the local poor. Terrett and his associates were overseers of the poor in Fairfax County in the early 1800s, and they claimed right to the land so that its proceeds could be applied to what they held was its original purpose. Before the Revolution, the Episcopal Church was established in Virginia on the English model, and therefore was charged with certain social duties such as poor relief; after the Revolution and of course the Virginia Statute of Religious Freedom, this arrangement is displaced, leaving the poor either to the charity of churches or to the care of secular authorities. Story holds with the vestrymen, recognizing in the vestry and the clergy control over the property of their church, as though they were a private corporation (in 1784 Virginia had incorporated churches, then in 1786, after the famous Statute, it un-incorporated them). Without settling whether the un-incorporation was constitutional, the Court noted that private gifts had been made to the church as well as public grants, and in any event, there was "vested an indefeasible and irrevocable title" in the church lands equal to any other title to property. The Revolution may have ended an exclusive privilege in the Episcopal Church to exercise ecclesiastical responsibility and authority, but "the dissolution of the form of government did not involve in it a dissolution of civil rights, or an abolition of the common law under which the inheritances of every man in the state were held," and if of every man, so of every association of men, including a church.[25] Four years before the more famous *Dartmouth College* case, then, the Court per Justice Story establishes the independence of churches as private entities from a state that, in assuming a former church function, demands right to church property for public use. Whether Story had such old arrangements in mind when he wrote in his *Commentaries* about the state's encouragement of Christianity is unclear. At least in this case he is willing to stop a state that might discourage churches by subsuming their former functions under its mantle.

Decided at the other end of Justice Story's career was *Vidal* v. *Girard's Executors*, a case in which the purported heirs of wealthy Philadelphia businessman Stephen Girard challenged his will to establish a school for orphans whose administration would be entrusted to the mayor and aldermen of that city. In his will, Girard had listed certain subjects of study, adding "I would have them taught facts and things rather than words or signs; and especially I desire that by every proper means a pure attachment to our republican institutions, and to the sacred rights of conscience as guaranteed by our happy constitutions shall be formed and fostered in the minds of the scholars," with the proviso, "I enjoin and require that no ecclesiastic, missionary, or minister of any sect whatsoever, shall ever hold or exercise any station or duty whatever in the said college; nor shall any such person ever be admitted for any purpose, or as a visitor, within the premises appropriated to the purposes of the said college."[26] Although the will went on to explain that his concern was to spare the children exposure to "clashing doctrines and sectarian controversy," the legal challenge asserted that by excluding the clergy, the will went against the public policy of the state of Pennsylvania, which had listed the suppression of vice as one purpose for incorporating the city which was now to serve as the school's trustee. Justice Story, however, upheld the will, with language that sounds remote to the modern ear but that fits cleanly with what we have read thus far. After acknowledging, with citation of a Pennsylvania blasphemy case, that "Christianity be a part of the common law of the state," he proceeds:

25 *Terrett* v. *Taylor*, 9 Cranch (13 U.S.) 43, 50 (1815).

26 *Vidal* v. *Girard's Executors*, 2 Howard (43 U.S.) 127, 184, 133 (1844).

> It is unnecessary for us, however, to consider what would be the legal effect of a devise in Pennsylvania for the establishment of a school or college, for the propagation of Judaism, or Deism, or any other form of infidelity. Such is not to be presumed to exist in a Christian country; and therefore it must be made out by clear and indisputable proof. Remote inferences, or possible results, or speculative tendencies, are not to be drawn or adopted for such purposes. There must be plain, positive, and express provisions, demonstrating not only that Christianity is not to be taught; but that it is to be impugned and repudiated.[27]

The exclusion of clergy does not mean that Christianity cannot be taught, much less that it would be criticized; it only means that if it is taught, it must be by lay teachers. From a "mere judicial view," nothing here is "inconsistent with the Christian religion, or . . . opposed to any known policy of the state of Pennsylvania."[28] As in *Terrett* many years before, Story both acknowledges the Christian background of society and decides the case as a matter of private right – now of a will, rather than an entity, and for the local government, rather than against it.

Turning to slavery, the appeal to background Christian principles is loud and clear in Story's 1822 Circuit Court decision in the admiralty case, *La Jeune Eugenie*. While deciding the case principally on factual grounds – that the ship, purporting to be French, was actually an American ship engaged in the slave trade fraudulently seeking to evade the American prohibition on that trade – Story includes a ringing denunciation of that trade:

> Now in respect to the African slave trade, such as it has been described to be, and in fact is, in its origin, progress, and consummation, it cannot admit of serious question, that it is founded in a violation of some of the first principles, which ought to govern nations. It is repugnant to the great principles of Christian duty, the dictates of natural religion, the obligation of good faith and morality, and the eternal maxims of social justice.[29]

But a serious question is raised three years later when Chief Justice Marshall decides for the Supreme Court in the case of *The Antelope* – with Justice Story's silent consent – that the law of nations does not forbid the slave trade, repugnant as that trade may be to natural law and to Americans and British by that time, so when Story writes to free the black rebels in the case of *The Amistad*, he rests his argument solely on the uncontroverted fact of their

27 Ibid., 198–199.
28 Ibid., 201.
29 William P. Mason, *Report of the Case of the Jeune Eugenie* (Boston: Wells and Lilly, 1822), 73.

original freedom and unjust kidnapping, without reference to Christianity or natural law.[30]

If in *La Jeune Eugenie* and *The Amistad* Justice Story decides in harmony with his own antislavery opinions, albeit upon facts determined according to law, in *Prigg* v. *Pennsylvania* he decides against them, and if the case did not ruin his reputation at home, it clearly damaged it.[31] At issue in the case was the constitutionality of a Pennsylvania personal freedom statute and of the Federal Fugitive Slave Act of 1793. Recognizing the force of *Somerset,* the 1772 English case that declared slavery unknown at common law and thus unrecognized on English soil, but also explaining that the federal Constitution was based on numerous compromises that should be interpreted clause-by-clause, Story allowed that while slavery could exist only as a result of a positive municipal law, the Constitution created a positive right of recapture in the Fugitive Slave Clause and, by saying fugitive laborers "shall be delivered," empowered congressional legislation to provide for the process, overriding contrary legislation in the states and indeed, for Story, prohibiting the states from passing any legislation on the subject whatsoever. Fidelity to the Constitution's text required this decision, Story argued; needless to say, there is no mention of Christianity or natural law this time.

LIVING FAITH OR LIVING CONSTITUTION?

As justice, professor, and author, Joseph Story was, one is tempted to say, an apostle of American constitutionalism in his age. His leading precedents remained good law for years after he left the bench, and some of his books remained in print for nearly a century, with his *Commentaries on the Constitution* receiving renewed attention in the controversies of the late twentieth century. The question of fidelity to the constitutional text in *Prigg* brings us back to the contrast between Justice Story and the modern originalist with which we began. An originalist would have to applaud Justice Story's principle for deciding *Prigg,* even while he is of course spared by the Thirteenth Amendment from ever having to confront such a case today. Originalism is attractive in part because it exhibits the virtue of fidelity to constitutional meaning, not least over personal prejudices or opinions. But if originalism is attractive because it displays the virtue of fidelity, might there not be other virtues required in a judge – who doubts there are, for example,

[30] *The Antelope,* 10 Wheaton (23 U.S.) 66 (1825); *The Amistad,* 15 Peters (40 U.S.) 518 (1841).

[31] *Prigg* v. *Pennsylvania,* 16 Peters (41 U.S.) 539 (1842); see Newmyer, *Supreme Court Justice Joseph Story,* ch. 10.

good judgment, not to mention justice – and if so, might the demands of these not sometimes override the imperative of strict fidelity? "The first and fundamental rule in the interpretation of all instruments," wrote Professor Story, "is, to construe them according to the sense of the terms, and the intentions of the parties." But, he proceeds to argue, "to give a reasonable construction to this instrument, as a constitution of government established for the common good, we must throw aside all notions of subjecting it to a strict interpretation, as if it were subversive of the great interests of society, or derogated from the inherent sovereignty of the people."[32] The text of the Constitution, after all, assigns to the federal courts jurisdiction over law and equity, and while the latter was obviously not meant to swallow the former, its recognition weighs against insistence on the letter of the law against all other claims to justice.

Could Justice Story's Christian constitutionalism have spared him enchainment to the text of the Constitution on the matter of slavery? While the Garrisonian Abolitionists despised the Constitution as a pact with the Devil, others such as Lysander Spooner, Salmon Chase, and Frederick Douglass developed an interpretation of the whole Constitution as a liberty document, and while no judge might adopt such a reading, it was useful politically, not least in indicating to so careful a lawyer as Abraham Lincoln a way to confine the rights of slavery in the Constitution in light of its general thrust toward freedom. Story allowed room for growth and development in the law – witness his applause for religious liberty, if not for the emerging form of state secularism – and he seemed to think the direction of development is implicit in Christianity itself, but the Christianity he elaborated was a particular strain that became increasingly unable to float above a sea of consensus while society became more religiously diverse, by permission of the Constitution itself. And of course on the question of slavery, the import of Christianity was deeply contested, not only across denominations, but within them.

To my mind, the liberty guaranteed by the Constitution is political liberty, and that entails the right of citizens of every faith to bring their witness to the public square in the making of laws and so inevitably as well in their application, together with their responsibility, often learned through bitter defeat in the political process, to explore possibilities for shared understanding and tolerable working arrangements in public and civic life, even when these cut against what one might wish for on the basis of one's religion's ideal. The Constitution is one of those arrangements, supported by Americans who differ on the truly first things, accepted by each community for their own reasons – and rightly interpreted on principles that respect that underlying consensus,

32 *Commentaries on the Constitution*, book 3, ch. 5, sect. 400, 423 (vol. 1, pp. 283, 300).

leaving ample room for political authorities to gather consent, not serving itself as an instrument of social transformation at judicial hands. Insofar as Justice Story sought at once to be faithful to the agreed-upon meaning of the framers' Constitution and "to follow truth, not as they saw it, but as we see it, fearlessly and faithfully,"[33] there is much to be learned from his endeavor, both where he succeeded and where he failed.

[33] Cf. above, p. 150, and note 11.

9

Harvard's Evangelist of Evidence: Simon Greenleaf's Christian Common Sense

Daniel David Blinka

Mention Simon Greenleaf's name to a throng of lawyers today, or, for that matter, a group of law professors, and you will receive mostly uncomprehending shrugs. This outcome is hardly surprising for a law professor who died in 1853. Lost in time is Greenleaf's standing as a founder of Harvard Law School, an innovative teacher, and a legal scholar whose treatise on evidence law dominated American courtrooms, law offices, and law school classrooms into the twentieth century.

Yet an online search quickly reveals Greenleaf's continuing resonance among evangelical Christians of today, mostly nonlawyers, who remain deeply impressed by an erudite essay he wrote about 170 years ago. The 1846 tract, entitled "The Testimony of the Evangelists," proved the historical truth of the Gospels by Greenleaf's application of the evidence rules that govern trials. Some internet tellings of the story are made more compelling by assertions that Greenleaf started his project as "an agnostic, some say atheist," who in the end was converted to Christianity through the force of his reason.[1]

Greenleaf, a devout evangelical Episcopalian, would be chagrined by his fall in professional standing but mortified by aspersions that he was an atheist. Greenleaf, though, was more than a pious lawyer. Historians are now plumbing the origins of modern trials with new insights into the role of religion. Examining the trial's "forgotten theological roots," historian John Q. Whitman has provocatively demonstrated the Christian origins of the reasonable doubt standard in the late eighteenth century.[2] Another forgotten

1 Simon Greenleaf, *An Examination of the Testimony of the Four Evangelists, By the Rules of Evidence Administered in Courts of Justice* (1846; microfilm, 2nd edn., London, 1847). Robert R. Edwards, "Is Simon Greenleaf Still Relevant?," last accessed November 26, 2016, www.creationstudies.org/Education/simon_greenleaf.html.

2 James Q. Whitman, *The Origins of Reasonable Doubt: Theological Roots of the Criminal Trial* (New Haven: Yale University Press, 2008), 2, 31.

taproot is Simon Greenleaf's significant, though mostly unappreciated, role in explicitly centering the modern trial on Christian footings. As we will see, Greenleaf consciously and conscientiously wove core tenets of evangelical Christianity into his hugely influential work on American evidence law and trials, an enduring achievement overlooked by many today but keenly appreciated by those sensitive to its tones.

I

Simon Greenleaf came of age in the early nineteenth century, a self-made man who the fictional Horatio Alger might envy for his drive, discipline, and success. For Greenleaf, however, the fortune sought was not monetary, although he did well professionally. Rather, he used his manifold talents to help lay a foundation for the American legal profession that drew deeply from his evangelical Christianity. Greenleaf's biography has yet to be written, but the outline of his life is reasonably clear.[3]

The year 1783 saw Great Britain's recognition of American independence in the Peace of Paris and Greenleaf's birth in Newburyport, Massachusetts. His bloodlines help explain both Greenleaf's deep commitment to nation-building and Christianity. Writing later in life, Simon recalled with evident pride that his father, Moses, was "altogether a soldier and nothing but a soldier." Moses fought in some of the "hottest of fights" in the Revolution's northern theater, also enduring the cold and hunger of Valley Forge. Honorably discharged in 1781, he tried his hand at "mercantile enterprises" with "disastrous" results, his son tenderly observing that his father had a "better genius for war, than for the arts of peace." Moses moved his family to the Maine district, then a part of Massachusetts, to try his hand at carpentry and farming in 1790.[4]

3 The biographical sketch is based on the following: Daniel D. Blinka, "The Roots of the Modern Trial: Greenleaf's *Testimony* to the Harmony of Christianity, Science, and Law in Antebellum America," *Journal of the Early Republic* 27 (2007): 293, 297 (citing sources); Daniel R. Coquillette and Bruce A. Kimball, *On the Battlefield of Merit: Harvard Law School, The First Century* (Cambridge: Harvard University Press, 2015); James Greenleaf, *Genealogy of the Greenleaf Family* (Boston: Frank Wood, 1896), 138–144, file:///C:/Users/ddbli/OneDrive/Documents/16%20Nov%202016%20(docs)/Data/Data%20(DDB)/History/Greenleaf%20chapter%20(2016)/genealogygreenloogreegoog.pdf; Alfred Konefsky, "Piety and Profession: Simon Greenleaf and the Case of the Stillborn Bowdoin Law School, 1850–1861," *New England Quarterly* 85 (2012): 695.

4 Harvard Law School, Simon Greenleaf Papers, Series V, 26–27 (family history), https://iiif.lib.harvard.edu/manifests/view/drs:46295797$1i .

Young Simon, however, was left behind in Newburyport under the tutelage of his maternal grandfather, the Rev. Jonathan Parsons, a Presbyterian minister who tended to the boy's education and spiritual well-being. While at the town's Latin school, Simon received a "thorough classical training" before rejoining his parents at age sixteen in New Gloucester, Maine. His time at the Latin school marked Greenleaf's only exposure to formal schooling before he joined the Harvard faculty in 1833. Intelligent, hardworking, and perhaps driven to avoid his father's financial struggles, Greenleaf largely taught himself what he needed to succeed.

In New Gloucester, Greenleaf chose law as his calling. He apprenticed in a local law office in 1801 and gained admission to the county bar four years later. Apprenticeship was the primary means of educating lawyers throughout the nineteenth century. Lacking structure and rigor, apprenticeship left talented law students largely to their own devices. As we will see, both Greenleaf and Justice Joseph Story organized the pedagogy of Harvard Law School as a response to the weaknesses of apprenticeships, and despite having surmounted them.

In 1808 Greenleaf set up practice in Portland, where "by his winning manners and persuasive style of speaking and address, accompanied by the skill and ingenuity of his arguments, [he] established his reputation … on a firm basis." When Maine gained statehood in 1820, the Supreme Judicial Court appointed Greenleaf the reporter for its decisions, a post he held until resigning in 1832. While maintaining a busy law practice, Greenleaf served two terms in the state legislature where he helped establish the state's government and formulate a code of law. As Maine's reporter for twelve years, he produced nine volumes of the court's decisions, their high professional quality earning him acclaim. Greenleaf's careful legal writings gained the notice and respect of Justice Story of the US Supreme Court, who later became a close friend and invited Greenleaf to join him at Harvard Law School.[5]

Greenleaf served on the faculty from 1833 until his retirement in 1848. Despite a heavy teaching load, administrative responsibilities, including student recruitment, and his own burgeoning scholarly writings, Greenleaf continued to practice law at a high level. Most notable was his victory before the Supreme Court in the landmark Charles River Bridge case, which is discussed later. Greenleaf's scholarship also won acclaim. He wrote the first American treatise on the law of evidence, which dominated the nineteenth-century doctrinal landscape long after his death. The evidence treatise, as we

[5] Greenleaf, *Genealogy*, 138.

will see, was built upon his same core Christian beliefs that he displayed in the "Testimony of the Evangelists."[6]

Although Greenleaf chose law over the ministry, the Rev. Parsons profoundly influenced his grandson. Greenleaf married Hannah Kingman in 1806 and had four children. One son, Patrick, left the law to become an Episcopalian minister. Their two daughters, Charlotte and Caroline, married Episcopalian ministers. Throughout his adult life, Greenleaf actively worked on behalf of the Episcopal church, especially its "low church," evangelical wing. He also wrote for the American Tract Society. Moving to Cambridge in 1833, Greenleaf later served as president of the Massachusetts Bible Society for many years. In the 1840s, he was instrumental in establishing the Protestant Episcopal Society for the Promotion of Evangelical Knowledge (PESPEK), a voluntary organization aimed at eradicating the "errors" then percolating throughout the Episcopal church by distributing books and tracts that would "prevent the silent and gradual disappearance of evangelical views." Greenleaf's own 1846 tract, "The Testimony of the Evangelists," proved beyond rational doubt, at least in his mind, the truth of the Gospels by applying evidence law. So deeply held were his evangelical beliefs that in 1851, two years before his death, Greenleaf resigned from the Episcopal church because of its perceived Romanism and pondered becoming a Baptist.[7]

Politically, it appears that Greenleaf followed his father, a "federalist of the Washington school." By the 1830s, Greenleaf was a staunch Whig whose beliefs transcended party politics. Whigs were committed to institutions that "helped them synthesize order with freedom and change." Greenleaf's own institutional commitments to moral reform are vividly seen in his leadership positions in the religious groups described above, but even more so in his rethinking of legal education and judicial institutions like the trial. Threaded throughout his work, as we will see, is Greenleaf's mastery of Scottish Common Sense philosophy, a core tenet of Whig and Christian evangelical thought.[8]

II

Historians seem not to know what to make of Greenleaf. Most often he is the "other guy" on the historical stage, overshadowed by more remarkable figures.

[6] Simon Greenleaf, *A Treatise on the Law of Evidence* (3 vols., 1842–1852).

[7] Blinka, "Roots," 311 (PESPEK); Konefsky, "Piety," 710.

[8] Greenleaf Papers, 26–27. Daniel W. Howe, *Making the American Self: Jonathan Edwards to Abraham Lincoln* (Cambridge, MA: Harvard University Press, 1997), 8–12, ch. 4.

Greenleaf's deeply held Christian beliefs are also too often overlooked completely or, when noted, considered an aspect of his private life and piety. One sees these oversights in historians' assessment of the Charles River Bridge case, Greenleaf's scholarship on evidence law, and his role at Harvard Law School.

The 1837 Charles River Bridge decision is a seminal case in American constitutional jurisprudence involving a dispute between two rival bridge companies. Decades earlier, the Massachusetts legislature had granted monopoly power to the Charles River Bridge company to finance a badly needed bridge connecting Boston and Cambridge. The legislature later launched the upstart Warren Bridge company for the express purpose of smashing that monopoly power in the name of free tolls. The case languished for six years before the Warren Bridge company retained Greenleaf, who successfully argued the case before the Supreme Court against the redoubtable Daniel Webster. The case came with baggage. Since Harvard profited from the Charles River Bridge, Greenleaf secured the reluctant consent of the university's leaders to argue, in effect, against Harvard's interests. Greenleaf's friend, colleague, and mentor, Joseph Story, bitterly dissented from the majority opinion by Chief Justice Taney that supported Greenleaf's position.[9]

Greenleaf's impressive performance is lost in time, at least in some legal histories. The case did not mark Greenleaf's ascent to the first rank of American lawyers, namely, the Storys, the Marshalls, and the Websters. Putting aside his bitterness, Justice Story privately praised Greenleaf's advocacy as having "honored Dane Hall" (Harvard Law School). Nonetheless, Greenleaf's performance has not guaranteed his legacy, even among lawyers. A leading historian of the Charles River Bridge case, Stanley Kutler, sees it as the triumph of an ideology of "creative destruction," the platform for nineteenth-century industrial capitalism. Historian Carl Brent Swisher's classic history of the Taney Court carefully recounts Greenleaf's lawyerly arguments but in the end attributes the outcome more to newly appointed Chief Justice Taney than Greenleaf's lawyering.[10]

While Greenleaf's contributions to the case may be debated, more intriguing is the silence about Greenleaf's Christianity among the case's historians. Kutler makes no mention of it even in his biographical sketch of Greenleaf. The omission is unfortunate because Greenleaf's evangelical faith was at one with his Whiggish drive to improve economic opportunities and his own

9 See Coquillette and Kimball, *Battlefield*, ch. 5.

10 Stanley I. Kutler, *Privilege and Creative Destruction: The Charles River Bridge Case* (New York: Norton, 1971). Carl B. Swisher, *History of the Supreme Court of the United States: Volume 5, The Taney Period, 1836–64* (New York: Macmillan, 1974), 79.

unassailable character. For example, after the Taney Court's decision, Greenleaf publicly stated that the late Chief Justice John Marshall essentially agreed with the Warren Bridge's position when the case was first argued years earlier. Kutler credits Greenleaf's story by underscoring how unlikely it would be for a man of Greenleaf's professional reputation to carelessly spread such a story unless it came from an unimpeachable source (perhaps Justice Story). Greenleaf's lawyerly standing aside, Kutler's argument is even more compelling if Greenleaf's devout evangelical Christianity is considered, not to mention his obsession with truth seeking. Swisher, too, focuses tightly on Greenleaf's lawyering but says nothing about his Christianity. The point is not that Greenleaf's Christianity impacted the case in some discernable way, but rather the complete omission of religion altogether when discussing Greenleaf. Religion is as irrelevant as, say, the color of Greenleaf's eyes.[11]

Similarly, Greenleaf's work on evidence has become an afterthought despite his lustrous nineteenth-century reputation. Greenleaf wrote the first American treatise on evidence law, which dominated legal doctrine and practice throughout the 1800s before being supplanted by John Henry Wigmore's evidence treatise in 1904. Ironically, Wigmore had revised an earlier edition of Greenleaf's treatise but decided a "fresh start" was in order. Wigmore eclipsed Greenleaf, just as Greenleaf had eclipsed earlier British treatise writers.[12]

William Twining's intellectual history of evidence law, while not unkind to Greenleaf, finds him less "systematically critical" than Wigmore, who integrated "the law of evidence and the principles of proof within a single theoretical framework." Greenleaf's treatise disappoints Twining on two fronts: it is a work written for law students and practitioners that struggled to "expound a consistent body of doctrine for a single, non-existent jurisdiction (the United States)." Wigmore, Twining notes, included "considerably more theoretical material." In sum, Greenleaf catalogued cases for practitioners, his treatise lacking critical rigor and any mooring in science.[13]

Like Kutler and Swisher, Twining too makes no mention of Greenleaf's religious beliefs or, for that matter, his "Testimony of the Evangelists." This is a missed opportunity because, as we will see, Greenleaf's work was explicitly based on the theoretical framework of Scottish Common Sense philosophy, which pervaded antebellum lay culture, Christianity, and science. While

[11] Kutler, *Privilege*, 178.

[12] William Twining, *Theories of Evidence: Bentham & Wigmore* (Stanford: Stanford University Press, 1985), 112, 123.

[13] Twining, *Theories*, 5, 123–124, 223, n. 17.

Wigmore consciously crafted evidence law as an esoteric doctrine based on prevailing scientific theories, Greenleaf's point was that evidence law was exoteric, deeply rooted in ways of thinking about the world that dominated popular thinking as well as the best minds of the time. Greenleaf's name may no longer appear in footnotes of case law and current day treatises, yet, as we will see, he remains the architect and engineer of modern evidence law; the scaffolding is his.

Recent scholars have been more attuned to Greenleaf's Christianity and its impact on his legal thought. In a rich article exploring the kinship between nineteenth-century natural science and legal science, Howard Schweber portrays Greenleaf as a significant figure, albeit a secondary one, in what he terms "Protestant Baconianism." The tradition had four features: (1) a faith in natural theology (in nature we find religious truth); (2) a commitment to inductive reasoning and taxonomy; (3) a belief in a "grand synthesis" of all knowledge; and (4) a claim that "science was a public undertaking that would produce moral and political uplift." Drawing on the insights of law professor Alfred Konefksy, Schweber places Greenleaf in all four facets. Greenleaf's treatise and the "Testimony of the Evangelists" are cited as examples of his use of nature to demonstrate the truths of Christianity, but Schweber's purpose is to fix Greenleaf's place in a larger story, not to focus on his unique blending of law, Common Sense, and evangelical Christianity.[14]

When considering the history of Greenleaf's beloved Harvard Law School, we see here too that he is overshadowed by the influence of Justice Story. Greenleaf's Christianity is also downplayed when not ignored altogether. Later we will consider Greenleaf's contribution to Harvard's success, but the present point is how historians have gauged it.

In the best books, chapter titles are carefully chosen and reveal an author's leanings. Charles Warren's 1908 history of Harvard Law School features two chapters entitled the "Story-Greenleaf" period that assess their joint contributions. Story has first billing but Greenleaf is an equal. An excellent 2015 history of Harvard Law School, *On the Battlefield of Merit*, seemingly finds no such equivalence. One chapter about Story's role is entitled "The School Saved" and another "Joseph Story's Law School in the Young Republic." Story is clearly center stage. Following Story's death, Greenleaf assumed undisputed leadership until his retirement, a story told in a chapter bearing the uninspiring title, "The Greenleaf Transition." One senses declension and

[14] Howard Schweber, "The 'Science' of Legal Science: The Model of the Natural Sciences in Nineteenth-Century American Legal Education," *Law and History Review* 17 (1999): 421, 423, 447.

disappointment. History is seldom kind to any "transition" figure; what happened before and after is what counts, and if the aftermath is ugly, as in Harvard's case, the implication is that our transition figure was not up to the task.[15]

Looking beyond chapter titles, these historians acknowledge, as we will see, that Greenleaf's workload and responsibilities at the law school dwarfed Story's. The school's success was Greenleaf's doing. Warren frequently mentions the mutual respect that bespoke their personal and professional relationship, including Story's warm support for Greenleaf's struggles to complete his great evidence treatise amidst his other responsibilities. When it was completed in 1844, Greenleaf dedicated the first volume to Story, who affectionately wrote his friend that "[b]ut for you, the School would never have attained its present rank." The *Battlefield of Merit* credits Greenleaf's "genius at institutional development." Yet here too the focus is on Story's "bold appointment" of Greenleaf, who so ably promoted "Story's vision" of legal education. Harvard Law School flourished under Greenleaf's "supervision" yet the critical factor was Story's "oversight" as "leader." In its closing thoughts on Greenleaf's contribution, however, the *Battlefield of Merit* reassesses somewhat, invoking insights by Schweber and Konefsky. The authors posit that "in key ways" Greenleaf was "Story's intellectual superior, and 'one of the most thoughtful and productive legal scholars of his age.'" In short, the authors' vacillations nicely capture the need to rethink Greenleaf's role at Harvard and in legal history.[16]

Although Story deserves great credit for Harvard Law School's early success, the overlooking of Greenleaf's evangelical Christianity by historians is more perplexing. Warren makes no mention of it, even when describing Greenleaf's life and "personality." "The Testimony of the Evangelists" appears in a footnote listing Greenleaf's "other legal works." The *Battlefield of Merit* makes more of his religion, but does not go quite far enough. It observes, for example, that Greenleaf was a "highly practical teacher and devoted Christian." Popular among students, his "deep religious convictions commanded their respect." Closer to the heart of the matter, the authors observe that "some of Greenleaf's most remarkable books," including "The Testimony of the Evangelists," grew from his deep religious faith. *Battlefield of Merit* also contends that Greenleaf's "Protestant Baconianism" worked toward "a fusion

[15] Charles Warren, *History of the Harvard Law School and of Early Legal Conditions in America* (2 vols., 1908; rep. New York, 1970), I: ch. 23 (1833 to 1836); II: ch. 25 (1837 to 1845). Coquillette and Kimball, *Battlefield*, chs. 4–6.

[16] Warren, *History*, II: 10, 18 (quoting Story). Coquillette and Kimball, *Battlefield*, 140–141, 157, 195.

of scientific thought and moral experiences" while presaging a "Progressive vision" of law.[17]

If the implication is that Greenleaf paved the way for secularization, he would be appalled. By not developing Greenleaf's deeply held evangelical Christianity and commitment to Scottish Common Sense thinking, the authors lost the opportunity to appreciate how Greenleaf's work fit within, and advanced, antebellum Whig culture. His originality lay not in any steps toward "Progressivism," but in his demonstration that law conformed to the mainstream popular and academic thinking of his time, especially evangelical Christianity.

III

In all ways, Harvard explains Greenleaf's greatest success during his lifetime and his significance today. Greenleaf built a national reputation at the Law School, which provided the impetus and occasion for his emergence as an important legal thinker. Without Harvard, one is hard pressed to imagine much interest in the man today; he would have likely remained a "prominent Maine lawyer" of the antebellum period. Nonetheless, to appreciate Greenleaf, one must understand how his Christianity pervaded all that he did at Harvard, animating his teaching, thinking, and writing.

Harvard Law School opened in 1817 but was floundering by the late 1820s. Harvard's solution was to clean house and start over. It reposed the School's leadership in Justice Joseph Story, whose national prominence on the Supreme Court and prodigious treatise writing would draw students and underwrite its quality, or so it was hoped. Story's top choice as his only colleague on the faculty was John Ashmun, a distinguished local lawyer who ran his own proprietary law school. Ashmun shuttered his school while drawing a number of his own student to join him at Harvard. It was a promising start, but Ashmun's death from tuberculosis the next year compelled Story to reach out to Simon Greenleaf as Ashmun's replacement in 1833. The pairing would be a happy one for both men, Harvard, and the legal profession.

By any measure, the Law School flourished under Story's and Greenleaf's tenures. Much of this is attributable to Greenleaf, an "institutional genius," as noted, who taught most of the courses while running the Law School's daily operations. Financially, the school showed a surplus by the late 1830s. Its two endowed chairs – the Royall chair held by Greenleaf and the Dane chair held by Story – helped defray their salaries which were supplemented by tuition

[17] Warren, *History*, I: 480–482; II: 122. Coquillette and Kimball, *Battlefield*, 149, 177, 195–200.

revenue of roughly $100 per student per annum. Moreover, the Dane donation had also paid for a new building, Dane Hall, which replaced the School's inadequate facilities with serviceable classrooms, a library, and offices.[18]

The surge in student enrollment accounted for the Law School's financial prosperity while further enhancing its growing national reputation. Its key competition was not other law schools, but the apprenticeship system, discussed further below, by which most aspiring lawyers learned their craft. Indeed, Harvard's $100 tuition was pegged to the cost of most apprenticeship relationships, a strategic move designed to neutralize cost as a factor for prospective students. The School aggressively recruited students nationally, drawing classes that were diverse, at least geographically. Greenleaf played an active role in recruiting. From 1835 to 1845, he steadily increased the advertising budget from about $140 to over $500 per year (equating to five students' tuition out of a class of about 150).[19]

It is tempting to speculate that perhaps part of Greenleaf's design for the "Testimony of the Evangelists" was to draw students from evangelical Christian backgrounds. The tract demonstrated the harmony of law with Christian values and beliefs while also allaying qualms about whether evangelicals would feel at home in Unitarian Cambridge or, for that matter, studying law. More to the point, the tract portrayed lawyers, properly prepared of course, as charged "to discover truth and separate it from error" in all walks of life.[20]

The Law School's innovative pedagogy also explains it success in drawing fledgling law students. Both Story and Greenleaf had learned law as apprentices in law offices, the dominant mode of legal education. And despite their respective successes, both found it lacking. An apprenticeship's value was hit-or-miss, depending on the quality of the lawyer–tutor relationship, available books, and the student's own diligence. Apprentices wrote "commonplace books," essentially copying down any wisdom they thought pertinent from the master lawyer or whatever books they read. Harvard's approach was quite different.[21]

Story's pedagogy, superbly implemented by Greenleaf, arose from the former's "vision" for legal education. First, the law was a "science." Second, legal education must be "cosmopolitan," that is, national and even international in scope. Third, the law school demanded men of "merit and

[18] Coquillette and Kimball, *Battlefield*, ch. 5.
[19] Ibid., 164–165, 174.
[20] Greenleaf, *Testimony*, vii (forward to the "Members of the Legal Profession").
[21] Coquillette and Kimball, *Battlefield*, 49–53.

character," just as the other professional schools for theology and medicine. Greenleaf and Story's pedagogy has been described as a "text-and-recite" method; students read learned legal treatises, including those written by their two professors, and were closely questioned in class about their understanding. Story's duties as a Supreme Court justice drastically limited his teaching availability, so Greenleaf shouldered most of the Law School's teaching load, including moot courts which simulated law practice. Students praised the high quality and rigor of Greenleaf's teaching. A young Rutherford B. Hayes, who would be elected president in 1876, wrote in his diary that Greenleaf was "very searching and logical in examination. It is impossible for one who has not faithfully studied the text to escape exposing his ignorance."[22]

Academic rigor went hand-in-hand with their Christianity; neither Greenleaf the evangelical nor Story the Unitarian saw any inconsistency between the common law and Christianity. Greenleaf openly espoused his evangelical beliefs throughout his years at Harvard. In 1834, in his inaugural address as Royall Professor, he unflinchingly declared that "the Christian religion is part of our common law, with the very texture of which it is interwoven."[23] David Cross, a student and later a New Hampshire judge, similarly recalled Greenleaf lecturing that "The Common Law is Christian; It has been baptized."[24] Earlier we saw that students respected Greenleaf's "deep religious convictions." For both Greenleaf and Story, the law, science, and religion were one. In his moving 1845 discourse on the life of Joseph Story, Greenleaf warmly praised his late mentor and friend for rebuilding Harvard Law School "purely for the advancement of the science of law" and for students "with high and just views of the dignity of their position as ministering officers in the temple of Justice, and above all, with a deep sense of their duty to the cause of learning and religion, and of their ultimate accountability to posterity and to God."[25]

Nor were such views restricted to formal discourses. When addressing students at the close of the 1846 spring term, Greenleaf's handwritten notes are replete with values shared by both Whigs generally and evangelical

22 Ibid., 141–142, 167. William P. LaPiana, *Logic and Experience: The Origins of Modern American Legal Education* (New York: Oxford University Press, 1994), 50 (Hayes quote).

23 Simon Greenleaf, *A Discourse Pronounced at the Inauguration of the Author as Royall Professor of Law in Harvard University* (Aug. 26, 1834), 24, https://play.google.com/books/reader?id=cpw8AAAAIAAJ&printsec=frontcover&output=reader&hl=en&pg=GBS.PA2.

24 Warren, *History*, II: 27 (quoting Cross).

25 Simon Greenleaf, *A Discourse Commemorative of the Life and Character of the Hon. Joseph Story* (Boston: Little and Brown, 1845), 39.

Christians. Students are expected to be "gentlemen" who know that "good lawyers" work to "advance the science" (of law) in ways that "give strength to institutions," thereby "promot[ing] public security, peace, and happiness." The "Duty of lawyers" is "to employ their influence on the side of virtue, and patriotism, and religion." They are to be "fellow ministers at the altar of Justice."[26] In sum, Christian – and Whig – values are seamlessly "interwoven" with the law.

One finds the same intellectual fabric in Greenleaf's scholarship, yet his own emergence as a scholar is impressive in and of itself. Joining Story at Harvard at age fifty, Greenleaf retooled himself, blossoming into an innovative thinker and writer at a point in life when many look to retire. His earlier writings in Maine, in which Story saw promise, were largely confined to dry case reports, not systematic thinking. Once at Harvard, and despite a heavy teaching load, his writings multiplied in number, complexity, and ambition.

It is here that we see how rigorous teaching sometimes stimulates scholarship. As early as 1834, after just one year teaching, Greenleaf confided to a young Charles Sumner, who sometimes filled in as an instructor, that he was dissatisfied teaching from the leading British evidence treatise by "Starkie." Greenleaf complained that "Starkie vexes me by his frequent obscurity, diffuseness, and want of method; and I sometimes resolve to write a compendium of the law of evidence myself."[27] In an 1838 letter to Sumner, Greenleaf had plainly emerged intellectually. He candidly lamented that his own lawyerly training had narrowed his outlook but that five years of teaching had yielded an epiphany:

> The result of wider and deeper researches is to make me less exclusively addicted to the Common Law . . .; in short, to lead me to regard the law . . . as a system of principles – of higher and holier origin than any codes whatever, though disclosed with more or less symmetry and beauty in the codes of all civilized nations.[28]

Thus, Greenleaf now looked at law as a science of "higher and holier origin," one consistent with Common Sense epistemology and methodology. These views are encompassed in his *Evidence* treatise, first appearing in 1842, which was far more than the "compendium" he had envisioned in 1834.

Greenleaf's intellectual retooling related to his close study of Scottish Common Sense philosophy and its application to the law. The "Common

[26] Greenleaf Papers, Harvard Law School, Box 21, folder 1, available at: https://iiif.lib.harvard.edu/manifests/view/drs:46293888$1i.

[27] Quoted in Warren, *History*, I: 491.

[28] Quoted in Warren, *History*, II: 4.

Sense tradition," observes historian Mark Noll, "dominated American intellectual life before the Civil War" while simultaneously "occup[ying] a major place in evangelical theology." There was no "conversion" experience for Greenleaf; Common Sense was at one with his long-held beliefs as an evangelical Christian. He now became its serious student. As an epistemology, Common Sense "cut the nerve of skepticism," recognizing that our "perceptions revealed the world to us directly." Methodologically, Common Sense embraced Francis Bacon: the "truths about consciousness, the world, or religion must be built by strict induction from irreducible facts of experience." Common Sense's epistemology was shared by the lay public and the erudite alike. Its methodology, however, appealed more narrowly to academics.[29]

Greenleaf used Common Sense as the scaffolding for modern evidence law – the rules governing trials. Unlike later legal scholars who used appellate cases as the basis for their induction, Greenleaf's "irreducible facts of experience" were drawn directly from the Common Sense tradition itself, which provided the law's principles for proof. Volume one of *Evidence* appeared in 1842. Its first ninety-seven sections, over one-seventh of the volume, set forth the core principles of proof, directly drawn from the Common Sense canon to bring order and consistency to evidence law. The great Chief Justice Lemuel Shaw of Massachusetts, an influential friend, publicly praised Greenleaf's "remarkable" achievement in presenting "the grounds and principles of the theory of proof in general, [rather] than as a detail of the rules of evidence."[30]

Greenleaf summed up his enormous debt to the tradition when identifying the three bases of "evidence": (1) "the disposition to believe"; (2) "our faith in human testimony, as sanctioned by experience"; and (3) "the known and experienced connexion subsisting between collateral facts or circumstances, satisfactorily proved, and the fact in controversy." He seamlessly blended technical issues of admissibility (What should the jury hear?) with the problem of proof itself (When is a fact "proved"?). The discussions of "moral evidence," "sufficient probability," and when facts are adequately "proved" are, for example, drawn from the core of the Common Sense tradition. When addressing the "general nature and principles of evidence," Greenleaf extensively quoted from Thomas Reid, a founder of the tradition, whose "profound" work explicitly rejected David Hume's skepticism. Of critical importance was the term "moral evidence," by which "matters of fact" are proved; it extended to all evidence drawn from the senses and thus obtained other than by

29 Mark A. Noll, "Common Sense Traditions and American Evangelical Thought," *American Quarterly* 37 (Summer 1985): 216, 222–223.

30 *Commonwealth* v. *York*, 50 Mass. 93, 106 (1845).

"intuition" or "demonstration" (e.g., mathematical truths). Whatever the allure of reason and abstraction, at bottom human experience and observation underlies all knowledge.[31]

Greenleaf's "faith in human testimony" depended on witnesses' credibility, namely, the accuracy of the testimony. While all people make occasional mistakes, deliberate deceit – lying, perjury – posed special legal and moral hazards. Weaving Christianity into the law of evidence, Greenleaf passionately championed oaths as a condition for testifying. A "religious sanction" was "an indispensable test of truth." One must believe "in the being of God, and a future state of rewards and punishment; that is, the Divine punishment will be the certain consequence of perjury." The oath provides the key benchmark of faith; "the law presumes that every man brought up in a Christian land, where God is generally acknowledged, does believe in him and fear him." Secular safeguards, such as concerns about one's character or social place, or even fear of prosecution, did not suffice. For similar reasons, the law punished blasphemy, which included a "profane scoffing at the Holy Bible."[32] So seriously did he take oaths, Greenleaf wrote that one convicted of perjury (lying under oath) should be forever barred from testifying, even when pardoned, because "to preserve the temple of justice from pollution, it repels from its portal the man who feareth not an oath."[33]

Greenleaf's "Testimony of the Evangelists" is, in many ways, the tour de force of his balancing of Christianity, Common Sense, and legal science. First published in 1846, a revised "corrected" edition appeared in 1847, the same year that Greenleaf launched PESPEK, the Episcopalian society for the "Promotion of Evangelical Knowledge." His "Testimony" demonstrated the power of Greenleaf's legal science to three groups that he hoped most to impress: the legal profession, the intellectual community, and evangelical Christians.

The essay opens by declaring its three-fold purpose: (1) the need to "investigate the truth of our religion," (2) by applying the same standards "readily conceded to every other branch of human science," namely, (3) "the tests to which other evidence is subjected in human tribunals." Reversing the order, one sees that Greenleaf essentially asserts that evidence is tested in "human tribunals," that these tests meet the standards of those in other branches of "human science," and that such sciences prove "the truth of our religion."

31 Greenleaf, *Treatise*, 1: § 1 and § 7.

32 Greenleaf, *Treatise*, 1: §§ 368–370; 3: § 68 (blasphemy).

33 Greenleaf Papers, 5–14, seq.7 (handwritten draft, essay on "crimen falsi"), http://pds.lib.harvard.edu/pds/view/45652160?n=7&;printThumbnails=no&oldpds.

Greenleaf's challenge was to apply his legal science to Mathew, Mark, Luke, and John: if the four evangelists "ought to be believed and have weight" in a "court of justice," they "ought to have weight and credit" outside the courtroom as well.[34]

To this end, Greenleaf first demonstrated the authenticity of the gospels as historical documents. Errors undoubtedly crept in through repeated copying, and poor translations distorted their words as well, but the law places the burden on the "objector to show them spurious," which they failed to do.[35] The heart of the essay, however, is Greenleaf's assessment of the gospel writers' credibility. The "ordinary affairs of life" require only "moral evidence." The "proper inquiry" is not whether oral "testimony may be false, but whether there is sufficient probability that it is true." Evidence must be "competent" and sufficient "to satisfy the mind and conscience of a man of common prudence and discretion" who would "venture to act upon the conviction in matters of the highest concerns and importance to his own interest." Greenleaf then closely examined the gospel writers' sincerity, their opportunity to observe what they reported, the "number and consistency of their testimony," its conformity to "experience," and how the evangelists' testimony coincided with "collateral and contemporaneous facts and circumstances."[36] In sum, the evangelists met the standard for moral evidence.

The language of Common Sense suffuses Greenleaf's "Testimony," particularly the references to "moral evidence" and "sufficient" proof, which had informed his *Evidence* treatise as well. William Paley, a key figure within the tradition who had also argued for the evangelists' credibility, is prominently featured. David Hume's skepticism about miracles is easily rebuffed by "plain and simple" facts perceived "by persons of common capacity and observation."[37] Legal science, then, conformed to the tenets of Common Sense, yielding the same outcome: The evangelists are worthy of belief. Yet Greenleaf took his conclusion one step further. The proof was so compelling that no trial was needed; rather, a judge applying evidence rules would direct a verdict in favor of the evangelists' truth. The rules, then, were of greater force than trials themselves.

Greenleaf personally saw to it that his "Testimony" reached prominent figures in American intellectual life, including James Walker, an expert on Common Sense and later Harvard's president, and Edward Robinson,

34 Greenleaf, *Testimony*, § 2 and § 3.
35 Greenleaf, *Testimony*, §§8–10.
36 Greenleaf, *Testimony*, §§ 26–27.
37 Greenleaf, *Testimony*, § 38.

a renown biblical scholar who drew upon geology and archaeology. Greenleaf's intent was to prove that legal science stood on the same plane as geology, philology, etc. The point was not that law offered insights unavailable to other sciences; rather, law was as rigorous as the other disciplines because all drew from the well of Common Sense.[38]

Not everyone took the point. Francis Bowen, a Harvard economist and moral philosopher, reviewed the "Testimony of the Evangelists" in the *New Englander*. In a generally favorable review, Bowen seconded most of Greenleaf's key arguments and even added to them; indeed, Bowen himself had written on the evidence of Christianity and had no quarrel with the law professor's conclusions.[39] He lamented, however, that Greenleaf had not "favored us with a summary of the historical evidence" followed by a "legal opinion of its credibility and sufficiency." Rather, the law professor's argument was "nothing more than that of Paley, drawn from the historical allusions[.]"[40] Yet that was Greenleaf's point: his "legal opinion" was identical to Paley's common sense of the matter. What occurred in courtrooms reflected the same standards of moral evidence found in sciences like geology and used by ordinary people in daily life.

IV

What do we make of Greenleaf's following among today's evangelical Christians in light of his obscurity among the legal profession? One focusing on citation counts in legal authority will quickly conclude that Wigmore, who died in the 1930s, remains far more influential than Greenleaf in evidence law. Yet such counts are deceiving when measuring influence. Greenleaf's impact on law remains substantial, unheralded by the legal profession but duly appreciated by lay people still drawn to his "Testimony." What then so attracts them?

Drawing from the deep wellspring of Common Sense, Greenleaf ensured that his antebellum legal science was consonant with both popular (lay) thought and contemporary science. Although its methodology, as we have seen, appealed mostly to intellectuals, its epistemology was shared by elites and the broader public alike. For this reason, Greenleaf built the foundation for his "Testimony" on the bedrock of Common Sense, a common ground

38 See Blinka, "Roots," 314–315.

39 Schweber, "Legal Science," 445. See Blinka, "Roots," 319–320 (discussing Bowen).

40 See Francis Bowen, "Greenleaf and Strauss: The Truth of Christianity," *The North American Review* 63 (Oct. 1846): 384–385.

shared by both intellectual elites and the Christian public, especially evangelicals. The message was straightforward: legal science proved the truth of the gospels and thus could be relied upon for determining truth more generally.

By the late nineteenth century, however, science had moved beyond Common Sense. The "natural science" that Greenleaf and Story's legal science so emulated had fallen out of academic fashion. Science had become self-consciously esoteric, the province of specialized education, inaccessible to a lay public – the antithesis of antebellum natural science.[41]

The new sciences seduced the legal profession as well. Wigmore supported all manner of forensic techniques, including psychology and psychiatry. The credibility of witnesses has always been the focus of evidence law. Greenleaf, as we have seen, looked to Common Sense's treatment of "moral evidence," but Wigmore believed modern science offered better solutions. Two examples suffice. Wigmore's evidence treatise strongly recommended that young girls who claimed sexual abuse should be examined by physicians or psychiatrists. In his words, "No judge should ever let a sex offense charge to the jury unless the female complainant's social history and mental makeup have been examined and testified to by a qualified physician." More generally, Wigmore overcame initial skepticism to endorse the use of "lie detectors" as a scientific means of quantifying credibility.[42]

Wigmore's prescriptions have come to nothing. Critics justly lambasted as misogynist and repressive Wigmore's biased assumptions that "young girls" are prone to lie about sexual abuse. Polygraphs too came to nothing; nearly all courts exclude their results as insufficiently reliable. The "lie detector's" legal standing is neatly summed up in the career path of one of its pioneers, William Marston, whom Wigmore supported. Marston abandoned polygraphy to make a fortune promoting his comic book champion Wonder Woman, whose magic lasso became the "ultimate lie detector." To this day, credibility is left to the lay jury's common sense and life experiences, just as Greenleaf had endorsed.[43]

Wigmore retains "credibility" today largely because most of his treatise built on Greenleaf's foundation. Modern science abandoned the tenets of Common Sense, especially its methodology, but its epistemology continues to resonate among the lay public and remains the core of modern evidence law. The term "moral evidence" is quaintly old-fashioned, even musty, yet

41 Schweber, "Legal Science," 456–457.

42 Ken Alder, *The Lie Detectors: The History of an American Obsession* (New York: Free Press, 2007), 92–93, 116–117. Leigh B. Bienen, "A Question of Credibility: John Henry Wigmore's Use of Scientific Authority," *California Western Law Review* 19 (1983): 235, 238.

43 Bienen, "Wigmore," 236. Alder, *Lie Detectors*, 191–195.

Greenleaf's assessment of the evangelists' credibility is something that both today's lawyers and the general public find familiar and even compelling. A witness' sincerity, opportunity to observe events, consistency, and plausibility remain factors contemplated by evidence law and lay factfinders. The concept of "character," anathema to modern psychology, remains central to evidence law, its ambiguities as comfortably familiar in today's popular thinking as it was in Victorian America.

It is ironic, then, that Greenleaf, who had so hoped to impress the intellectuals of his own time, made his lasting impression by centering his legal science on an epistemology that still resonates among the lay public and the legal profession. This is evidenced by his own "Testimony's" currency today. Greenleaf understood that the legitimacy of his legal science required that it be calibrated to prevailing popular culture. And so it remains nearly 200 years later.

V

The modern trial is accurately portrayed as an objective search for the truth, yet historians are coming to see its deep theological roots and how they affected rules and practices long-deemed secular. As historian James Q. Whitman has discerned, Christian doctrine profoundly influenced the structure of jury trials in the early Republic.[44]

Greenleaf persistently harked on the importance of separating "error" from truth; it appears in his Royall discourse of 1834, as well as in his "Testimony" and even in his informal remarks to students at the term's end in 1846 ("the true office of counsel is to reflect the truth"). Yet Greenleaf's search for truth, in whatever setting, was always consistent with Christian thinking. So essential was it that Greenleaf consciously embedded core principles of evangelical, Common Sense thinking into the epistemology of evidence law, where they remain today.

Whitman has skillfully explored how broader currents of "moral theology" deeply affected modern doctrine, particularly, the reasonable doubt standard. It is ironic, then, that he singles out the year 1783 as an "important date."[45] For 1783 marks not only British recognition of American independence and key developments in Anglo-American criminal trials, but also Greenleaf's birth. In short, 1783 was not an endpoint or culmination, but rather a marker in the process by which Christianity shaped the law.

44 Whitman, *Origins*, 31.
45 Ibid., 199–200.

10

John Marshall Harlan the Elder

Linda Przybyszewski

Long before he was appointed to the United States Supreme Court in 1877, John Marshall Harlan was a teacher of religion, a fact that illuminates his life in the law. He taught young women in Sunday school while a lawyer in Kentucky, and organized a class for adult men at the New York Avenue Presbyterian Church from 1896 until his death in 1911, which also ended his tenure on the Court.[1]

We have no notes of what Bible verses Harlan discussed, and no jottings to tell us how he interpreted the Good Book for his students. Harlan's private letters offer us a little more on his religious faith, but an even richer source is the record of the other kind of teaching he did: legal teaching. Two night students at Columbian (now George Washington) University took down his lectures on constitutional law in 1897 and 1898, and these notes made their way back to the Harlan family.[2] They shed a surprising amount of light on how Harlan's religious beliefs intertwined with his view of his country and its laws, especially the origins of his famous dissents in favor of civil rights for African-Americans.

From these lectures, we learn that Harlan came to understand the Civil War as part of God's plan to free the nation from the sin of slavery. Harlan's belief that he had a role in this divine plan explains the determination behind his lonely judicial dissents in favor of civil rights for the new African-American citizens. Harlan understood the course of American history by applying to historical events an approach used in reading the Bible. Called "typology,"

[1] Malvina Shanklin Harlan, *Some Memories of a Long Life, 1854–1911* (New York: Modern Library, 2002), 40.

[2] For an annotated version of the lectures, see "Justice John Marshall Harlan: Lectures on Constitutional Law," ed. Josh Blackman, Brian L. Frye, and Michael McCloskey, *George Washington Law Review Arguendo* 81 (2013): 12–341. This chapter refers to that edition as Harlan Lectures.

this approach identified events in the Hebrew Bible as foreshadowing events in the New Testament; the earlier events are types to be repeated. So, with God's help, first, the American Revolution overthrew the tyranny of kings and nobles; then, the Civil War overthrew the tyranny of slavery. The American nation became a type for the world: it would spread the example of equality across the globe. Typology made order from the political chaos through which Harlan struggled as a Kentucky slaveholder turned Civil War Union officer turned civil rights champion. Lastly, we learn from the lectures that he believed in legal formalism which holds that the meaning of the law exists outside of history and judges discover it when they ponder specific legal cases. Harlan had the same approach to the logical problems posed by traditional theology and by legal formalism; he refused to trouble himself much about them.

Justice David J. Brewer once teasingly said of Harlan that he "goes to bed every night with one hand on the Constitution and the other on the Bible, and so sleeps the sweet sleep of justice and righteousness."[3] Harlan did see both Bible and United States Constitution as "supreme" in all matters that fell under them.[4] Yet only one of the biographies of Harlan does more than shuffle his religious life off to one side in the usual chapter on "off-the-bench" activities included in most judicial biographies.[5] But religion and law were intertwined in Harlan's life.

John Marshall Harlan was born in Kentucky in 1833 to Eliza Harlan, the daughter of farmers, and James Harlan, a Whig Party politician, lawyer, and state attorney general. James named his son in honor of Chief Justice John Marshall in the hopes he would also become a lawyer. At eight, John Harlan was enrolled in the Sabbath school of the First Presbyterian Church of Frankfort, Kentucky, and he continued to be affiliated with Presbyterianism for the rest of his life.[6]

3 Justice Brewer speech, in "John Marshall Harlan's Twenty-Fifth Anniversary of the United States Supreme Court Banquet Program," John Marshall Harlan Papers, University of Louisville.

4 "James B. Morrow, 'Talks with Notable Men,' *Washington Post*, Feb. 23, 1906" (Interview with JMH), typescript, John Marshall Harlan Papers, Library of Congress, hereafter JMH Papers, LC.

5 See Linda Przybyszewski's full treatment of Harlan's religion and the law lectures in *The Republic according to John Marshall Harlan* (Chapel Hill: University of North Carolina Press, 1998) versus Loren P. Beth, *John Marshall Harlan: The Last Whig Justice* (Lexington: University Press of Kentucky, 1992) and Tinsley E. Yarbrough, *Judicial Enigma: The First Justice Harlan* (New York: Oxford University Press, 1995).

6 William H. Averill, *A History of the First Presbyterian Church, Frankfort, Kentucky: Together with the Churches in Franklin County, in Connection with the Presbyterian Church in the United States of America* (Cincinnati: Monfort & Co., 1902), 226, 241. Since John Harlan's son

His father James owned some half dozen slaves who worked in the house and its gardens. Kentucky was a small-farm state that sold slaves down river to work on the plantations of the Deep South. James was an ally of Henry Clay, the great senator from Kentucky, who urged the end of slavery through gradual emancipation. James Harlan also brought what were called freedom suits – lawsuits brought on behalf of people who claimed to be unlawfully held in bondage – but he was no radical on slavery. Freedom suits reinforce the legality of slavery: they claim these particular people are held wrongly in slavery; all the other slaves are held legally.

By the time the Whig Party fell apart in the 1850s under the pressure of arguments over the future of slavery in the western territories, John Harlan had made himself a name as a political speaker and become a lawyer. He fell briefly into the Know-Nothing Party which hoped to make anti-immigrant policies the crucial national issue, but by the four-way election of 1860, Harlan was part of the Constitutional Union Party which hoped to preserve the Union as it was with the Constitution's protections for slavery. This was not a wild idea. After all, even Abraham Lincoln made it clear that, however much he disproved of slavery on moral grounds, and wanted it barred from the western territories, he was willing to allow the states to determine the laws within their own borders. President Lincoln refused to make emancipation a war aim early on precisely because he did not want to alienate the voting men of the border states. Lincoln is supposed to have said that he would like to have God on his side, but he *must* have Kentucky.

So, John Harlan the slaveholder joined the Union Army along with about 30,000 other Kentucky men. He raised his own regiment, the 10th Kentucky infantry in the fall of 1861, but saw little action. Then, on January 1, 1863, the Emancipation Proclamation officially declared free all slaves held in disloyal territory as part of Lincoln's strategy for winning the war. Harlan resigned his commission that year in response to his father's death in order to salvage the family law firm.

Harlan may not have resigned because of the Emancipation Proclamation, but he certainly disapproved of it. He campaigned against Lincoln in the 1864 presidential election and reminded his audiences in Kentucky and Indiana that the war was fought for the Union, not for emancipation. He called the Thirteenth Amendment, which freed the slaves, "a flagrant violation of the right of self-government."[7] When General John M. Palmer continued to

Richard studied at Princeton Seminary, the most conservative of Presbyterian seminaries, it is likely that John was always a member of an Old School Presbyterian Church.

7 Quoted in E. Merton Coulter, *The Civil War and Readjustment in Kentucky* (Chapel Hill: University of North Carolina Press, 1926), 279–280.

recruit enslaved men into the Union Army after the end of the war because joining up freed them and their families, John Harlan was Kentucky's attorney general and had Palmer indicted for violating the state's slave code in 1866. Even as Harlan was arguing hopelessly for the Union as it was, white terrorism broke out in Kentucky.

Around 10,000 white Kentucky men had fought for the Confederacy and now they came home and many of them were angry. With the blessing of the Democratic Party, they formed into gangs and began wreaking violence upon whites and blacks across state. Blacks from Harlan's hometown of Frankfort reported in 1868 that white gangs rode over the countryside "going from county to county spreading terror wherever they go, whipping, ravishing and killing our people without provocation."[8]

The Harlans had always told themselves that they upheld the rule of law *and* the white supremacy which the law enshrined; they told themselves that their practice of white supremacy under slavery had been benign, even kind. But after the Civil War, the rule of law meant a newly amended Constitution, an end to slavery, citizenship for the freed people, whereas white supremacy meant arson, murder, and rape. Harlan chose the rule of law over white supremacy, but he would continue to believe that Anglo-Saxons were particularly good, or ought to be, at upholding the rule of law, and this racial belief would limit his work for civil rights.

By 1868, Harlan had joined the Republican Party. He ran for governor in 1871 and 1875 and rode through the state giving speeches that denounced white terrorism. "These KuKlux are enemies of all order," he declared in 1875. Anyone who opposed the exercise of black civil rights "is no friend of the law, is an enemy of our free institutions."[9] When hecklers in the crowd first challenged him on his record, Harlan admitted he had changed his mind. "It is true that I was at one time in my life opposed to conferring these privileges upon the freedman," he told a crowd in Kentucky, "but I have lived long enough to feel and declare, as I do this night, that the most perfect despotism that ever existed on this earth was the institution of African Slavery. I rejoice that it is gone! I rejoice that the Sun of American Liberty does not this day shine upon a single human slave upon this continent!"[10] Harlan lost both gubernatorial elections, but he had made himself into a leading southern

8 W. A. Low, "The Freedmen's Bureau in the Border States," in *Radicalism, Racism, and Party Realignment: The Border States during Reconstruction*, ed. Richard Orr Curry (Baltimore: Johns Hopkins University Press, 1969), 245–264, 256.

9 Quoted in editorial, "General Harlan's Republicanism," *Louisville Daily Commercial*, November 1, 1877, typed copy, JMH Papers, LC.

10 Ibid.

Republican politician. When the Kentucky delegation to the Republican convention gave its support to Rutherford B. Hayes for president in 1876, Harlan caught Hayes's eye. Hayes asked him to serve on the commission sent to Louisiana in 1877 to sort out a disputed state election, and then nominated him to the Supreme Court later that year.

In order to make sense of the enormous changes that he and the nation had experienced, Harlan told stories about his father and his country that made it seem as though both had always been on the righteous side of history. John's wife, Malvina Shanklin Harlan, offered the most elaborate version of this story about James: "One Sunday morning, on his way to church, he passed in the main street a company of slaves that were being driven to the 'Slave Market' in a neighboring town. The able-bodied men and women were chained together, four abreast, proceeded by the old ones and the little 'pickaninnies,' who walked unbound." In charge of "this pitiful procession" was a slave-driver who handled a long whip, "every blow from which drew blood." James Harlan saw before him "the awful possibilities of an institution" which separated husband from wife, parent from child.[11]

Faced with this horror, what did James Harlan the slaveholder do? He walked into the middle of the street, shook his finger in the face of the slave-driver and said, "'*You are a damned scoundrel. Good Morning, sir.*' After having thus relieved his feelings, he quietly pursued his way to the House of Prayer."[12] We may have hoped for something a bit more dramatic, but do not underestimate the significance of a curse on a Sunday morning in the 1840s to a pious Presbyterian. Malvina Harlan concluded her story with this: "To those who heard and saw him that day, there was no suggestion of profanity in his language. Like some Old Testament prophet, he seemed to be calling down Heaven's maledictions upon the whole institution of Slavery."[13] We know that the Harlans did in fact buy and sell slaves, but this family story placed James on the side of the righteous who had not. So too John Harlan placed himself there when he recalled in his law lectures "practices that were horrible to the rights of the Christian man," and spoke feelingly of how the slave trade separated families.[14]

11 MSH, *Memories of a Long Life*, 20–21.

12 Ibid., emphasis in original.

13 MSH, *Memories of a Long Life*, 20–21. DNA analysis in the fall of 1999 done at my request with help from Eugene A. Foster, who organized the testing of the descendants of Sally Hemings/Thomas Jefferson, revealed no kinship between the sole living male descendant of Robert J. Harlan, a mixed-race slave freed by James Harlan, and three male descendants of James Harlan who did match one another. On the original controversy, see James W. Gordon, "Did the First Justice Harlan Have a Black Brother?," *Western New England Law Review* 15 (1993): 159–238.

14 Harlan Lectures, May 7, 1898, p. 342.

The larger, national story which John Harlan told the students in his constitutional law class followed the type of story he told of his father. In each case, the more complicated and uglier truth was replaced with a myth that foretold the end of slavery as part of a Divine plan. Harlan depicted the founding fathers as reluctant slaveholders. He pointed to the Declaration of Independence, "our political Bible," with its proclamation of equality as proof.[15] The founders' unwillingness to use the word "slave" in the Constitution was proof of their plan for future generations to destroy slavery. And the *Dred Scott* case in 1857 was part of this plan. In truth, it was a test case brought by proponents of anti-slavery, who wanted the Supreme Court to determine whether or not a slave was made a free man when he entered free territory. The result was a decision that shocked many. The Court not only declared that Congress had no power to ban the spread of slavery into the territories, but Chief Justice Roger B. Taney wrote that so far as the law was concerned, a black man, even if free, had no rights which a white man was bound to respect.[16]

Northerners in general and anti-slavery people in particular found the decision appalling at the time, but, looking back, Harlan made it into a crucial step toward emancipation. First, he spoke of "particular things which have occurred as Providences." George Washington was one such "special Providence," so were Thomas Jefferson, Lincoln, and General Ulysses S. Grant. Of each of them, we can say "that no other man could have performed the work he did." *Dred Scott* was another: "that case was a work of special Providence to this country, in that it laid the foundation of a civil war, which, terrible as it was, awful as it was in its consequences in the loss of life and money, was in the end a blessing to this country in that it rid us of the institution of African Slavery."[17] In a letter written to one of his sons on his birthday in 1880, Harlan explained the Civil War was the nation struggling for its life against the work of traitors, "but in another sense, it was struggling for a new life which would come after the destruction of slavery."[18] Like the Protestant believer, the United States suffered from an original sin, but was reborn. The country set an example for the world. It was "a light to guide the oppressed of all lands in their struggle for freedom," as he told members of the Union League in 1888.[19]

15 Harlan Lectures, October 21, 1898, p. 29.

16 *Dred Scott* v. *Sandford*, 60 U.S. 393 (1857).

17 Harlan Lectures, March 12, 1898, p. 265.

18 John M. Harlan to James S. Harlan, November 1880, JMH Papers, LC.

19 JMH, Speech at Chicago Union League Banquet, February 22, 1888, John Marshall Harlan Papers, University of Louisville, hereafter JMH Papers, UofL.

This view of the nation's history lay behind Harlan's dissents from Supreme Court decisions that limited the civil rights of black Americans. In the *Civil Rights Cases* in 1883, the Court was asked to rule whether the new constitutional amendments that prohibited slavery and granted black citizenship barred the owners of railroads, hotels, theaters, and other public accommodations from segregating or excluding people by race. The majority of the Court decided that the Thirteenth Amendment's ban on slavery did not affect segregation or exclusion, nor were the private actions of individual property owners affected by the Fourteenth Amendment's prohibitions on action by the states that deprived citizens of their privileges and immunities, of due process, or of the equal protection of the law.

No one had raised the *Dred Scott* case in the proceedings, but Harlan pointed to it to prove that before the war, even free blacks had no rights that white men were bound to respect. Segregation and exclusion had been allowed before the war only because blacks were members of a slave race, he reasoned. When the Thirteenth Amendment ended slavery, it established "universal civil freedom."[20] Discrimination in accommodations offered to the public were doubly barred when blacks gained citizenship with the Fourteenth Amendment. Dissenting alone, Harlan spoke "with tones of feeling" and "even struck the desk before him in his earnestness."[21]

In deciding the *Civil Rights Cases*, the Court had left unanswered the question of whether these constitutional amendments barred the states themselves from enacting laws that discriminated by race. So, a group of black men in New Orleans decided to bring a suit to challenge a Louisiana law that required "equal but separate accommodations" for the races. This became *Plessy* v. *Ferguson* in 1896. Again, the Court upheld discrimination while Harlan dissented alone. The state law was constitutional, held the Court, because it did not touch civil rights, but only so-called social rights, an odd logic since presumably when the state acts, the act is civil by definition. In justifying its reasoning, the Court allowed the state of Louisiana to rely on "the established usages, customs and traditions of the people" – which were racist, of course – "and with a view to the promotion of their comfort, and the preservation of the public peace and good order."[22]

Harlan dismissed all of the Court's legal precedents as meaningless – those from before the Civil War were irrelevant and those directly after the war were

20 *Civil Rights Cases*, 109 U.S. 3, 34 (1883).

21 Clipping, "Harlan for President," *Louisville Evening Post*, October 16, 1894, Family Scrapbook (*Income Tax Case*), JMH Papers, UofL.

22 *Plessy* v. *Ferguson*, 163 U.S. 537, 550 (1896).

tainted by racism. Again, he referred to *Dred Scott*, the decision he thought of as a "special Providence." Harlan argued that the Thirteenth and Fourteenth Amendments had overturned these precedents by prohibiting the slavery and discrimination which Taney had upheld in *Dred Scott*. He appealed to whites, as whites, to uphold the achievements of the Civil War and to fulfill the American mission. Anglo-Saxons had long told themselves that their race had a special ability to establish free, democratic governments under the rule of law. "Every true man has pride of race," Harlan wrote, but the peculiar racial superiority of whites was best expressed by obedience to the laws governing their free government, and under this government that meant respecting the legal rights of the black race. In words that became famous, Harlan wrote: "in the view of the Constitution, in the eye of the law, there is in this country no superior, dominant ruling class of citizens. There is no caste here. Our Constitution is color-blind and neither knows nor tolerates classes among citizens." By allowing the states to incorporate racial prejudice into law, the Supreme Court had betrayed the providential mission set out by the founders, a mission taken one step further by the Civil War generation which had destroyed slavery. These hopes for the American mission explain the anger and sorrow with which Harlan wrote in *Plessy*, "We boast of the freedom enjoyed by our people above all other peoples. But it is difficult to reconcile that boast with a state of the law which, practically, puts the brand of servitude and degradation upon a large class of our fellow-citizens, our equals before the law." The doctrine of separate-but-equal could not justify the Court's decision: "The thin disguise of 'equal' accommodations for passengers in railroad coaches will not mislead any one, nor atone for the wrong this day done."[23]

Boasting of freedom was what Anglo-Saxons, "the custodians of the principles of liberty which must prevail to the end," should be able to do according to Harlan.[24] This is why he became so excited at the idea of the United States as liberator during the Spanish-American War and so disappointed when it became clear that America was becoming an empire that ruled other peoples. Great naval victories might be achieved on the Fourth of July in 1898, he wrote President William McKinley. Filipino insurgents who balked at American rule instead of independence were like the Confederates who fired on Fort Sumter, Harlan told the president.[25] But his war fever subsided once he realized that the American administration wanted to hold onto new territories,

23 *Plessy* v. *Ferguson*, 163 U.S. 537, 559, 562 (1896).

24 Harlan Lectures, October 14, 1897, p. 16.

25 On Harlan's war fever and cure, see Przybyszewski, *The Republic according to John Marshall Harlan*, 125ff.

as dependent colonies, not as future American states. So upset was Harlan when a decision on tariff laws raised the question of the status of Puerto Rico, he confided to William Howard Taft in 1901 that "I stayed away from church to do the work" of writing his dissent on a Sunday. "Horrible!" he wrote.[26]

Harlan was writing the first of several dissents to a group of decisions called the Insular Cases. These cases determined the legal status of the several territories newly won from Spain. Did their inhabitants have all the rights guaranteed in the US Constitution? To Harlan, it was clear that they had to, while other Americans, leery of peoples they considered untutored in or unfit for self-government, were not sure. Justice Henry B. Brown had written in his majority opinion in *Downes* v. *Bidwell* that it was enough for the administration to rely upon "principles of natural justice inherent in the Anglo-Saxon character which need no expression in constitutions or statutes to give them effect."[27] Harlan pointed out that the American founders had fought Anglo-Saxons across the Atlantic and written a constitution precisely in order to protect their rights. If Americans no longer wanted to ensure justice for all, Harlan wrote, amend the Constitution. Harlan dissented again when the Court majority determined that the right to trial by jury did not extend to the territory of the Philippines. His brethren were applying the Constitution as though it read, "The trial of all crimes, *except in cases of impeachment, and except where Filipinos are concerned,* shall be by jury." Such an idea was "revolting" to his mind.[28] In a speech at a mass meeting on foreign missions at the General Assembly of the Presbyterian Church in the USA in 1905, Harlan spoke unhappily of imperialism: "We have tacked upon our republican system a colonial system, covering races who are practically our subjects – can never be our fellow-citizens."[29] This remark indicates another limit to Harlan's understanding of race. While he saw African-Americans and assimilated Native-Americans as included in the civil and political regime of the United States, Harlan balked at granting citizenship to Chinese-Americans because they were pagans and "a race utterly foreign to us and never will assimilate with us" whose parents simply happened to be upon

26 JMH to William Howard Taft, July 22, 1901, William Howard Taft Papers, Library of Congress.

27 *Downes* v. *Bidwell,* 182 U.S. 244, 280 (1901). Harlan had voted with the majority in the first Insular Case, *Delima* v. *Bidwell,* 182 U.S. 1 (1901). For a recent defense of Harlan's dissents, see Eric Schepard, "The Great Dissenter's Greatest Dissents: The First Justice Harlan, the 'Color-Blind' Constitution and the Meaning of His Dissents in the 'Insular Cases' for the War on Terror," *The American Journal of Legal History* 48.2 (2006): 119–146.

28 *Dorr* v. *United States,* 195 U.S. 138, 156 (1904). Harlan had also dissented when the Court declared that the Bill of Rights did not apply to Hawaii in *Hawaii* v. *Mankichi,* 190 U.S. 197 (1903).

29 "The General Assembly," *The Interior* 36 (1905), 655.

American soil for their birth.[30] Harlan objected to imperialism both because it led to violations of the Constitution *and* involved peoples whose citizenship troubled him because of their race. Because Harlan's views of Anglo-Saxon identity were the source of his civil rights jurisprudence, modern scholars are bound to be disappointed when they go looking for the natural rights egalitarian they expect.[31]

Harlan used less explicitly religious rhetoric in his judicial decisions than he did in his public talks and private papers, and this has misled some scholars into underestimating the role of his faith in his understanding of the law. Take his ruling on Sunday laws. On the one hand, American Protestants objected generally to anything that looked like a union of church and state as smacking of Roman Catholic popery, yet insisted that the Sunday be kept holy (and quiet) by people who did not share their faith. Judges like Harlan found ways to admit and dismiss the religious character of Sunday laws at the same time. In 1896, Harlan upheld a law that punished a railroad superintendent for sending out a freight train on a Sunday in Georgia. He admitted that "the day on which the running of freight trains is prohibited is kept by many under a sense of religious duty."[32] Notice they "kept" the day, an echo of the distinctive language of the King James Version of the Bible which commands believers, "To Remember the sabbath day, to keep it holy."[33] Yet Harlan justified the statute entirely in terms of the state's interest in providing its citizens with a day of rest in order to keep them healthy. It is a mistake to take this secular language as proof of Harlan's indifference to quiet Sundays as a Christian duty that the law should protect.[34]

Off the bench, Harlan made plain his insistence on keeping the Sabbath holy, scolded his fellow citizens for failing to do so, and made himself a fine example of a public advocate of Sabbatarianism for other Presbyterians. Harlan denounced Sunday dinners in Washington as "an outrage" on a day

30 Harlan joined Justice Melville W. Fuller's dissent in *United States* v. *Wong Kim Ark*, 169 U.S. 649 (1898); see Harlan Lectures, March 19, 1898, p. 268 on the Chinese. Harlan dissented when the Court refused citizenship to an assimilated Native American in *Elk* v. *Wilkins*, 112 U.S. 94 (1884).

31 See Earl M. Maltz, "Only Partially Color-Blind: John Marshall Harlan's View of Race and the Constitution," *Georgia State University Law Review* 12:4 (June 1996): 973–1016; and Gabriel J. Chin, "The *Plessy* Myth: Justice Harlan on the Chinese Cases," *Iowa Law Review* 82 (Oct. 1996): 151–182.

32 *Hennington* v. *Georgia*, 163 U.S. 299, 304 (1896) which was followed in *Petit* v. *Minnesota*, 177 U.S. 164 (1900).

33 Exodus 20:9.

34 See Steven K. Green, who concluded Harlan "was not sympathetic" to the idea of the Christian nation, in Green, "Justice David Josiah Brewer and the 'Christian Nation' Maxim," *Albany Law Review* 63. 2 (1999), 469.

that "should be devoted to other and higher things." He blamed foreign diplomats used to the livelier (and Catholic) "Continental Sunday" who saw nothing wrong with dinner parties, golf games, and musicales.[35] He condemned Sunday mail delivery as a violation of a holy day, and warned that "A people without a Sabbath have a rotten social organization and cannot exert a beneficent or permanent influence upon the world."[36]

Patriotism and religious faith blended throughout Harlan's life. In 1903, he presided over the celebration of the New York Avenue Presbyterian Church's 100th anniversary which President Theodore Roosevelt and other Washington notables attended. Harlan was serving as a church elder then. The arches within the church were decorated on one side with a banner with the words, Christ, King, Kingdom and Covenant, the other boasted the seal of the Presbyterian Church in the USA and the words *Christus Levatus Salvator*, while the middle arch held aloft an American flag. Harlan opened the event by asking everyone to sing "Onward, Christian Soldiers," which he called "the battle hymn of the Christian Church." He ended the event by asking all to join the choir in "My Country, 'tis of thee" which ends with these lines: "Long may our land be bright/ With freedom's holy light;/ Protect us by Thy Might, Great God, our King." In between, he made much of the fact that the church had preserved the very pew where regularly sat Abraham Lincoln, the "Martyr President," "the Saviour of his Country."[37]

Harlan identified Presbyterianism with his country. It was a faith historically and peculiarly suited to republics. For "it teaches man to read the Bible, and invited every one to freely utter his opinions ... " and "teaches him to resist, as did his fathers, any authority that would assume to trample upon the rights of man." Harlan pointed to the American Revolution when Presbyterian elders and pastors played key roles in politics and battles, and English opponents complained of the Presbyterian Rebellion. It was a fact, said Harlan, "there was no Presbyterian Tory to be found anywhere during the Revolution." He noted the parallels between the US Constitution and the Presbyterian Constitution. Both protected the individual from "arbitrary power."[38]

35 Quoted in Presbyterian Church in the USA General Assembly, *Minutes of the General Assembly of the Presbyterian Church in the United States of America*, new series, v.11 (1911), 46.

36 Clipping, *Christian Observer*, n.d., JMH Papers, UofL; Morrow, "Talks with Notable Men."

37 New York Avenue Presbyterian Church, *The Centennial of the New York Avenue Presbyterian Church. Washington, DC, 1803–1903* (Washington, DC, 1904), 9–10, 66, 99–100, 92, 96.

38 John Marshall Harlan, "The Court in the American System of Government," *The Westminster* 30 (Apr. 8, 1905): 9–11, 10, a speech to the Presbyterian Social Union of Philadelphia.

Harlan exaggerated these links, of course, but his views made it all the easier for him to see his life's work as a spiritual and legal whole.

Race raised questions for Harlan as a Presbyterian as well as a judge, and his work in both religion and law demonstrates both his effort on behalf of civil rights and its limits. We see the righteousness in 1905 when the Washington City Presbytery met to vote on whether the larger Presbyterian Church in the USA, of which it was a part, should welcome in the Cumberland Presbyterian Church which was all white and wanted to stay that way. Organizing presbyteries by race instead of place offended Harlan who "put himself on record" against separate presbyteries "even if the whites and blacks agree mutually to have them." (Some blacks might have agreed to separation so they might avoid white racists and hang onto power within predominantly black presbyteries.) "Let us," said Harlan, "stand in the way of the fathers and say to the world that as far as our church is concerned, we are race blind and color blind." Harlan used the word "fathers" to speak of both the American founders and the church fathers, and called for color-blindness in both law and religion. "Long continued applaud ... followed those noble words," reported a black newspaper, but the Washington presbytery voted to accept segregation in the church, and "thus put itself on record in favor of this ecclesiastical infamy."[39]

Harlan may have been the "grand old friend of the Afro-Americans," as the black newspaper put it, but he was unwilling to confront the more controversial kinds of race-mixing. In *Cumming* v. *Richmond Board of Education* in 1899, Harlan refused to grant an injunction to make the public school board close its white high school until it had re-opened its black high school. He described the board's shifting of monies to the black grammar schools as a good-faith effort, noted the presence of private black high schools that charged no more tuition than the public one had charged, and suggested the petitioners would have done better to have asked that the black high school be re-opened than the white one closed. The terse opinion in *Cumming* reads nothing like Harlan's impassioned dissents in favor of civil rights, such as *Berea College* v. *Commonwealth of Kentucky* from 1908. In fact, when faced with a statutory attack on interracial Berea College, an integrated, Christian, private college in Kentucky, Harlan invoked "the Almighty" Himself in his dissent. If a legislature could violate a teacher's God-given ability to impart knowledge regardless of race, warned Harlan, then it could bar "the assembling of white and colored children in the same Sabbath-school" or "at the communion table in the same Christian church." Despite this bold and angry

39 Archibald H. Grimké, "WHITED SEPULCHRE," *The New York Age*, vol. XVIII, issue 36, April 20, 1905, p. 1.

language, Harlan made a point in *Berea College* of saying that he was not ruling on "public schools, established at the pleasure of the State ...."[40] But surely, if it was wrong constitutionally and spiritually to separate children in Sunday school, was it not just as wrong to separate them in grade school?

We can see the same wobbly logic in 1905, when Harlan served on the Standing Committee on Freedmen of the Presbyterian General Assembly. One of almost two dozen ministers and elders, Harlan did not write the committee report but one imagines he influenced it. The report repudiated the then-popular idea that blacks should be funneled into education for manual labor in favor of giving blacks "an equal chance" to become laborers, artisans, doctors, teachers, preachers, and leaders. Yet it also rejected "assimilation as destructive as it is repugnant," then asked "can two races live together, and both be independent and their identify be preserved?" Yes, the committee answered, "look at the Jew."[41] The awkwardness of urging blacks to be both Christians and like Jews betrays the difficulty even well-meaning whites had in imagining whites and blacks as civic equals with entirely separate social lives.

The most intimate of social interaction – marriage – had almost come before the Court two decades earlier. *Pace* v. *Alabama* challenged the constitutionality of a law that punished interracial marriage (as did most American states), and punished interracial sexual partners outside of marriage more harshly than those of the same race.[42] In this instance of extramarital relations, the unanimous Court reasoned that both the white and black partner were punished equally, and upheld the law. Harlan voted here for a doctrine of separate but equal that he would reject years later in *Plessy* v. *Ferguson*.

Interracial sexual relations were the third rail of nineteenth-century politics – too dangerous to touch – and raised the specter of sexual abuse and sin as well as white fears of interracial mixing. The Rev. Francis J. Grimké, a fellow Presbyterian, and one of the mixed-race nephews of Angelina and Sarah Grimké, the famous white abolitionist workers, told a story in 1916 about Harlan that shows how both men deflected talk of social equality. Grimké was writing in response to a letter from a white minister who accused him of advocating "intermarriage of the races" in a sermon that did no such thing. Grimké scolded the man for worrying about interracial marriage when he should be worrying about "the illicit

40 *Berea College* v. *Commonwealth of Kentucky*, 211 U.S. 45, 68 (1908).

41 Presbyterian Church in the USA, *Minutes of the General Assembly of the Presbyterian Church in the United States of America*, new series s.2 v.5 no.1 (1905): 63.

42 *Pace* v. *Alabama*, 106 U.S. 583 (1883).

intercourse between the races, which has gone on for centuries, and still goes on."[43] Then he told about a talk Harlan had given in which Harlan recounted how he had faced the question while still a Republican politician in Kentucky. When Harlan argued for political and civil equality for blacks, a man charged him with advocating social equality as well. "The man who made the charge, was at that very time, living with a colored woman," according to Harlan. "If that isn't social equality, what is it? . . . If I was teaching social equality, he certainly was practicing it." So Harlan both denied he was interested in social equality and identified it with interracial immorality and sexual exploitation, issues which the Grimké family had long struggled against. The Grimké brothers were born of a slave mother and the white man who owned her, but did not marry her, and their white half-brother sold them as slaves after their father's death. But while Harlan avoided addressing anti-miscegenation laws, the Grimkés fought them on principle.

Of course, when Harlan shied away from addressing issues of social equality, he created inconsistencies in his legal record of civil rights. To conclude that he only cared about "the largely symbolic efforts" of de-segregating public accommodations which affected the lives of a handful of middle-class blacks, as one scholar writes of him, is to ignore other decisions.[44] In *Clyatt* v. *United States*, Harlan concurred in a case involving peonage – the binding of people to work out their debts, an attempt to recreate slavery in another form – insisting that the facts disclosed "barbarities of the worst kind against these negroes."[45] And Harlan dissented in another debt peonage case when the Court refused to rule on the constitutionality of the law itself because he was so eager to destroy peonage laws.[46]

Harlan lived by the overarching legal philosophy of legal formalism which held that the rules of law transcended time. This was an approach to law that reflected his religious faith. As he told his constitutional law students in 1897, "there is little or no scope for originality" in what he could tell them.[47] The courts simply applied the law as circumstances came before them. What to do when history presented Harlan with constitutional illogic? It clearly did so

43 Sol. C. Dickey to F. J. Grimké, February 7, 1916, and Francis J. Grimké to Sol. C. Dickey, February 11, 1916, in Francis J. Grimké, *The Works of Francis J. Grimké*, 4 vols. (Washington, DC: Associated Publishers), 4:148–149.

44 J. Morgan Kousser, "Separate but Not Equal: The Supreme Court's First Decision on Racial Discrimination in Schools," *Journal of Southern History* 46 (1980): 17–44, 42.

45 *Clyatt* v. *United States*, 197 U.S. 207, 223 (1905).

46 *Bailey* v. *Alabama* (I), 211 U.S. 452 (1908); the Court finally condemned the peonage law in *Bailey* v. *Alabama* (II), 219 U.S. 219 (1911) with Harlan voting with the majority.

47 Harlan Lectures, October 14, 1897, p. 14.

when he tried to explain to his students how West Virginia had been made a state out of the existing state of Virginia in clear violation of Article 4, Section 3 of the US Constitution. Harlan tried several ways, but finally gave up by saying, "I am not sure that I understand myself on that question."[48] To admit that the Constitution had been violated by the very government that it created would have meant acceptance of the philosophy of legal realism which holds that the law changes with the vagaries of humankind. At their most cynical, legal realists say that the law depends on what the judge had for breakfast. A judge happy with his bacon and eggs will give one kind of ruling; a judge who grumbled over his toast will issue another kind. Harlan found legal realism impossible to accept even when legal formalism placed him in a logical muddle.

We can see humility more than muddle in Harlan's thought when theological questions arose as they did when one of his college-age sons asked him about eternal punishment. The degree or extent of the punishment "is not a question which need concern us very much in this life," wrote Harlan in reply. Yet he did turn to the Bible to find as much of an answer as he could. He recounted to his son the story of the rich man who was surprised to find himself in hell while the beggar Lazarus was in Abraham's bosom. But he advised him: "I do not bother my brain with these subtle inquiries" for "if we could solve them all we should know as much as God does . . . ."[49] Harlan stressed the limits of human reason in both law and religion.

Harlan's ideal for judgeship came from the Bible, a book that certainly stresses human frailty. When one of the district judges in the Harlan's federal circuit stepped down from the bench, Harlan turned for appropriate words to the First Book of Samuel and quoted to him from what must be one of the first recorded judicial retirement speeches.[50] Samuel went before all Israel and asked if he had been a righteous judge. "Witness me before the Lord and before his anointed: whose ox have I taken? Or whose ass have I taken or whom have I defrauded? Whom have I oppressed? Or of whose hand have I received any bribe to blind my eyes therewith? And I will restore it to you." None was the answer. Samuel had neither oppressed nor defrauded, nor "taken aught of any man's hand." Samuel's was an ideal that Harlan may never have reached, but it guided his life in the law.

48 Harlan Lectures, April 2, 1898, p. 290.

49 Quoted in Beth, *John Marshall Harlan*, 149–150. The Bible story is from Luke 16:26.

50 We have the district judge's letter, not Harlan's; Romanzo Bunn to JMH, January 18, 1905, JMH Papers, UofL; I Samuel 12:3–4.

11

Judicial Conservatism and Protestant Faith: The Case of Justice David J. Brewer

Linda Przybyszewski

David J. Brewer is responsible for the most famous, or infamous, declaration on religion and the law by a justice of the United States Supreme Court in the late nineteenth century. *Church of the Holy Trinity* v. *United States* had nothing to do with religious liberty laws. It was a test case to draw attention to the objectionable features of a federal immigration statute by asking that the government apply it to an English minister recently hired by an Episcopalian church in New York City. Drawing on rules of judicial interpretation, and considering the intent of Congress in passing the law, Brewer refused to apply it to the new pastor in 1892. Congress had been discussing the problems of imported manual laborers and not men of the cloth when it passed the law, Brewer noted.[1] "But beyond all these matters" of congressional intent in regulating labor, he continued, "no purpose of action against religion can be imputed to any legislation, state or national, because this is a religious people . . . this is a Christian nation."[2] From Christians celebrating Brewer's words, "there was so much twanging of the joyous harp," according to one critic at the time.[3] Now, legal scholars rightly point out that the proof Brewer offered for his Christian nation declaration was not particularly impressive – a strange hodge-podge of religious pronouncements drawn from American history – but they err in trying to dismiss it as *obiter dicta*, that is, as judicial chatter having nothing to do with the rule in the case.[4]

[1] Congress exempted ministers before the case was decided, see Carol Chomsky, "Unlocking the Mysteries of Holy Trinity: Spirit, Letter, and History in Statutory Interpretation," *Columbia Law Review* 100 (May 2000): 901–956, 935–938.

[2] *Church of the Holy Trinity* v. *United States*, 143 U.S. 457, 465, 471 (1892). See also Linda Przybyszewski, "Judicial Conservatism and Protestant Faith: The Case of Justice David J. Brewer," *Journal of American History* 91 (Sept. 2004): 471–496.

[3] Letter to the Editor, W. A. Croffut, "Nations Have No Religion," *The Washington Post*, March 20, 1905: 9

[4] See Leo Pfeffer, *Church, State, and Freedom* (rev. edn., Boston: Beacon Press 1967), 86; Michael J. Brodhead, *David J. Brewer: The Life of a Supreme Court Justice, 1837–1910*

Brewer's Christian nation declaration is important not as sound legal doctrine, but as telling evidence of how many nineteenth-century Protestant judges viewed their country and its laws. Questions of religious liberty rarely appeared before the Supreme Court at this time, and explicit religious language was equally rare in Brewer's judicial decisions, yet religious faith was an important element in judicial thought. It undergirded the Court's opposition to certain new kinds of economic regulation as an interference with the right of a man to use his God-given faculties to get ahead.[5] The Court's rulings provoked an especially loud national outcry in 1895. That year, it held that the Sherman Anti-Trust Act could not be used against a giant firm that controlled 98 percent of the country's sugar-refining business.[6] Then, Justice Brewer delivered an opinion that upheld the federal government's power to interfere in a railroad strike through the courts in the name of interstate commerce; and Eugene Debs, leader of the American Railway Union, spent six months in prison for contempt of court.[7] The Court also struck down the federal income tax as unconstitutional.[8] While Brewer praised the anti-income tax opinion as "majestic and immortal," that decision sparked a nation-wide campaign to amend the Constitution to make it possible for Congress to pass income tax laws that eventually succeeded in 1913.[9] Legal critics of the time gave the Court led by Chief Justice Melville Weston Fuller from 1888 to 1910 a reputation for heartless and mindless jurisprudence.

Following the lead of Justice Oliver Wendell Holmes, Jr., who dissented from the labor regulation case of *Lochner* v. *New York* in 1905, it has been all too easy for critics of the Fuller Court then and scholars now to dismiss judicial conservatism as a form of Social Darwinism.[10] In fact, it was religious

(Carbondale: Southern Illinois University Press, 1994), 111; Stuart Banner, "When Christianity Was Part of the Common Law," *Law and History Review* 16 (Spring 1998): 27–62, 42–43. Justice Rufus W. Peckham treated the Christian nation doctrine as one of the legal rules found in *Holy Trinity* in *United States* v. *Laws*, 163 U.S. 258, 264 (1896).

5 Women were denied the same freedom of contract for their own protection; see *Muller* v. *Oregon*, 208 U.S. 412 (1908).

6 *United States* v. *E. C. Knight Co.*, 156 U.S. 1 (1895).

7 Debs violated the federal circuit court order to desist from leading the strike, see *In re Debs*, 158 U.S. 564 (1895); the US attorney general had also deputized men to run the trains.

8 The income tax case was heard twice in *Pollock* v. *Farmers' Loan and Trust* (I), 157 U.S. 429 (1895), *Pollock* v. *Farmers' Loan and Trust* (II), 158 U.S. 601 (1895).

9 This is the Sixteenth Amendment to the US Constitution. David J. Brewer, *The Income Tax Cases and Some Comments Thereon, An Address Delivered on the Invitation of the Faculty, before the Graduating Class of the Law Department of the State University of Iowa, at the Annual Commencement, June 8, 1898* (Iowa City: State University of Iowa, 1898), 4.

10 See *Lochner* v. *New York*, 198 U.S. 45 (1905), which misled Richard Hofstadter in his *Social Darwinism in American Thought, 1860–1915* (Philadelphia: University of Pennsylvania Press,

faith, not the new science of evolution, that men like Brewer depended on when they struck down laws designed to protect workers. Justice Brewer directly contradicted the idealization of brute force which made the rounds in the evolutionary theories of Charles Darwin and Herbert Spencer by having his calling cards read "Right Is Might."[11] Nor was Brewer shy about touting Christianity as essential to the American Republic. In 1905, he published the lectures that he gave at Haverford College as *The United States A Christian Nation*.[12]

That volume is merely the tip of the iceberg. Brewer began publishing in the 1880s with publications like *The Western Homestead*, went on to religious publications such as the *Sunday School Times* and the *Ram's Horn*, and secular ones like the *Atlantic Monthly*. Brewer spoke to bar associations, insurance agents, and West Point cadets. He wrote on the Bible, on lynching, and on the sacred rights of property, making him an unparalleled source of conservative judicial thinking. But his writings off the bench have been neglected by scholars. As a result, one could remark that Brewer's legal decisions were "sustained by a spirit *approaching* religious faith" (emphasis added) when his other writings make clear that his judicial decisions were sustained *by* religious faith.[13] Brewer's writings offer us a way to delve into the religious foundation of conservative legal thought during an era "when religion was not just something to think about," as one scholar of religion puts it, "but was a *way* of thinking."[14] Brewer's discussions of the law of private

1944), and in turn influenced such scholars as Arnold Paul, *Conservative Crisis and the Rule of Law: Attitudes of Bar and Bench, 1887–1895* (Ithaca: Cornell University Press, 1960), 22–23, n. 10; and William Wiecek, *The Lost World of Classical Legal Thought: Law and Ideology in America, 1886–1937* (New York: Oxford University Press, 1998), 82–85. For a correction, see Joseph Frasier Wall, "Social Darwinism and Constitutional Law with Special Reference to *Lochner* v. *New York*," *Annals of Science* 33 (Sept. 1976): 457–480, 465–476; and Robert C. Bannister, *Social Darwinism: Science and Myth in Anglo-American Social Thought* (Philadelphia: Temple University Press, 1979).

11 Joseph Gordon Hylton defended Brewer in "David Josiah Brewer and the Christian Constitution," *Marquette Law Review* 81 (Winter 1998): 417–425.

12 David J. Brewer, *The United States a Christian Nation* (Philadelphia: J. C. Winston, 1905), which prompted Hassler's book noted below and "NATION NOT CHRISTIAN: DR. SILVERMAN SAYS SO: Justice Brewer's Book Criticised by Jewish Rabbi," *New-York Tribune*, February 26, 1906: 5; "ARE WE A CHRISTIAN NATION?" *Reformed Church Messenger* 75.26 (June 28, 1906): 4; and Isaac Hassler, *A Reply to Justice Brewer's Lectures: "The United States a Christian Nation"* (Philadelphia: Young Men's Hebrew Association of Philadelphia, 1908).

13 Owen M. Fiss, *Troubled Beginnings of the Modern State, 1888–1910* (New York: Macmillan, 1993), 56.

14 C. John Sommerville, "Secular Society/Religious Population: Our Tacit Rules for Using the Term 'Secularization,'" *Journal for the Scientific Study of Religion* 37.2 (1998): 249–253, 253.

property and criminal responsibility most clearly demonstrate the effect of religious faith on the making of law, while his vision of the coming millennium lay back of his forays into international law.

David Josiah Brewer's background made him the perfect justice to preach to the nation on how law relied upon religion. He was born abroad in what is now part of Turkey because his parents were Congregationalist missionaries, the Reverend Josiah Brewer and Emilia Field, the daughter of a minister. His uncles on his mother's side include David Dudley Field, who led the movement for legal codification, and Stephen J. Field, who sat on the US Supreme Court from 1863 to 1897. Brewer attended Wesleyan College and finished his degree at Yale College in 1856. He read law in the office of his uncle D. D. Field and graduated from Albany Law School in 1858. He went west to practice law where he also helped organize the First Congregational Church of Leavenworth, Kansas.[15] He served first as a state judge and was later elected to the Kansas Supreme Court where he served from 1871 to 1884. He joined the ranks of federal judges with an appointment to the Eighth Circuit Court in 1884 and stayed there until he was nominated to the US Supreme Court in 1889. Brewer and Justice Rufus W. Peckham became the center of a conservative voting bloc until his death in 1910.[16]

When Brewer declared that the United States was a Christian nation, he seemed aware of yet unconcerned by the complicated story of religion in America. In truth, the United States was led and peopled by a mix of religious believers from the start. Many were Christians who thought the new state governments should tax to support all the various churches, like Patrick Henry who led an unsuccessful fight to do that in Virginia. Others, like Thomas Jefferson, were Deists who thought Jesus Christ an exemplar among ethical teachers, but dismissed the miracles in the Bible as fables. Jefferson wanted government to keep its hands off individuals and their beliefs. Some Christians agreed, including Baptists in New England, who were appalled that any government would lay its sullied hands on religious faith through taxation even in support of churches. In Virginia, the crucial opponents rounding up signatures on petitions to stop Henry's tax plan were evangelicals. The religious revivals that followed the founding generation gathered more Americans into the churches, but the churches themselves multiplied and divided throughout the nineteenth century. Nor did the skepticism of men like Jefferson ever disappear. Arguments over the exact role religion should play in the Republic continued as the population grew more diverse with the

15 On Brewer's religious activities, see Brodhead, *David J. Brewer*, 9.

16 On Brewer's influence, see Fiss, *Troubled Beginnings*, 33.

arrival of hundreds of thousands of Catholics following the potato famine in Ireland in the 1840s.

Brewer's choice of documents in *Church of the Holy Trinity* drew upon this mixed history. He pointed first to a colonial grant from 1584 that barred the entry of anyone save Church of England followers. Some of his quotations announced more broadly that early Americans had acted upon "Christian faith" like the Pilgrims on the Mayflower in 1620. Other quotations announced that the purpose of a colony was to protect "Freedom of Consciences" as did the charter of privileges of William Penn in 1701. Some documents that Brewer quoted spoke of God and failed to mention Christ at all, like the Declaration of Independence and the Illinois Constitution of 1870. Brewer ended by quoting the First Amendment to the United States Constitution prohibiting an establishment of religion and guaranteeing the free exercise of religion. Despite the wide variety of positions on religion found in these documents, Brewer claimed "there is no dissonance in these declarations."[17]

There was no dissonance to Brewer's mind because of the way he thought about his faith and freedom. Like many American Protestants of the nineteenth century, Brewer equated religion with Christianity, Christianity with Protestantism, and Protestantism with religious freedom despite the many exceptions to all of these equations before and during his lifetime. At the end of the *Church of the Holy Trinity* decision, he argued that a law barring a foreign Catholic cardinal or a Jewish rabbi from immigrating into the United States would be just as objectionable as applying the labor law now before the Court to the Episcopalian minister.[18] But if "American life as expressed by its laws, its business, its customs, and its society" added up to a Christian nation according to Brewer, why bother with immigrating rabbis at all?[19] After all, that a Christian state needed an established church privileged by government was a common enough idea in many of the original American colonies. But later American Protestants needed to address the First Amendment's ban on a national established church. They did so by making that ban into an essential way of proving the Christian character of the nation. Brewer called the ban on an established church "one of the highest credentials to the title of a Christian nation." Why? Because "the great thought of the Master"– as Brewer often called Jesus Christ – "was that over the human

17 *Church of the Holy Trinity v. United States*, 143 U.S. 457, 466–470 (1892).

18 Ibid., 472.

19 Ibid., 471.

soul there was no earthly sovereign." The First Amendment ban on an established church proved the Christian nature of the American Republic, "where everyone is welcome."[20]

Precisely because Brewer, and many other Protestants, believed both in the United States as a Christian nation and in the United States as a nation devoted to religious liberty, they had trouble when the first belief led them to impose their religious practices on others, while the second belief led them to deny they were doing exactly that. For example, state Sabbath laws punished anyone for keeping their shops open on Sundays even when their own faith required closing up shop on Saturdays as was the case for Jews and others. State judges denied a religious motive for such laws, and the Supreme Court agreed in 1896 that the state was merely looking after the health of workers in passing Sunday laws.[21] But such efforts troubled those who found themselves in the minority. Brewer's comment in *Church of the Holy Trinity* about an immigrating rabbi did not reassure American Jews who were appalled by his Christian nation declaration and the book expanding on the argument in 1905.[22] One wrote that, while the majority of Americans might be Christians, the Constitution was meant to restrict "the brutal exercise of its power by a majority."[23]

Brewer's Christian faith actually reflected the evolution of religion in the modern era and its diversity. Although his father had been trained at Andover Seminary when it was trying to recapture older Calvinist traditions, Justice Brewer was a liberal member of the Congregational Church who coped with modern challenges without giving up belief in God or the Bible. He dismissed traditional Christian doctrines, like original sin and eternal damnation, going so far as to joke that a man who worried himself about the Calvinist doctrine of predestination was merely suffering from an attack of acute indigestion.[24] Brewer did not read the Bible literally although he thought it contained eternal truths of morality. For example, Jesus may or may not have been

20 David J. Brewer, *American Citizenship* (New York: Charles Scribner's Sons, 1902), 21–22. For a similar logic, see the Reverend Sanford H. Cobb, *The Rise of Religious Liberty in America: A History* (New York: Macmillan, 1902), 528.

21 The Supreme Court echoed the health argument in *Hennington* v. *Georgia*, 163 U.S. 299, 304 (1896).

22 See Robert T. Handy, *Undermined Establishment: Church-State Relations in America, 1880–1920* (Princeton: Princeton University Press, 1991), 175–176; "Justice Brewer on Cranks," *The Washington Post*, January 28, 1894: 4; Edward Thomson, "ART. VII.–THE RELATION OF RELIGION TO OUR GOVERNMENT," 15 no. 2 *The Methodist Review* (Nov. 1899): 930.

23 Hassler, *A Reply to Justice Brewer's Lectures*, 20.

24 David J. Brewer, *American Citizenship* (New York: Charles Scribner's Sons, 1902), 92.

born of a virgin, wrote Brewer, but Jesus's words came directly from God. Brewer found ways to explain that both natural science and religion were true. For example, when it came to judging whether Joshua had made the sun stand still, Brewer argued that science described "these phenomenon as they are," while the Bible described them "as they appear[ed]" to people at the time.[25] Most Bible passages that people disputed were actually parables, he explained. So the six days of creation in the Book of Genesis, for example, were "but an outline sketch of the gradual fitting up of the world for the habitation of man, the general truth of which science continues to affirm."[26]

Brewer also yielded to some of the challenges to traditional Christianity made by the higher critics of the Bible. They treated the Good Book as they did any other book: by studying it as a historical document created at a certain point in time. Brewer acknowledged that the Bible contained human errors through "interpolations," "additions and omissions," and chronological inaccuracies. But he insisted that "it contains the truth of God."[27] Brewer was not a zealot for his own beliefs. He explained that he had become tolerant of the views of other Christian believers after his many years teaching Sunday school. Theology, creeds, and church government were less important than what Brewer called religion and life. There may be many different Christian churches, he wrote in 1904, but we "are all Christians."[28]

If Brewer could reconcile his more modern faith with natural science, he had a harder time with certain strains of the new social sciences which challenged traditional beliefs about individual free will and the role government should play in the economy. His religious faith served as a bulwark against new economic regulation. In law, businesses considered to be affected with a public interest, such as transportation companies, had long been considered subject to government regulation, and many state legislators saw changes in the size and scope of the commercial economy in the nineteenth century as reason to extend those regulations to other kinds of companies. Many Americans also wanted government protection for workers faced with enormous and powerful corporations with whom they could hardly bargain as equals. While the Court and Brewer upheld most of the regulations that came before them, both struck down enough important state and federal laws to rile reformers.[29]

25 David J. Brewer, "Science v. the Bible," clipping, folder 228, box 7, Brewer Family Papers, Manuscripts and Archives, Yale University Library. Hereafter cited as Brewer Family Papers.

26 David J. Brewer, "What I Have Gained from Bible Teaching," *The Congregationalist and Christian World* 89.49 (Dec. 3, 1904): 813–814.

27 Ibid.

28 Ibid.

29 See Hylton, "Brewer and the Christian Constitution," 423–424.

Brewer became known in 1892, and among later scholars, for his dissent from *Budd* v. *New York* in which he dismissed the idea that grain elevators were affected with a public interest and subject to regulation with this remark: "the paternal theory of government is to me odious." Just as important, although often ignored, was his paraphrase of the Apostle Paul: "There is scarcely any property in whose use the public has no interest. No man liveth unto himself alone, and no man's property is beyond the touch of another's welfare."[30] Because of the conventions about how judges should write their opinions while serving on the bench, such Bible quotations show up rarely in Brewer's more than 600 legal opinions.

But they show up constantly in Brewer's public talks and they make clear that his judicial conservatism stood on a bedrock of biblical interpretation. For example, Brewer made his religious vision of the legal profession abundantly clear in his off-the-bench talks. He explained in one address that law "seeks to incarnate in human life those lofty conceptions which dwell in the mind of the Infinite, to make real the purposes of justice and to bring nearer the promised day" of the Second Coming of Christ.[31] When he spoke to the Baltimore Bar Association in 1903, he urged the lawyers before him to serve the Republic in words becoming a preacher: "It is written by the finger of the Almighty on the everlasting tablets of the universe that no nation can endure and prosper into the web and woof of whose life does not run one thread, and that the golden thread of equal, absolute and universal justice."[32] Not that they should expect to achieve that absolute justice in their lifetimes, but they should aim for it. Brewer's prestigious position on the bench was flourished by the religious press as a sign of the influence of faith. When *The Congregationalist and Christian World* published his article on "What I Have Gained from Bible Teaching" in 1904, the accompanying headline read "A Personal Testimony from a Member of the Supreme Court."[33] Behind

30 *Budd* v. *New York*, 143 U.S. 517, 549 (1892); Romans 14:7 (AV); Brewer was not following the text: the Apostle Paul was suggesting that Christians not criticize one another's decisions as to which Jewish laws to follow, because it was God's business, and not theirs. For more of Brewer's opinions on price regulations, see *Reagan* v. *Farmer's Loan and Trust Company*, 154 U.S. 362 (1894), *Interstate Commerce Commission* v. *Cincinnati, New Orleans & Texas Pacific Ry.*, 167 U.S. 479 (1897), *Cotting* v. *Kansas City Stock Yards Co.*, 183 U.S. 79 (1901), and his dissent from *Armour Packing Co.* v. *U.S.*, 209 U.S. 56 (1908).

31 David J. Brewer, "The Good Time Coming, or the Final Triumph of Justice and Peace," (address delivered in Birmingham, Alabama) typescript, Nov. 22, 1906, 7, folder 178, box 5, Brewer Family Papers.

32 David J. Brewer, clipping, "Justice Brewer's Eloquent Words," (address to the Baltimore Bar Association), Dec. 2, 1903, Scrapbook III, 14, Brewer Family Papers.

33 David J. Brewer, "What I Have Gained from Bible Teaching," *The Congregationalist and Christian World* 89.49 (Dec. 3, 1904): 813–814.

all of Brewer's judicial efforts lay his belief that he was doing God's work on the bench.

Both Christ and Christianity rejected coercion, Brewer argued, and government should do the same when it came to property rights. Some of his religious invocations in defense of property rights bordered on the bizarre. In 1891, when Brewer defended private property as a sacred right to be protected by the courts from "public attack" in the form of economic regulation, he pointed to two things: the Declaration of Independence *and* to the Book of Genesis "when Eve took loving possession of even the forbidden apple."[34] If Brewer could extend his worries about protecting private property to include even the apple that got humankind thrown out of the Garden of Eden, no one will be surprised to learn that he was eager to protect breweries from state laws targeting the vice of intemperance. Brewer struck down such laws while serving on lower courts, a position that the Supreme Court rejected before his arrival.[35] Brewer invoked other Bible passages more straightforwardly as when he brought up the Good Samaritan as an example of the value of private charity while condemning laws protecting labor.[36] Labor unions which tried to bargain for higher wages and government regulation of property, explained Brewer to the New York Bar Association in 1893, "in spirit, if not in letter, violate both the Eighth and Tenth Commandments."[37] With such a powerful spiritual command behind him, Brewer acted confidently to contain what he considered to be the threatening forces of socialism as embodied in new state laws.

While the Court ruled regularly on cases involving interstate commerce and labor regulations on constitutional grounds, it ruled rarely on criminal law in the nineteenth century. It was only in the twentieth century that the Court determined that the US Constitution required the states to extend the protections found in the Bill of Rights to criminal defendants. This opened up the possibility of state criminal cases being appealed to federal courts long after Brewer's time on the Court. But Brewer had a chance to rule on criminal cases early in his career while serving as a judge in Kansas. He was "particularly

34 David J. Brewer, *Protection to Private Property from Public Attack, an Address Delivered before the Graduating Classes at the Sixty-Seventh Anniversary of the Yale Law School on June 23rd, 1891* (New Haven: Hoggson & Robinson, printers, 1891), 4.

35 See *Intoxicating Liquor Cases*, 25 Kan. 751 (1881); *State* v. *Walruff*, (C.C. D. Kans.) 26 Fed. 178 (1886); and *State* v. *Mugler*, 29 Kan. 252 (1883) and *Mugler* v. *Kansas*, 123 U.S. 623 (1887).

36 David J. Brewer, "Address on Charity, in behalf of the Citizens Relief Association and the Associated Charities of the District of Columbia," typescript, 1906, pp. 4, 3, 13, folder 179, box 5, Brewer Family Papers.

37 David J. Brewer, "The Nation's Safeguard," *New York State Bar Association Proceedings and Committee Reports* (16th Annual Meeting) (Albany, 1893), 39.

stern," according to his biographer.[38] Brewer was able to put this attitude into practice while on the US Supreme Court in the 1890s, when several dozen cases came up on appeal from trials from federal territory. These trials had been held in the Western District of Arkansas before the notorious "hanging judge" Isaac Parker. The Court reversed twenty-seven of these convictions because Parker's instructions prejudiced the jury against the accused, and Brewer dissented from nine of these reversals. Brewer saw no reason to grant a new trial for murder if the accused was possibly as young as fourteen and his ability to distinguish right from wrong unproven,[39] or because the prosecuting district attorney had pointed out that an accused man's wife was not by his side during the trial,[40] or if there was some doubt that the prisoner had been present and able to challenge the selection of jurors.[41]

Brewer thought the other justices were fussing over procedural trifles while men got away with murder. Legal prosecutions often went too slowly to satisfy an "excited" community, he complained in an editorial in *Leslie's Weekly* in 1903.[42] Such delays led to a rise in lynchings, he wrote. Like many white Americans, Brewer blamed most lynchings on a white mob eager to destroy "the Black beast" guilty of raping a white woman, but he wanted proper trials nonetheless. Swifter trials would help as would an end to appeals in criminal cases, he reasoned. In response to the uproar which greeted the latter suggestion, Brewer expanded on his argument in *The Independent* later that year. There was "very little danger" of an innocent man being condemned, Brewer explained, because of all the protective measures built into a jury trial. Courts of appeal could still choose to hear cases at their discretion; they merely would not have to hear every claim of imagined wrongs made by a creative defense attorney. Brewer added that any wrongs done in trial courts would be righted because any community in which "injustice prevails" would find itself "cursed."[43]

Brewer's religious faith underlay his skepticism of criminal appeals in two ways. First, his understanding of sin allowed him to place the responsibility for crime solely on the free choices of individuals. Second, when the idea that crime can only be explained by individual choices was challenged, he turned to the Last Judgment as an ultimate court of appeal.

38 Brodhead, *David J. Brewer*, 34.
39 *Allen* v. *United States*, 150 U.S. 551 (1893).
40 *Graves* v. *United States*, 150 U.S. 118 (1893).
41 *Lewis* v. *United States*, 146 U.S. 370 (1892).
42 Brewer, "Plain Words on the Crime of Lynching," *Leslie's Weekly* 97 (Aug. 20, 1903), 182.
43 David J. Brewer, "The Right to Appeal," *The Independent* (Oct. 1903), 2547, 2550.

People in the Atlantic world had long thought of crime and sin in the same instant. The leading American treatise writer on criminal law and medical jurisprudence in the nineteenth century was also an ordained Episcopal priest who once quoted the Apostle Paul in order to explain that mortals choose to sin.[44] But the modern era offered new challenges to this view. French criminologists noticed in the early nineteenth century that social forces, not individual choices, seemed to determine the rate of crime. When the price of bread soared, so did crime. When it fell, so did crime.[45] These so-called moral statistics clearly moved in tandem. If economic forces determined the number of crimes committed on any given day, were criminals guilty or mere pawns of fate? And law-abiding citizens, were they innocent or lucky? Moral statistics implied the latter. Other social scientists added to the discussion. Italian doctor turned criminologist Cesare Lombroso argued in 1876 that some criminals were simply born that way, while Richard Louis Dugdale came out in 1877 with a book detailing the criminal exploits of an American family called the Jukes. Dugdale traced their pauperism, disease, and criminality over generations. His explanations included heredity – one bad ancestress in the Revolutionary period – and a kind of moral statistic – living in a rural backwater in New York that offered few ways out of poverty.[46]

Brewer would have none of it. He was well aware of these new ideas, but rejected them in the name of religion. In a 1903 talk on the early American theologian Jonathan Edwards, Brewer insisted that crime was crime and not "simply mistake," sin was sin and not "only error." God has given us all free will to choose one or the other, he declared, no matter what scientists were writing about the forces of "heredity and environment."[47] A year later, Brewer developed a stronger defense against science in a talk he called "The Religion of a Jurist." Speaking to an audience of Congregationalists in the Old South Church in Boston in 1904, he declared himself willing to admit that "absolute justice ... should take into account the difference caused by heredity and environment for which individuals are not responsible." However, this changed nothing in the courtroom because humankind cannot do absolute justice,

44 Francis Wharton, quoted in Herbert Hovenkamp, "Insanity and Criminal Responsibility in Progressive America," *North Dakota Law Review* 57.4 (1981): 541–575, 546.

45 See Ysabel Rennie, *The Search for Criminal Man: A Conceptual History of the Dangerous Offender* (Lexington, MA: Lexington Books, 1978), 34–37.

46 See R. L. Dugdale, *"The Jukes": A Study in Crime, Pauperism, Disease, and Heredity* (New York: G. P. Putnam's Sons, 1877); and Arthur E. Fink, *Causes of Crime: Biological Theories in the United States, 1800–1915* (Philadelphia: University of Pennsylvania Press, 1938).

47 David J. Brewer, "Address on Jonathan Edwards and the freedom of the will," typescript, Oct. 5, 1903, pp. 12, 14, folder 195, box 5, Brewer Family Papers.

he explained. The effects of larger social or natural forces upon the criminal "must be ignored" by a judge. Why ignored? Because a judge cannot examine the souls standing before him the way natural scientists can examine things in the material world. As a result, mere mortals can never do absolute justice. But God could and would. To prove this, Brewer argued, "The inevitable failure of justice in this life is an assurance of a life to come." Now, this logic may have sounded far less comforting to men facing a hanging judge in Arkansas territory than it did to Brewer, but he was borrowing a theological argument dating back to the Middle Ages.

Brewer took a page from Anselm, archbishop of Canterbury, who reasoned that God must exist since all people can conceive of a perfect being. Brewer argued, in effect, that since all people can conceive of absolute justice, it must exist. Just not now, not here on earth, and not in his courtroom. He summed up his account of the religion of a jurist with this: "So out of my judicial experience, and looking through the glass of my life-work, I have learned to see in the cross the visible symbol of faultless justice, and in the resurrection of Christ the prophecy and truth of its final triumph."[48] Much had happened in theology since Anselm died in 1109, and nineteenth-century American Protestants were more likely to prove there was a Creator by pointing to the wonders of the natural world around them. But it was not the wonders of the legal system that Brewer needed to explain, but its limitations. So, the argument from design, as it was called, might prove the existence of God but not the troubles with the legal system's failure to do justice. This is why Brewer had to reach back to the *a priori* argument of Anselm for a way to explain his judicial choices. Out of his own mortal failings, Brewer found his proof of God's absolute justice.

Like justice, history was part of God's larger plan too, and the United States played a crucial role in it. Speaking to members of the Young Men's Christian Association in 1904, Brewer first praised them for the association's ecumenical character which brought all Christians together regardless of their particular church, and then gave his version of the last four hundred years of history. The European races were at first belligerent and ignorant, and Christianity was "largely buried beneath a mass of superstitions" while "the Bible was a chained book" under the rule of the Catholic Church. Then, three providential events occurred. The first two events were typical items in Protestant accounts of history: printing with movable type was invented by Gutenberg and the chained Bible was freed as a result of the Reformation. Brewer's third event was peculiarly American and somewhat at odds with the idea popular among

[48] David J. Brewer, "The Religion of a Jurist," *Outlook* 80 (June 24, 1905): 533–536.

Protestants that the Reformation itself introduced religious liberty into history. Brewer's third event was the discovery of America. There in America, Brewer explained, religious refugees might find shelter. The first of these refugees were the Puritans of New England who fled the Church of England because they thought it insufficiently Protestant and still tainted by Catholic practices. But Puritans had hardly welcomed other religious refugees; in fact, they barred people of other faiths from their territories. These more complicated facts could not stand in the way of the powerful myth of the Reformation and the Republic spun by Brewer. He took these three events as proof "that in the councils of eternity it was thought out long before man began to be, that here in the Republic, in the Providence of God, should be worked out the unity of the race – a unity made possible by the influences of education and the power of Christianity."[49] Christianity was so powerful in its appeal that it could take people immigrating from different countries, with different religions, or no religion at all and form them into one faith and one people, making the United States into a successful country. In words that proved that Jews were right to shy at the Christian nation declaration, Brewer added, "so if we can bring the 76,000,000 American people into the bonds of a single religious faith," then the "unity of the country is forever secured."[50] Of course, that single religious faith was Christianity, and presumably Protestantism.

The United States fulfilled God's plan not only by existing as a Christian nation, but by leading the international movement for peace which Brewer saw as an effort that helped hasten the Second Coming of Christ. Brewer gave numerous speeches at the Mohonk Conferences on international arbitration which began in 1895. Scholars tend to divide the many members of peace organizations, which included such well-known men as William Howard Taft and Woodrow Wilson, into two groups. They were either peace activists who worked in the name of God, or lawyers of a more secular turn of mind.[51] But this simple divide underestimates how religious faith could include legal work within its ken. Brewer saw religion as crucial to legal work for peace and legal work for peace as God's work.

49 David J. Brewer "Address to the YMCA," typescript, Oct. 16, 1904, p. 6, folder 157, box 4, Brewer Family Papers. For a similar account of the timing of America's discovery by someone whose work Brewer's father would have known, see the discussion of Edwards Amasa Park's views in Perry Miller, *The Life of the Mind in America from the Revolution to the Civil War* (San Diego: Harcourt Brace Jovanovich, 1965), 58.

50 Brewer "Address to the YMCA," 3.

51 See C. Roland Marchand, *The American Peace Movement and Social Reform, 1898–1918* (Princeton: Princeton University Press, 1972), xii; and Irwin Abrams, "The Emergence of the International Law Societies," *Review of Politics* 19 (July 1957), 361–380.

For example, in 1896, Brewer used one of the peace advocates' favorite passages from the Bible in a talk on improvements that should be made in legal education. The prophet Isaiah was scolding the nation of Israel for the evil it had done. Isaiah warned that God would come to judge Israel, and after He rebuked them, "they shall beat their swords into plowshares, and their spears into pruning hooks; nation shall not lift up sword against nation, neither shall they learn war any more."[52] It will be the lawyer who will bring on that "glad day," said Brewer, by helping to ensure that all international disputes will be settled in courts of law or "some great international court."[53]

In 1905, Brewer recounted a story at Mohonk of an American delegation at the First Hague Conference in 1899, the first of two international peace conferences where several treaties were negotiated. The delegation had brought a wreath to the tomb of Hugo Grotius, a Dutch writer crucial to the development of international law, on the Fourth of July. Standing there, it was as if they heard a voice "bidding the peace conference be brave and true and trustful in that Power in the Universe which works for Righteousness."[54] Brewer ended this speech with lines from a hymn from 1850 by Edmund Hamilton Sears: "Traveler, lo, The Prince of Peace,/ Lo, the Song of God is come!"[55] Titled officially as "The Angel's Song," the hymn is better known for its opening line, "It came upon a midnight clear."

Brewer continued to write on the coming millennium up until his death in 1910, four years before the horrors of World War I began, but he was no naïf. For all his repeated avowals of confidence in the eventual return of Christ and the dawn of the millennium, he also warned his listeners that they might not live to see the day. With the world now bending "under the weight of ever-increasing armaments," he explained in 1905, that blessed day might remain only a dream for him and his listeners.[56]

52 Isaiah, 2:4.

53 David J. Brewer, "A Better Education the Great Need of the Profession," *American Lawyer* 4 (Jan. 1896), 13, 12.

54 David J. Brewer, "The Enforcement of Arbitral Awards," in Edward Everett Hale and David J. Brewer, *Mohonk Addresses* (Boston: Published for the International School of Peace, Ginn and Company, 1910), 115.

55 Ibid.

56 Ibid.

12

John T. Noonan, Jr.: Catholic Jurist and Judge

Charles J. Reid, Jr.

BIOGRAPHICAL INTRODUCTION

John T. Noonan, Jr. was born into an upper-middle class Catholic family in Boston, Massachusetts, in 1926. He had fond recollections of the faith of both of his parents. His mother taught him to pray. His father, a successful attorney, was devoted to Lourdes, the French shrine renowned for its curative powers, and believed in the possibility of miracles, although he simultaneously asked tough and penetrating questions about Catholicism. Noonan's parents were ecumenical rather than parochial in their view of the world, but this did not lessen their commitment to their beliefs. Mass attendance "was a matter of course, never questioned, never neglected."[1]

Noonan was educated not in the Catholic school system, but in the leading secular institutions of the day – the Unitarian-infused Rivers Country Day School, and Harvard College. Admitted to Harvard in 1944, Noonan graduated in 1946, *summa cum laude*, his studies accelerated because of World War II.[2] Following graduation, Noonan took a year to study literature and philosophy in Cambridge, England. He had the opportunity to interview T. S. Eliot and travel to Rome to meet with George Santayana.[3] All the while, his faith was deepening, maturing. "I returned from Cambridge," Noonan reflected, "conscious that for me Catholicism was the strongest force in my life and equally conscious that I had never studied it as a subject."[4]

[1] John T. Noonan, Jr., *The Lustre of Our Country: The American Experience of Religious Freedom* (Berkeley: University of California Press, 1998), 16.

[2] Kevin Starr, "Judge John T. Noonan, Jr.: A Brief Biography," *Journal of Law and Religion* 11 (1994): 151, 152–156.

[3] John T. McGreevy, "A Case of Doctrinal Development: John T. Noonan, Jurist, Historian, Author, Sage," *Commonweal*, November 17, 2000, 12, 13.

[4] John T. Noonan, Jr., "My Philosophical Education," *Proceedings of the American Catholic Philosophical Association* 69 (1995): 29, 30.

Noonan determined to enroll at the Catholic University of America, where he proved to be a brilliant student. After showing an early interest in biblical criticism – he published two articles in the field[5] – he selected a topic from medieval scholasticism for his doctoral dissertation. He would explore the question of doctrinal change presented by the evolution of the usury doctrine. He received his PhD in 1951, and subsequently published a revised and substantially expanded version of his dissertation as *The Scholastic Analysis of Usury*.[6]

By this time, however, he had moved on to a career in the law. He graduated from Harvard Law School in 1954, worked as a staff attorney for a year under Dwight Eisenhower's National Security Advisor Robert Cutler, and then entered the private practice of law in Boston. He nevertheless had time for a detour into public life, winning election as chairman of the Brookline Redevelopment Authority, defeating among others future Massachusetts Governor and presidential candidate Michael Dukakis.[7]

In 1961, Noonan was recruited to join the faculty of the Notre Dame School of Law. The timing was fortuitous. The Second Vatican Council opened in 1962, and Noonan became involved in the affairs of the Council. His research on contraception led to the publication of a major book on the topic and to appointment on a papal advisory commission on the subject.[8] In 1967, Noonan joined the faculty of Boalt Hall, at the University of California, where he benefitted from the very generous bequest made by Lloyd Robbins for the study of Roman and canon law.[9]

JOHN NOONAN AS LEGAL HISTORIAN AND MORALIST

John T. Noonan, Jr. was a giant in at least two very different areas of public life. One might begin with the field of academic inquiry in which he first established his reputation – the history of the moral and legal teachings of the Catholic Church. His books on usury and contraception were path-breaking. *Contraception* was not only massively researched, with its carefully reasoned argument that contraception might be licit within marriage, it helped to frame

5 John T. Noonan, Jr., "Renan's Life of Jesus: A Re-Examination," *Catholic Biblical Quarterly* 11 (1949): 26–39; and John T. Noonan, Jr., "Hegel and Strauss: The Dialectic and the Gospel," *Catholic Biblical Quarterly* 12 (1950): 136–152.

6 John T. Noonan, Jr., *The Scholastic Analysis of Usury* (Cambridge, MA: Harvard University Press, 1957).

7 Noonan, *Lustre of Our Country*, 37.

8 Starr, "Judge John T. Noonan," 168–170; cf., John T. Noonan, Jr., *Contraception: A History of Its Treatment by the Catholic Theologians and Canonists* (Cambridge, MA: Harvard University Press, 1965).

9 Starr, "Judge John T. Noonan," 171.

the debate for the 1960s and beyond.[10] For his efforts, Noonan won the John Gilmary Shea award for the best work of Catholic history in 1965.[11]

Seven years later, there appeared another prize-winning book, *Power to Dissolve.*[12] This book represented a shift in the way Noonan did history. Noonan did not limit himself to recounting the development of ideas, as he had in his first two volumes, but provided instead a narrative focused on persons – litigants, their lawyers, and the judges who decided their petitions for nullity in the matrimonial courts of the Catholic Church. Cautiously, Noonan stated the case for reconciling divorced and remarried Catholics to the Church[13] – a process that Pope Francis has recently advanced in his apostolic exhortation, *Amoris Laetitia.*[14]

These three monumental publications would have been sufficient to establish the lifetime reputation of most scholars. Noonan, however, was poised to move to the next phase of his career. He followed these three works with a major study of personalist jurisprudence, *Persons and Masks of the Law.*[15] And he followed that work with a series of more specific historical investigations that allowed him to apply the lessons he taught in *Persons and Masks.* These included works on slave law;[16] abortion;[17] bribery and public corruption;[18] religious liberty;[19] and constitutional power.[20] At the close of

10 Leslie Woodcock Tentler, "Breaking the Silence: Sex, Gender, and the Parameters of Catholic Intellectual Life," in *In the Lógos of Love: Promise and Predicament in Catholic Intellectual Life*, ed. James L. Heft and Una M. Cadegan (New York: Oxford University Press, 2016), 100, 107, 121–122.

11 "Report of the Chairman of the Committee on Program," *Catholic Historical Review* 52 (1966): 86, 88.

12 John T. Noonan, Jr., *Power to Dissolve: Lawyers and Marriages in the Courts of the Roman Curia* (Cambridge, MA: Harvard University Press, 1972). Cf., "Report of the Committee on the John Gilmary Shea Prize," *Catholic Historical Review* 59 (1973), 43.

13 "[C]reative innovations," Noonan wrote in the Preface, "have been organic … the evolution has not ended." Noonan, *Power to Dissolve*, xix.

14 Joshua J. McElwee, "Vatican Cardinal: *Amoris Laetitia* Allows Some Remarried to Take Communion," *National Catholic Reporter*, February 14, 2017.

15 John T. Noonan, Jr., *Persons and Masks of the Law: Cardozo, Holmes, Jefferson, and Wythe as Makers of the Masks* (Berkeley: University of California Press, 2002) (reprint, with new preface, of 1976 edition).

16 John T. Noonan, Jr., *The Antelope: The Ordeal of the Recaptured Africans in the Administrations of James Monroe and John Quincy Adams* (Berkeley: University of California Press, 1977).

17 John T. Noonan, Jr., *A Private Choice: Abortion in America in the Seventies* (New York: The Free Press, 1979).

18 John T. Noonan, Jr., *Bribes* (New York: Macmillan, 1984).

19 John T. Noonan, Jr., *The Believer and the Powers That Are: Cases, History, and Other Data Bearing on the Relation of Religion and Government* (New York: Macmillan, 1987); and Noonan, *The Lustre of Our Country*.

20 John T. Noonan, Jr., *Narrowing the Nation's Power: The Supreme Court Sides with the States* (Berkeley: University of California Press, 2002).

this line of publications, Noonan returned to questions of Church history, exploring the paradox of doctrinal stability and doctrinal change in his book, *A Church That Can and Cannot Change*.[21]

And again, this list of publications would suffice to enshrine most scholars in the academic pantheon of all-time greats. Noonan, however, was engaged in a second career for at least the latter part of this period, that of a federal appellate judge.[22]

JOHN T. NOONAN, JR., AS JUDGE

In the 1970s, John Noonan was widely acknowledged as among the nation's most forceful and articulate defenders of the right of the unborn to life. Thus he wrote, summarizing his understanding of the Catholic position on abortion: "Once conceived, the [fetus] was recognized as man because he had man's potential. The criterion for humanity, thus, was simple and all-embracing: if you are conceived by human parents, you are human."[23]

Noonan was nominated by President Ronald Reagan for a seat on the Ninth Circuit Court of Appeal in part because of the strength of his pro-life views. For that reason, his nomination encountered some opposition in the fall of 1985.[24] Republican Senator Robert Packwood announced that he could not support the nomination.[25] Even so, Noonan was able to secure the unanimous approval of the Senate Judiciary Committee and was easily confirmed to the bench in December 1985.[26]

He took senior status in 1996 and served until his death in April 2017. While on the bench, Noonan authored numerous leading opinions, too many to list comprehensively here. A brief sampling suffices. In *Kyllo* v. *United States*, he dissented from a majority opinion upholding the use of thermal imaging to search for drug laboratories.[27] Noonan's view was subsequently ratified by the

21 John T. Noonan, Jr., *A Church That Can and Cannot Change: The Development of Moral Teaching* (Notre Dame: Notre Dame University Press, 2005).

22 "John T. Noonan, Jr.," in John R. Vile, ed., *Great American Judges: An Encyclopedia*, vol. I (Santa Barbara: ABC-CLIO, 2003), 618.

23 John T. Noonan, Jr., "An Almost Absolute Value In History," in *The Morality of Abortion: Legal and Historical Perspectives*, ed. John T. Noonan, Jr. (Cambridge, MA: Harvard University Press, 1970), 1, 51.

24 "Litmus Test for John Noonan," *Sacramento Bee*, October 18, 1985; and "UC Anti-Abortion Activist Chosen for Appeals Court," *Los Angeles Times*, October 13, 1985.

25 "Packwood to Fight Judge Confirmation," *Los Angeles Times*, October 14, 1985.

26 Starr, "Judge John T. Noonan," 175.

27 *Kyllo* v. *United States*, 190 F. 3d 1041 (9th Circuit, 1999) (Noonan, J., dissenting).

United States Supreme Court.[28] In *Lazo-Majano* v. *INS*, Noonan read the asylum and refugee laws expansively to protect the immigration status of a woman fleeing the endemic violence of the El Salvadoran civil war.[29] This opinion has now achieved near classic status in immigration-law circles.[30]

In *Harris* v. *Vasquez*, he opposed the execution of Robert Alton Harris, arguing that his right to an independent psychiatric assessment had been violated,[31] a position that has now been vindicated by the United States Supreme Court.[32] In *Compassion in Dying* v. *Washington*, he upheld the State of Washington's law prohibiting physician-assisted suicide,[33] an outcome subsequently sustained by the United States Supreme Court.[34] In *Mockaitis* v. *Harcleroad*, finally, Judge Noonan relied on the Religious Freedom Restoration Act to rule that a prisoner's visit with a priest-confessor could not be tape-recorded.[35] His judicial record transcended partisan boundaries and focused on the doing of justice in the particular case.[36]

Noonan's career was clearly rich and multi-layered. It is impossible to do justice to the entirety of his contributions – to religion, to Church, to history, to jurisprudence, to American case law – in a single chapter. Selectivity is required. I have chosen to focus on Noonan's contributions to jurisprudence. That is, I would like to pose the question, how did he understand the nature and functions of law?

"MASKED MEN"

Noonan's major work on jurisprudence is his book *Persons and Masks of the Law*. It is a book that must be read, however, in context with his other essays and studies on legal philosophy. And if one does so, one will quickly realize that even though *Persons and Masks of the Law* is written in a secular key and contains very few citations to religious sources, it is nevertheless a book steeped in Catholic jurisprudential thought. To appreciate this dimension of his work,

28 *Kyllo* v. *United States*, 533 U.S. 27 (2001).
29 *Lazo-Majano* v. *INS*, 813 F. 2d 1432 (9th Circuit, 1987).
30 See, e.g., John Noonan's own assessment of the case's history. John T. Noonan, Jr., "*Lazo-Majano*: Alive, Well, and Thriving at Twenty-Seven," *Harvard Human Rights Journal* 28 (2015): 1–10.
31 *Harris* v. *Vasquez*, 901 F. 2d 724 (9th Circuit, 1990).
32 *McWilliams* v. *Dunn*, 137 S. Ct. 1790 (2017).
33 *Compassion In Dying* v. *Washington*, 49 F. 3d 586 (1995).
34 *Washington* v. *Glucksberg*, 507 U.S. 702 (1997).
35 *Mockaitis* v. *Harcleroad*, 104 F. 3d 1522 (9th Circuit, 1997).
36 Norman Dorsen, "John T. Noonan, Jr.: Renaissance Man in the Catholic Tradition," *Notre Dame Law Review* 76 (2001): 843, 845–846.

it is probably best to begin with an essay Noonan published in 1974 in the *Proceedings of the American Catholic Philosophical Association*. Entitled "Masked Men,"[37] this short study reconsiders a question classically posed by Thomas Aquinas: Suppose a judge who knows the defendant before the bench is innocent; suppose further that the defendant has been convicted publicly, through perjured testimony, of a capital offense. Must the judge order the defendant's execution?[38]

Thomas tried to evade giving an affirmative answer. Perhaps, he suggested, the judge might rigorously cross-examine the perjuring witnesses as Daniel had and so reveal their dishonesty.[39] Or perhaps, he might forward the case to his superiors.[40] Shift the responsibility, Thomas thought, and let others carry out the execution, since they would have no knowledge of the defendant's actual innocence. But where the judge cannot take these steps, he may, as a last resort, order the defendant's execution. The guilt, Thomas declared, would be on perjurers and not on the judge.[41]

Noonan saw this answer as an evasion of responsibility. "Verbally, Thomas has maintained that it is never lawful to kill the innocent; substantively, in an exceptional case he has permitted one man to kill another who is innocent."[42] There was no divine mandate that ordered the judge to kill, nor did the first principles of natural law require it. The judge killed for no other reason than his "social role[]."[43] And imagine the horror the innocent defendant would experience, being compelled to execution at the hands of a judge like this! The flaw in Thomas's reasoning, Noonan asserted, was his sharp division between the public and private selves of the human person.

Thomas knew better than to draw such an arbitrary line, of this Noonan was convinced. A search of Thomas's voluminous writings reveals that he knew that the human person truly was indivisible. "A person is a whole" was the clear thrust of Thomas's teaching.[44] The human person as conceived by Thomas Aquinas was capable of "self-possession, self-identity, personality."[45]

37 John T. Noonan, Jr., "Masked Men: Person and Persona in the Giving of Justice," *Proceedings of the American Catholic Philosophical Association* 48 (1974): 228–237.

38 Thomas Aquinas, *Summa Theologiae*, 2a 2ae, q. 64, art. 6.

39 Ibid., q. 64, art. 6, responsio 3. Cf., *Daniel* 13:42–62 (Daniel's cross-examination of the lecherous elders in the trial of Susanna).

40 Thomas Aquinas, *Summa Theologiae* 2a 2ae, q. 64, art. 6, responsio 3.

41 Ibid.

42 Noonan, "Masked Men," 229.

43 Ibid., 231.

44 Ibid., 232.

45 Mariasusae Dhavamony, *Subjectivity and Knowledge in the Philosophy of Saint Thomas Aquinas*, Analecta Gregoriana, vol. 148 (Rome: Gregorian University Press, 1965), 34.

So conceived, the human person could also exercise agency and moral responsibility.[46] This unified sense of self could not be shattered without the loss of the entire person. Dismembered, the human person does not exist. A severed arm or leg or head cannot constitute a person. And neither can a person whose private and public selves wage war against each other.

Noonan took special note of the noun Thomas used to describe the human person, *persona*. The noun was ambiguous. It might signify both a living, flesh-and-blood human being, and the masks worn by actors in the theater.[47] The word might simultaneously refer to authentic human reality or a charade.[48] Was it possible that in distinguishing between public and private personae Thomas was betrayed by the tensions and ambiguities embedded in the vocabulary he used? Not likely. He was too refined a thinker for that to occur.

There remained, therefore, the problem, how can one unite that which Thomas found it necessary to separate? How can a judge be restored to wholeness, to integrity in its deepest, most original sense of the word? Dissatisfied with the limits of the medieval scholastic writers, Noonan turned for additional guidance to two twentieth-century Catholic Francophone philosophers, Étienne Gilson and Jacques Maritain.[49]

For Gilson, Christianity opened up new horizons in understanding not only the integrity but the transcendence of the human person. Consider the contrast with Platonism, he wrote. Platonism deals with ideal types, even of persons. Humanity, the species is real. The individual, on the other hand, is accidental, contingent, dependent on a whole set of converging circumstances.[50] This is true even of the great philosopher Socrates. Socrates was nothing more than an example of an extreme but recognizable type – the great inquiring mind, the towering intellect.[51] All of his accomplishments, however, availed him nothing. Like all persons, Socrates was destined to die and to pass through the great transmigration of souls which Plato envisioned as the fate of all human beings.[52]

46 Martinez Hewlett, "What Does It Mean to Be Human? Genetics and Human Identity," in *Human Identity at the Intersection of Science, Technology, and Religion*, ed. Nancey Murphy and Christopher C. Knight (New York: Routledge, 2016) (reprint of 2010 edition), 147, 161–162.

47 Noonan, "Masked Men," 232.

48 Donnalee Dox, *The Idea of the Theater in Latin Christian Thought: Augustine to the Fourteenth Century* (Ann Arbor: University of Michigan Press, 2004), 68.

49 Noonan, "Masked Men," 235–236.

50 Étienne Gilson, *The Spirit of Mediaeval Philosophy (Gifford Lectures)*, A. H. C. Downes, tr. (New York: Charles Scribner's Sons, 1936), 190.

51 Ibid.

52 Erland Ehnmark, "Transmigration in Plato," *Harvard Theological Review* 50 (1957): 1–20.

Christianity, however, was forced to confront the enduring individuality and distinctiveness of every man and woman. This was made necessary by its central premise, belief in the resurrection of the dead. St. Paul, of course, wrote that "if the dead are not raised, then Christ has not been raised."[53] Early Christian writers like Athenagoras speculated on the significance of the resurrection[54] and Gilson made much of this speculation. For Gilson, following these ancient writers, "[n]othing could be more resistant than an individuality of this kind."[55] It was the resurrection of the body that conferred on the human person integrity, distinctiveness, respect, wholeness, transcendence, and even immortality itself.[56]

Still, Gilson and the resurrection only helped Noonan part of the way in his quest to resolve Aquinas's dilemma. It gave him the robust concept of personhood that his jurisprudence demanded. But he still required something more to answer Thomas's sharp division of the person into public and private aspects.

To satisfy this requirement, he turned to Jacques Maritain. Maritain's life spanned the worst portions of the twentieth century. He witnessed the senseless blood-letting of World War I, the rise of fascism in Italy, the totalitarianism of the Stalinist period, and the genocidal frenzies of Nazi Germany.[57] Few intellectuals had his personal acquaintance with all of the horrors of the twentieth century.

Such experiences left Maritain a realist about human nature and its proclivity to sin. He knew well the evil that violence in the name of ideology might perpetrate.[58] At the same time, however, he was an optimist about the possibility of arriving at just social arrangements.[59] He placed tremendous

53 1 *Corinthians* 15:16.

54 Athenagoras, *De Resurrectione* 15.6–7. In Athenagoras, *Legatio and De Resurrectione*, William R. Schoedel, ed. and tr. (Oxford: Clarendon Press, 1972). Athenagoras's authorship of the *De Resurrectione* is now disputed. For arguments pro and con, consult Vladimir Kharlamov, *Theosis: Deification in Christian Theology* (Cambridge: James Clarke and Co., 2006), 1: 67, 80–81 and note 85.

55 Gilson, *Spirit*, 193.

56 Carol Collier, *Recovering the Body: A Philosophical Story* (Ottawa: University of Ottawa Press, 2013), 87–88.

57 Marcello Flores, "History and Memory: The Perception of Totalitarianism in Italy in a Comparative Perspective," in *Totalitarian and Authoritarian Regimes in Europe: Legacies and Lessons from the Twentieth Century*, ed. Jerzy Borejsa and Klaus Ziemer (New York: Berghahn Books, 2006), 70, 72. Cf., Bernard Doering, "Maritain and America – Friendships," in *Understanding Maritain: Philosopher and Friend*, ed. Deal Wyatt Hudson and Matthew J. Mancini (Macon: Mercer University Press, 1987), 37, 39–55 (detailing Maritain's friendship with Saul Alinsky and his criticism of capitalism).

58 Dennis McCann, "Reinhold Niebuhr and Jacques Maritain on Marxism: A Comparison of Two Traditional Models of Practical Theology," *Journal of Religion* 58 (1978): 140, 154–164.

59 Julie Clague, "'A Dubious Idiom and Rhetoric': How Problematic Is the Language of Human Rights in Catholic Social Thought?" in *Catholic Social Thought: Twilight or Renaissance?*, ed. Jonathan Boswell et al. (Leuven: Leuven University Press, 2000), 125, 132–133.

hope in a renewed Christendom, believing it might provide an effective rebuttal to scientific racism, scientific socialism, and even the terminal emptiness of consumer capitalism.[60]

There was much in Maritain for Noonan to use. In his response to Aquinas, he found especially helpful the way in which Maritain deployed the concept of mask. Quoting Maritain, Noonan wrote: "One of the most instructive chapters of a Christian philosophy would deal with what I might call the intermingling of masks and offices. Not only is the part of iniquity often played under the mask or figure of justice, but masks of iniquity can fill and mar the roles of justice."[61]

Noonan now had the elements he needed to construct his own brand of personalist jurisprudence. From the classical Christian commitment to the resurrection of the body he developed the unyielding, irreducible dignity of every human person; from Gilson, he acknowledged its scholastic formulation; and from Maritain, came the recognition that office might be used to conceal the humanity of those who claimed to act in the name of goodness, or truth, or righteousness, but who instead visited upon the innocent and unwary the horrors of injustice – barbarity, brutality, and viciousness in the place of fair and just and equitable judgment.

While this essay was published two years before *Persons and Masks* and was not referenced by Noonan in its pages, it properly stands as an introduction to that larger inquiry. For when Noonan spoke of persons in *Persons and Masks*, the concept of person he was utilizing was that stubbornly transcendent being so eloquently described in this earlier essay, just as when he wrote of masks, it was Maritain's dark vision of the agent of injustice that he had in mind.

A JURISPRUDENCE OF RULES

"The life of the law," Oliver Wendell Holmes wrote on the opening page of his history of the common law, "has not been logic; it has been experience."[62] Holmes continued: "The felt necessities of the time, the prevalent moral and political theories, intuitions of public policy, avowed or unconscious, even the prejudices which judges share with their fellow-men, have had a good deal

60 Jonas Kurlberg, "The Moot, the End of Civilisation and the Re-Birth of Christendom," in *Modernism, Christianity, and Apocalypse*, ed. Erik Tonning et al. (Leiden: E. J. Brill, 2015), 222, 225–232.

61 Noonan, "Masked Men," 236 (quoting Jacques Maritain, *True Humanism* (New York: Charles Scribner's Sons, 1938), 223).

62 Oliver Wendell Holmes, *The Common Law* (Boston: Little, Brown, and Company, 1881), 1.

more to do than the syllogism in determining the rules by which men should be governed."[63]

This paragraph clearly promises a particular kind of book. Holmes's word choices – "experience," "felt necessities," personal "prejudices" – suggest that he meant to tell the story of the generations of persons who crafted the common law. What did they think? What was their vision of the ideal society? What were their hidden biases and forbidden desires? A reader who knew nothing of what was to follow would expect an account of the external factors, from great philosophical movements to flawed and finite personalities, that shaped the law's movement.

Of course, that is not the book that Holmes wrote. His book, rather, is an account of the development of legal doctrine from which the human element was almost entirely purged. To Noonan, Holmes gave a body of accreted rules life, personality, sentience, even will. He thereby turned the law into a "personification," and simultaneously "overlooked the actual people in the process. The jar and motion of their experience was replaced by the imaginary adventures of the law."[64]

Persons and Masks of the Law, Noonan made clear, was intended to reverse that emphasis. "No person itself," Noonan answered Holmes, "[the law] lives in persons."[65] The great writers on jurisprudence had neglected that insight. John Austin wrote of power and command,[66] Roscoe Pound spoke of social engineering,[67] but neither they nor anyone else had investigated the relationship of personhood and the law.

Noonan was quick to state that by making personhood a central concern of his jurisprudence he did not mean to disparage the significance of rules. Abolish rules, establish government by personal decree, and tyranny follows. And so Noonan insisted that institutions succeeded because of their impersonality. "Rules delineate the boundaries of the office. Rules create the roles within which the officeholder acts with authority."[68] In litigation, furthermore, the judge is properly expected to behave impartially. The scholastic tradition condemned the "respect of persons" as a kind of corruption "and

63 Ibid.

64 Noonan, *Persons and Masks*, 3 ("personification") and 4 ("overlooked").

65 Ibid., 4.

66 John Austin, *The Province of Jurisprudence Determined* (London: John Murray, 1832), 1–5; and T. R. S. Allan, *The Sovereignty of Law: Freedom, Constitution, and Common Law* (Oxford: Oxford University Press, 2013), 137.

67 Roscoe Pound, "The Need of a Sociological Jurisprudence," *The Green Bag* 10 (1907): 607, 611–612; and Linus J. McManaman, "Social Engineering: The Legal Philosophy of Roscoe Pound," *St. John's Law Review* 33 (1958): 1–47.

68 Noonan, *Persons and Masks*, 15.

peculiarly the sin of the judge."[69] Indeed, the effective functioning of government depends upon rule-based order: "Where monsters have appeared in American government, they have appeared to issue from the sleep of rule."[70]

PERSONS AND MASKS

Still, Noonan wrote, rules must be understood in relation to persons. Rules do not exist as reifications, as abstractions possessing independent life and vitality. A simple thought experiment illustrates the point: How does one distinguish between the Federal Rules of Civil Procedure and the Code of Hammurabi? In the first case, persons take the federal rules seriously as normative and apply them in order to secure the efficient functioning of the contemporary judiciary. The Code of Hammurabi, on the other hand, might have served to guide the legal process of the long-ago past but today it is studied as an artifact of another age. Persons make the difference as to which book of rules is given effect and which is safely ignored: "Rules of law are formed by human beings to shape the attitude and conduct of human beings and applied by human beings to human beings. The rules are communications uttered, comprehended, and responded to by persons ... They exist as rules – not as words on paper – in the minds of persons."[71]

There are certainly situations, Noonan conceded, in which the application of a rule is swift and automatic. The uncontested traffic violation is the classic example of such a circumstance.[72] But contested litigation is another matter. There, rival litigants do battle over a given rule's scope, meaning, and applicability. Persons matter greatly in such a contest. A sympathetic litigant stands a better chance of prevailing than a scoundrel. A self-assured, articulate witness is likely to be more persuasive than a fearful, inarticulate mumbler. A lawyer who knows how to prepare a case, present evidence, pose questions, will be at an advantage over "his adversary."[73]

Not only litigants and their counsel matter, but so do the judges who conceptualize and craft the rules. As Immanuel Kant observed, "there is no rule for applying a rule."[74] Which rules to apply, which to limit, which to

69 Ibid., 16.
70 Ibid.
71 Ibid., 4.
72 Ibid., 5.
73 Ibid.
74 So Harold Berman paraphrased Kant. Harold Berman, in *Law and Language: Effective Symbols of Community*, ed. John Witte, Jr. (Cambridge: Cambridge University Press, 2013), 80.

distinguish, or which to overlook, these are questions that the judge answers in main part by consulting his or her value system.[75] It is thus a short step from accepting this truth to acknowledging that law is not, and cannot be, neutral.[76] Noonan knew this and so rejected the proposition that "a neutral universe ... governed by rules exists."[77]

In making this claim, Noonan had no intention of following the path of Marxists or critical legal scholars who moved from similar premises to theorizing about the class struggle or denouncing the oppressiveness and the incoherence at the heart of the prevailing legal order.[78] And he certainly did not mean to defend judicial relativism. He wished, rather, to set forth the values and principles that persons should bear in mind as they apply rules to the lives and welfare of their fellows.

But first Noonan had to confront the problem of "masks." When Thomas Aquinas taught that a judge might order the execution of a defendant he knew to be innocent, he revealed himself as principally concerned with institutional roles, even at the cost of an innocent life. The innocent person – the panic and dread such a person must feel at knowing how she or he was to die – was blotted from view. This exercise in willfully turning a blind eye Noonan described as putting on a "mask." He now wished to explore this operation at greater length.

Masks, Noonan makes plain, are not roles. Roles are a routine feature of life. Indeed, human interaction is usually mediated not directly, but through the roles persons assume in the various dimensions of their lives.[79] Lawyers, legislators, litigants, judges, and others find their roles in the legal order defined by custom, expectation, and vocabulary.[80]

A mask is different. "The image of the mask suggests that the true self is separated from an alien person that is the product of legal reasoning."[81] Masks,

75 Robert A. Destro, "'Engines of the Ruling Party': Political Correctness, 9/11, and the Politics of Culture," in *The Crisis of Religious Liberty: Reflections from Law, History, and Catholic Social Thought*, ed. Stephen M. Krason (Lanham: Rowman and Littlefield, 2015), 85, 90–91.

76 Gary A. Olson, *Justifying Belief: Stanley Fish and the Work of Rhetoric* (Albany: State University of New York Press, 2002), 49–52.

77 Noonan, *Persons and Masks*, xviii.

78 Ibid., 23.

79 Helen Harris Perlman, *Persona: Social Role and Personality* (Chicago: University of Chicago Press, 1968), 3.

80 James R. Elkins, "The Legal *Persona*: An Essay on Professional Masks," *Virginia Law Review* 64 (1978), 735, 737–741.

81 Kristin Bumiller, *The Civil Rights Society: The Social Construction of Victims* (Baltimore: Johns Hopkins University Press, 1988), 62.

so conceived, are a perversion of role. They occur when we carry our roles to impermissible extremes.

Imagine an American company that exercised effective control over a nominally independent central American state. Imagine that company utilized its commanding position within that state to tamper with land titles and effectively seize the property of a rival company. That rival sought recourse under the antitrust laws in American courts. But now imagine a sitting United States Supreme Court justice ruling in favor of the first, more powerful company because he refused to look behind the concept of sovereignty to examine the messy facts. The case was *American Banana Company* v. *United Fruit Company*.[82] The nominally sovereign central American state was Costa Rica. The judge was Oliver Wendell Holmes. And the mask was Holmes's use of sovereignty as a near "theological" concept to obscure the corrupt domination the United Fruit Company was already exerting in central American politics.[83]

THE MASKS OF THE POWERFUL AND THE POWERLESS

How do we know whether we have donned a mask and have begun to exceed our assigned roles? Or, how do we know whether we have placed a mask over another human being, concealing that individual's identity in the name of some greater good we self-righteously seek to accomplish? On the other hand, how can we tell whether we are fulfilling our duties and doing exemplary work?

Noonan did not give his readers checklists to follow or handy guideposts to consult when answering these questions. He did not believe in easy, one-size-fits-all formulas. And for good reason. Checklists, guideposts, formulas, and labels can all too often amount to substitutes for thought, and become an excuse for a failure to engage in self-critical reflection.[84] We follow the approved forms, neglect to undertake critical analysis, and think that we can thereby rest easy.[85]

82 *American Banana Company* v. *United Fruit Company*, 213 U.S. 347 (1909).

83 Noonan, *Persons and Masks*, 108. Cf., Marcelo Bucheli, "Multinational Corporations, Totalitarian Regimes, and Economic Nationalism: United Fruit Company in Central America, 1899–1975," *Business History* 50 (2008): 433–454.

84 Loren P. Beth, "Civil Liberties and the American Supreme Court," *Political Studies* 6 (1958): 134, 143 (on Justice Felix Frankfurter's aversion to formulas in constitutional law); and *Carlton* v. *Estelle*, 480 F. 2d 759, 761 (5th Circuit, 1973) (opinion of Judge Griffin Bell criticizing "labels" as "substitutes for thought").

85 Ronald F. King and Thomas S. Langston, "Narratives of American Politics," *Perspectives on Politics* 6 (2008): 235, 248–249 (calling for the jettisoning of tired formulas and the employment of greater narrative self-awareness in political analysis).

Noonan answered these three questions through narrative. Noonan, it has been said, "is a story-teller. He is an attentive story-teller, tracing out the history, listening carefully, sifting painstakingly. He takes the characters and the plot seriously."[86]

There are advantages to using narrative in this way. Human beings are story-tellers who define their lives and worlds and moral codes through narrative.[87] Our distinctiveness and our self-awareness as human beings are the product of reflection on how we have developed over time.[88] Historical narrative is an extension of these basic insights and its open-endedness constitutes a rich font of lessons.[89]

There is, furthermore, a dialogic quality to narrative as the historian – and his or her readers – mentally recreate the narrated events and empathize with the historical personages.[90] And while any good narrative provides an accurate reconstruction of events, our response to narrative is shaped by the questions it puts to us and by the circumstances of our lives.[91] Narrative history, seen in this light, is like a parable. Both narratives and parables have a moral richness to them. They engage the emotions and prompt curiosity, inquiry, and, finally, self-reflection.[92]

Noonan was well aware of these insights and it is no surprise therefore that *Persons and Masks* is replete with narrative reconstructions. I shall discuss one such narrative, Noonan's recreation of *Palsgraf* v. *Long Island Railroad Company*.[93] It is a lavishly told story, but I will focus on only a few of its aspects.

86 Stanley Hauerwas and Richard Church, "The Art of Description: How John Noonan Reasons," *Notre Dame Law Review* 76 (2001): 849, 863.

87 Mark B. Tappan and Lyn Mikel Brown, "Stories Told and Lessons Learned: Toward a Narrative Approach to Moral Development and Moral Education," *Harvard Educational Review* 59 (1989): 182–205.

88 R. Daniel Wadhwani and Geoffrey Jones, "Schumpeter's Plea: Historical Reasoning In Entrepreneurship Theory and Research," in *Organizations In Time: History, Theory, Methods*, ed. Marcelo Bucheli and R. Daniel Wadhwani (Oxford: Oxford University Press, 2014), 192, 208–209.

89 Kenneth J. Gergen, "Narrative, Moral Identity, and Historical Consciousness," in *Narrative, Identity, and Historical Consciousness*," ed. Jürgen Straub (New York: Berghahn Books, 2005), 99–119.

90 Karsten R. Stueber, "The Psychological Basis of Historical Explanation: Reenactment, Simulation, and the Fusion of Horizons," *History and Theory* 41 (2002), 25–42.

91 Keith Oatley, "Emotions and the Story Worlds of Fiction," in *Narrative Impact: Social and Cognitive Foundations*, ed. Melanie C. Green et al. (New York: Psychology Press, 2013), 39, 40 ("biography [and] narrative history" are like fiction in the emotions aroused and the lessons instilled).

92 Noonan knew, with the biblical critics, that "[t]he reader is active, not passive, and contributes to the production of textual meaning." James L. Ressguie, "Reader-Response Criticism and the Synoptic Gospels," *Journal of the American Academy of Religion* 52 (1984): 307, 308.

93 Noonan, *Persons and Masks*, 111–151; cf., *Palsgraf* v. *Long Island Railroad Company*, 248 N.Y. 339, 162 N.E. 99 (1928).

At an important level, as Noonan tells it, *Palsgraf* involved the jarring intersection of wealth and poverty, intellectual ambition, and terrible misfortune. The judges who heard the case were wealthy men. This was especially so at the highest appellate level, the New York Court of Appeals. "All were members of the upper middle class, the sons of prosperous fathers."[94] Noonan thus posed an implicit question: It is a truism that prosperous men and women find it difficult to grasp the true condition of the poor – the indignities of poverty, the petty humiliations, the absence of opportunity, the constriction of choice, the loss of freedom, the soul-crushing inability to meet financial obligations. Could Benjamin Cardozo, the author of the *Palsgraf* opinion, step outside the comfort and affluence of his exalted station in life and empathize with Helen Palsgraf's strained financial circumstances?

Noonan provides important details concerning Mrs. Palsgraf. She was a custodial worker "and the mother of three children."[95] Her younger two children, aged "fifteen and twelve, were with her at the time of the accident."[96] It was late August and she was hoping to give them a few moments of relaxation at Rockaway Beach, at the southern edge of Queens.[97] There is no mention of a husband and it is likely that Mrs. Palsgraf was separated.[98] She made a little more than $400.00 annually, was chronically behind on her bills,[99] and struggled as an anonymous, voiceless member of the urban proletariat of the 1920s.[100]

Benjamin Cardozo recited what has been received as the generally accepted version of the facts: Helen Palsgraf and her two children were standing at the far end of a railroad station. At the other end, a man tried to board a moving train, slipped, and was assisted by two guards. The man dropped a package of fireworks, which exploded. The explosion's shockwave toppled a set of scales onto Mrs. Palsgraf, injuring her.[101]

This description likely contains significant errors and distortions. It was probably the rush of an escaping crowd or damage to the platform that caused the scales to fall on Mrs. Palsgraf.[102] Cardozo, furthermore, implied that there

94 Noonan, *Persons and Masks*, 133.

95 Ibid., 126.

96 Ibid.

97 J. G. Deutsch and Michael H. Hoeflich, "Legal Duty and Judicial Style: The Meaning of Precedent," *St. Louis University Law Journal* 25 (1981): 87, 91.

98 Noonan, *Persons and Masks*, 126.

99 Ibid., 125.

100 Frank Stricker, "Affluence For Whom? Another Look at Prosperity and the Working Classes in the 1920s," *Labor History* 24 (1983): 5, 8–9.

101 *Palsgraf* v. *Long Island Railroad*, 248 N.Y. at 340–341.

102 William H. Manz, "*Palsgraf*: Cardozo's Urban Legend?" *Dickinson Law Review* 107 (2002): 785, 792–795.

was a great distance, perhaps hundreds of feet, between Palsgraf and the accident, when it was likely that she was no more than ten to thirty feet from the explosion.[103] And the injuries she suffered were not primarily physical, but principally in the form of psychological trauma.[104]

And if the facts were messier than Cardozo acknowledged, the legal question was also closer. Cardozo's formulation of the rule is well known: "Negligence is not actionable unless it involves the invasion of a legally protected interest."[105] As Cardozo saw it, the accident was unforeseeable and the railroad employees owed no duty of care to Palsgraf. She should therefore bear her own loss.[106]

Cardozo's formula, however, was not self-evidently correct to the other judges who heard the case. A jury had awarded Mrs. Palsgraf $6,000.00, a verdict which was sustained by the trial-court judge.[107] The Appellate Division ruled by a margin of three-to-two in favor of Palsgraf.[108] And at the level of the Court of Appeals, Cardozo prevailed but by a bare majority of four-to-three. Judge William Andrews authored a strong dissent, arguing for a broader conception of duty.[109] Noonan identified further defects with Cardozo's reasoning and proposed yet a different solution to the case.[110]

An actual majority of the judges who heard the case, in other words, not counting Cardozo, sided with Palsgraf.[111] In light of the closeness of the question, and the split on the bench, Noonan was particularly disturbed by one aspect of Cardozo's ruling: his decision, which was entirely discretionary, to tax Helen Palsgraf "costs in all courts."[112] This was where wealth and poverty and Cardozo's intellectual ambition combined to mask Palsgraf's humanity.

Noonan reminded readers the impact such a gratuitous award would have had on Palsgraf: "It is probable that costs in all courts amounted to $350.00,

103 Richard A. Posner, *Law and Literature* (Cambridge, MA: Harvard University Press, 2009), 429.

104 Richard A. Posner, *Cardozo: A Study in Reputation* (Chicago: University of Chicago Press, 1990), 35–36.

105 *Palsgraf* v. *Long Island Railroad*, 248 N.Y. at 341.

106 Ibid., at 341–346.

107 Noonan, *Persons and Masks*, 130–131.

108 *Palsgraf* v. *Long Island Railroad Company*, 222 A.D. 166, 225 N.Y.S. 412 (1927).

109 *Palsgraf* v. *Long Island Railroad*, 248 N.Y. at 349 (Andrews, J., dissenting) ("Due care is a duty imposed on each one of us to protect society from unnecessary danger, not to protect A, B, or C alone"). Ibid.

110 Noonan, *Persons and Masks*, 136–139. Noonan argued for a restitution-based theory of recovery "for injuries which [were the] inevitable by-product" of running commuter railroads. Ibid., 137.

111 Ibid., 144.

112 *Palsgraf* v. *Long Island Railroad*, 248 N.Y. at 347.

not quite a year's income for Helen Palsgraf. ... The effect of the judgment was to leave the plaintiff, four years after her case had begun, the debtor of her doctor, who was still unpaid; her lawyer, who must have advanced her the trial court fees at least; and her adversary, who was now owed reimbursement for expenditures in the courts on appeal. Under the New York statute, the Long Island could make execution of the judgment by seizing her personalty."[113]

Noonan accordingly condemned Cardozo: "Only a judge who did not see who was before him could have decreed such a result."[114] What was the proximate cause of the mask Cardozo used to conceal the human impact of this needless award? Noonan attributed it to Cardozo's desire to establish the rule in *Palsgraf*, which in truth had been closely contested by other judges, as prevailing legal doctrine.[115] The award of costs was required, as Noonan saw it, as a means of signaling Cardozo's confidence in the rule.[116] Cardozo's intellectual pride thus blinded him to the grim realities that Helen Palsgraf faced.

Cor ad cor loquitur

Justice, St. Augustine wrote, is "love serving only the one loved."[117] Noonan quoted this passage to explain how Cardozo's opinion in *Palsgraf* failed as a matter of law, policy, and even simple justice.[118] It was a point Noonan returned to in the preface to the 2002 edition of *Persons and Masks*: "The central problem, I think, of the legal enterprise, is the relation of love to power. We can often apply force to those we do not see, but we cannot, I think, love them. Only in the response of person to person can Augustine's sublime fusion be achieved."[119]

Love and justice, how is such a fusion possible? The personalist tradition, of which Noonan's book is an excellent restatement, provides some suggestive possibilities.[120] Love for the personalist, it has been suggested, should reflect "divine love," which is "not impartial, but universally partial."[121] If we imitate God's love, and truly love others without reservation, or distinction, or

113 Noonan, *Persons and Masks*, 144.

114 Ibid., 150.

115 Ibid.

116 Ibid., 150–151.

117 Donald X. Burt, *Friendship and Society: An Introduction to Augustine's Practical Philosophy* (Grand Rapids: William B. Eerdmans, 1999), 49.

118 Noonan, *Persons and Masks*, 137.

119 Ibid., xx.

120 For one such synthesis, see the encyclical of St. John XXIII, *Pacem In Terris* (1963), paras. 4–38.

121 Stephen G. Post, "The Tradition of *Agape*," in Stephen G. Post et al., eds., *Altruism and Altruistic Love: Science, Philosophy, and Religion* (Oxford: Oxford University Press, 2002), 51, 57.

discrimination, then we should be open to understanding their perspectives through conversation. Thus Emmanuel Mounier, Jacques Maritain's younger and tragically short-lived collaborator, proposed to unite love and justice through "engagement that opens up towards the other person in critical dialogue."[122]

Dialogue in a personalist context, furthermore, is a commitment not only to meet with or engage with others in some abstract sense, but to see to their well-being in the particularities of their lives: "We don't exist for ourselves; we exist with and for each other."[123] And so finally the personalist is equipped through empathetic dialogue to work for the betterment of those with whom he or she comes into contact.[124]

These twin premises – critical, considerate dialogue and the improvement of others' welfare through meeting their concrete needs – are also crucial to understanding Noonan's work. Let us take the question of dialogue first. For Noonan, legal interpretation constitutes a kind of dialogue between the interpreter and the creator of a text. In a law review article published a decade after *Persons and Masks*, Noonan posed the question: "What makes a judge great?" and answered that inquiry by insisting that greatness is achieved through "respect and affection for persons."[125]

Affection can, of course, be demonstrated in face-to-face encounters, among friends, colleagues, and intimates. But it can also be revealed in the good will and deference a judge shows to the legal documents he or she is called upon to construe. "Texts," Noonan wrote, "do not speak for themselves."[126] They are, in that sense, unlike human beings in conversation. "If a person is speaking to you and is misunderstood, no hermeneutic hiatus develops .... Correction is instantaneous. 'You missed my meaning. You haven't got the point. You didn't hear what I said.'"[127]

The great temptation of those who interpret the law is to regard legal texts as somehow different from this everyday form of human interaction. Lawyers who have an interest in representing their client will find ambiguities in a will where none exist; statutes will be given novel constructions; lacunae will be

[122] Jacob Dahl Rendtorff, *French Philosophy and Social Theory: A Perspective For Ethics and Philosophy of Management* (Dordrecht: Springer, 2014), 48.

[123] Walter Cardinal Kasper, *That They May All Be One: The Call to Unity Today* (London: Continuum, 2004), 35.

[124] Stephen J. Pope, *The Evolution of Altruism and the Ordering of Love* (Washington, DC: Georgetown University Press, 1994), 24–26.

[125] John T. Noonan, Jr., "Education, Intelligence, and Character in Judges," *Minnesota Law Review* 71 (1987): 1119, 1120.

[126] Ibid.

[127] Ibid.

found in contracts where the parties thought their meaning was complete and clear.[128] Much of this misconstrual is possible because of a power disparity between text and interpreter. A willful interpreter, seeking advantage, can exploit the words on a page, overpower them, make them say what was never actually intended. After all, "[t]exts are inert."[129] "Mute and uncomplaining, a text cannot retort, 'I'm misunderstood.'"[130]

Noonan's remedy for this problem is to remain ever vigilant to the human reality that stands behind every printed word. "Texts are after all only the memorial of a person's thoughts. The person is not there to offer instantaneous correction .... But behind the words the person can be glimpsed, seen, appreciated. The person did have a meaning. Whoever loves him or her will not try to replace that meaning with someone else's."[131]

Thus Noonan sees a kind of personalist dialogue as constituting the core of legal interpretation. Respect matters. This respect can be face-to-face, or it can span generations, even centuries and millennia.

But dialogue is insufficient by itself. For Noonan, love must finally eventuate in action. One might consider another article he authored, in 1981, shortly after completing *Persons and Masks*, as illustrating the action that is required of the judge.[132] This article posed a series of questions: How might one characterize the Catholics who had served on the Supreme Court up to that time? Were there any who qualified as great? Did their Catholic identity make any difference in their judicial conduct?

Noonan offered balanced and fair-minded answers to these questions. Joseph McKenna was singled out for the humanity of his opinion in *Weems* v. *United States*.[133] Pierce Butler's silent dissent in the notorious *Buck* v. *Bell* decision also came in for notice.[134] Roger Taney, on the other hand, was criticized for "the judicial catastrophe" of *Dred Scott* v. *Sandford*.[135]

Noonan, however, reserved his greatest admiration for Frank Murphy, who spent a mere nine years on the Supreme Court (1940–1949). A one-time Mayor of Detroit, Governor of Michigan, and Governor General of the Philippines,

128 Ibid.

129 Ibid.

130 Ibid.

131 Ibid.

132 John T. Noonan, Jr., "The Catholic Justices of the United States Supreme Court," *The Catholic Historical Review* 57 (1981): 369–385.

133 Ibid., 372. Cf., *Weems* v. *United States*, 217 U.S. 349 (1910).

134 Noonan, "Catholic Justices," 377. Cf., *Buck* v. *Bell*, 274 U.S. 200 (1927).

135 Noonan, "Catholic Justices," 379. Cf., *Dred Scott* v. *Sandford*, 19 How. (60 U.S.) 393 (1857).

Murphy was no stranger to the corridors of power.[136] But Murphy knew better than to always let power have its way.

For Noonan, this point was driven home in Murphy's dissent in *Korematsu* v. *United States*.[137] The infamous Japanese internment case, *Korematsu* was the product of blind panic and bigotry: an irrational fear swept the West Coast following the Pearl Harbor attack that no Asian American could be trusted.[138] Best they be confined in desert encampments where they could threaten no one.[139]

Ignominiously, a Supreme Court majority upheld President Franklin Roosevelt's decision to intern some 120,000 Americans of Japanese ancestry.[140] Murphy, however, dissented, asserting that the policy of internment "[fell] into the ugly abyss of racism."[141] "[T]his racial restriction," Murphy added, "is one of the most sweeping and complete deprivations of constitutional rights in the history of this nation."[142] All Americans, Murphy concluded, "are kin in some way by blood or culture" and all alike "must accordingly be treated at all times as the heirs of the American experiment."[143]

For Noonan, this opinion was the practical expression of biblical commandment: "The message of Paul to the Galatians that there was no discrimination in the Lord found here a constitutional counterpart in an American Catholic heart."[144]

What, then, is love for John Noonan? It is not mere sentimentality. It is not an uncritical embrace of another person's misdeeds or a heedless and empty mock forgiveness of trespasses. It is not an abandonment of standards. It is, on the other hand, a due regard for individuals as they have expressed themselves in texts and actions that extend across time. It is a willingness to take persons

136 One source ranks Murphy among the ten best all-time mayors of a big city. Melvin G. Holli, *The American Mayor: The Best and the Worst Big-City Leaders* (University Park, PA: Pennsylvania State University Press, 1999), 151. He was appointed Governor General of the Philippines in part because of his Catholicism. James T. Fisher, *Communion of Immigrants: A History of Catholics In America* (Oxford: Oxford University Press, 2007), 105.

137 Noonan, "Catholic Justices," 383–385.

138 Alexander Wohl, *Father, Son, and Constitution: How Justice Tom Clark and Attorney General Ramsey Clark Shaped American Democracy* (Lawrence: University Press of Kansas, 2013), 29–32.

139 Gerald Stanley, "Justice Deferred: A Fifty-Year Perspective on Japanese Internment Historiography," *Southern California Quarterly* 74 (1992): 181–206.

140 The 120,000 included some 70,000 American citizens. Debra Lyn Bassett, "Comment On Chapter Four: Toward a Nonracial Sovereign," in *Sovereignty, Emergency, Legality*, ed. Austin Sarat (Cambridge: Cambridge University Press, 2010), 228, 236.

141 *Korematsu* v. *United States*, 323 U.S. 215, 233 (Murphy, J., dissenting).

142 Ibid., 235.

143 Ibid., 242.

144 Noonan, "Catholic Justices," 385; cf. *Galatians* 3:28.

seriously – in their thoughts and intentions, in their words and deeds, in the wholeness of their being. For sure, Noonan was not afraid to call a monster by that name. But he was equally conscious of the admixture of base and exalted motives which cohabit uneasily within everyone's minds and hearts.

Noonan frequently employed the language of "heart speaking to heart" when he invoked this idea of love. At the close of his reconstruction of the slave-trading case *The Antelope*, Noonan wrote that "every so often in a human heart the ice will crack, and a human person will acknowledge his responsibility for other human persons he has touched."[145] In his study of Shakespeare's Sonnets, he admonished the reader to "[h]ear with your heart."[146] In *A Church That Can and Cannot Change*, he noticed the centrality of the heart in Jesus's love commandments.[147]

Noonan's acknowledged source for this formulation is John Henry Cardinal Newman. *Cor ad cor loquitur* – "heart speaks to heart" – these were the words that Newman selected as his motto upon being made a cardinal.[148] When Newman wrote of the heart, it has been shown, his purpose was to reject the dichotomy "that man is distinguished mainly by his intellect and his will."[149] "The primary fulfillment of the human person," for Newman, "is an affective fulfillment."[150] It is our hearts, our affective selves, that draw us closer. We love God, and so we wish to know and to conform to God's will.[151] So also, it is our hearts, our emotion-laden selves, that allow us to "feel great compassion for a needy person."[152] We become fully human, we aspire to be our best, we give lovingly to others, we are generous with our time and wealth, we engage the world with tenderness and compassion, when our hearts are fully committed.[153]

When Noonan closed *Persons and Masks of the Law* with the fervent hope that "[p]ersons speak to persons, heart unmasked to heart" he seemed to have a similar thought in mind.[154] Law surely is an enterprise that engages the

145 Noonan, *The Antelope*, 159.

146 John T. Noonan, Jr., *Shakespeare's Spiritual Sonnets* (North Charleston: CreateSpace, 2011), 5.

147 Noonan, *A Church That Can and Cannot Change*, 12–14.

148 Mary Beth Ingham, "*Cor ad cor loquitur*: Re-fashioning the Imagination Around Love," in *The Newman-Scotus Reader: Contexts and Commonalities*, ed. Edward J. Ondrako (New Bedford, MA: Academy of the Immaculate, 2015), 447, 447.

149 John F. Crosby, *The Personalism of John Henry Newman* (Washington, DC: The Catholic University of America Press, 2014), 69.

150 Ibid.

151 Ibid., 70.

152 Ibid., 71.

153 Harold L. Weatherby, *Cardinal Newman in His Age: His Place in English Theology and Literature* (Nashville: Vanderbilt University Press, 1973), 177.

154 Noonan, *Persons and Masks*, 167.

reason – it is through our reason that we solve legal puzzles and serve the best interests of clients. And law is surely also an expression of will. What else do judges do in their courtrooms or lawmakers in their legislative assemblies than express their commanding will? But if law is only that, if it is only reason and will, we lose sight of persons. To keep persons firmly in view, we must cultivate our affective sides. We must keep open our hearts. That, for Noonan, is the path to true justice.

13

The Integrative Christian Jurisprudence of Harold J. Berman

John Witte, Jr.

BIOGRAPHICAL SKETCH

Harold Berman (1918–2007) was one of the great polymaths of American legal education, and a pioneer of the study of law and religion. He studied at Dartmouth College with German intellectual, Eugen Rosenstock-Huessy. After studying legal history for a year at the London School of Economics under T. F. T. Plucknett, he pursued his LL.B. and M.A. in History at Yale, but was interrupted by military service in World War II from 1942 to 1945, where he served as a cryptographer, breaking Russian code for the Allied Forces in Europe. He began his teaching career at Stanford Law School in 1947, but the following year moved to Harvard Law School, where he taught until 1985, retiring as the James Barr Ames Professor of Law. He also served for twenty-five years as Founding Director of Harvard Law School's Liberal Arts Fellowship Program in Law. Berman moved to Emory Law School in 1985, serving as the first Robert W. Woodruff University Professor of Law. At Emory, he was also Fellow in Russian Studies at The Carter Center, Founding Director of the American Law Center in Moscow, and Senior Fellow of the Center for the Study of Law and Religion. He remained an active scholar and lecturer until his final, eighty-ninth year, and was famous for being at the office six and a half days a week, taking off only Sunday mornings for worship.

For the first three decades of his career, Berman's principal scholarly focus was on the Soviet legal system and the law of East–West trade. He developed new courses, testified frequently before courts, commissions, and Congress, and traveled regularly to Europe and the Soviet Union – fifty-five times to Russia alone. He produced a massive body of scholarship in this early period, including his famous *Justice in the U.S.S.R.* (1950; rev. edn. 1963). In these first decades Berman also developed a keen interest in bringing legal education into college courses and into the public mainstream. These interests he distilled in three signature titles: *On the Teaching of Law in the Liberal Arts Curriculum* (1956), *Law and Language: Effective Symbols of Community* (1964, 2013), and *The Nature and Functions of Law* (1958; 6th ed. 2004). Extending the classroom globally, he orchestrated a series of public lectures on the fundamentals of law that were broadcast throughout the world on Armed Forces Radio, and then published in multiple languages as *Talks on American Law* (1961).

In the last three decades of his career, Berman shifted his main scholarly and teaching focus to legal philosophy, legal history, and law and religion. He produced a series of path-breaking volumes, most notably *The Interaction of Law and Religion* (1974), *Law and Revolution: The Formation of the Western Legal Tradition* (1983), *Faith and Order: The Reconciliation of Law and Religion* (1993), and *Law and Revolution II: The Impact of the Protestant Reformations on the Western Legal Tradition* (2003). He left a scholarly legacy of twenty-five books and 458 articles, translated into eighteen languages.

Berman was a man of firm Christian faith, a stance that earned him the scorn of his family and some of his colleagues. He was born into a conservative Jewish family in Connecticut, but at the age of twenty-one he had a Damascene experience. He was visiting Germany at the time, but when Hitler announced on the radio that Germany had invaded Poland, Berman feared for his life as a Jew and fled to France. En route on a late night train in an empty carriage, he later reported:

> I thought that Hitler's invasion of Poland would lead to the total destruction of human civilization. I felt as one would feel today if all the major powers were to become involved in a full-scale nuclear war. I was shattered – in total despair. There, alone on that train, Jesus Christ appeared to me in a vision. His face reminded me of one of the Russian icons that I would later see – heavily scarred and tragic – not suffering, but bearing the marks of having suffered. I suddenly realized that I was not entitled to such despair, that it was not I, but another, God himself, who bore the burden of human destiny, and that it was rather for me to believe in him even though human history was at an end. When the train arrived in Paris early that morning, I walked straight to the Notre Dame cathedral, and I prayed a personal prayer to God for the first time in my life.[1]

This conversion permanently alienated Berman from his Jewish family. His overt Christian faith and interest in discussing it publicly often alienated his

[1] Harold J. Berman, "Judeo-Christian Versus Pagan Scholarship," in *Finding God at Harvard: Spiritual Journeys of Thinking Christians*, ed. Kelly Monroe (Grand Rapids: Zondervan, 1996), 292, 295.

colleagues as well. Even in his last days, Berman was smarting that his Harvard Law School colleagues simply ignored his early book *The Interaction of Law and Religion* that he sent to each of them. He was also irritated that his decanal hero, Erwin Griswold, would not let him teach a new course in Canon Law for credit. Berman found a warmer reception at Emory, but even this university faculty, devoted to interdisciplinary study and located in the Bible belt, was skeptical about the study of law and religion.

Berman remained an ecumenical Christian throughout his adult life, though he remained proud of his Jewish heritage: "God made me both root and branch," he often said, referring to Paul's description of Jews and Christians in Romans 9–11. While he worshipped regularly in the Episcopal Church, he loved to attend Russian Orthodox services when in Russia, where the "splendor and pathos of the ikons" and liturgy overwhelmed him.[2] In his final years he worshipped in a small church for the homeless in Atlanta. Both at Harvard and Emory, he led the community in annual Christmas caroling while playing the accordion with gusto. He was a strong supporter of the National and World Council of Churches and Christian Legal Society, and dabbled in interreligious movements like Moral Rearmament and the Parliament of World Religions.

Berman was an avid Bible reader, and he read the Christian classics, though he was impatient with technical theology. For the twenty-five years we worked together, we often shared morning devotions. He read the Old Testament in the Hebrew of his youth, and insisted that I read the New Testament from John Calvin's French Bible. We would sometimes spend a week discussing a single passage, like the opening verse of the creation story: "The Spirit of God moved upon the face of the waters." Who was this Spirit, and how did it relate to the third member of the Trinity? What was motion before creation set the laws of motion? Is water a pre-creation substance, and did God create that, too, suggesting more than one creation? And on and on the conversation went, often sending both of us to commentaries and the reception history of individual biblical texts.

MAIN SCHOLARLY THEMES

Faith and Law. Throughout his long career, Berman had the remarkable ability to think above, beyond, and against the times. In the 1950s and 1960s, the dominant Cold War logic taught that the Soviet Union was

[2] Harold J. Berman, "Christianity and Democracy in the Soviet Union," in *Christianity and Democracy in Global Context*, ed. John Witte, Jr. (Boulder: Westview Press, 1993), 292.

a lawless autocracy. Berman argued to the contrary that the Russians did follow rules and would always honor contracts and treaties that were fairly negotiated.[3] His views prevailed and came to inform various nuclear treaties, trade agreements, and East–West accords. In the 1970s and 1980s, the conventional belief persisted that the Middle Ages were the dark ages as the West waited impatiently for Enlightenment and modernization. Again Berman argued the contrary, insisting that the medieval era was the first modern age of the West and the founding era of the Western legal tradition.[4] This view is now standard lore. In the 1980s and 1990s, jurists fought fiercely over whether legal positivism or natural law or some other perspective was the better legal philosophy. Berman called for an integrative jurisprudence that reconciled these views with each other and with other perspectives on law, particularly historical jurisprudence.[5] This view now prevails in a world dedicated to interdisciplinary legal study. And, in the 2000s, with the world hell-bent on waging "a clash of civilizations," Berman called for a world law, grounded in global structures and processes, and universal customs and principles of peace, cooperation, and reconciliation.[6] This view holds much more promise than the jingoism and jihadism of the past two decades.

"First it was Russian law, then it was Western law, now it is world law. What's next, cosmic law?" This is how Professor Berman's beloved wife, Ruth, once summarized for me (with a blend of exasperation and astonishment) the stages of Berman's legal career. There is keen insight in this statement. For Berman, every legal system – even the budding legal system of the world – must ultimately be founded upon cosmic commandments and contemplation, divine examples and exemplars. Berman often predicted that those legal systems that build on immanent and material foundations alone would ultimately fail. The spectacular failure of the Soviet legal system in the late

3 Harold J. Berman, *Justice in the U.S.S.R.*, rev. edn. (Cambridge, MA: Harvard University Press, 1963); ibid., *The Russians in Focus* (Boston: Little Brown, 1953, repr. ed. 1969).

4 Harold J. Berman, *Law and Revolution: The Formation of the Western Legal Tradition* (Cambridge, MA: Harvard University Press, 1983).

5 See esp. Harold J. Berman, "Toward an Integrative Jurisprudence: Politics, Morality, History," *California Law Review* 76 (1988): 779–801; ibid., *Faith and Order: The Reconciliation of Law and Religion* (Grand Rapids: Wm. B. Eerdmans, 1993), 239–310.

6 Harold J. Berman, "Integrative Jurisprudence and World Law," in *Rechtstheorie: Theorie des Rechts und der Gesellschaft: Festschrift für Werner Krawietz zum 70. Geburtstag*, ed. Manuel Atienza et al. (Berlin: Duncker & Humblot, 2003), 3–16; ibid., "Faith and Law in a Multicultural World," in *Religion in Global Civil Society*, ed. Mark Juergensmeyer (Oxford: Oxford University Press, 2005), 69–89; ibid., "World Law: An Ecumenical Jurisprudence of the Holy Spirit," *Theology Today* 63 (Oct. 2006): 365–374.

twentieth century was ample vindication of his insight into the essential religious foundations of law.

Berman repeated this message in China, too, when in 2006, as a still energetic 88-year old, he gave a series of lectures on law to packed houses in a dozen universities. One of his Chinese respondents asked whether one needed to believe in God in order to have a just legal order. "It would certainly help!" Berman quipped immediately. "But no," he went on diplomatically:

> You don't necessarily have to believe in God, but you have to believe in *something*. You have to believe in law at least. If you can't accept God, then just focus on the law that God has written on all of our hearts. Even children intuitively sense this law within us. Every child in the world will say, "That's *my* toy." That's property law. Every child will say, "But you *promised* me." That's contract law. Every child will say, "It's not my fault. He hit me first." That's tort law. Every child will say, "No, I didn't; *ask him*." That's evidence law. Every child will say, too, "Daddy said I could." That's constitutional law. Law ultimately comes from our human nature, and our human nature is ultimately an image of God, the source of all law.[7]

Such views reflect, in part, Berman's lifelong effort to integrate his religious faith with his legal learning. In his chapel talks delivered in the Harvard Memorial Church, Berman contrasted "the wisdom of the world" with "the wisdom of God." The wisdom of the world, he declared, "assumes that God's existence is irrelevant to knowledge, and that truth is discoverable by the human mind unaided by the Spirit." Jewish and Christian wisdom, by contrast, "seeks God's guidance ... in order to discover the relationship between what we know and what God intends for us." Knowledge and intellect are "intimately connected with faith, with hope, and with love." "God does not call us to be merely observers of life; rather he calls all of us – even the scholars in all that we do – to participate with him in the process of spiritual death and rebirth which is fundamental religious experience."[8]

Dialogue and Reconciliation. Early on, Berman made clear that dialogue was essential to our relationships with God, neighbor, and self, and that language was an essential sinew of all our relationships, including our legal relationships. The God of the Bible is a God of words, Berman believed. "In the beginning was the Word, and the Word was with God, and the *Word was*

7 Berman reported this familiar classroom saying to me after his return from China. See also Meredith Hobbs, "Translating Western Law into Chinese; Emory Professor Harold J. Berman Toured China, Speaking to Halls Packed with Chinese Students," *The Fulton County Daily Report* 117 (June 1, 2006): 1.

8 Berman, *Faith and Order*, 319–322.

God," reads John 1. "In the beginning God created the heavens and the earth," Genesis 1 reads. And he did so by speech: "And God *said*, 'Let there be' . . . ." is how each day of creation starts. When it came to the creation of men and women, it was by dialogue, by conversation, first among the members of the Trinity, then between God and humanity: "Let *us* make man in our image, after our likeness," the Trinitarian God says to its members. And thereafter, God "walked and talked" with the man and the woman whom he created, though he talked with no other creature. For Berman, humans, created in the image of God, are endowed with not only reason, will, memory, and faith, but also the capacity for language and dialogue with each other and with God.

> If we see Christianity as a dialogue which God has initiated with man, I think we can see that Christians are called to transform this dialogue into a dialogue also among men, in which we are brought into relationships with each other, so that we share common convictions, undertake common tasks, and recognize a common authority. . . . All life is a great conversation, a discourse, a speaking together, which goes back to the very beginning, to God Himself.[9]

Dialogue was key, in Berman's view, to reaching and teaching reconciliation, and for building community both locally and globally. Both Jewish and Christian theology, he reminded his readers, teach that persons must reconcile themselves to God, neighbor, and self, overcoming the alienation of original sin. For Berman, building on St. Paul, this meant that there can be "no real division between Jew and Gentile, slave and free, male and female"[10] – or, for that matter, black and white, straight and gay, old and young, rich and poor, citizen and sojourner. For every sin that destroys our relationships, there must be grace that reconciles them. For every Tower of Babel that divides our voices, there must be a Pentecost that unites them and makes them understandable to all.[11]

Such spiritual sentiments could shackle the narrow-minded. They liberated Berman from conventional habits of mind and traditional divisions of knowledge. He challenged Max Weber, Karl Marx, and Jeremy Bentham for their separation of fact and value, is and ought.[12] He criticized Alexander Solzhenitsyn for his contradistinction of law and morals, law and love.[13] He

9 Harold J. Berman, *Law and Language: Effective Symbols of Community*, ed. John Witte, Jr. (Cambridge: Cambridge University Press, 2013), 161.

10 Galatians 3:28; Ephesians 2:14–15; Colossians 3:10–11.

11 See Tibor Várady, "Afterword: From Babel to Pentecost," in Berman, *Law and Language*, 163–185.

12 Berman, *Justice in the U.S.S.R.*, 15–24; ibid., *Faith and Order*, 239, 280; ibid., *Law and Revolution*, 538, 546; ibid., *Law and Language*, 23–26, 65–82.

13 Berman, *Faith and Order*, 314, 381; ibid., *The Interaction of Law and Religion* (Nashville: Abingdon Press, 1974), 81–105.

fought against the divisions of the very world itself into East and West, old and new, developed and undeveloped. His favorite jurists were Gratian, Matthew Hale, and Joseph Story, who wrote concordances of discordant canons.[14] His favorite philosophers were Peter Abelard, Philip Melanchthon, and Michael Polanyi, who developed integrative holistic philosophies.[15] "The era of dualism is waning," Berman wrote in 1974. "We are entering into a new age of integration and reconciliation. Everywhere synthesis," the overcoming of false opposites, is "the key to this new kind of thinking and living." Either-or must give way to both-and. Not subject versus object, not fact versus value, not is versus ought, not soul versus body, not faith versus reason, not church versus state, not one versus many, "but the whole person and whole community thinking and feeling, learning and living together" – that is the common calling of humankind.[16]

Berman applied this gospel of reconciliation and integration most vigorously to his legal studies. He called for the reintegration of the classic schools of legal positivism, natural law theory, and historical jurisprudence – which, in his view, had been artificially separated since God was cast out of the legal academy. Pre-Enlightenment writers, he argued, were not only natural law theorists, who believed that "God implanted reason and conscience in the minds of men in the hearts of men." They were also legal positivists and historical jurists who "believed that God ordained earthly rulers with the power to make and enforce laws, and in addition that the history of law represents the providential fulfillment of God's providential plan" of bringing justice and order in this fallen world. They reconciled these natural, positivist, and historical dimensions of law "by finding their common source in the triune God, who himself is an all-powerful law-maker, a just and compassionate judge, and the inspirer of historical change in legal as in other social institutions."[17] It is no longer possible to appeal to a common belief in a triune God or to a Christian anthropology that emphasizes the integration of reason, will, and memory in human nature, Berman lamented. But jurists, especially those trained in interdisciplinary legal study, can still see the enduring power and utility of reconciling the historical, rational, and voluntarist elements of law, both in individual cases and doctrines, and in the legal system as a whole.

14 Berman, *Law and Revolution*, 144–148; ibid., *Faith and Order*, 170ff.; ibid., *Law and Revolution II: The Impact of the Protestant Reformations on the Western Legal Tradition* (Cambridge, MA: Harvard University Press, 2003), 100–130.
15 Berman, *Law and Revolution*, 132; ibid., *Law and Revolution II*, 77–80.
16 Berman, *Interaction*, 113.
17 Berman, *Faith and Order*, 292.

Berman called further for the reconciliation of law and religion. Their separation was, for him, a theological "heresy" and a jurisprudential "fallacy" that cannot survive in the new era of synthesis and integration. "Despite the tensions that exist in all societies between religious faith and legal order, they inevitably interact, and neither can maintain its vitality independently of the other. At the highest level, surely the just and the holy are one, and our sense of each rests partly on our sense of the other." "[L]aw and religion stand or fall together," he wrote. "[I]f we wish law to stand, we shall have to give new life to the essentially religious commitments that give it its ritual, its tradition, and its authority – just as we shall have to give new life to the social, and hence the legal, dimensions of religious faith."[18]

Berman's vision of the dialogical interaction of law and religion was rooted in his critique of prevailing positivist concepts of law and privatist concepts of religion that dominated the legal academy in his day. Many jurists, he argued, conceive of law simply as a body of rules and statutes designed to govern society. They conceive of religion simply as a body of doctrines and exercises designed to guide private conscience. Law has no place in the realm of religion. Religion has no place in the public square. Such definitions, Berman insisted, are altogether too narrow for us to recognize the mutual interdependence of law and religion: "Law is not only a body of rules; it is people legislating, adjudicating, administering, and negotiating." It is a living process, a functional process of allocating rights and duties, of resolving conflicts, of creating channels of cooperation among a variety of different individuals and institutions. Law is rules, plus the social articulation, implementation, and elaboration of those rules. Religion is not only a set of doctrines and exercises of the private conscience, of the individual heart. It is also "people manifesting a shared intuition of and collective concern for the ultimate meaning and purpose of life" – for "the idea of the holy." Religion involves creeds, cults, codes of conduct, and confessional communities. It involves beliefs plus the social articulation, implementation, and elaboration of those beliefs.[19]

Every society needs both law and religion, Berman argued. Law helps to give society the structure, the order, the harmony, the predictability it needs to "maintain inner cohesion. Law fights against anarchy." Religion helps to give society the faith, the visions, the destiny, the telos it needs "to face the future. Religion fights against decadence" and malaise. Law and religion also need each other. Law gives religion its order and stability as well as the organization

[18] Ibid., jacket description and p. 13.

[19] Berman, *Interaction*, 23–30.

and orthodoxy it needs to survive and flourish. Religion gives law the spirit and vision as well as the sanctity and sustenance it needs to command obedience and respect. Without religion, law tends to decay into empty formalism. Without law, religion tends to dissolve into shallow spiritualism.[20]

Time and History. Berman's talk of the death of dualism and the birth of an age of reconciliation points to his further belief in a teleological, if not providential, view of history. Both Jewish and Christian theology, he reminded his readers, teaches that time is continuous, not cyclical, that time moves forward from a sin-trampled garden to a golden city, from a fallen world to a perfect end time. Berman was convinced that slowly but surely all the peoples of the world would come into contact with each other, and ultimately, after revolutionary struggle and even apocalyptic explosion, would seek finally to be reconciled with each other forever.[21]

Berman's grand account of evolution and revolution in Western legal history, set out in his *Law and Revolution* series, is rooted in this basic belief about the nature and pattern of time. There is a distinctive Western legal tradition, he argued, a continuity of legal ideas and institutions, which grow by accretion and adaptation. The exact shape of these ideas and institutions is determined, in part, by the underlying religious belief systems of the people ruling and being ruled. Six great revolutions, however, have punctuated this organic gradual development: the Papal Revolution of 1075, the German Lutheran Reformation of 1517, the English Puritan Revolution of 1640, the American Revolution of 1776, the French Revolution of 1789, and the Russian Revolution of 1917. These revolutions were, in part, rebellions against a legal and political order that had become outmoded and ossified, arbitrary and abusive. But, more fundamentally, these revolutions were the products of radical shifts in the religious belief-systems of the people – shifts from Catholicism to Protestantism to Deism to the secular religion of Marxist-Leninism. Each of these new belief systems offered a new eschatology, a new apocalyptic vision of the perfect end-time, whether that be the second coming of Christ, the arrival of the heavenly city of the Enlightenment philosophers, or the withering away of the state. Each of these revolutions, in its first radical phase, sought the death of an old legal order to bring forth a new order that would survive the Last Judgment. Eventually, each of these revolutions settled down and introduced fundamental legal changes that were ultimately subsumed in and accommodated to the Western legal tradition.

20 Ibid., 31–47.

21 Ibid., *Interaction*, 119–120; ibid., *Law and Revolution*, 166–172.

In this new millennium, Berman believed, the Western legal tradition is undergoing a profound integrity crisis, graver and greater than any faced in the past millennium. The old legal order of the West is under attack both from within and from without. From within, Western law is suffering from the critical and cynical attacks relentlessly issued by jurists and judges. These legal skeptics have dismissed legal doctrine as malleable, self-contradictory rhetoric. They have depicted the law as an instrument of oppression and exploitation of women, of minorities, of the poor, of the different. They have derided the legal system for its promotion of the political purposes of the powerful and the propertied. This assault from within the law, from within the legal academies and within the courts – devoid as it is of a positive agenda of reconstruction – reflects a cynical contempt for law and government, a deep loss of confidence in its integrity and efficacy. The secular priests of the law, its officials and its educators, no longer seem to believe in what they are doing.

From without, the radical transformation of economic life and the rapid acceptance of new social forms and customs, many born of Eastern cultures and the global South, have stretched traditional Western legal doctrines to the breaking point. Each of the major branches of Western law – contracts, property, torts, family, criminal, commercial, and constitutional law – have transformed several times over in the past two generations. Many of these changes may well have been necessary to modernize the law, to conform it to contemporary social needs and ideals, to purge it of its obsolete ideas and institutions. But as a consequence, Western law – always something of a patchwork quilt – has become more of a collection of disjointed pieces, with no single thread, no single spirit holding it in place and giving it integrity and direction. This also has led to profound disillusionment with and distrust of the law.[22]

For Berman, these are signs of end times. We are reaching the end of the Western legal tradition, as we have known it. Western law is dying, he wrote, a new common law of all humanity is struggling to be born out of the counter-forces of violent balkanization, radical fundamentalism, and belligerent nationalism that now beset us all. Western law, rooted in the soils and souls of Christianity, Judaism, and their secular successors, will have a place in this new common law of humanity. But so will the laws of the East and the South, of the tribe and the jungle, of the country and the city, each with its own belief system. What needs to be forged in this new millennium is a comprehensive new religious belief system, a new pattern of language and ritual, a new

[22] Berman, *Law and Revolution*, 33–41, 538–559; ibid., "The Crisis of Legal Education in America," *Boston College Law Review* 26 (1985): 347–352.

eschaton that will give this common law of humanity its cohesion and direction.

Toward the end of his life, Berman emphasized the role of the Holy Spirit in bringing about this global reconciliation. Echoing the medieval mystic, Joachim of Fiore, Berman divided human time into three long eras. The first era before Christ was the age where God the Father dominated. The second era, just ending has been the age of God the Son. This third and final age is the age of the Holy Spirit. As Berman put it in a sermon in 2001:

> God has worked in history to bring all the peoples of the world, finally, into a world economy, with world communications, and the beginning of a world society, with world law, and ultimately, in the third millennium of the Christian era, into a world community .... It is hard for me to doubt the providential character of this historical development, which appears to be the culmination of more than five thousand years of human history .... As we experience the gradual creation of a world order, with a common economic and legal structure, we must recognize that a central ingredient of that process is a commitment to the higher spiritual truth that transcends all loyalties of blood and soil. Such a common commitment, or faith, is needed to hold together people of different nations, different cultures, and different religions. It is an inchoate faith, lacking in dogmas. It is a belief in a sacred spiritual reality that is guiding the process by which the destiny of humanity, its ongoing history on this planet, is to be fulfilled. This Age of the Holy Spirit, the third millennium in the history of Christianity, is an ecumenical age. In it, all who share a belief in a Spiritual Presence, both theists and non-theists, all who speak the language of a higher spiritual faith, all who seek a higher truth, are called to join in giving a foundation of ritual, tradition, authority, and universality to the emerging common law of mankind.[23]

A streak of mystical millenarianism colors Berman's legal historical method – much of it already conceived while he was a young man witnessing the carnage of World War II and still brimming with the heady instruction of his college mentor, Rosenstock-Huessy. Description and prescription run rather closely together in his account, and occasionally stumble over each other. Historical periods and patterns are rather too readily equated with providential plans and purposes. The doctrine of God becomes ever more diffuse, even faintly pantheistic. But here we have one of the deepest sources of many of Berman's insights and ambitions as a Christian legal scholar. He was, as he put it in a 1966 letter to Rosenstock, on a scholarly "pilgrimage."

[23] Harold J. Berman, "The God of History: A Sermon Delivered at Emory Law School," April 13, 2001 (Good Friday), 2–3 (on file in Emory Law School Library Archives).

> It is a very long, slow, hard journey. It goes through law and language, history, comparison of legal systems and cultures, the Great Revolutions, the communification [sic] of the nations, trade between planned and market economies, the hard struggle for peace, the reconciliation of man to his destiny and to God . . . . I have hope that I can make meaningful and important what you have taught me—and can possibly rescue a good deal of scholarship and make a contribution to peace—by showing, first, that American law is a human, creative response to the continued danger of disintegration and alienation, and that law altogether is a great hope for uniting mankind. But law, to fulfill this hope, must be felt to be Speech, and a response to God's Word.[24]

EVALUATION AND IMPACT

Berman did pioneering work in the fields of Soviet legal studies, comparative legal history, legal philosophy, and law and religion. His *Justice in the U.S.S.R.* (1950, 1963) and related texts showed the profound impact of the founding beliefs of Marxist-Leninism on all aspects of Russian public, private, penal, and procedural law, but also the profound dependence of Soviet law on the fundamental legal postulates of the Western legal tradition. Russian and Anglophone scholars alike continue to cite this work as the standard introduction to the Soviet legal system.[25] His early work on *Law and Language* (1964) offered a timeless statement about the intricacies of legal translation, transmission, and transplantation over time and the essential role and power of law and legal language in building culture and community both locally and globally. This work, together with *The Nature and Functions of Law* (1958), laid an early foundation for interdisciplinary legal study in general, and more particularly the modern fields of comparative hermeneutics, literary theory, legal philology, and semiotics.[26] His *Interaction of Law and Religion* (1974) demonstrated that law has a religious dimension, that religion has a legal dimension, and that a just society depends on the healthy interaction of these two fundamental dimensions of life. This book helped to launch the modern law and religion movement, now embracing several hundred law professors, with dozens of centers, programs, journals, and associations around the world.[27] And his

24 Harold J. Berman, Letter to Eugen Rosenstock-Huessy (Apr. 17, 1966) (on file in the Emory Law School Library archives).

25 See William E. Butler, Peter B. Maggs, and John B. Quigley, Jr., *Law after Revolution* (New York: Oceana Publications, 1988).

26 John Witte, Jr. and Christopher J. Manzer, "Introduction," to Berman, *Law and Language*, 1–35.

27 See John Witte, Jr., "The Study of Law and Religion in the United States: An Interim Report," *Ecclesiastical Law Journal* 14 (2012): 327–354.

volumes on *Law and Revolution* (1983 and 2003) demonstrated the immense power of Christianity in shaping and reshaping the fundamentals and fine legal points of the Western legal tradition, particularly during the High Middle Ages, the Protestant Reformation, and the English Revolution. These volumes helped mainstream legal history, particularly the history of medieval canon law, and encourage interdisciplinary approaches to historical legal studies, not only in the West, but throughout the world. The English edition of *Law and Revolution I* attracted some five dozen reviews. Its publication in European languages prompted reviewers to herald the book as a map of the genesis and genius of a united European legal culture.[28]

Guido Calabresi, Dean of Yale Law School, wrote in 1996: "Harold Berman is a giant, whose work defies the banalities of the age and allows us to take their measure. In a scholarly world drifting toward the particularistic exploration of 'unique' contexts, Berman points in a different direction – toward holistic descriptions of entire systems of legal thought .... Berman's work, and especially his *Law and Revolution*, will endure when almost everything is forgotten. He is the only American who might be paired with Max Weber in the depth of his historical and comparative understanding of the remarkable character of legal modernity."[29] This is a widely shared sentiment among Berman's peers. Berman has been variously called "our new Blackstone,"[30] "the founder of the modern discipline of law and religion,"[31] the author of "path-breaking and myth-shattering historical narratives."[32] His first *Law and Revolution* volume in particular not only won the Scribes Award from the American Bar Association, but also attracted long and laudatory reviews from leading historians in leading law journals at Harvard, Yale, Columbia, Chicago, Michigan, Cornell, Oxford, and Cambridge. While technical medieval legal historians found a good number of mistakes, misjudgments, and exaggerations in this vast work, no one doubted the profundity and power of Berman's broader historical narrative. Mirjan J. Damaška, for example, wrote in a lengthy review essay in the *Yale Law Journal* that

28 See, e.g., Uwe Wesel, "Die Revolution von 1075: Zu Harold J. Berman's bahnbrechender Studie," *Zeit Online* (30 August 1991). See further Symposium, "Harold Berman, Law and Revolution Revisited," *Rechtsgeschichte/Legal History* 21 (2013): 156–229.

29 Jacket Endorsement for Howard O. Hunter, ed., *The Integrative Jurisprudence of Harold J. Berman* (Boulder: Westview Press, 1996).

30 Gary L. McDowell, "Review of Berman, *Law and Revolution*," *American Political Science Review* 78 (1984): 577–578.

31 Thomas L. Shaffer, "Law and Religion," *Christian Legal Society Quarterly* 9 (1989): 26.

32 David S. Caudill, "Review of Berman, *Faith and Order*," *Journal of Law and Religion* 16 (2001): 716.

Berman's "account of the birth of Western law is an impressive achievement, a towering contribution to comparative legal history ..., indispensable to anyone who wishes to understand the distinctive features of Western civilization."[33]

Most significant for this volume was Berman's insistence on taking his Christian faith directly into his legal studies, and showing the power of biblical texts, tropes, and traditions for understanding the basics of legal reality. In his historical work, he worked with familiar biblical teachings on law – the role of the created order, natural law, and the Decalogue in the construction of Western legal theory; the role of biblical passages on the "two swords," "keys of the kingdom," and "render unto Caesar" in the development of Western constitutionalism; the role of biblical injunctions to "honor promises" or "flee fornication" in the construction of Western contract and family law; the role of justice and mercy in rendering legal judgment, or giving aid to the poor, needy, and sojourner; and much more. More creative and original was his use of biblical teachings on time, speech, judgment, and reconciliation to call for an integrative jurisprudence and world law, and to construct a providential theory of history that focused on the role of fundamental beliefs and shifting root metaphors in the formation and transformation of the Western legal tradition.

Berman worked hard to build institutions to continue and amplify this work, particularly in the field of law and religion. In the early 1980s, he helped establish the Council on Religion and Law that gave rise to the *Journal of Law and Religion*, which is still the standard journal in the field. He helped create the Law and Religion Section of the Association of American Law Schools, which now includes some 500 law professors among its members. He helped build the Christian Jurisprudence project of the Christian Legal Society, an early effort that brought law professors and practitioners into common cause. And he worked with Frank Alexander and me to build the Center for the Study of Law and Religion at Emory, now in its thirty-seventh year of operations.[34] As part of this effort, Berman also generously – and rigorously! – mentored hundreds of students who worked in the fields of law and religion and legal history. More than 8,000 students sat in his courses over sixty years, and

33 Mirjan J. Damaška, "How Did it All Begin?" *Yale Law Journal* 94 (1984–1985): 1807, 1824.

34 See history of the Center in April L. Bogle and Ginger Pyron, *When Law and Religion Meet: The Point of Convergence* (Grand Rapids: Wm. B. Eerdmans Publishing, 2007) and updates on http://clsr.law.edu.

scores of them became law professors throughout the world. Berman ultimately considered this his greatest accomplishment. At a late-life dinner celebrating his career, he proclaimed: "Though 'my sins be like scarlet' let my books continue to be read; and though I fall and fade, let my many students continue to soar beyond me."

14

Antonin Scalia: Devout Christian; Worldly Judge?

Thomas C. Berg*

Antonin Scalia, justice of the US Supreme Court from 1986 to his death in 2016, was a towering figure in jurisprudence and legal culture. Using his powerful intellect and trenchant writing style, Scalia reshaped debates over legal interpretation, most successfully in his insistence that judges reading a statute should focus on its text rather than the legislative debates over it or the generalized goals it might be said to promote.[1] In constitutional cases, Scalia was less consistently the victor, and frequently a dissenter. But he was the most eloquent and prominent proponent of the idea that the Constitution should be interpreted according to its "original meaning," the public meaning of its words at the time of adoption. He preferred, in his droll phrasing, a "dead Constitution," whose linguistic meaning is fixed until changed by formal amendment, over a "living Constitution" that unelected judges can manipulate as they wish.[2]

Scalia also became unusually controversial in the broader culture. His eloquence inspired generations of lawyers and students convinced by his judicial philosophy. And many people who opposed his judicial opinions nevertheless admired their razor-sharp prose. But some critics thought his attacks on other justices' positions tipped into incivility, and some went so far as to dismiss him – unfairly, as I will discuss – as merely a political ideologue whose jurisprudential method was pure pretext for a doctrinaire conservatism.

* For comments on drafts, I thank Robert Delahunty, Michael Paulsen, and the participants in the faculty works-in-progress colloquium at St. Thomas.

1 See, e.g., Antonin Scalia, *A Matter of Interpretation: Federal Courts and the Law* (Princeton: Princeton University Press, 1997). In Justice Elena Kagan's words, Scalia "taught everybody how to do statutory interpretation differently.... [W]e're all textualists now." "The Scalia Lecture: A Dialogue with Justice Kagan on the Reading of Statutes," (Nov. 25, 2015), 8:09, 8:28, http://today.law.harvard.edu/in-scalia-lecture-kagan-discusses-statutory-interpretation/.

2 See, e.g., Scalia speech at University of Fribourg, (Mar. 9, 2006), unofficial transcript at www.pegc.us/archive/Supreme_Court/scalia_fribourg_20060308.txt.

Either way, his combined intellectual impact and cultural resonance may ultimately place Scalia in history alongside such iconic judges as Blackstone, Holmes, and Brandeis.[3]

Most relevant for this study, Scalia was a devout Christian: a traditional Catholic who set forth his Christian beliefs, characteristically, with frankness, pungency, and wit. At a 1996 prayer breakfast, he exhorted attendees to wear the label "fools for Christ" and "pray for the courage to endure the scorn of the sophisticated world."[4] In a 2013 interview with *New York* magazine, he made clear that the Devil "is a real person" whose presence is less explicit today than in biblical stories only because "he's gotten wilier."[5] Scalia frequently told the story of how, during his undergraduate oral examinations at Georgetown University, he was asked the most significant event in history; he answered the Battle of Waterloo, whereupon the professor "shook his head sadly and said, 'No, Mr. Scalia. The Incarnation.'" The lesson the young Scalia drew: "'[Never] separate your religious life from your intellectual life. They're not separate.'"[6]

And yet this most publicly devout justice also frequently made clear that his beliefs had nothing to do with his judicial role. His job, he emphasized, was merely to apply the meaning of the text without regard to policy considerations or moral values, including religious values. "I'm a worldly judge," he told a Catholic audience in Rome in 1996. "I just do what the Constitution tells me to do."[7] He frequently denied there was "any such thing as a Catholic judge," adding: "The only article in faith that plays any part in my judging is the commandment 'Thou Shalt Not Lie.'"[8] Even as he vigorously dissented from the constitutional right to abortion, he emphasized that he did not do so because he viewed abortion as immoral: "If I genuinely thought the Constitution guaranteed a woman's right to abortion, I would [rule] the other way."[9]

3 See Brian Christopher Jones and Austin Sarat, "Justices as 'Sacred Symbols': Antonin Scalia and the Cultural Life of the Law," *British Journal of American Legal Studies* 6 (May 2017), 13–14, https://papers.ssrn.com/sol3/papers.cfm?abstract_id=2871469.

4 "Supreme Court Justice Tells Christians: Be Firm on Faith," *Orlando Sentinel*, April 13, 1996, http://articles.orlandosentinel.com/1996-04-13/news/9604121157_1_unmarried-couples-mormon-temple-welcoming-immigrants.

5 Jennifer Senior, "In Conversation: Antonin Scalia," *New York*, Oct. 6, 2013, http://nymag.com/news/features/antonin-scalia-2013-10/.

6 Joan Biskupic, *American Original: The Life and Constitution of Supreme Court Justice Antonin Scalia* (New York: Sarah Crichton Books, 2009) (quoting interview with Scalia, Jan. 28, 2008).

7 http://robertaconnor.blogspot.com/2016/03/justice-scalia-at-gregorian-university.html.

8 George P. Matysek, Jr., "Scalia Urges Christians to Have Courage," *Catholic Review*, Oct. 25, 2010, www.archbalt.org/justice-scalia-urges-christians-to-have-courage/.

9 Ibid.

These statements present a puzzle: did Scalia end up separating his religious life from his jurisprudence, the core of his intellectual life, or was he still somehow a distinctively Christian judge? The solution, I'll suggest, lies in distinguishing his first-order legal conclusions, which were driven largely (although not solely) by his judicial method, from his second-order choice of that method, which may well have reflected his outlook on the world, including his faith.

BIOGRAPHY

Antonin Scalia was the only child of a Sicilian-American immigrant father and a first-generation Italian-American mother.[10] Salvatore Eugene Scalia was an intellectually intense professor of Romance languages, an expert on Dante and other texts; Catherine Scalia came from a voluble Sicilian family that had produced several politicians. His parents' personalities were both evident in Antonin. He attended Jesuit schools in New York City in the 1940s and 50s, the heyday of the pre-Vatican-II Catholic enclaves in American cities. His education "established his academic prowess, entrenched his regard for Catholicism, and reinforced his rule-oriented nature."[11] He then went to Georgetown, graduating as valedictorian; to Harvard Law School, graduating magna cum laude; and to a large Cleveland law firm. In the meantime he married Maureen McCarthy, an equally devout Radcliffe graduate, and began raising a family of, ultimately, nine children.

Leaving private practice after six years, Scalia taught law in two stints, at Virginia and Chicago, separated by service in the Nixon and Ford executive branches. As an academic, he specialized in administrative law and was an early advisor to the Federalist Society, the law-student organization that soon became influential in conservative legal and policy circles. As a government official, he defended presidential prerogatives on matters from congressional oversight to domestic wiretapping.[12] President Reagan appointed Scalia to the US Court of Appeals for the District of Columbia Circuit in 1982 and to the Supreme Court in 1986.

Scalia's Senate confirmation to the high Court was unanimous, but on the bench he quickly became a lightning rod for his strongly articulated views on

[10] Details of Justice Scalia's early life are drawn largely from Biskupic, *American Original*, 11–32.

[11] Ibid., 21.

[12] Ibid., 49–57.

the Constitution. He also drew attention, and mixed reactions, for straightforwardly stating his Christian beliefs. When he told attendees at the 1996 prayer breakfast that modern elites scorned them as fools, a *Washington Post* columnist groused that Scalia had a "martyr complex" and had "joined the ranks of those Christians who … fantasize that secular society is persecuting them";[13] Barry Lynn of Americans United for Separation of Church and State claimed that Scalia's speech "clearly undermines public confidence in his objectivity regarding religious controversies."[14] Scalia's defenders answered that he was merely quoting St. Paul and that he had every right to speak on public issues – as other justices spoke – as long as he avoided commenting on pending cases.[15] "The idea that a Supreme Court justice's statement of his own religious beliefs is somehow a threat to the First Amendment," wrote Michael Paulsen and Steffen Johnson, "is simultaneously naïve and itself a threat to freedom of speech and religion."[16]

A later instance of Scalia's public religious statements, his 2013 *New York* interview, gives a taste of his firm beliefs and zestful banter:

> [*Leans in, stage-whispers.*] I even believe in the Devil.
>
> **You do?**
>
> Of course! Yeah, he's a real person. Hey, c'mon, that's standard Catholic doctrine! Every Catholic believes that.
>
> ***Every* Catholic believes this? There's a wide variety of Catholics out there …**
>
> If you are faithful to Catholic dogma, that is certainly a large part of it. …
>
> **Isn't it terribly frightening to believe in the Devil?**
>
> You're looking at me as though I'm weird. My God! Are you so out of touch with most of America, most of which believes in the Devil? I mean, Jesus Christ believed in the Devil! It's in the Gospels! You travel in circles that are so, *so* removed from mainstream America that you are appalled that anybody would believe in the Devil! Most of mankind has believed in the Devil, for all of history. Many more intelligent people than you or me have believed in the Devil.[17]

13 Colman McCarthy, "Martyrs in Their Own Minds," *Washington Post*, April 23, 1996, www.washingtonpost.com/archive/lifestyle/1996/04/23/martyrs-in-their-own-minds/8884f015-20a4-4243-8b03-d91a895ff719/?utm_term=.870bc3fe2d3f.

14 Robert A. Sirico, "Scalia's Dissenting Opinion," *Wall Street Journal*, April 19, 1996, A12 (quoting Barry Lynn).

15 Michael Stokes Paulsen and Steffen N. Johnson, "Scalia's Sermonette," *Notre Dame Law Review* 72 (1997): 863, 867–873.

16 Ibid., 874.

17 Senior, *supra* n.5.

SCALIA THE "WORLDLY JUDGE"?

His positivist, "limited sources" jurisprudence

Scalia's jurisprudence, which can only be briefly summarized here, had four major components. The first two were textualism and originalism, which he often combined: he advocated reading legal texts, statutory and constitutional, according to the meaning their words had for the public at the time of their enactment.[18] For constitutional interpretation, he sometimes added consideration of legal tradition: patterns of enactments and practices since the time of the founding.[19] Finally, he had a strong preference for categorical rules over fact-sensitive standards or balancing tests: "the rule of law," he argued, required "a law of rules."[20] His overall method was positivist in its focus on legal texts; above all it rejected various sources of interpretation, such as inquiries into "fundamental" moral or social values, that Scalia believed left judges too much room to enforce their personal views. As such, he epitomized what Kent Greenawalt has called the "limited sources" approach to judicial decision-making.[21]

As Scalia said, this approach made him a "worldly" judge: he often disclaimed any reliance on his religious beliefs. He criticized the Court vigorously for finding that Colorado's constitutional amendment overriding local gay-rights laws reflected animus toward homosexuality; but he took pains to add that he would not "indulge in … official praise for heterosexual monogamy, because I think it no business of the courts (as opposed to the political branches) to take sides in this culture war."[22] In *Planned Parenthood* v. *Casey*, after attacking the Court's reaffirmation of abortion rights, he emphasized that "[t]he States may, if they wish, permit abortion on demand, but the Constitution does not *require* them to do so."[23]

18 Scalia, *supra* n.1, 38 ("What I look for in the Constitution is precisely what I look for in a statute: the original meaning of the text[.]").

19 See, e.g., *Rutan* v. *Republican Party of Ill.*, 497 U.S. 62, 95–96 (1990) (Scalia, J., dissenting) (defending traditional patronage practices against First Amendment scrutiny); *Michael H.* v. *Gerald H.*, 491 U.S. 110, 121–24 (1989) (plurality opinion) (limiting substantive due process rights to those deeply rooted in specific legal traditions).

20 Antonin Scalia, "The Rule of Law as a Law of Rules," *University of Chicago Law Review* 56 (Fall 1989): 1175–1188.

21 Kent Greenawalt, *Private Consciences and Public Reasons* (Oxford: Oxford University Press, 1995), 141–142.

22 *Romer* v. *Evans*, 517 U.S. 620, 652 (1996) (Scalia, J., dissenting).

23 *Planned Parenthood* v. *Casey*, 505 U.S. 833, 979 (1992) (Scalia, J., concurring in the judgment in part and dissenting in part) (emphasis in original).

Scalia's emphasis on distinguishing law from the judge's moral preferences provided the foundation for his constitutional method: it was a key argument for focusing on the text's original meaning rather than its current societal meaning. Originalism, although not perfect, was "the lesser evil" because it was less prone to "the main danger in judicial interpretation of the Constitution": judges' inclination to "mistake their own predilections for the law."[24] Scalia emphasized that "[a]voiding this error is the hardest part of being a conscientious judge; perhaps no conscientious judge ever succeeds entirely." He rejected nonoriginalism because "it plays precisely to this weakness. It is very difficult for a person to discern a difference between those political values that he personally thinks most important, and those political values that are 'fundamental to our society.'"[25]

Judges up for confirmation are expected to avow that they will disregard their own preferences and follow the Constitution. Scalia took the vow,[26] but he went further and built his general interpretive approach around it. He also defended it before religious audiences who pressured him to make less separation between his jurisprudence and basic elements of Catholic faith, such as natural law. In his 1996 Rome address, to theologians at the Gregorian University, he answered a question whether he would have enforced Nazi anti-Semitic laws by saying he would have resigned from the bench – "[b]ut I would certainly not have the power to invalidate them because they are contrary to the natural law. I have been appointed to apply the Constitution and positive law. God applies the natural law."[27] In another exchange, at the University of Chicago Divinity School, he emphasized: "I try mightily to prevent my religious views or my political views or my philosophical views from affecting my interpretation of the laws, which is what my job is about."[28] He told his biographer, Joan Biskupic: "I am always reading a text and trying to give it the fairest interpretation possible .... How can my religious views have anything to do with that? ... I have religious views on [abortion]. But they have nothing whatsoever to do with my job."[29]

24 Antonin Scalia, "Originalism: The Lesser Evil," *University of Cincinnati Law Review* 57 (1989): 849, 863.

25 Ibid.

26 See quotes in Sanford Levinson, "The Confrontation of Religious Faith and Civil Religion: Catholics Becoming Justices," *DePaul Law Review* 39 (1990): 1047, 1064.

27 Antonin Scalia, "Left, Right, and the Common Good," at http://robertaconnor.blogspot.com/2016/03/justice-scalia-at-gregorian-university.html.

28 "Scalia Calls Death Penalty Constitutional, Not Immoral," Pew Research Center: Religion & Public Life, Feb. 4, 2002, www.pewforum.org/2002/02/04/scalia-calls-death-penalty-constitutional-not-immoral/.

29 Biskupic, *American Original*, 191 (citing Death Penalty Address, http://pewforum.org/deathpenalty/resources/transcript3.php; interview with Scalia, May 1, 2008).

On the issue of separating legal interpretation from personal beliefs, Scalia's critics fired at him from two sides. Many, especially in the dominant liberal side of the legal academy, doubted that he separated his personal beliefs from his judicial decisions. Others, including some in the traditional religious world with which he sympathized, worried that he had separated his faith too greatly from his decisions.

Did Scalia actually vote his religious/moral views?

Many observers charged that Scalia's originalism was a cover for his personal preferences. They pointed out that he sometimes omitted any originalist analysis in his opinions, or reached results difficult to square with originalism (more about this shortly). They concluded that Scalia "departs radically from his chosen theory when it suits his fancy":[30] that "[w]hen original meaning does not support the result they want to reach," Scalia and the other conservative justices "tend to ignore it, making it difficult to take their professions of originalism seriously."[31]

In one especially barbed commentary in 2007, Geoffrey Stone attacked the five Court members who had just voted to uphold the federal ban on "partial-birth" abortions.[32] Observing that "[a]ll five justices in the majority ... are Catholic," Stone charged them with "fail[ing] to respect the fundamental difference between religious belief and morality."[33] It was "painfully awkward" and "mortifying to have to point this out," he claimed, "[b]ut it is too obvious, and too telling, to ignore."[34] He quoted the Court's statement in *Casey* that "[o]ur obligation is to define the liberty of all, not to mandate our own moral code,"[35] and he concluded: "It is sad that Justices Roberts, Scalia, Kennedy, Thomas and Alito have chosen not to follow this example."[36]

30 Gene R. Nichol, "Justice Scalia and the *Printz* Case: The Trials of an Occasional Originalist," *University of Colorado Law Review* 70 (1999): 953, 969–971 (pointing to cases involving takings of private property, free exercise of religion, standing to sue, and race-based affirmative action).

31 Andrew Koppelman, "Phony Originalism and the Establishment Clause," *Northwestern University Law Review* 103 (2009): 727, 729.

32 Geoffrey R. Stone, "Our Faith-Based Justices," Huffington Post, April 20, 2007, www.huffingtonpost.com/geoffrey-r-stone/our-faithbased-justices_b_46398.html (discussing *Gonzales* v. *Carhart*, 550 U.S. 124 (2007)).

33 Ibid.

34 Ibid.

35 *Casey*, 505 U.S. at 850.

36 Stone, *supra*.

Stone's charge was a severe overreach, at the very least as applied to Scalia, whose position in the abortion cases was fully explicable by his constitutional methodology. Whatever may be said about the constitutional right to abortion, it is hard to find it in the Fourteenth Amendment's text (the Due Process Clause speaks of procedural, not substantive, protections) or its original meaning (in 1868, 30 of the 37 states had criminal abortion laws, many of them recently enacted[37]). And Scalia believed unenumerated privacy rights were illegitimate in general, not just regarding abortion. There was no warrant to assert that the Catholic justices put the dictates of their faith above their best understanding of American law – a toxic suggestion that reintroduced charges of disloyalty leveled at American Catholics in the past.[38]

Scalia reached results on constitutional interpretation concerning abortion, and other issues, that were likely consistent with his religious, moral, and political beliefs. But that does not prove he reached the results because of those beliefs rather than his constitutional methodology.[39] Later I consider whether his choice of methodology itself arose from his religious worldview. But that is a different question from whether his methodology was a mere pretext for voting his personal views.

Scalia clearly reached some results that conflicted with his personal views.[40] He often pointed to the decisions he wrote holding that criminal defendants have the right to confront witnesses against them in court, even when the witness's out-of-court statement is reliable[41] and even when the witness is a vulnerable child.[42] Scalia also provided the crucial fifth vote in rulings that the First Amendment protected protesters who burned the American flag.[43] "If it were up to me," he said, "I would put in jail every

37 See, e.g., Joseph W. Dellapenna, *Dispelling the Myths of Abortion History* (Durham: Carolina Academic Press, 2006), 315–320 (compiling the statutes).

38 See, e.g., Mark S. Massa, S.J., *Anti-Catholicism in America: The Last Acceptable Prejudice* (New York: Crossroad Publishing, 2005).

39 Michael Stokes Paulsen, "The Supreme Greatness of Justice Antonin Scalia," *Public Discourse*, March 15, 2016, www.thepublicdiscourse.com/2016/03/16612/ (arguing that Scalia "did not allow his personal or political views to dictate his legal interpretations, even if sometimes they coincided").

40 In the words of constitutional commentator, and political liberal, Jeffrey Rosen, "[T]he case against Scalia as an inconsistent originalist fails to acknowledge the many occasions on which his constitutional conclusions did indeed diverge from his policy preferences." Jeffrey Rosen, "What Made Antonin Scalia Great," *The Atlantic*, Feb. 15, 2016, www.theatlantic.com/politics/archive/2016/02/what-made-antonin-scalia-great/462837/.

41 See, e.g., *Crawford* v. *Washington*, 541 U.S. 36 (2004) (overturning murder conviction); *Melendez-Diaz* v. *Massachusetts*, 557 U.S. 305 (2009) (overturning drug-dealing conviction).

42 *Coy* v. *Iowa*, 487 U.S. 1012 (1988).

43 *Texas* v. *Johnson*, 491 U.S. 397 (1989); *United States* v. *Eichman*, 496 U.S. 310 (1990).

sandal-wearing, scruffy-bearded weirdo who burns the American flag .... But I am not king."[44]

Nevertheless, Scalia also gave his critics ammunition, because he reached results in a number of prominent cases that seemed at odds with originalist methodology. For example, he treated virtually all affirmative-action measures benefiting minorities as violations of the Fourteenth Amendment, despite evidence that the same Congress that passed the Amendment in 1868 also instituted race-based benefits such as the Freedmen's Bureau.[45] Instead of grappling with what such evidence indicated about the original meaning, Scalia's opinions condemned affirmative action on the broad, moralistic ground that racial discrimination of any kind is "'illegal, immoral, unconstitutional, inherently wrong, and destructive of democratic society.'"[46] That is the language of a "living Constitution," not of original meaning.

In other cases too, Scalia reached results that seem questionable under the original-meaning criterion while providing no originalist arguments for them. He wrote the Court's opinion preventing Congress from authorizing citizens to sue in federal court on behalf of the public,[47] even though several such public actions were recognized at the time of the founding.[48] He joined the ruling that stretched Congress' interstate commerce power – already enlarged over founding-era principles – to allow federal prosecution of a woman who grew medical marijuana in her home solely for her medicinal use.[49] He joined the ruling stopping the Florida presidential recount in *Bush* v. *Gore*,[50] based on (among other things) the Fourteenth Amendment's Equal Protection Clause, even though the weight of evidence of original public meaning shows that "political" rights such as voting fell within the Fifteenth Amendment, not the Fourteenth.[51]

Even from this evidence, it would be unfair to conclude that Scalia's methodology was mere cover for his personal views. Recall that on significant

44 Quoted in Scott Bomboy, "Justice Antonin Scalia Rails Again about Flag-Burning 'Weirdoes,'" *Constitution Daily*, Nov. 12, 2015, http://blog.constitutioncenter.org/2015/11/justice-antonin-scalia-rails-again-about-flag-burning-weirdoes/.

45 Eric Schnapper, "Affirmative Action and the Legislative History of the Fourteenth Amendment," *Virginia Law Review* 71 (1985): 753, 796.

46 *City of Richmond* v. *J. A. Croson Co.*, 488 U.S. 469, 521 (1989) (Scalia, J., concurring in the judgment) (quoting Alexander Bickel, *The Morality of Consent* (1975), 133).

47 *Lujan* v. *Defenders of Wildlife*, 504 U.S. 555 (1992).

48 Cass R. Sunstein, "What's Standing after *Lujan*? Of Citizen Suits, 'Injuries,' and Article III," *Michigan Law Review* 91 (1992): 163, 170–179.

49 *Gonzales* v. *Raich*, 545 U.S. 1 (2005).

50 531 U.S. 98 (2000).

51 See, e.g., Akhil Reed Amar, "Bush, Gore, Florida, and the Constitution," *Florida Law Review* 61 (Dec. 2009): 946, 965.

subjects such as criminal procedure and free speech rights, he followed principles to results that surely conflicted with his preferences. Even the questionable rulings have potential methodological explanations. Sometimes the result arguably fit the original public meaning of the Constitution's words as set forth in dictionaries or legal texts – Scalia's criterion – even if it did not square with founding-era practices. Thus, perhaps the public in 1868 understood the Fourteenth Amendment to state a principle of "colorblindness," even if Congress sometimes departed from the principle.[52]

Some of Scalia's other decisions reflect other elements in his methodology besides original meaning. His majority opinion in *Employment Division* v. *Smith* eliminated Free Exercise Clause challenges to "neutral and generally applicable laws," not because of the clause's text or original meaning (which *Smith* did not investigate), but because such challenges required judges to balance religious and governmental interests, something they could not do, he said, in a principled way. There his jurisprudential preference for categorical rules acted as trump card. In other decisions, like the medical-marijuana case, he arguably accepted precedents whose results he would not have reached initially. Indeed, he acknowledged that he was a "faint-hearted originalist" who "would adulterate [the method] with the doctrine of *stare decisis*," meaning some decisions would stand even if scholars "demonstrate[d] unassailably that [they] got the meaning of the Constitution wrong."[53]

The problem, however, is that Scalia often failed to explain these results, or his application of different aspects of his methodology in different cases. He never confronted the challenge that color-conscious practices during the Reconstruction era posed for his position that the Fourteenth Amendment required colorblindness. "The issue is not . . . whether an originalist case could possibly be made for colorblindness. It's whether Scalia had made the case, or even tried to."[54] Nor did he develop a theory of *stare decisis* to explain when to accept nonoriginalist precedents – or even extend them, as in *Bush* v. *Gore* and the medical-marijuana decision. Without such a criterion, giving weight to

[52] Moreover, the Reconstruction programs overwhelmingly benefited persons – newly freed slaves – who had directly suffered racial discrimination under the authority of federal and state law. Even Scalia was willing to allow race-conscious remedies in such cases. *Croson*, 488 U.S. at 524 (Scalia, J., concurring in the judgment). But cf. Schnapper, *supra* n.45, 796 (Reconstruction programs did not "screen individual black participants to assure that they were actual victims").

Also in Scalia's defense, his inconsistencies were noticeable precisely because his methodology gave relatively clear criteria to which he himself could be held accountable – "something that is not true of all, or even most, Supreme Court justices." Paulsen, *supra* n.39.

[53] Scalia, "Originalism: The Lesser Evil," 861.

[54] Mitchell Berman, "The Tragedy of Justice Scalia," *Michigan Law Review* 115 (2017): 783, 806.

precedent threatens to reintroduce the judicial discretion that Scalia sought to exclude. In short, Scalia gave powerful witness to the importance of objectivity in judging and interpretation, but – like most of us – he sometimes weakened the credibility of his own witness.

Did he wrongly fail to integrate his religious/moral views?

Justice Scalia also had critics on the religious side, who complained that his posture of judicial neutrality on moral and cultural issues was misguided – that he failed to implement moral principles on which the Constitution itself rests. While social conservatives generally admired him, some objected to Scalia's declaration that if the popular institutions in a democracy want abortion rights, a judge has no ground to stand in their way.[55] On the religious left, some people criticized him for upholding death sentences, allegedly in violation of Catholic teaching that capital punishment was immoral.[56]

Scalia stated that if faced with a conflict between the dictates of the Constitution and his faith, he would resign.[57] He never faced that conflict over abortion rights, since he believed it did not exist. But he said he would have faced it over the death penalty, which he clearly believed was constitutional, had he also believed it was immoral under Catholic teaching. In a 2002 address, he argued that a judge could not affirm a death sentence – even a Supreme Court justice reviewing a penalty decreed by a state – without becoming "part of the criminal-law machinery that imposes death."[58] He would therefore face a conflict of conscience if he were bound by "the encyclical *Evangelium Vitae* and the new Catholic catechism . . ., according to which the death penalty can only be imposed to protect rather than avenge, and since it is (in most modern societies) not necessary for the former purpose, it is wrong." But, he said, he disagreed with the recent teaching, since it went against centuries of earlier doctrine and failed to take into account the state's role as instrument of God's vengeance.[59] "I am happy to have reached that

55 See, e.g., Robert A. Connor, "Justice Scalia and Yogi Berra: A Matter of Interpretation," *American Journal of Jurisprudence* 41 (1996): 165, 187–88 (arguing that Scalia's statement overlooks the natural-law grounding of American constitutional democracy).

56 See, e.g., David Gibson, "Should Justice Scalia Resign?," *Commonweal*, Sept. 30, 2011, www.commonwealmagazine.org/blog/should-justice-scalia-resign.

57 See Levinson, *supra* n.26, 1064; Scalia, "Left, Right, and the Common Good," *supra* n.27.

58 Antonin Scalia, "God's Justice and Ours," *First Things*, May 2002, www.firstthings.com/article/2002/05/gods-justice-and-ours.

59 Ibid. ("[T]he major impetus behind the modern aversion to the death penalty is the [erroneous] equation of private morality with governmental morality . . . . [According to St. Paul, government, unlike the individual,] is the 'minister of God' with powers to 'revenge,' to

conclusion," he said, "because I like my job, and would rather not resign."[60] Here again, Scalia's constitutional view – which was clearly defensible based on legal text and tradition – coincided with his traditionalist moral view.[61]

Conservative commentator Christopher Wolfe defended Scalia's posture of judicial neutrality but raised two narrower criticisms.[62] First, Scalia could do more in his opinions to offer moral defenses of the laws he was upholding as constitutional. Although Wolfe accepted the limited-sources approach under which the morality of a law was irrelevant to its constitutionality, he worried that this approach created "a profound asymmetry in the Court's cases [involving] culture war issues." Liberal constitutional method itself incorporated moral arguments – both *Roe* and *Casey* "make an argument for a women's right to choose to have an abortion" – while the dissents, based in judicial restraint, merely "point out that the Constitution [leaves the] matter to the states. There has never been a Court opinion that attempts to explain why abortion or homosexuality is wrong."[63] Wolfe worried about the Court's "educative impact," its power not just to decide cases but to "help shape [public] opinions." Cultural conservatives suffered "a great disadvantage" in such debates, "with their views on the substantive issues at stake muffled." He suggested that conservative justices, while upholding traditionalist laws based on

'execute wrath,' including even wrath by the sword."). He added "that the more Christian a country is the *less* likely it is to regard the death penalty as immoral," which he "attribute[d] to the fact that, for the believing Christian, death is no big deal." Ibid. (emphasis in original). The last assertion is questionable, overlooking the very substantial abolition of the death penalty in Catholic-dominated Latin America. See www.deathpenaltyinfo.org/abolitionist-and-retentionist-countries.

60 Ibid.

61 Setting aside whether Scalia was correct about the morality of capital punishment or the status of Catholic moral teaching on it, his claim that he was morally complicit in death sentences seems questionable – at least when he would be engaging (as he usually would be) in habeas corpus review of the constitutionality of a state sentence. A federal judge is arguably no more complicit in allowing a state to proceed with a constitutionally permissible execution than in allowing a state to proceed with a liberalized abortion law – which Scalia said he would do, but which permits (according to pro-life premises) killing of unborn persons. Cf. John T. Garvey and Amy B. Coney, "Catholic Judges in Capital Cases," *Marquette Law Review* 81 (1998): 303, 330–31 ("Saying that the Eighth Amendment does not authorize intervention [in a capital case, on appeal or habeas,] is not equivalent to enforcing or approving what [the legislature] has done."). Scalia argued that judges were more complicit in allowing killing by government than by private persons – but one might counter that executions are far less numerous and involve guilty rather than innocent persons.

62 See Christopher F. Wolfe, "Some Religiously Devout Justices, Civil Religion, and the Culture War," *Marquette Law Review* 81 (1998): 427.

63 Ibid., 434.

constitutional text or history, should mention moral or policy arguments for them as well.[64]

Scalia later moved in the direction Wolfe suggested. For example, in *Stenberg* v. *Carhart*,[65] where the Court struck down a state "partial-birth" abortion ban somewhat broader than the later federal ban, Scalia dissented and attacked such abortions with a passion he had never expressed before in an opinion. He called the method "so horrible that the most clinical description of it evokes a shudder of revulsion"; he called it "absurd" to claim that the Constitution, designed to "'secure the Blessings of Liberty to ourselves and our Posterity,' prohibits the States from simply banning this visibly brutal means of eliminating our half-born posterity."[66] Such language was actually part of a progression in which Scalia became less self-restrained – call it less self-censoring – over time.

Wolfe's second criticism was that Scalia sometimes "fail[ed] to distinguish more carefully what might be called his 'judicial positivism' from a broader 'legal positivism'":

> So concerned does he appear to be with denying judicial discretion untethered to the positive law – a completely defensible position for a moral traditionalist – that the language he uses at times suggests a much broader (and completely indefensible) positivism, i.e., that what the majority does is right because the majority does it.[67]

This tendency to conflate philosophical and legal positivism appeared in Scalia's wide-ranging 1996 address to the Gregorian theologians.[68] He began by making a sharp distinction between the goals of Christianity and those of the civil state: he denied that any particular form of government was most conducive to the "Christian common good," that is, to "increasing the love of God or the chances of salvation." Government, he said, "is not meant for saving souls, but for protecting life and property and assuring the conditions for physical property." He questioned Christian socialism in particular, criticizing the equation of government redistribution with Christian charity: "[T]he transformation of charity into legal entitlement has produced both donors without love [since they pay taxes under compulsion] and recipients

64 Ibid., 435. Wolfe suggested stating the moral arguments as third-party hypothetical questions: "What are we judges to say to those who argue ... [here state a trenchant case for a moral traditionalist public policy]?").

65 530 U.S. 914 (2000).

66 Ibid., 953 (Scalia, J., dissenting) (quoting US Const., Preamble).

67 Wolfe, 439.

68 Scalia, "Left, Right, and the Common Good," *supra* n.27.

without gratitude." And he noted that in the United States, government-provided services from orphanages to schooling "cannot be intermingled with Christian teaching or even, increasingly, with Christian morality."[69] He concluded that he was claiming

> not that a government of the right is more Christlike, only that there is no reason to believe that a government of the left is. To tell you the truth, I don't think Christ cares very much what sort of political system we live under. He certainly displayed very little interest in that subject during his time among us, as did his apostles. Accordingly, we should select our economic and political systems on the basis of what seems to produce the greatest material good for the greatest number, and leave theology out of it.[70]

Scalia's reasoning on these points, though sharp and provocative, was certainly debatable. As questioners remarked, Catholic theology historically has not made the "very strong distinction [Scalia drew] between the temporal things being assigned to the world and the spiritual things being assigned to God." That dichotomy, one questioner said, reflected "a Protestant way of understanding it, whereby the world is . . . a place of sin" governed by will, not by natural law or reason as Catholic moral theology holds.[71] Nor, others objected, does Christian theology treat the "natural man" as solely an "economic actor," or the purpose of secular government as solely to protect material interests.

In response, Scalia reemphasized statements in the New Testament that separate the claims of God from those of civil institutions: "Render unto Caesar the things that are Caesar's"; "Slaves, obey your masters." Both Jesus and St. Paul, he said, were more concerned with faithfulness and salvation than with the form of government under which Christians lived.[72] But these arguments, too, are debatable. Christianity was too small a movement in New Testament times to influence government; but both the Old Testament and post-Constantinian Christian political theology have much to suggest concerning government's role in promoting justice in society.

Scalia agreed that moral propositions play a role in a democracy, but only, he said, through the arguments of citizens who try to convince a majority, "which will then have its effect upon the government." He denied that democracy itself supplied substantive values: "I don't know how you can argue on the basis of democratic theory that the government has a moral obligation to do something that is opposed by the people." Because "[t]he

69 Ibid.
70 Ibid.
71 Ibid.
72 Ibid.

whole theory of democracy ... is that the majority rules," the state "protect[s] minorities only because the majority determines that there are certain minorities or certain minority positions that deserve protection .... Otherwise you do not want a democracy, you want a king to decide what is right."[73] But these assertions, too, are questionable. They overlook the argument that even minimally effective operation of the democratic process probably depends on certain substantive values like equal citizenship, free debate, and some basic education.[74] Scalia's assertions also overlook that in a democratic republic policy is made by representatives who can exercise independent judgment during their terms – as Edmund Burke famously advocated[75] – before submitting themselves again to voters.

Scalia ultimately conceded that his case for positivism in decision making was stronger for judges than for legislators. "Maybe," he said, "my very stingy view ... of the role of natural law and Christianity in the governance of the state comes from the fact that I am a judge, and it is my duty to apply the law."[76] It makes perfect sense that judges should confine themselves to positive law while – even in a democracy – legislators vote their moral conscience between elections and the state's legitimacy rests on natural justice, not simply majority rule. As some questioners at the Gregorian noted, although Scalia made "philosophical or theological" claims about the limited nature of the democratic state, in truth he was defending a narrower claim: what he was "allowed to do as a judge" within the "determined historical and constitutional context ... of the United States."[77] His assertions about the nature of the state, although not necessarily wrong, raised many more complexities than did his assertions about the judicial role.

Did Scalia's religious commitments drive his methodology?

If Scalia maintained a principled, albeit imperfect, adherence to positivist methodology, that merely pushes the question back one step: did his Christian commitments influence him to adopt that methodology? The crudest connection would be for a traditionalist to choose to read legal texts according to

73 Ibid.

74 See, e.g., John Hart Ely, *Democracy and Distrust: A Theory of Judicial Review* (Cambridge, MA: Harvard University Press, 1980), 93–94, 152–153 (free debate, equal respect); Frank Michelman, "Welfare Rights in a Constitutional Democracy," *Washington University Law Quarterly* 1979 (1979): 659, 677.

75 Edmund Burke, "Speech to the Electors of Bristol," Nov. 3, 1774, http://press-pubs.uchicago.edu/founders/documents/v1ch13s7.html.

76 "Left, Right, and the Common Good," *supra* n.27, Q&A session.

77 Ibid.

their original meaning, one often fixed in the distant past, because he values the judgments of the past over those of today. But again, it is unfair to charge Scalia with being crassly result-oriented.

A subtler, although still speculative, account came from law professor George Kannar in an article published early in Scalia's Supreme Court tenure. Even then, Scalia had already departed from "conservative" results in some cases; this suggested, Kannar said, that "a facile focus on [Scalia's] supposed 'result-orientation'" was unfair, and that his methodology arose "from sources in his character running deeper than his specifically political convictions."[78] Kannar located Scalia's methodological commitments – to text, history, and categorical rules – in, among other things, his pre-Vatican-II Catholic education. Quoting Garry Wills, Kannar argued that Catholic schooling, through documents like the Baltimore Catechism, transmitted the Church's historical teachings, but with relatively little emphasis on understanding the broad historical context and far more on mastering categories and "'a vast terminology,' all in the service of a life-absorbing, habit-forming 'urge to codify reality and capture it in rules.'"[79] Since legal education at the time also emphasized mastering relatively formal categories, Scalia's schooling overall "promote[d] an exceptionally strong respect for 'the rules laid down.'"[80] Kannar suggested additional sources of Scalia's positivist approach to law, including his father's reverence for the literal meaning of texts.[81]

Hypotheses about formative influences on a justice are inevitably speculative. But Scalia's emphasis on the importance of decision-making by rules, and on the dangers of giving discretion to unelected judges, pervaded his writing both on jurisprudence and on other matters. It seems reasonable to hypothesize that it stemmed from premises at the core of his outlook on the world. Such core premises characteristically reflect a mixture of influences: family background, education, and in the case of a devout and intellectually engaged believer like Scalia, religious faith.

Kannar briefly mentioned "original sin" in discussing Scalia's religious formation,[82] and more might be said on how Christian teachings about human temptations could have helped incline Scalia toward condemning judicial discretion. As Reinhold Niebuhr has described, the Bible describes

78 George Kannar, "The Constitutional Catechism of Antonin Scalia," *Yale Law Journal* 99 (1990): 1297, 1309.

79 Ibid., 1315 (quoting Garry Wills, *Bare Ruined Choirs: Doubt, Prophecy, and Radical Religion* (1972): 16, 32).

80 Ibid., 1315.

81 Ibid., 1319–1320.

82 Ibid., 1309.

the characteristic sin of the mighty as pervasive pride and self-deception; for the "worldly wise" (intellectuals) in particular, this means the pretension that one's perspective is universal rather than partial.[83] This fits well with Scalia's warning that the "main danger" for judges is their inclination to "mistake their own predilections for the law."[84] It fits with his frequent impulse to treat the views of the Court, and of elites in general, as overinflated bubbles to be punctured.[85] Scalia, wrote law professor John Jeffries, "is informed by [among other things] a sharp distrust of easy promises about a better world."[86] From this perspective, constitutional mandates claim a dangerous finality, because they are so hard to revise – but legislative decision-making has the virtue of "corrigibility," in its "openness to revision by citizens' exercise of the vote."[87]

Kannar properly emphasized that there is no single "Catholic" (let alone "Christian") inclination on a matter as complicated as interpreting legal texts. Scalia's particular Catholic formation and outlook may have helped make him skeptical of judicial discretion. But justices formed by a more philosophical version of natural law may be inclined to think that constitutionally recognized general concepts such as equality or private property have a moral logic capable of elucidation in particular cases.[88] And justices formed by a Christian concern for the vulnerable may be inclined to emphasize the Constitution's guarantees of protection and equality for minority groups and unpopular perspectives.

A CASE STUDY: SCALIA ON CHURCH AND STATE

A Christian judge is particularly likely to have some interests in cases before him involving religious liberty and church–state relations. Scalia articulated

83 See, e.g., Reinhold Niebuhr, *The Nature and Destiny of Man, v. 1: Human Nature* (New York: Scribner, 1941), 186–207.

84 Scalia, "Originalism: The Lesser Evil," 863.

85 For example: "[T]he point at which life becomes 'worthless,' and the point at which the means necessary to preserve it become 'extraordinary' or 'inappropriate,' are neither set forth in the Constitution nor known to the nine Justices of this Court any better than they are known to nine people picked at random from the Kansas City telephone directory." *Cruzan* v. *Director, Missouri Dept. of Health*, 497 U.S. 261, 293 (1990) (Scalia, J., concurring).

86 John C. Jeffries, Jr., "Tribute," *New York University Annual Survey of American Law* (2006): 11.

87 H. Jefferson Powell, *The Moral Tradition of American Constitutionalism* (Durham: Duke University Press, 1993), 289.

88 See, e.g., Michael J. Perry, *The Constitution, the Courts, and Human Rights* (New Haven: Yale University Press, 1982) (non-economic rights); Hadley Arkes, *The Return of George Sutherland: Restoring a Jurisprudence of Natural Rights* (Princeton: Princeton University Press, 1997) (private property).

strongly held opinions on the subject under both religion clauses of the First Amendment, free exercise and non-establishment. His opinions make an interesting case study in the complex relation between his personal inclinations and his constitutional methodology.

As to the Free Exercise Clause, as already noted, Scalia wrote the controversial opinion for the Court in *Smith*, eliminating protection for religious conduct when it conflicts with "neutral law[s] of general applicability."[89] Because *Smith* omitted any inquiry into the original meaning of "free exercise," critics saw the ruling as another example of Scalia's selectivity in following his methodology.[90]

Whether *Smith*'s rule conflicted with Scalia's personal views on religious freedom protections is also a complex question. He voiced concern about secular government's increasing pressure on religious life; for example, he praised Catholic colleges that march to a different tune than society's and suggested that a student-funded gay-rights group at Georgetown had been "imposed upon [the university] by a questionable court decree."[91] Despite this, in *Smith* his rule-oriented methodology led him to adopt a principle that greatly weakened constitutional challenges to such impositions. But he was also clear that legislatures could enact religious exemptions: *Smith* suggested that these were "permitted, or even desirable."[92]

Scalia was deeply committed to *Smith* as a methodological matter, but he also may have had confidence in 1990 that the political branches would respect religion, including traditional Catholicism, and accommodate it generously in statutes and regulations. Recently, such confidence has become questionable; traditionalist Christianity faces increasing governmental and social pressure from progressive views on sexual morality and from growth among the religiously unaffiliated. In his later years, Scalia voted to protect traditional religious claimants against non-discrimination suits by clergy (*Hosanna-Tabor Church & School* v. *EEOC*[93]) and against the Obamacare contraception-coverage mandate (*Burwell* v. *Hobby Lobby Stores*[94]). But it is

89 494 U.S. 872, 877 (1990).

90 Several years after the fact, Scalia set forth an originalist defense of *Smith*. *City of Boerne* v. *Flores*, 521 U.S. 507, 537-44 (1997) (Scalia, J., concurring in part). In the same case, Justice O'Connor presented the originalist case against *Smith*, and in favor of some constitutionally mandated exemptions. Ibid., 549–564 (O'Connor, J., dissenting).

91 Jeffrey Gold, "Catholic Universities Neglect Their Mission," Assoc. Press. Pol. Serv., March 6, 1997, 1997 WL 2506558 (Scalia speech at Seton Hall University).

92 494 U.S. at 890; see also *Texas Monthly* v. *Bullock*, 489 U.S. 1, 29–45 (1989) (Scalia, J., dissenting).

93 132 S. Ct. 694 (2012).

94 134 S. Ct. 2751 (2014).

unfair to conclude that he changed his tune because religious conservatives needed protection. *Hobby Lobby*, for example, is consistent with *Smith* because it was decided under religious freedom legislation, not the Free Exercise Clause.[95] With respect to religious freedom, as in other areas, Scalia seemed to adhere to methodological principle in disregard of certain of his personal preferences – although other preferences of his arguably made him comfortable with the result.

In cases involving claims of government "establishment of religion," Scalia's position was simpler. He voted to reject such challenges in every one of the twenty-three merits cases before the Court during his tenure.[96] He repeatedly urged the Court to adopt rules that would allow more room for religious influences in public life, from official prayers or symbolic displays to religious speech in public schools to government funding of religious schools. "Those who wrote the Constitution," he argued, "believed that morality was essential to the well-being of society and that encouragement of religion was the best way to foster morality":[97] thus government actions favoring religion were not establishments unless they either were coercive or made more specific religious assertions than simply acknowledging a creator.[98] He based this conclusion on the original public meaning of "establishment," as shown by government acknowledgments of religion in the founding period.[99] Although his reading of the history is open to challenge in some respects,[100] Scalia doubtless held it sincerely and based it on close study.

At the same time, Scalia was surely comfortable as a policy matter with government acknowledgment of religion. As he wrote, with considerable passion, in dissenting from the Court's invalidation of prayers at public school graduation ceremonies:

95 *Hosanna-Tabor* is more difficult to reconcile with *Smith*, since both cases involved constitutionally mandated exemptions from general laws. The best defense of Scalia's vote is his preference for rules over standards: *Hosanna-Tabor* adopted a categorical bar against religious leaders suing their employers for employment decisions, while *Smith* rejected a more open-ended balancing test for free exercise exemptions generally.

96 From *Edwards* v. *Aguillard*, 482 U.S. 578 (1987), through *Town of Greece* v. *Galloway*, 134 S. Ct. 1811 (2014).

97 *McCreary County* v. *American Civil Liberties Union*, 545 U.S. 844, 887 (2005) (Scalia, J., dissenting).

98 Ibid., 893–894.

99 See ibid., 886–989, 895–899; *Lee* v. *Weisman*, 505 U.S. 577, 632–636 (1992) (Scalia, J., dissenting).

100 See, e.g., *Van Orden* v. *Perry*, 545 U.S. 677, 722–735 (Stevens, J., dissenting); *Weisman*, 505 U.S. at 612–616, 622–626 (Souter, J., concurring).

> Church and state would not be such a difficult subject if religion were, as the Court apparently thinks it to be, some purely personal avocation that can be indulged entirely in secret, like pornography, in the privacy of one's room. For most believers it is *not* that, and has never been. Religious men and women of almost all denominations have felt it necessary to acknowledge and beseech the blessing of God as a people, and not just as individuals . . . . [Moreover,] nothing, absolutely nothing, is so inclined to foster among religious believers of various faiths a toleration – no, an affection – for one another than voluntarily joining in prayer together, to the God whom they all worship and seek.[101]

In short, the Establishment Clause was an area where Scalia's historical and traditionalist approaches to interpretation easily coincided with his own policy views.

CONCLUSION

"No one on the contemporary Court spoke out on religion before audiences as Scalia did."[102] Simultaneously, no justice articulated a methodology that so clearly claimed to separate judicial conclusions from religious beliefs. But Antonin Scalia was an integrated personality. His personal and intellectual orientation to the world did not (usually) dictate his conclusions, but it almost certainly influenced his adoption of the methodology that he applied and so powerfully defended.

[101] See, e.g., *Weisman*, 505 U.S. at 645–46 (Scalia, J., dissenting).
[102] Biskupic, *American Original*, 188.

15

The Insights and Transitions of Mary Ann Glendon

Paolo G. Carozza

INTRODUCTION

Mary Ann Glendon first encountered the thought and work of the twentieth-century Canadian Catholic philosopher and theologian Bernard J. F. Lonergan, S.J., through her Jesuit colleagues at Boston College in the 1970s. Lonergan sought to discern a path through the turbulence and confusion of the modern era by taking the inheritance of the Catholic intellectual tradition, especially Thomism, and appropriating within it the achievements of both modern philosophy (particularly Kant) and also of the human and natural sciences. His most famous work, *Insight: A Study of Human Understanding*,[1] turned its attention to the dynamic structure and processes of human knowledge, judgment, and decision, and inquired in particular how human beings gain that spark of "insight" that constitutes a new and significant step forward in understanding reality. Not unlike Aquinas's assimilation of classical philosophy into his integrative theology nearly a thousand years earlier, Lonergan's approach aimed to avoid being either reactionary or acritical with respect to his contemporary world. Glendon frequently invokes Lonergan's observation that

> There is bound to be formed a solid right that is determined to live in a world that no longer exists. There is bound to be formed a scattered left, captivated by now this, now that new development, exploring now this and now that new possibility. But what will count is a perhaps not numerous center, big enough to be at home in both the old and the new, painstaking enough to work out one by one the transitions to be made, strong enough to refuse half measures and insist on complete solutions even though it has to wait.[2]

[1] Bernard J. F. Lonergan, *Insight: A Study of Human Understanding*, ed. Frederick E. Crowe and Robert M. Doran (Toronto: University of Toronto Press, 1992).

[2] Bernard J. F. Lonergan, *Collection*, ed. Frederick E. Crowe and Robert M. Doran (Toronto: University of Toronto Press, 1988), 245.

Glendon has described herself explicitly as trying to work in the spirit of that approach.[3] Her prolific and broad-ranging scholarly contributions, as well as her multiple forays into public service on behalf of the United States and the Holy See, can be best understood not as the systematic development or application of a particular jurisprudential school of thought, but rather as the painstaking work of pursuing a series of insights into the transitions to be made in law and in society, across a broad range of discrete topics, at the turn of the twenty-first century. That is not to say that there are not also persistent and coherent themes that animate and unite her work, especially ideas that resonate deeply with Catholic social thought. As the focus of her attention shifted from labor and property law to family law, the legal profession, constitutional law, and international human rights, she has remained persistently concerned with the role and importance of mediating institutions of civil society, especially families. She has consistently maintained an understanding of the systemic relationships between law and society handed down from Max Weber through her mentor, Max Rheinstein. And she has insisted on the unique importance of comparative methods to help arrive at a sound balance between universal ideals of justice, liberty, and dignity, on the one hand, and the value of the diversity and particularity of local communities in which human life takes concrete shape and flourishes, on the other.

LIFE

Mary Ann Glendon's passion for the questions of law, politics, and society that have occupied her life can be traced back clearly to her early years in the town of Dalton, in western Massachusetts, where she was born in 1938. A stereotypical small New England town such as those with which Alexis de Toqueville began his famous study of democracy in America, Dalton contained strong communities of both Congregationalist and Roman Catholic Christians. Glendon's parents bridged the two in their marriage and family: her father Martin Glendon was Catholic; her mother Sarah Pomeroy Glendon was a Congregationalist who faithfully kept her promise to raise their children as practicing Catholics.[4] In the local public school, both the Protestant and Catholic children would join together in saying the Lord's Prayer (although Glendon humorously noted that the latter would stop after " . . . and deliver us from evil" while their Protestant schoolmates continued

[3] Mary Ann Glendon, "Author's Preface," in *Traditions in Turmoil* (Ann Arbor: Sapientia Press, 2006), xii.

[4] Mary Ann Glendon, "Why I'm Still a Catholic," in *Traditions in Turmoil*, 399–408, 408.

with "For thine are the kingdom ... ," before all reunited again with "Amen").[5] The two sides of her family also represented different political leanings, both of which would later find echoes in Glendon's life: her mother's ancestors fought in the Revolutionary War and the Civil War and her grandfather Theodore Pomeroy was chairman of the town's Republican Committee; her father was the first Irish-Catholic Democrat to chair the local Board of Selectmen.[6] "I'm half Irish and half Yankee," she would say.[7] Glendon's lifelong concern with the family life, the religious communities, and the practices of local democracy that all serve as "seedbeds of virtue"[8] and schools of citizenship can easily be seen as having germinated and been cultivated from her earliest years in the New England soil of the Berkshires.

She was a precocious child. Her father, a reporter for the local newspaper, the *Berkshire Eagle*, assigned her to cover the local baseball team starting at age twelve, and she continued to work as a budding journalist for the paper for many years. At around the same time, she began to be aware of the intellectual side of Catholicism, principally through the literary works of novelists and poets who took Christianity seriously. At age eleven or twelve she also read all of the works of Graham Greene, then turned to Evelyn Waugh, Fyodor Dostoyevsky, T. S. Eliot, and Gerard Manley Hopkins.[9] Socially and politically, she was inspired by the work and witness of Dorothy Day.[10]

Glendon left Dalton for Mount Holyoke College at age sixteen, and after one year there received a full scholarship to attend the University of Chicago, where she finished her BA and continued on to the University of Chicago Law School. There she was one of only four women in the student body, continued to excel in her studies, and finished her law degree at the unusually young age of twenty-one. At the University of Chicago she met a number of prominent scholars and professors who, even if not themselves Christian, were appreciative of the deep intellectual heritage of the Christian tradition and nurtured in her a familiarity with thinkers such as Augustine and Aquinas.[11]

The most important relationship of all for Glendon's future as a jurist was with Max Rheinstein, who became her mentor and close friend. Rheinstein, a German émigré, the son of Protestant Christian parents of Jewish ancestry,

5 Mary Ann Glendon, "The Twain Meet in Dalton," *Berkshire Eagle*, December 28, 1979.

6 Dick Lehr, "Mary Ann Glendon," *Boston Globe*, December 11, 1996, C1.

7 Lehr, "Mary Ann Glendon."

8 Mary Ann Glendon and David Blankenhorn, eds., *Seedbeds of Virtue: Sources of Competence, Character, and Citizenship in American Society* (Lanham: Madison Books, 1995).

9 Glendon, "Why I'm Still a Catholic," 400–401.

10 Mary Ann Glendon, interview by Paolo Carozza, September 2, 2016 (notes on file with the author).

11 Glendon, "Why I'm Still a Catholic," 401–402.

and an eminent comparative law scholar, had been a pupil of Max Weber. He helped to instill in Glendon a Weberian sensibility for the sociological dimensions of legal systems and "gave great encouragement to rising scholars like ... me at a time when women got very little encouragement in legal circles," Glendon later recalled.[12] He later invited her to join him as coauthor on some of her first scholarly works.

Glendon continued her studies under Rheinstein with a Master of Comparative Law at the University of Chicago, and complemented her education with a period of study and work in Europe, including for the European Economic Community in Brussels. When she returned to the United States in 1963, despite her outstanding academic record, she was unable to get a job practicing law in New York City, experiencing first hand the difficulty of being a young woman trying to enter a still very traditionally male profession. She did become a lawyer with a prominent Chicago law firm – only the second woman ever hired there – where she practiced for five years, but her experience undoubtedly contributed to her lifelong sensitivity toward the challenges facing women in contemporary society. Similarly, her work as a *pro bono* lawyer in the civil rights movement in the early 1960s, working for voting rights and defending jailed civil rights workers in Mississippi, both reflected and fed her thirst for equal justice and the rule of law. She attributes this concern directly to both her parents (who had taken her at age nine to witness the reality of segregation in the South) and her Christian faith.[13] Politically, she remained throughout this period and until the mid-1970s a Democrat, which she saw as the "party of work, family, church, and community."[14]

In 1970, Glendon married Edward Lev, a Jewish labor lawyer, continuing the constant openness to ecumenical and interfaith encounters and dialogue that has marked her entire life. Lev supported the Catholic upbringing of their three daughters.[15]

Glendon began her academic career at Boston College Law School, as the first woman on that faculty, in 1968. She gradually rose to national and international prominence as a legal scholar, moving in 1986 from Boston College to Harvard Law School, where she is currently the Learned Hand Professor of Law. She has received widespread recognition for her scholarly work, winning prestigious awards for her books and becoming the president of

12 Mary Ann Glendon, "The Adventure of Comparative Law," unpublished lecture delivered June 17, 2013 (text on file with the author).
13 Glendon, interview.
14 Lehr, "Mary Ann Glendon."
15 Glendon, "Why I'm Still a Catholic," 408.

the International Association of Legal Science, a member of the International Academy of Comparative Law, and a member of the American Academy of Arts and Sciences. She received the National Humanities Medal in 2015.

In addition to her scholarly career, Glendon has achieved great prominence both as a public intellectual and in various forms of public service to the Holy See and to the United States. Glendon's public profile beyond the world of legal academics emerged in a decisive way in the 1990s, first as her work on controversial public issues such as abortion and divorce became more widely known, and then as she increasingly wrote books and articles intended for a broader, lay audience. She was a regular contributor to *First Things*, an influential journal on issues relating to religion and public life, where she also served on the editorial board and had a close friendship with its founder, the Reverend Richard John Neuhaus.[16] Her work had also been attracting attention within the Vatican, and in 1994 Pope John Paul II appointed her as one of the inaugural members of the new Pontifical Academy of Social Sciences, which she later served as President from 2004 to 2014. In 1995, the pope also asked her to lead the diplomatic delegation of the Holy See to the Fourth World Conference on Women in Beijing, China, a position which brought her significantly more into the public light. President George W. Bush appointed Glendon to the US President's Council on Bioethics in 2001, and as the United States Ambassador to the Holy See in 2008 (a post she retained for one year). She continues to provide significant public service to both the United States and the Holy See today, both as a Commissioner of the US Commission on International Religious Freedom and also as a member of the Board of Supervisors of the Institute of Religious Works (the "Vatican Bank").

SCHOLARLY WORK[17]

Glendon's career as a scholar began in collaboration with Max Rheinstein, particularly in the comparative study of property and estate law.[18] However, she describes her first academic interest as being principally in the field of comparative labor law.[19] Quite early on in her time at Boston College, however, she turned her attention to questions of family law, and made her first major scholarly contributions by examining the intersection of family,

16 Many of Glendon's *First Things* essays have been republished in *Traditions in Turmoil*.

17 Although referring occasionally to other materials, this section draws primarily on Glendon's books to illustrate the arc of her development as a jurist.

18 Max Rheinstein and Mary Ann Glendon, *The Law of Decedents' Estates* (New York: Foundation Press, 1971).

19 Glendon, interview.

property, and the state.[20] As Glendon has described it, her interest in the area was not so much in family *law* as such, but rather in the family as a social institution that carries a tradition.[21] As she put it, "family and marriage are pre-legal institutions that were not invented by law but are inherent in the human species, although not peculiar to it."[22]

Glendon explored the rapid and profound upheaval in the structures and patterns of family life and their relationship to law and the state through a trio of books. The first, *State, Law and Family*, compares changes in family law in the United States, England, Germany, and France to "place . . . the changes of special aspects of family life and family law into the broad and comprehensive context of an inquiry into the transformation of the relationship between the family and the state."[23] The book shows the ways that the family and the state, as basic institutions of society, are shifting their respective roles in the fulfillment of human needs.[24] She elaborated and updated that work in a "successor" volume, *The Transformation of Family Law* (1989). The latter traces the changes that took place in family law beginning in the 1960s in order to reflect on the implications for the future of the family as an institution in society. In this account, Glendon observes a "historic shift in the relationship of the state to the family," and comments that the intense legislative activity that immediately preceded the book "formalized and systemized transforming trends that had long been diffuse and partially realized in law."[25] *The New Family and the New Property*, written in between the first book and its successor volume, explores the shifting relative importance of family, work, and government as determinants of wealth and status. Glendon traces the legal developments of both marriage relationships and employment relationships to show a broad shift in the relative importance of work and family as focal points of standing and security in society. She also highlights the then-emerging reliance on the state, through administrative law, to provide or distribute the "new properties" for families, including upon the dissolution of marriages.[26]

20 Mary Ann Glendon, *State, Law and Family: Family Law in Transition in the United States and Western Europe* (Amsterdam: North-Holland, 1977); Mary Ann Glendon, *The New Family and the New Property* (Toronto: Butterworths, 1981); Mary Ann Glendon, *The Transformation of Family Law: State, Law, and Family in the United States and Western Europe* (Chicago: University of Chicago Press, 1989).

21 Glendon, interview.

22 Glendon, *State, Law and Family*, 3.

23 Max Rheinstein, "Foreword," in Glendon, *State, Law and Family*, viii.

24 Rheinstein, "Foreword," viii.

25 Glendon, *The Transformation of Family Law*, 37.

26 Glendon, *The New Family and the New Property*.

Several overarching themes emerge in her work on family law, three of which can be highlighted here. First, her sociological sensibilities lead her to emphasize the connection between different aspects of society including family life, work and employment, and personal property, and to emphasize that changes in law "may be important evidence of changes that are taking place in family structure and social structure, especially in the world of work."[27] Second, she shows an enduring commitment to integrating the study of different branches of law in order to reveal larger social realities: "if one breaks down the artificial barriers between the various fields of private or civil law, the knowledge gained in each area may deepen one's understanding of every other and bring out connections that would otherwise remain invisible from within the confines of usual categories."[28] And third, she reveals a deep concern over the impact of the shifting conceptual frameworks of marriage and work on the common good of society and the role of the state.

A second area of scholarly interest for Glendon, which occupied her principally in the early part of the 1980s, has been in the methods of comparative law as a discipline. The textbook that she coauthored at this time,[29] which in turn drew from separate articles she had written in the same period,[30] exemplifies a vision of comparative law consistent with her larger vision of law and society. Eschewing more constrained formalist, procedural, or taxonomic approaches found elsewhere in the comparative law literature, Glendon's introduction to Romano-Germanic (or "civil law") legal systems has at least three notable broad features that characterize her intellectual mindset as a whole. First, it emphasizes that law operates as a *tradition*. Glendon uses the idea of a "tradition" in a sense explicitly drawing on the work of the philosopher Alasdair MacIntyre: "A living tradition then is an historically extended, socially embodied argument, and an argument precisely in part about the goods which constitute that tradition. Within a tradition the pursuit of goods extends through generations, sometimes through many generations."[31] Glendon sees the civil law tradition as

27 Mary Ann Glendon, "The New Family and the New Property," *Tulane Law Review* 53 (1978–1979): 705.

28 Glendon, "The New Family and the New Property," 708.

29 Mary Ann Glendon, Michael Wallace Gordon, and Christopher Osakwe, *Comparative Legal Traditions* (St. Paul: West Publishing, 1st edn. 1985). Glendon was responsible for the authorship of Part I ("Introduction to the Comparative Study of Law") and Part II ("The Civil Law Tradition").

30 For example, Mary Ann Glendon, "The Sources of Law in a Changing Legal Order," *Creighton Law Review* 17 (1984): 663–698.

31 Alasdair MacIntyre, *After Virtue* (Notre Dame: University of Notre Dame Press, 1981), 207, as quoted in Mary Ann Glendon, Michael Wallace Gordon, and Christopher Osakwe, *Comparative Legal Traditions* (St. Paul: West Publishing, 2nd edn. 1994), 17.

one of the few great traditions of law, but even more importantly sees the idea of tradition in this sense as essential to understanding law as a whole, and law's relationship to the future and past of our society, community, and democracy. A second feature is Glendon's emphasis on the systemic interactions of a broad range of social actors and institutions – confirming and continuing Glendon's indebtedness to Max Weber's legacy. Her text formulates a legal tradition as composed in a complex way by the dynamics of history, by institutional structures such as legislatures and all levels of courts, by distinct actors such as judges and lawyers and scholars (including their processes of education, selection, and formation), by documents and the rules they embody (e.g., constitutions and codes), by sets of procedures that direct human behavior in preestablished ways, and by a dynamic, socially situated hermeneutic practice that unites and carries forward in time all of these other elements.[32] The third distinctive feature of her approach, consistent with her prior work on the evolution of the family and the state, is her interest in using law to identify and understand better the large, long-term, structural changes in society that the twentieth century had wrought.[33]

From 1987 to 1994, Glendon published a series of three books that marked a number of transitions in her trajectory as a scholar and public intellectual. While taking up questions, themes, and methods explored in some way in her earlier work, each of these is written for a broader audience, and indeed had a wider impact on public debate in the United States. The first was *Abortion and Divorce in Western Law*,[34] which in some ways continued her interest in family law and its relationship to societal transformations, as well as her attentiveness to comparative methods. In it, Glendon compares the way that abortion and divorce are treated in a variety of Western European countries and in the United States. She underscored what she calls "the American Difference" – a way of regulating both areas that reveals a greater emphasis on individual rights, a more atomistic conception of freedom and self-determination, and a correspondingly diminished sense of social responsibility, especially for the weak and vulnerable members of society.[35] *Abortion and Divorce* led very directly to Glendon's turn in these years toward constitutional law more generally. The individualistic rights-based discourse of the United States she identified there became the direct subject of her 1991 book *Rights*

32 See, e.g., "Table of Contents," in Glendon, Gordon, and Osakwe, *Comparative Legal Traditions* (1st edn.).

33 See, e.g., Glendon, "Sources of Law in a Changing Legal Order."

34 Mary Ann Glendon, *Abortion and Divorce in Western Law: American Failures, European Challenges* (Cambridge, MA: Harvard University Press, 1987).

35 Glendon, *Abortion and Divorce in Western Law*, Chapter 3.

Talk,[36] a highly influential critique of certain "dialects" of rights (prevalent at the time especially in the United States) that tend to make absolute claims, to isolate the lone rights-bearer from any sense of community or sociality, and to ignore the responsibilities that are complementary to rights in a well-ordered free society. Again, Glendon uses comparative perspectives to broaden our horizons: her exploration of less libertarian and more communitarian understandings of rights in other constitutional systems are the foil for advocating a reexamination of the way that the peculiarly American style of rights talk might be coarsening our political discourse more generally.[37] The third book in this period turns to a different subject: the legal professions. In *A Nation under Lawyers*,[38] Glendon continues to explore the relationship between law and broad social transformations. Here, Glendon dives more deeply into one critical piece of the overall structures of traditions of law mentioned earlier, focusing in turn on lawyers, judges, and scholars, and reflecting on the ways in which deep changes in the professions put at risk the American democratic experiment. Characteristically, however, Glendon aims less at exposing the pathologies and more at affirming the creative approaches that may provide a way forward: "I have tried to look not just for what may be amiss but for what is sound, healthy, and capable of development."[39]

As noted earlier, Glendon's more publicly visible work, especially on abortion and on rights talk, brought her increasingly into the eye of Pope John Paul II as well, and led among other things to her appointment as the head of the Holy See's diplomatic delegation to the 1995 UN World Conference on Women. In her scholarly work, this was accompanied by a parallel shift of her gaze toward international human rights law. Especially following the work in comparative constitutional law that began with her studies of abortion and rights discourse, and significant academic articles on other fundamental rights questions like freedom of religion[40] and economic and social rights,[41] it was a small stretch for her to take up international human rights documents and institutions as well. But having by then begun a style of work that was more directed at a broad and lay audience, and always having shown her propensity for good storytelling and for the intimate human dimensions of large social

36 Mary Ann Glendon, *Rights Talk* (New York: Free Press, 1991).

37 Glendon, *Rights Talk*, Chapter 7.

38 Mary Ann Glendon, *A Nation under Lawyers: How the Crisis in the Legal Profession Is Transforming American Society* (New York: Farrar, Straus and Giroux, 1994).

39 Glendon, *A Nation under Lawyers*, 14.

40 Mary Ann Glendon and Raul F. Yanes, "Structural Free Exercise," *Michigan Law Review* 90 (1991): 477–550.

41 Mary Ann Glendon, "Rights in Twentieth-Century Constitutions," *University of Chicago Law Review* 59 (1992): 519–538.

phenomena, Glendon chose to focus her work on the framers of the Universal Declaration of Human Rights (UDHR), particularly through the eyes and life of Eleanor Roosevelt.[42] In *A World Made New*, Glendon combines original archival work on the genesis of the Universal Declaration with new biographical research on many of the principal protagonists involved in the birth of the post-war human rights project at the United Nations, and produces what is probably the most definitive study to date of the origins of the UDHR. Consistent with her past work, she uses the narrative also to explore larger questions looming over social life in our era: the meaning of universality in a global and pluralistic world, the fragility and yet hopefulness of our efforts to seek and achieve the common good, and the centrality of human dignity – understood in an integral way – to the generative possibilities of law and politics.

Glendon's most recent book (as of the writing of this chapter), *The Forum and the Tower*,[43] continues in the vein of *A World Made New* insofar as she explores large ideas through the narratives of individual lives. With each chapter focusing on the life of a significant historical figure who in some way straddled the worlds of scholarship and politics (Plato, Machiavelli, Burke, Weber, and many others), the book is an extended reflection on the relationship between the academy, the tower of intellectual life, and the public square, the realm of politics. It reflects, at least implicitly, Glendon's own trajectory as a scholar whose work brought her over time to act in the forum of public life in significant ways.

THE PLACE OF CHRISTIANITY

In all of the richness of Mary Ann Glendon's work as a scholar of the law, the place of her Christian faith is both pervasive and yet difficult to place and to describe. As described earlier, she was raised a practicing Catholic and has been a person of faith since her childhood. She had absorbed much of the contemporary literary tradition of Christianity already by her early teen years and had become familiar with many of the philosophical and theological giants of Christianity while an undergraduate at the University of Chicago. The Second Vatican Council and the encyclicals of Pope John XXIII were memorable and important moments in her formation and education.[44]

[42] Mary Ann Glendon, *A World Made New: Eleanor Roosevelt and the Universal Declaration of Human Rights* (New York: Random House, 2001).

[43] Mary Ann Glendon, *The Forum and the Tower: How Scholars and Politicians Have Imagined the World, from Plato to Eleanor Roosevelt* (Oxford: Oxford University Press, 2011).

[44] Glendon, "Why I'm Still a Catholic," 402.

Clearly, therefore, she was steeped throughout her formative years in Catholic sensibilities and perspectives. Yet, by her own self-description, she did not set out in any way to be a "Catholic lawyer," and insists that for much of her early career she was not self-consciously "Christian" in her scholarly work and did not give much thought to the relationship between her religious beliefs and the subject matter of her study in the law.[45] She does not consider herself to have been closely familiar with Catholic social thought until well after she had launched her scholarly career.[46] But when she did encounter it in a more direct way, beginning in the 1970s, she says she felt like Molière's *Bourgeois Gentilhomme*, who discovered late in life and to his delight that he had been speaking prose all along.[47]

Two things in particular would seem to have brought that strong but diffuse and unfocused background presence of Christianity in her thought into more sharpened relief. The first was participating in the interdisciplinary discussions around philosophy and theology at Boston College, and especially the immersion with colleagues there into the work of Bernard Lonergan. Glendon notes with gratitude the importance of this experience to her faith, thanking Fr. Joseph Flanagan, S.J., the longtime chairman of Boston College's Philosophy Department for the critical role that he played in her faith and intellectual formation[48] (and dedicating one of her books to him as well).[49] She describes it as "endowing me with a bit of Ignatian spirituality" as well.[50] Even more specifically, it must be supposed that the emphasis that Lonergan places on the self-awareness of one's own dynamic of knowing and judging must have made Glendon more self-conscious of the Catholic Christian framework that she brought, theretofore perhaps more unconsciously, to all her work.

The second catalyzing factor was the pontificate of John Paul II and his monumental corpus of teachings. It would be impossible to overstate the influence of both his thought and his personal relationship with Glendon on her life as a Christian and as a jurist. As she has put it in discussing her relationship to the Church, "Thank you, Lord, for the utterly inestimable gift of faith, and for the privilege of having lived in the time of John Paul the Great."[51]

45 Glendon, Interview.
46 Ibid.
47 Ibid.
48 Glendon, "Why I'm Still a Catholic," 408.
49 Glendon, *Abortion and Divorce in Western Law*.
50 Glendon, "Why I'm Still a Catholic," 408.
51 Ibid.

Viewed through the eyes of her readers, and especially scholarly readers, her Christian faith has similarly been paradoxically both very evident and hidden. On the one hand, it is of course common knowledge that Glendon is a prominent *Catholic* intellectual, who has played important public roles for the Catholic Church and has written and spoken very openly about her faith for at least the last thirty-five years. At the same time, as her writing has been seen and received by other scholars, the role of Christianity in her juridical work has seldom, if ever, been addressed in any academic literature. More generally, although at the level of one or another specific book or article each of her scholarly works has provoked considerable commentary and reaction, there is no work to speak of, neither a monograph nor even an edited collection, nor any full biography of her life beyond brief newspaper accounts, that attempts to understand and evaluate Glendon's scholarly work as a comprehensive and integrated whole.[52] To some extent that may simply be due to its recent vintage: other scholars have not yet had the distance and time to take up and digest as a whole the work of this still-active legal scholar. But the difficulty of seeing Glendon's work in its entirety, and therefore the distinctive place of Christianity throughout it, is more than just a question of time; it is also due to the eclectic breadth of her scholarship, both in the subject areas she has tackled over her career and in the methods she has used. Her books and articles have ranged over public law and private law in a multiplicity of different legal systems; property law, labor law, and family law; legal and political history; multiple aspects of constitutional law and international human rights; law and religion; the judiciary and legal interpretation; bioethics and biographies; and more. Jurisprudentially, she explicitly acknowledges that she is not, and has never sought to be, associated with any distinctly identifiable "school" of thought in law.[53]

Making a first attempt at surveying Glendon's work as a whole does, nevertheless, reveal certain constant themes and sensibilities that can reasonably be linked to her Catholic Christian formation and frame of mind. They can be grouped around five poles.

[52] The closest attempt is a law review article by Donald Kommers, though it focuses only on her work in constitutional law: Donald P. Kommers, "The Constitutionalism of Mary Ann Glendon," *Notre Dame Law Review* 73 (1998): 1333–1354. There are two collections of articles in law review symposia honoring Glendon: *Notre Dame Law Review* 73.5 (1998); and *Duquesne Law Review* 52.1 (2014). Although many of these articles critically engage pieces of Glendon's work, all focus only on one or another aspect of her corpus, and none discuss the role of Christianity or religious faith generally in her thought and writing.

[53] Glendon, interview.

The first begins precisely with that diversity (we might say "catholicism") of methods in her work noted above. The starting point of her work is almost always comparative, although always using the comparative method to immerse herself sympathetically in another frame of reference and then from there to look with fresh and critical eyes back on herself and the unique virtues and the persistent faults of American law and society.[54] Beyond her self-reflective comparativism, her jurisprudential methods are quite wide-ranging. Glendon consistently employs the knowledge gleaned from the social sciences to inform her work, grounding the scholarly inquiry in data from sociology and economics, yet in her work the empirical is always deployed in the service of the larger normative questions; she is not in any way an empiricist in a narrow sense. At the same time, her work shows a frequent assimilation of the more interpretive turn that some of the social sciences took in her lifetime. She often cites approvingly the cultural anthropologist Clifford Geertz, who described law as a "distinctive way of imagining the real" requiring an exercise in cultural hermeneutics, and she sometimes shows a predilection for the narrative approaches reminiscent of law and literature scholars.[55] *Abortion and Divorce in Western Law* is a bravura display of both empirical and hermeneutic methods in union with each other, using social science data in support of her larger goal of interpreting how the law in these areas both reflect and constitute us as a community.[56] In a parallel way, Glendon's work has always insisted on the systemic understandings of law, culture, and politics – like her social science approach generally, an inheritance from Weber and Rheinstein – and yet consistently exhibits her penchant for addressing large structural and historic questions through the highly personal biographies of exemplary individuals.[57] At the broadest level, it is not far-fetched to connect this breadth of methods to her decidedly Catholic frame of mind, whether one describes it in terms of Pope Benedict XVI's exhortation to an "openness to the full breadth of reason," or Luigi Giussani's insistence that the methods of reason must conform to the object of our inquiry and that reason consists in openness to the totality of the real, or Lonergan's call to work out the

54 Glendon frequently cites an aphorism by Fernand Braudel: "Live in England for a year and you will not learn much about the English. But when you return to France you will see, in the light of your surprise, that which had remained hidden to you because it was so familiar." See, e.g., Mary Ann Glendon, "Why Cross Boundaries?," *Washington and Lee Law Review* 53 (1996): 971, 976.

55 Glendon, *Abortion and Divorce in Western Law*, 8–9.

56 For example, Glendon, *Abortion and Divorce in Western Law*, especially Introduction and Chapter 3.

57 For example, Glendon, *A Nation under Lawyers*; Glendon, *A World Made New*; Glendon, *The Forum and the Tower*.

transitions of modernity one by one with the entirety of methods of human knowledge in play, or Alasdair MacIntyre's emphasis on the unity of all knowledge being the distinctive hallmark of a Catholic scholarly community.[58] Evocatively, Glendon ends her book on the legal professions with an appeal to return to a grounding in *reason*:

> How to wrest the strands of freedom and order from the chaos of history? How to assure that neither will overwhelm the other? How to weave those wavering cords into sturdy fabrics that our successors will admire even as they fashion them anew? "Reason," say the ancient voices. "Reason, now and always, the life of the law."[59]

A second notably Catholic emphasis in Glendon's work is her use of the idea of "tradition," understood in the dynamic, temporally extended and socially embodied sense in which MacIntyre describes it.[60] Lonergan, too, emphasizes the role of tradition in knowledge and human development, arguing that human authenticity requires taking tradition, in the sense of an inherited social and cultural fabric, seriously – that is, being faithful to it by both appropriating its values and also criticizing its inadequacies and shortcomings.[61] Glendon consistently thinks in terms of such traditions and applies this understanding of tradition not only to her study of Western law in both its civil law and common law branches[62] but also generally to her analysis of cultural and political life.[63]

A third cluster of features in Glendon's collected work that is certainly inspired and fed by her Christian faith is her constant focus on the dignity of the human person, especially as manifest in the poor and the weak. From her pro bono work in the civil rights movement as a young lawyer, to her earliest scholarly work on family law that consistently emphasized the economic

58 Pope Benedict XVI, "Faith, Reason and the University: Memories and Reflections," Lecture at the University of Regensburg, September 12, 2006, w2.vatican.va/content/benedict-xvi/en/speeches/2006/september/documents/hf_ben-xvi_spe_20060912_university-regensburg.html; Luigi Giussani, *The Religious Sense* (Montreal: McGill-Queen's University Press, 1997), 4–5, 12–22; Lonergan, *Collection*; Alasdair MacIntyre, *God, Philosophy, Universities: A Selective History of the Catholic Philosophical Tradition* (Lanham: Rowman and Littlefield, 2009), Chapter 19.

59 Glendon, *A Nation under Lawyers*, 294.

60 MacIntyre, *After Virtue*, 207; Alasdair MacIntyre, *Three Rival Versions of Moral Enquiry: Encyclopaedia, Genealogy, and Tradition* (Notre Dame: University of Notre Dame Press, 1990).

61 Bernard J. F. Lonergan, "First Lecture: Religious Experience," in *A Third Collection: Papers By Bernard J. F. Lonergan*, ed. Frederick E. Crowe (New York: Paulist Press, 1985), 113–128.

62 Glendon, Gordon, and Osakwe, *Comparative Legal Traditions*.

63 Glendon, *Traditions in Turmoil*.

implications for vulnerable women and children of legal and social changes, to her advocacy of the dignity of the unborn and the terminally ill, to her defense of the universality of human rights, all of her work speaks consistently of the unbounded value of every individual human being. Glendon has openly observed that her stances on issues as diverse as abortion, labor issues, economic policy, immigration, intergenerational solidarity, and ecology – positions which have at different times put her at odds with both liberals and conservatives – are all rooted in the Catholic social tradition's core concern for the dignity of the person.[64]

The reference to Catholic social thought foregrounds a fourth aspect of Glendon's work that has strongly Christian roots to it: her insistence throughout her life to the importance of the mediating institutions of civil society, and the interrelated attentiveness to maintaining a healthy balance between the individual and communities. Lived out in her upbringing and her affection for small-town New England ways, reinforced by her Tocquevillian inclinations (Tocqueville himself, of course, being unmistakably Catholic in his outlook on American democracy), and consolidated in the central emphasis on subsidiarity in Catholic social thought (and particularly strongly in the teaching of Pope John Paul II, who influenced her so much), Glendon's concern for families and local communities of education, aid, and support is probably the most consistent thread woven throughout every stage of her work. Her critique of certain dialects of rights, her vigorous defenses of freedom of religion, and her analysis of the decadence of the legal professions all share a common concern for the ways these either support or undermine the "schools of citizenship" of our democracy and the "seedbeds" of civic virtues.[65] She is a fierce critic of the pathologies of excessive individualism, yet celebrates human diversity and vigorously defends the civil and human rights that are essential to the protection of individual liberty. At a very deep and unarticulated level, Glendon's constant sensitivity to the relationship of individual to community, insisting on the essential need for and complementarity of both, might be seen as a manifestation in the world of the Christian experience of the divine as Trinitarian, a complete unity of distinct Persons.[66]

Fifth and finally, Glendon's work consistently displays the paradoxical but characteristically Christian awareness of both human brokenness and fragility, and also the unfinished work of redemption already at work in the world,

64 See generally Glendon, *Traditions in Turmoil*; Lehr, "Mary Ann Glendon."

65 Glendon and Blankenhorn, *Seedbeds of Virtue*.

66 Cf. Luigi Giussani, *Why The Church?* (Montreal: McGill-Queen's University Press, 2001), 166–167.

which is ever cause for hope. Always realistic, she is a conservative with no nostalgic illusions of a past to be recaptured. Equally, she indulges in no utopianism even as she affirms that law pursues a transcendent ideal and as she looks for new ways of addressing the vexing problems that twentieth-century social upheavals have left in the foyer of the twenty-first century. From this realism comes her insistence on the importance of craftsmanship within the tradition of the common law, and the restraints that it fosters, as well as her trenchant critique of the dangers of a judicial imperialism and a legal elitism that separates law from its wider social base and that makes it more ideological and more vulnerable to the interests of the wealthy and powerful.[67] Glendon's very Christian awareness of the fragility and promise of our human efforts is captured well by her description of the statue by Arnaldo Pomodoro at the United Nations Headquarters in New York:

> A gift from the government of Italy, it consists of an enormous sphere of burnished bronze, suggesting a globe. The sphere is pleasing to behold, even though it startles with its imperfection. There are deep, jagged cracks in its golden-hued surface, cracks too large ever to be repaired. Perhaps it's cracked because it's defective (like the broken world), one thinks. Or maybe (like an egg) it has to break in order for something else to emerge. Perhaps both. Sure enough, when one peers into the gashes on its surface, there is another brightly shining sphere coming along inside. But that one is already cracked, too!
>
> Whatever is going on inside those spheres, it does not seem to be all chance and accident. There is a tremendous sense of motion, of dynamism, of potency, of emergent probabilities. And so it has been with the human rights project. Yes, the enterprise is flawed. . . . [But] men and women of goodwill can make a difference. The imaginations, actions, decisions, sacrifices, and personal examples of countless individuals have helped to bolster the chances of reason and conscience against power and interest.[68]

CONCLUSION

Mary Ann Glendon has self-consciously directed her work as a jurist toward a Lonerganian ideal of seeking and pursuing one insight at a time in one area of law after another, in an effort to work out painstakingly the transitions that are required in an era when the inherited Christian foundations that have sustained Western legal traditions for the last thousand years seem increasingly tenuous and unconvincing to the world. This has made her contributions to

67 Glendon, *A Nation under Lawyers*.
68 Glendon, *A World Made New*, 240–241.

legal scholarship broad and varied yet still thematically and intellectually coherent, and very infused with a Christian ethos that is, however, seldom explicitly confessional in her scholarship. On the occasion of a seminar held in honor of her seventy-fifth birthday, Glendon reflected on the "adventure" of her own life as a comparative law scholar by invoking the motto of the French *Société de la Législation Comparée: jus unum, lex multiplex, universa curiositas.*[69] It is in the end an apt synthesis of her own work as well, including its deeply Catholic Christian perspective: in Glendon's vision and life, the law, justice, and right are one (*jus unum*), giving universality and unity to human experience and pointing to the divine source of it all; but laws as expressed in social reality are diverse (*lex multiplex*), reflecting the embodied, incarnated, creaturely human life in which we inescapably live and seek to realize the good; and we strive to bring the two into harmony through the insatiability and dynamism of our human longing for knowledge (*universa curiositas*).

69 Glendon, "The Adventure of Comparative Law."

16

A Reformed Liberalism: Michael McConnell's Contributions to Christian Jurisprudence

Nathan S. Chapman*

> Americans mix Christianity and liberty so completely in their mind that it is nearly impossible to make them conceive one without the other; and, among them, this is not one of those sterile beliefs that the past bequeaths to the present and that seem more to vegetate deep in the soul than to live.[1]
>
> – Alexis de Tocqueville

Michael McConnell is one of the most influential jurists of his generation. As a scholar, judge, lawyer, and public intellectual, he has championed a modest legal conservatism that emphasizes judicial restraint, robust religious liberty, and space for religious voices in the public square. And he has done so as one of a handful of evangelical Christians in the upper echelons of the legal academy.[2]

Most of McConnell's scholarship focuses on constitutional law and theory. Much of it explores how the US Constitution protects religion. By contrast, relatively little of his work discusses the influence that religion has, or ought to have, on American constitutionalism. Nevertheless, in a handful of essays, McConnell has sketched a jurisprudence that emphasizes the continuities of Reformed (Calvinist) Christian theology, classical liberalism, and early US constitutionalism. McConnell's "reformed liberalism," as this essay calls it, contrasts with secular liberalism, which dominates contemporary political theory, and with the views of liberalism skeptics. Though McConnell does not fully develop a political theology, his view resembles other contemporary approaches to Christian liberalism, especially in its cautious optimism about republican constitutionalism.

* Thanks to Will Baude, Sam Bray, Daniel Dreisbach, and Mark David Hall for comments on prior drafts, and to T. J. Striepe for excellent library assistance.

1 Alexis de Toqueville, *Democracy in America: Historical-Critical Edition of "De la démocratie en Amérique,"* ed. Eduardo Nolla, trans. James T. Schleifer (Indianapolis: Liberty Fund, 2010), 1:476.

2 See Alan Wolfe, "The Opening of the Evangelical Mind," *The Atlantic* (Oct. 2000).

For the most part, reformed liberalism does not surface in McConnell's other scholarship. This should be unsurprising; for McConnell, there is little daylight between the insights of Reformed theology, classical liberalism, the political assumptions of the founding generation, and the demands of contemporary constitutional decision-making. McConnell's theology is therefore consistent with, though it may not motivate, his constitutional jurisprudence.

This essay proceeds as follows: (I) a biographical sketch; (II) an introduction to McConnell's account of reformed liberalism; and (III) an overview of McConnell's major contributions to constitutional jurisprudence, with an analysis of how they correspond to reformed liberalism. At the outset, a brief word about my relationship with McConnell: I worked with him for three years at Stanford University's Constitutional Law Center, we have coauthored an article, and we are friends, but this essay is based entirely on information that is publicly available.

I

McConnell's career was exceptional from the start. He grew up in Kentucky, graduated in 1976 from Michigan State University's James Madison College, and attended the University of Chicago Law School. Geoffrey Stone, a leading First Amendment scholar, said that McConnell "was one of the very few students I had that I knew I wanted to hire on the faculty within a few weeks of his arrival." "[I]n hope of somewhat moderating Mike's very strong conservative bent," Stone "arranged clerkships after law school with the same two judges for whom [he] had clerked, both of whom were very liberal."[3]

Stone got everything he wanted except a political conversion. McConnell clerked for two of the most renowned federal judges, J. Skelly Wright on the DC Circuit Court of Appeals and William Brennan on the United States Supreme Court. In 1985, he returned to teach at his alma mater.

McConnell was aware that he was part of a "counter-revolution in legal thought."[4] Since the New Deal, left-liberals had dominated American constitutional jurisprudence, especially in the academy.[5] As McConnell explained in a 1987 essay in *Policy Review*, for generations liberal judges had deferred to legislation that advanced their ideals and, in the name of a "living

[3] Eric Herman, "Former U of C prof on everyone's short court list: socially conservative judge has earned backing of liberals," *Chicago Sun-Times* (July 11, 2005), 65.

[4] Michael W. McConnell, "The Counter-Revolution in Legal Thought: Four Conservative Ideas Are Setting the Terms of Debate," *Policy Review* (Summer 1987): 18.

[5] See generally Laura Kalman, *The Strange Career of Legal Liberalism* (New Haven: Yale University Press, 1998).

Constitution," had invalidated legislation that did not. "Today," however, "conservative ideas increasingly set the terms of debate."[6] Specifically, McConnell explained that there were four schools of conservative legal thought, each with its own principles and tensions with the others: "traditional jurisprudential conservatives," focused on judicial restraint; "libertarians," committed to "individual liberties" and "hostility to big government"; "the law and economics movement," with a "rigorous pursuit of economic efficiency"; and "social conservatives," attached "to community and traditional moral values."[7]

The University of Chicago was ground zero for the conservative legal movement, leading the development of law and economics theory and boasting several influential libertarians. At the time, however, and to this day, McConnell was one of the only members of an elite law school faculty to write constitutional scholarship as a social conservative.[8] Given his intellectual background, and his position at Chicago, it is unsurprising that McConnell's scholarship has often bridged the four schools of conservative thought, emphasizing their overlapping commitments and deemphasizing the tensions among them. As one historian has noted, McConnell has served as a link between otherwise disparate conservative groups.[9] While he has self-consciously sought to build intellectual consensus, McConnell has occasionally taken positions that put him at odds with other conservative thinkers, especially libertarians. He has, for instance, consistently defended the constitutionality of legislative prohibitions on conduct such as abortion and physician-assisted suicide that are difficult to square with contemporary libertarianism.

At Chicago, McConnell's constitutional jurisprudence began to take shape. Against "living constitutionalists," he argued for judicial adherence to the historical understanding of the constitutional text. Against those who demanded a strict separation of church and state, he developed a subtle account of the Religion Clauses centered on the accommodation of private religious exercise. And against those who would shove religious views to the margin of public life, he argued for the priority of religious practice, expression, and political engagement. As this essay suggests, for McConnell, each of

6 McConnell, "The Counter-Revolution," 18.

7 Ibid.

8 During this era Stephen Carter, Professor at Yale Law School, also wrote as a social conservative. See Stephen L. Carter, *The Culture of Disbelief: How American Law and Politics Trivialize Religious Devotion* (New York: Doubleday, 1993).

9 Ann Southworth, *Lawyers of the Right: Professionalizing the Conservative Coalition* (Chicago: University of Chicago Press, 2008), 45–46, 201 n.9.

these positions is supported by classical liberalism, which in turn is supported by reformed Christian theology.

In 1997, McConnell took a position teaching law at the University of Utah. He taught there for five years before President George W. Bush nominated him to a vacancy on the Tenth Circuit Court of Appeals. Although liberal groups opposed his appointment based on his positions on abortion and religious liberty, he received broad support from law professors, liberal and conservative alike, and the Senate unanimously voted to confirm him.

On the court, McConnell sat on panels with other appellate judges, reviewing the decisions of trial courts that raised a variety of legal issues. From 2002 to 2009 he authored 90 opinions. The Supreme Court considered four of them, agreeing with McConnell's opinion in each.[10] According to many accounts in the media, McConnell was on President George W. Bush's "short list" of potential Supreme Court appointees, but that was not to be.[11] In 2009, McConnell stepped down from the bench and joined the faculty of Stanford Law School, where he is the Director of the Stanford Constitutional Law Center.

As McConnell's career has taken him from one institution to another, he has maintained several commitments. First, he has consistently practiced law at the highest level. Before entering the academy, he served as Assistant General Counsel for the Office of Management and Budget, which oversees the economics of the federal government, and as Assistant to the Solicitor General, the office of the Department of Justice that argues before the Supreme Court on behalf of the federal government. While teaching, McConnell has worked with Kirkland & Ellis and Mayer, Brown, & Platt, two of the most prestigious litigation groups in the nation, authored numerous briefs, and personally argued fifteen cases before the Supreme Court, including a number of important religious liberty cases.[12] Considering his practice alone, McConnell has had an extraordinary career in the law.

[10] See *Pleasant Grove City* v. *Summum*, 555 U.S. 460 (2009) (holding that a city's decision to accept one privately donated monument and reject another did not violate the donors' free speech rights); *Fernandez-Vargas* v. *Gonzalez*, 548 U.S. 30 (2008) (interpreting a provision of an immigration statute); *Begay* v. *United States*, 553 U.S. 137 (2008) (holding that driving while intoxicated, a felony under New Mexico law, is not a "violent felony" under the federal Armed Career Criminal Act); *O Centro Espirita Beneficiente Uniao do Vegetal* v. *Ashcroft*, 546 U.S. 418 (2006) (holding that a religious group has a statutory right to use otherwise illegal hallucinogenic tea for ceremonial purposes).

[11] David Newman and Emily Bazelon, "The Supreme Court Shortlist: The Views of the Likely Candidates," *Slate* (July 1, 2005).

[12] See *Christian Legal Soc'y* v. *Martinez*, 130 S.Ct. 2971 (2010) (holding, contrary to McConnell's client, that the University of California Hastings School of Law could defund the Christian Legal Society student group because it imposed requirements on its members and leadership

Second, McConnell has consistently spotted talent and mentored young lawyers. After working with an especially gifted editor of the *Harvard Law Review*, McConnell suggested him for a position at the University of Chicago. That's how Barack Obama got his first job after law school.[13] As a professor and judge, McConnell has mentored hundreds of young lawyers, a number of whom now hold tenure-track positions in leading law schools.

Third, McConnell has always been engaged in civic leadership. He has served on boards of directors for a variety of schools, clinics, and religious liberty committees. From 2007 to 2009 he was an elder at First Presbyterian Church (USA), Salt Lake City.

II

Though McConnell's greatest influence as a scholar has been in the field of constitutional jurisprudence, he has also sketched the outline of a political theory that this essay refers to as "reformed liberalism." According to McConnell, reformed Protestant theology, classical liberalism, and the principles that animated the framing of the US Constitution are mutually reinforcing. This vision is distinctive among modern political theorists and casts light on McConnell's constitutional jurisprudence.

At the outset it is worth noting where McConnell's account differs from dominant secular and Christian political theories. By the end of the twentieth century, liberals welcomed "liberty of conscience" as a right to maintain private religious *beliefs*, but sought to all but banish those beliefs from the public sphere.[14] (Since 9/11, some liberals have begun to rethink religion's proper place in public discourse.)[15] While liberalism was abandoning

that effectively excluded sexually active gays and lesbians); *Mitchell* v. *Helms*, 530 U.S. 793 (2000) (holding that the First Amendment did not prohibit the federal government from making loans to religious schools for "secular, neutral, and non ideological" programs); *Rosenberger* v. *University of Va.*, 515 U.S. 819 (1995) (holding that the Free Speech Clause prohibits the University of Virginia from declining to fund a student periodical simply because it has a religious viewpoint); *Jimmy Swaggert Ministries* v. *Bd. of Equalization*, 493 U.S. 378 (1990) (holding, contrary to McConnell's client, that the First Amendment does not prohibit a state from imposing a sales tax on a Christian ministry's publications).

13 Jodi Kantor, "Teaching law, testing ideas, Obama stood apart," *New York Times* (July 30, 2008).

14 See John Rawls, "The Idea of Public Reason Revisited," *University of Chicago Law Review* 64 (1997): 765; Richard Rorty, "Religion as Conversation-Stopper," in *The Ethics of Citizenship: Liberal Democracy and Religious Convictions*, ed. J. Caleb Clanton (Waco: Baylor University Press, 2009).

15 See *An Awareness of What is Missing: Faith and Reason in a Post-Secular Age*, ed. Jurgen Habermas, trans. Ciaran Cronin (Cambridge: Polity Press, 2010); Mark Lilla, *The*

Christianity, some Christian thinkers returned the favor. Because the modern liberal state has rejected traditional moral reasoning, academics such as Alasdair MacIntyre have argued that its pretense to the pursuit of justice is not only incoherent but also manifestly unjust.[16] Others contend that the liberal state, as it has come to claim the exclusive loyalty of its citizens and to depend on the exercise of violence, is inconsistent with the demands of Christian discipleship.[17] Against both of these approaches to the relationship of religion and liberalism, McConnell has emphasized the compatibility, even symbiosis, of robust religious exercise and limited government.

In "Old Liberalism, New Liberalism, and People of Faith," McConnell identified four "doctrines of Christianity" that "point in the direction of liberalism," and argued that, "historically, liberalism was a product of those Christian impulses."[18] He thus united Christian belief and the classical liberalism that influenced the constitutional framers, paving the way for a constitutional jurisprudence that complements reformed Protestant theology. The four doctrines and their liberal implications are: (1) the doctrine of sin and the separation of powers; (2) the doctrine of "two kingdoms" and the separation of church and state; (3) the doctrine of individual conscience and religious liberty; and (4) the priesthood of all believers and personal equality. The last two, as McConnell explained in a speech before the Vatican, are especially central to reformed Protestantism.[19]

According to McConnell, "[p]erhaps the most fundamental connection between liberalism and Christianity is their common belief in the pervasive and ineradicable nature of sin."[20] Sin, in the Christian tradition, is not only the failure to live up to God's commands, but, perhaps more importantly, the

Stillborn God: Religion, Politics, and the Modern West (New York: Alfred A. Knopf, 2007). Some non-religious liberals have been more sanguine about the possibility of religious engagement in public discourse. See Jeffrey Stout, *Democracy and Tradition* (Princeton: Princeton University Press, 2004).

16 See Alasdair MacIntyre, *After Virtue: A Study in Moral Theory* (Notre Dame: University of Notre Dame Press, 1981).

17 See Stanley Hauerwas, *The Peaceable Kingdom: A Primer in Christian Ethics* (Notre Dame: University of Notre Dame Press, 1983); John Howard Yoder, *The Politics of Jesus* (Grand Rapids: Wm. B. Eerdmans, 1972).

18 McConnell, "Old Liberalism, New Liberalism, and People of Faith," in *Christian Perspectives on Legal Thought*, ed. Michael W. McConnell, Robert F. Cochran, Jr., and Angela C. Carmella (New Haven: Yale University Press, 2001), 6–7.

19 McConnell, "Theological Foundations of the Religion Clauses of the First Amendment to the United States Constitution," in *Secolarismo e Liberta Religiosa*, ed. Jorge Rodriguez (1998), 193, 194 ("Many of the same concerns for Christian liberty that inspired Protestant Christians to deny the ecclesiastical authority of Rome, rightly or wrongly, also lay behind their denial of the civil and ecclesiastical authority of their own legislatures in matters of religion.").

20 McConnell, "Old Liberalism," 7.

inability to do so without God's grace. McConnell linked the doctrine of sin to "[t]he central insight of liberal politics," "that all human beings and human institutions are prone to abuse of power. That is why liberal constitutionalism insists on dividing power and on creating checks and balances."[21]

To illustrate liberalism's assumption of human fallibility, McConnell pointed to *The Federalist*.[22] One of the key principles of the United States Constitution, explained John Jay, James Madison, and Alexander Hamilton, is the distribution of power among three federal departments and between the federal government and the states. By this vertical and horizontal division of power, a "double security arises to the rights of the people." Each government, and each department in that government, will seek its own power; none will have it absolutely. In this way, Madison wrote, "ambition [will] be made to counteract ambition."[23]

By linking the doctrine of sin to *The Federalist*, McConnell subtly suggests that human sinfulness is reflected not only in classical liberalism, but also in the logic and structure of the US Constitution. As an apology for the Constitution by some of the men who had a hand in drafting it, *The Federalist* is a starting point for jurists who seek the original understanding of the constitutional text. McConnell thus connected the dots between reformed Protestantism, liberalism, and the original understanding of the US Constitution.

The doctrine of sin leads McConnell to contrast "Christian politics" with "utopian politics." Because "[w]e will not bring about the Kingdom of Heaven on this earth through our political efforts," "Christian politics should be antiutopian in character." "Utopian politics" is "dangerous and deceptive," even "a kind of idolatry," because it falsely promises governmental solutions to fundamental human problems but leads inevitably to "tyranny." Power, unchecked, begets abuse. Christians and classical liberals alike "take human nature as given, and make modest efforts to improve community life at the margin."[24]

The second Christian doctrine that McConnell identified as part of the "liberal theory of government" is the doctrine of two kingdoms, the view that God has divided authority over human affairs between the church and the secular government. The doctrine of two kingdoms developed over the course of western political theology, from Augustine of Hippo to John Calvin. In the

21 Ibid., 7.
22 Ibid., 7.
23 *The Federalist* No. 51 (Madison), in *The Federalist (The Gideon Edition)*, ed. George W. Carey and James McClellan (Indianapolis: Liberty Fund, 2001), 268.
24 McConnell, "Old Liberalism," 8.

hands of the Protestant reformers, it was understood to be God's distribution of jurisdictional authority between temporal rulers and the church. Neither had complete control over human affairs, and each had limited control over the other.

The most obvious application of this doctrine in liberal theory is the separation of church and state. Thus, McConnell argues, "[t]he two-kingdoms view is at the heart of our First Amendment."[25] For this he cites John Locke, who translated the reformed Protestant version of the doctrine of two kingdoms into an argument for religious liberty.[26]

McConnell suggested another constitutional implication of the Christian doctrine of two kingdoms: a general commitment to a limited government. "If the state does not have power over the church, it follows that the power of the state is limited." Thus the "separation of church from state is the most powerful possible refutation of the notion that the political sphere is omnicompetent."[27] In "Old Liberalism" he does not elaborate on this connection, and that is probably just as well. The doctrine of two kingdoms was not, at bottom, about limited government. It was about understanding the allocation of authority between two governments. Christian thought does not postulate a realm beyond government; the question is who governs what.

"A third theological notion at the foundation of liberalism," McConnell argues, "is the idea of primacy of conscience." Championed by Martin Luther and John Calvin, the reformed notion is that each individual is responsible for determining and responding freely to God's will by faith. While this notion was politically destabilizing, it also held the seeds of religious freedom. As liberal theorists concluded, "it is literally impossible as a theological matter for government power to improve a citizen's spiritual state."[28] Put differently, "coerced faith is no faith at all."[29]

McConnell discusses the Virginia "act for establishing religious freedom" as an example of the primacy of conscience at work in the founding-era liberal political project. Thomas Jefferson, a Deist, authored the bill, which was a precursor of the First Amendment.[30] The bill ended state-mandated contributions to churches. The first paragraph, which spells out the bill's

25 Ibid., 10.

26 Ibid., 11.

27 Ibid., 10. See Michael W. McConnell, "Religion and Its Relation to Limited Government," *Harvard Journal of Law and Public Policy* 33 (2010): 943; Michael W. McConnell, "Non-State Governance," *Utah Law Review* 2010 (2010): 7.

28 McConnell, "Old Liberalism," 13.

29 McConnell, "Theological Foundations," 199.

30 See *Everson* v. *Bd. of Ed.*, 330 U.S. 1 (1947). For an argument that Jefferson's bill did not influence those who drafted and ratified the First Amendment, see Mark David Hall,

assumptions, is a powerful statement of the theological underpinnings of the liberal commitment to religious freedom:

> Whereas, Almighty God hath Created the mind free; That all attempts to influence it by temporal punishments or burthens, or by civil incapacities tend only to beget habits of hypocrisy and meanness, and therefore are a departure from the plan of the holy author of our religion, who being Lord, both of body and mind yet chose not to propagate it by coercions on either, as was in his Almighty power to do so . . .[31]

Elsewhere McConnell relied on these concepts to urge the Vatican to "appreciate the significance of beginning the argument for religious liberty unashamedly with the proposition that Almighty God hath made the mind free, and to join with Elisha Williams in his insistence that Christ be King in His own Kingdom."[32]

In "Old Liberalism," McConnell further argues that the doctrine of conscience "implies and leads to liberty in other matters essential to human flourishing: each person is free not just to worship but to pursue the good life in the manner and season most agreeable to his or her conscience." "To the extent that God's will affects all of life," he argues, "then the principle of freedom must apply to all of life."[33] Given his commitment to *Christian* conscience, however, McConnell disavowed libertinism, which may arise from agnosticism about the good. In the "early liberal conception," he writes, "freedom was the freedom to do the right."[34] This emphasis puts reformed liberalism in tension with the libertarian offshoots of classical liberalism.

The final Christian doctrine that McConnell identified as an influence on classical liberalism is the "priesthood of all believers."[35] As the Apostle Paul put it, Christ died for all; in him "[t]here is no longer Jew or Greek, there is no longer slave or free, there is no longer male and female."[36] For the Protestant reformers, the doctrine of spiritual equality had implications for salvation and for the nature of the church. They believed the Bible to be "a sufficient revelation of the truth to all men, and that all have the capacity to read and understand it without the mediation of earthly authorities." Thus "all people

"Madison's Memorial and Remonstrance, Jefferson's Statute for Religious Liberty, and the Creation of the First Amendment," *American Political Thought* 3 (2014): 32–63.

31 William Lee Miller, *The First Liberty: Religion and the American Republic* (Washington, DC: Georgetown University Press, 2003): 255–257.

32 Ibid., 203.

33 McConnell, "Old Liberalism," 14.

34 Ibid., 15.

35 Ibid., 15.

36 Galatians 3:28 (New Revised Standard Version).

are equal in the most fundamental sense – in their capacity to perceive the will of God and to act upon it."[37]

The ecclesiastical implications of the priesthood of all believers had a direct influence on classical liberal theories of popular sovereignty and constitutionalism. Equality of spiritual judgment implied equality of responsibility for church affairs. From this premise arose the reformed doctrine of covenant, "wherein a group of individuals constitute themselves as a body by mutual consent, based on shared convictions, with God as witness and ultimate authority."[38]

The conceptual as well as the historical connections between the doctrine of covenant and liberal theories of political sovereignty are clear. As McConnell explains:

> In its secular garb, the notion of covenant lies behind the political idea of the consent of the governed. If all persons are equally capable of perceiving the good and acting on it, then no one has a natural right to rule over another, and just government can be based only upon consent. In this sense, democracy was a secularization of the movement away from a hierarchical church structure and toward congregational ecclesiology.[39]

Enter the United States Constitution, the first national charter to memorialize and implement popular sovereignty. In the early years of the republic, McConnell noted, reformed theology, classical liberalism, and constitutionalism walked hand in hand. Religion was not relegated to private, non-political affairs. Rather it provided the conceptual and moral underpinning for liberal republicanism. The expansion of equality and enfranchisement owed as much to the theology and religious fervor of the Great Awakenings as to the anthropology of the Enlightenment.[40]

McConnell's account of "reformed liberalism," though merely a sketch, is innovative. While other Christian thinkers have developed more elaborate theories attempting to integrate Christianity and contemporary liberalism, McConnell's deserves to be read alongside them.[41] Few have given more

37 McConnell, "Old Liberalism," 15.

38 Ibid., 15. See Michael W. McConnell, "Calvinism and Liberty: Reformed influences on America's founding principles," review of *The Reformation of Rights: Law, Religion, and Human Rights in Early Modern Calvinism*, by John Witte, Jr., *Books and Culture* (Jan./Feb. 2009).

39 McConnell, "Old Liberalism," 16; see Gordon Wood, *The Radicalism of the American Revolution* (New York: Vintage, 1991), 230, 235.

40 McConnell, "Old Liberalism," 17; see Nathan O. Hatch, *The Democratization of American Christianity* (New Haven: Yale University Press, 1989).

41 See Nicholas Wolterstorff, *The Mighty and the Almighty: An Essay in Political Theology* (Cambridge: Cambridge University Press, 2012); Eric Gregory, *Politics and the Order of Love: An Augustinian Ethic of Democratic Citizenship* (Chicago: University of Chicago Press, 2008); Oliver O'Donovan, *The Ways of Judgment* (Grand Rapids: Wm. B. Eerdmans,

thought to the Protestant bases of religious liberty,[42] or done more to develop a constitutional jurisprudence that aligns with an account of Christian liberalism.[43]

III

McConnell's greatest contributions to constitutional jurisprudence have been sustained arguments for religious liberty, for an equal place for religion in public life, and for judicial deference to the democratic process where the Constitution is silent about contested moral issues. For each, he appeals to history, American constitutional tradition, and fundamental principles of republican political theory. Each of these themes is consonant with, though independent of, his notion of reformed liberalism.

A. *Religious Accommodations*

McConnell is perhaps best known in the legal academy for his scholarship on religious liberty. Early in his career he developed a theory of religious liberty that "changed the terms of debate."[44] Since mid-century, the Supreme Court had held that government action with the purpose or primary effect of advancing religion violated the Establishment Clause.[45] Many scholars defended this view by arguing that the Religion Clauses required "strict separation" between church and state.

But McConnell noticed that as the government reaches into nearly every facet of public life, it regulates conduct by individuals and groups that, though not originating with the government, nonetheless occurs in public. When the government organizes and regulates private conduct that occurs in public – schools, churches, public events, and the like – must the government ignore, or even be hostile toward, the religious exercise of those parties? McConnell

2008); Charles Mathewes, A *Theology of Public Life* (Cambridge: Cambridge University Press, 2007).

42 See Nicholas Wolterstorff, "A Religious Argument for the Civil Right to Freedom of Religious Exercise, Drawn from American History," *Wake Forest Law Review* 36 (2001): 535; John Witte, Jr., "The Essential Rights and Liberties of Religion in the American Constitutional Experiment," *Notre Dame Law Review* 71 (1999): 372.

43 See H. Jefferson Powell, "The Earthly Peace of the Liberal Republic," in *Christian Perspectives*; H. Jefferson Powell, *The Moral Tradition of American Constitutionalism: A Theological Interpretation* (Durham: Duke University Press, 1993).

44 Mark Tushnet, "Accommodation of Religion Thirty Years On," *Harvard Journal of Law & Gender* 38 (2015): 1, 7–8.

45 *Lemon* v. *Kurtzman*, 403 U.S. 602 (1971).

argued that some government action that facilitates religion does not amount to an establishment of religion, but rather is best understood to *accommodate* private religious exercise in a way that is entirely consistent with the Religion Clauses.[46]

The theory made sense of a number of longstanding American traditions and statutes that would have violated a strict separation of church and state but that, given the government's breadth of regulation, could be reformulated as accommodations of religion. Take for instance the government's provision of religious chaplains for members of the military or prisoners. On the one hand, the government's employment of military and prison chaplains promotes religion – especially among those who are particularly vulnerable to the government's exercise of power. On the other hand, when the government assigns someone to a ship, base, or prison, it deprives him of access to his minister, congregation, and religious practices. Rather than giving a particular religious belief or practice the state's imprimatur, then, providing a chaplain accommodates the sailor, soldier, and prisoner's private religious exercise.

McConnell's theory also at least partially reconciles the Supreme Court's doctrine under the Establishment and Free Exercise Clauses. At the time, the Court held that the Free Exercise Clause requires an accommodation from a governmental regulation that imposes a substantial burden on religious exercise when the regulation was unnecessary to achieve a compelling governmental interest.[47] This interpretation of the Free Exercise Clause probably – ironically – amounted to a violation of the Court's interpretation at that time of the Establishment Clause, which prohibited the government from acting with the purpose or principal effect of advancing religion. A theory of government accommodations reconciles exemptions for religious exercise with a commitment to the government's neutrality among religions by explaining that even-handed accommodations simply remove government-imposed burdens from religious exercise rather than promoting a particular religious belief or practice.

McConnell also wrote a book-length article arguing that the original history of the Free Exercise Clause is consistent with the view that the Clause requires accommodations from general laws that burden religious exercise.[48] At the

46 Michael W. McConnell, "Accommodation of Religion," *Supreme Court Review* 1985 (1985): 1; Michael W. McConnell, "Accommodation of Religion: An Update and a Response to the Critics," *George Washington Law Review* 60 (1992): 685.

47 *Sherbert* v. *Verner*, 374 U.S. 398 (1963).

48 Michael W. McConnell, "The Origins and Historical Understanding of Free Exercise of Religion," *Harvard Law Review* 103 (1990): 1409; see Michael W. McConnell, "Establishment and Disestablishment at the Founding, Part I: Establishment of Religion," *William and Mary*

time, the article would have reinforced the Court's interpretation of the Free Exercise Clause. That changed, however, the same year the article appeared.

In the landmark decision *Employment Division* v. *Smith* (1990), the Supreme Court held that the Free Exercise Clause does not provide an accommodation from a religiously neutral law of general applicability, regardless whether the law imposes a substantial burden on religious exercise.[49] The case was about whether members of a Native American church who used peyote as a sacrament were entitled to an accommodation from laws prohibiting the possession and use of controlled substances. Departing from longstanding doctrine, the Court said no, and it has never backed away from this decision. The political backlash to the case was swift and decisive. A near-unanimous Congress passed and President Clinton signed the Religious Freedom Restoration Act (RFRA). The Act reinstated accommodations from laws that unnecessarily place a substantial burden on religious exercise.[50] From the beginning the Act has received criticism from scholars who believe that it amounts to an unconstitutional establishment of religion. While McConnell's historical review of free exercise did not convince the Court to keep its doctrine of accommodations under the Constitution, it nonetheless provided crucial support for the constitutionality of government efforts, like RFRA, that provide such accommodations by statute.

Although McConnell rarely expressly makes the connection, his theory of religious accommodations is consistent with his view of reformed liberalism. He painstakingly reviewed the history of the Free Exercise Clause, concluding that accommodations were consistent with that history, though acknowledging that it may not have required them. By doing so, he tied contemporary accommodationism directly to the political theory that animated the founding era, which he believes to be consistent with reformed liberalism. For those who may be unmoved by evidence of the founders' commitment to religious accommodations, however, McConnell also provided an important conceptual argument that linked contemporary accommodations to the founders' broader understanding of the government's role in public life. "[T]he old paradigm of 'strict separation' under the Establishment Clause has had to give

Law Review 44 (2003): 2105. McConnell's *Harvard Law Review* article prompted several rebuttals of his interpretation of the history. See Ellis West, "The Right to Religion-Based Exemptions in Early America: The Case of Conscientious Objectors to Conscription," *Journal of Law and Religion* 10 (1993–1994): 367–401; Philip A. Hamburger, "A Constitutional Right of Religious Exemption: An Historical Perspective," *George Washington Law Review* 60 (1992): 915.

49 *Employment Division* v. *Smith*, 494 U.S. 872 (1990).

50 Pub. L. No. 103–141, 107 Stat. 1488 (1993), codified at 42 U.S.C. § 2000bb through 42 U.S.C. § 2000bb-4.

way to such ideas as 'equal access,' 'neutral funding,' and 'accommodation.'" Otherwise the government's steady growth "would have been a relentless engine of secularization."[51] McConnell thus suggests that religious accommodations, though not widely practiced at the founding, may be more consistent with classical liberalism, and thus with the spirit of reformed Protestantism, than would a continuing commitment to a strict separation of church and state.[52]

B. Religious Reasons in Public Discourse

McConnell has also been one of the most influential legal scholars to respond forcefully to the argument that religion has no place in public discourse. That theory, advanced most famously by the philosopher John Rawls, holds that members of a liberal democracy are obligated to give one another reasons that could, in principle, be acceptable to others.[53] According to some versions of this notion, a citizen may not advance religious reasons for law or policy because non-believers could not accept them.[54] The principle has important implications. All legislation should be based on non-religious reasons, including, somewhat ironically, perhaps, legislation that facilitates religious exercise. More importantly, perhaps, the notion relegates religion to a sphere of private belief and exercise, expelling it from public discourse about politics and morality, whether in journals, classrooms, political campaigns, or ballot boxes.

McConnell has forcefully opposed this account of liberalism, maintaining instead that citizens are entitled to give one another their reasons for favoring or opposing public policy, even when those reasons are based on religious beliefs. Indeed, citizens are entitled to recruit others to their religious views, including their views about public policy. Religious reasons are neither more nor less susceptible than any other kinds of reasons of

[51] McConnell, "Old Liberalism," 21.

[52] Ibid., 23–24.

[53] Rawls, "Public Reason"; John Rawls, *Political Liberalism* (New York: Columbia University Press, 2005).

[54] John Rawls originally advanced such a view of "public reason." A number of critics noted that this view would have eliminated the religious arguments of abolitionists and civil rights advocates. Rawls therefore revised his view to permit a citizen to advance a reasonable religious doctrine in public reasoning so long as she also advances a "public reason" sufficient to support her point. See Rawls, *Political Liberalism*, xlix–l; see generally John Rawls, "The Idea of Public Reason Revisited," *University of Chicago Law Review* 64 (1997): 765–807.

gaining the assent of those who do not share all of the presumptions that underlie them.[55]

A chief implication of McConnell's view is that the government should not disfavor private religious education or students' exercise of religion within public schools. Schools are the nurseries of public discourse. When the government puts a thumb on the scales against religious education or private religious exercise it systematically marginalizes religious voices in the public sphere for generations. The history of American public education and its use as a tool to promote the majority's religious sentiments is long, complicated, and turns a great deal on local norms. McConnell's theory of accommodations emphasizes that the First Amendment should be understood to require the government to provide even-handed support for education regardless of the parents and student's religious commitments. He has thus supported public vouchers so that poorer parents may choose to send their children to private religious schools.[56] The current model, in which the government supplies only a religion-free education, gives only the wealthy the opportunity to educate their children according to their religious beliefs.

Within public schools, too, McConnell has argued for the right of students to fully exercise their religions. In an important free speech and free exercise case before the Supreme Court, he successfully argued that religious student groups at public universities have the same right to use public funds to discuss their viewpoints that others have to discuss non-religious viewpoints.[57]

McConnell's argument that religion should have a place in public discourse is in line with his view of reformed liberalism. Reformed liberalism holds that God's sovereignty and care for humans are the most important bases of human decision making, and responding to God's truth and love will naturally shape one's views of public policy. Rather than sidelining religion, or assuming that it has uniform implications for public policy, reformed liberalism makes space for people to advance religious views – including the

[55] Michael W. McConnell, "Five Reasons to Reject the Claim that Religious Arguments Should be Excluded from Democratic Deliberation," *Utah Law Review* 1999 (1999): 639; Michael W. McConnell, "Secular Reason and the Misguided Attempt to Exclude Religious Argument from Democratic Deliberation," *Journal of Law, Philosophy and Culture* 1 (2007): 159.

[56] Michael W. McConnell, "Education Disestablishment: Why Democratic Values Are Ill-Served by Democratic Control of Schooling," in *Nomos XLII: Moral and Political Education*, ed. Stephen Macedo and Yael Tamir (New York: New York University Press, 2002): 87; Michael W. McConnell, "The Selective Funding Problem: Abortions and Religious Schools," *Harvard Law Review* 104 (1991): 989.

[57] *Rosenberger* v. *University of Virginia*, 515 U.S. 819 (1995).

space to disagree about religion and to dispute its implications for the common good.

C. *Judicial Humility and Democracy*

McConnell's most broadly applicable contribution to constitutional jurisprudence has been to consistently urge the Supreme Court to exercise judicial humility. He has been one of a handful of scholars arguing for judicial self-restraint during an era when the Court has confidently asserted its authority to enforce constitutional limits on the government even when those limits do not have a clear foundation in the Constitution's text and history.

The Supreme Court's constitutional interpretation, McConnell argues, should hew closely to the Constitution's text and historic understanding.[58] When those touchstones do not foreclose a policy decision embodied in an act of Congress or a state law, the Court should defer to the People's policy preferences. The principles underlying the Constitution suggest that, where the Constitution is silent, or can reasonably be read to authorize certain legislation, the People should have their way. The Constitution creates a government by the People, not by the Court. When the Court enforces the Constitution, it is enforcing the will of the People expressed in that document. When it ventures beyond the Constitution's text, the Court usurps the People's authority to govern themselves.[59]

Put differently, policy determinations on contested moral issues that the Constitution's text and history do not resolve should be resolved from the bottom up, not from the top down. Republican constitutionalism is messy. It presumes the People will disagree about matters of first importance. And it provides that the People themselves will resolve those disputes through their duly elected representatives, subject to constant revision through continuing public debate. When the Court invalidates a law regulating conduct about which people have moral disagreements, such as abortion, it ends democratic engagement of the issue. The only way for the People to take the issue back from the Court is to enact a constitutional amendment, something the Constitution itself makes a difficult task. The People should not have to gain

[58] Michael W. McConnell, "On Reading the Constitution," *Cornell Law Review* 73 (1988): 359; McConnell, "Time, Institutions, and Interpretation," *Boston University Law Review* 95 (2015): 1745.

[59] See Michael W. McConnell, "The Importance of Humility in Judicial Review: A Comment on Ronald Dworkin's 'Moral Reading' of the Constitution," *Fordham Law Review* 65 (1997): 1269.

a supermajority to govern themselves according to the terms of their fundamental charter.[60]

One of the longstanding disputes in constitutional law is whether, when, and why the Court should enforce individual rights that the Constitution does not expressly enumerate. While McConnell has generally argued that the People should have a free hand when the Constitution is silent, he has also argued that some rights may arise from longstanding practices of the people themselves – practices that the law has uniformly protected or allowed though the Constitution does not mention them. A family's right to raise and educate its own children may be one example.[61] By the same token, McConnell has argued that a number of rights the Supreme Court enforces against the states under the auspices of the Due Process Clause of the Fourteenth Amendment have little basis in the legal traditions and practices of the people.[62] Such rights, he suggests, should have their source ultimately in the People, usually through the constitutional text they adopt, or, at a minimum, through unspoken expectations based on longstanding legal tradition.[63]

McConnell has been even-handed about the implications of judicial humility. From early in his career he has argued against the legitimacy of the Court's abortion jurisprudence on the ground that it lacks a firm basis in constitutional text, history, and tradition. This may be an unsurprising position for a social conservative. However, McConnell has been equally critical of "conservative" Supreme Court decisions when they do not arise from the Constitution's text and history. For instance, McConnell defended Chief Justice Roberts's decision, controversial among some conservatives, to uphold the "individual mandate" provision of the Affordable Care Act under Congress' Taxing Power.[64] "Roberts's deft opinion," he wrote, "strikes a mighty blow for conservative constitutionalism, while bolstering the court's moral authority and reminding the country of the difference between law and

60 Michael W. McConnell, "The Role of Democratic Politics in Transforming Moral Convictions Into Law," *Yale Law Journal* 98 (1989): 1503; see Michael W. McConnell, "Institutions and Interpretation: A Critique of *City of Boerne* v. *Flores*," *Harvard Law Review* 111 (1997): 153.

61 *Pierce* v. *Society of Sisters*, 268 U.S. 510 (1925).

62 Nathan S. Chapman and Michael W. McConnell, "Due Process As Separation of Powers," *Yale Law Journal* 121 (2012): 1672.

63 Michael W. McConnell, "The Right to Die and the Jurisprudence of Tradition," *Utah Law Review* 1997 (1997): 665; Michael W. McConnell, "Ways to Think About Unenumerated Rights," *University of Illinois Law Review* 2013 (2013): 1985.

64 *Nat'l Fed. of Ind. Bus.* v. *Sebelius*, 132 S.Ct. 2566 (2012).

politics."[65] Likewise McConnell criticized the Court for invalidating part of the Voting Rights Act because he believed it rested on legal reasoning the conservative justices "made up."[66]

McConnell's case for modest judicial review corresponds to reformed liberalism. All people, not just an elite class of lawyers and judges, have an equal right to determine the norms that will shape their society. The government's role is limited to enforcing those norms the People enact into law, subject to the strictures the People have imposed on the government through a written compact.

Where McConnell promotes a modest judicial review of government conduct that might restrict unenumerated rights, his jurisprudence is in tension with the principles and aims of a more libertarian approach to US constitutionalism. This is, perhaps, the most important area of disagreement between McConnell and some other conservative legal scholars: in the name of popular sovereignty he has argued that the government should have latitude to restrict a wide range of individual conduct. This, too, is consistent with reformed liberalism, for it ensures that the People themselves are a check on the ambitions of a governing class, even a governing class of libertarians.

CONCLUSION

McConnell's most enduring contributions to Christian jurisprudence are impossible to estimate. He is, one hopes, far from the close of his career. Perhaps he will more fully elaborate a theory of reformed liberalism and relate it to his contemporary constitutional jurisprudence. Or perhaps he will continue to call for a more modest approach to judicial review. However he spends the remainder of his career, one can be sure that he will continue to advance, through his scholarship, lawyering, teaching, and op-eds, the "one point" he has "tried to make" "for most of [his] professional life": "the only tolerance worth having is tolerance for different understandings of the truth. A toleration based on skepticism, indifference or relativism is no tolerance at all."[67] A reformed liberalism indeed.

65 Michael W. McConnell, "Chief Justice Roberts crafts a ruling more conservative than it looks." *Reuters* (June 29, 2012).

66 Nina Totenberg, "Whose Term Was It? A Look Back At the Supreme Court" (includes an interview with Michael McConnell), *National Public Radio: Morning Edition* (July 5, 2013).

67 Michael W. McConnell, "We Worship the Same God You Do," in *Professors Who Believe: The Spiritual Journeys of Christian Faculty*, ed. Paul M. Anderson (Downers Grove: InterVarsity Press, 1998), 204.

17

The Jurisprudence of Robert P. George

Gerard V. Bradley

Robert P. George holds America's most prestigious academic position in public law, the McCormick Professorship of Jurisprudence at Princeton University. (The initial holder of that Chair was Woodrow Wilson. He was followed by such luminaries as Edward S. Corwin and Alpheus T. Mason.) George has done important scholarly work in constitutional law and theory, as well as in moral and legal philosophy. He is America's pre-eminent academic defender of the basic justice of traditional morals laws[1] (such as the legal regulation of pornography),[2] as well as what were until recently consensus positions on the nature, meaning, and social importance of marriage,[3] and the equal protection of the laws of homicide for all human persons from conception until natural death.[4] George has been an especially prominent defender of laws defining marriage as the conjugal union of husband and wife, and opponent of laws denying legal protection to children in the womb. In these (and other) matters his work is distinctive not only for the vigor of his advocacy, but also for the extraordinary depth and sophistication of his arguments for the positions he defends. George is

1 The best synoptic presentation of his views is "The Concept of Public Morality," *The American Journal of Jurisprudence* 45 (2000): 17–31.

2 See, e.g., Chapter Six of *The Clash of Orthodoxies* (Wilmington: ISI Books, 2001).

3 See, e.g., *What Is Marriage? Man and Woman: A Defense* (with S. Girgis and R. Anderson) (New York: Encounter Books, 2012), and *Conjugal Union: What Marriage Is* (with P. Lee) (Cambridge and New York: Cambridge University Press, 2014).

4 George's published writings in defense of all innocent human lives against intentional destruction are legion. See, e.g., *Embryo: A Defense of Life* (with C. Tollefsen) (New York: Doubleday, 2008); "Embryo Ethics," *Daedalus* (Spring, 2008); "The Wrong of Abortion" (with P. Lee), in *Contemporary Debates in Applied Ethics*, ed. A. Cohen and C. Wellman (Hoboken: Blackwell Publishers 2005) 13–26; and "Life as an Evil; Death as a Good: Dualism and Callahan's Inversion," in *Set No Limits: A Rebuttal to Daniel Callahan's Proposal to Limit Healthcare for the Elderly*, ed. G. Bradley and R. Barry (Chicago: University of Illinois Press, 1991), 15–28.

one of America's most effective defenders of the freedom of conscience, of which religious liberty is the central part.[5]

Besides his scholarly work in these areas, George has served in important public posts pertinent to them, such as membership on the United States Commission on Civil Rights (1993–1998), the President's Council on Bioethics (2002–2009), and the United States Commission on International Religious Freedom (2012–2016) – including two years as Chair.

George is a highly visible American public intellectual. His contributions to American political discourse in favor of the *public* importance of Judeo-Christian ethical principles, and of the moral truths contained in the Decalogue, are unsurpassed. *The New York Times Magazine*, in a lengthy profile of George, described him as "this nation's most influential conservative Christian thinker."[6] George is a devout Catholic, and a leading lay member of the church, which he has served faithfully in many ways, including as a trusted episcopal advisor and confidant.

The relationship between George's Christian beliefs and his jurisprudential *thought*[7] might strike some, however, as a bit paradoxical. There is no doubt that his faith in Jesus Christ includes his affirmation of manifold truths about all that there is (visible and invisible), and about the human person, his true good, what God wills for him, and the prospects and conditions for human persons to enjoy eternal life in Heaven.[8] His Christianity is not, in other words, merely an affair of the heart (think of the "liberal" Christianity of Schleiermacher). Nor is it a "narrative" of group identity and customs, so common among those Christians afflicted with a non-foundationalist epistemology (think of Stanley Hauerwas). Much less is it a personal spiritual brand (think of millennials). For George, Christianity is a worldview, an accurate account of the cosmos, a correct understanding of reality. For him,

5 See especially, *Conscience and Its Enemies* (Wilmington: ISI Books, 2013).

6 David D. Kirkpatrick, "The Conservative-Christian Big Thinker," *New York Times Magazine*, Dec. 16, 2009.

7 Which is not to speak of its influence upon *him*, for Professor George's scholarly work as well as his political and legal activism have been profoundly shaped by his Catholic faith, and after that by his deep sense of personal vocation; that is, to his discernment of how Christ wishes him to deploy his manifold gifts in the service of others, and thereby to help assemble material for the Kingdom of God.

8 In his Address to the 2014 National Catholic Prayer Breakfast, for example, Professor George challenged his listeners to be "unashamed of the Gospel," to witness to its truths without fear of the reprisal which very likely would follow. He further observed that "not long ago" it was different: "Biblical and natural law beliefs about morality were culturally normative; they were not challenges to cultural norms. But those days are gone. What was once normative is now regarded as heretical – the moral and cultural equivalent of treason."

Christianity includes many true propositions about matters germane to human well-being in society.

George steadily maintains too that political life and legal theory are to be open to the *entirety* of truth. He unequivocally endorses the "perfectionism" of the central pre-liberal tradition of political philosophy (even as he has reshaped some aspects of it, and provided it with a fresh foundation): sound politics and good law are concerned with helping people to lead genuinely moral, upright, and valuable lives.

Yet, George writes: "I want to show that Christians and other believers are right to defend their positions on key moral issues as *rationally* superior to the alternatives proposed by secular liberals and those within the religious denominations who have abandoned traditional moral principles in favor of secularist morality."[9] "My criticism of secular liberal views is not that they are contrary to faith; it is that they fail the test of reason."[10]

Any useful account of the influence of Christianity upon Robert George's thought lies here, in a supple description of the dialectic between, on the one hand, the truths of faith as revealed and authoritatively proposed by the magisterium of the church and the endowments of reason to which that faith attests, and, on the other hand, the fallibility and limitations of reason (including in its powers of reflection upon moral, political, and fundamental legal principles) in man's fallen state, to which the truths of the faith also attest. Simply put, George's Christian faith leads him to see that reason is both powerful and limited and that both reason's power and limits must be taken into account in theorizing about the common good, political life, and the role of law in the establishment and maintenance of just and humane laws and institutions.

Perhaps this helps to explain why George, who has absorbed and endorsed key aspects of the teachings of classical and medieval philosophers, is also a defender of Madisonian republican constitutional principles aimed at checking and limiting power and promoting what contemporary political theorists have labeled "deliberative democracy."

I

Robert P. George was born in Morgantown, West Virginia, on July 10, 1955, the eldest of five boys born to Catherine and Joseph George. His mother is the daughter of Italian immigrants. His father, a decorated World War II combat

9 Preface to *Clash of Orthodoxies*. Textual emphasis is in the original.

10 Ibid.

veteran who became a successful wine and spirits broker and real estate investor, is the son of Syrian immigrants. "Robby" (as he is almost universally known) is a "cradle" Catholic, raised in a devout home. All five George boys were altar servers and four were liturgical musicians.

George attended both public and Catholic schools in Morgantown. Four of the boys – Robby included – earned graduate degrees from Oxford University, and the same four became lawyers. The other brother earned graduate degrees from Harvard and Yale and became a businessman. Three of the lawyers are partners in the Charleston, West Virginia, law firm of Robinson & McElwee, where Robby is "of counsel."[11] As a teenager, George became a bluegrass banjo player and a guitarist. Before he left home for college he played regularly with local bands in coffee houses, fairs, and in local "rod and gun" clubs.

George studied moral and political philosophy at Swarthmore. He was elected student body president, and continued to play professional-quality strings in various ensembles on and around campus. One professor who greatly influenced him, and who remains a good friend, is James Kurth. A political scientist who was then a man of the secular left but who later became an evangelical Christian, Kurth was more than an intellectual mentor. He encouraged what later would probably be lamented as George's lack of "political correctness" on cultural issues, by his own example of feisty yet respectful dissent from campus orthodoxies.

While in high school in West Virginia, George became politically engaged. He was, perhaps inevitably, a Democrat, given his family's links to coal miners and to immigrant-Catholic culture. He worked in the 1972 McGovern campaign, and served as an alternate delegate to the 1976 Democratic convention at Madison Square Garden. He thought that he was destined for a public life, if not for political office. He considered himself a liberal, though strongly pro-life, as were many nationally prominent Democrats in these years immediately after *Roe* v. *Wade*. The sexual revolution was in full swing, but American politics were not yet roiled by a culture war over marriage and the family, so his traditional views on these matters did not mark him as a Party outlier. He remembers being a "dissenter," however, on these questions at Swarthmore.[12]

College is formative for nearly everybody. Often it changes dramatically one's anticipated trajectory toward and through adult life. It surely did for George, in two different but equally vital ways. One was an epiphany when he read Plato's *Gorgias* in a political theory seminar. "Before reading that

11 "Of counsel" means that an attorney who may not be a salaried employee of a firm nevertheless has a regular relationship working with it.

12 P. Wachter, "A Mind on the Right," *Swarthmore College Bulletin*, January 2009.

dialogue, never in my wildest dreams would I have thought of pursuing an academic career," George recalled. He began to see education as the process of coming to "understand more deeply the truth about oneself and the world." Socrates engendered in George a most profound respect for the truth: "The conclusion that Socrates takes us to" in that dialogue "is that you'd be better off losing an argument when you're wrong than winning it," George later told an interviewer for a Swarthmore publication.[13] He decided to pursue a career in the realm of argument and ideas.

The second was meeting Cindy Schrom, also Swarthmore Class of 1977, when they were both sophomores. It was, at least for him, love at first sight. A Jewish woman from the New York suburbs, Cindy married George in an interfaith Jewish–Catholic service (with the approval of the Catholic Church) in the Andover Chapel at Harvard University, while George was working on his doctoral degree at Oxford. Shortly after they were wed, he was diagnosed with thyroid cancer, for which he was successfully treated over a period of a few years. They were blessed with two children – David and Rachel.

After Swarthmore, George attended Harvard Law and Divinity Schools, obtaining the Master of Divinity and *juris doctor* degrees. He thereafter matriculated at Oxford University, where he obtained his doctorate. (Later, Oxford would confer upon him the degrees of Bachelor of Civil Law and Doctor of Civil Law.) At Oxford from 1981 until 1985, George's supervisor was John Finnis, then (and now) the world's leading natural law legal philosopher.

George's doctoral thesis centered upon natural law and the legal enforcement of morals. Parts of that thesis inform his first book, *Making Men Moral: Civil Liberties and Public Morality* (*MMM*). In the dissertation (but not the book) he criticized Germain Grisez and Joseph Boyle's *Life and Death with Liberty and Justice* (1976) as excessively libertarian. His analyses and prescriptions (as developed in *MMM* and sustained in the years since) make greater room for the just legal enforcement of true moral norms than for Grisez and Boyle. (Their thought moved toward George's later on.) George and Finnis too continue to respectfully disagree about matters of detail on the legal enforcement of morals: Finnis affirms the existence of a slightly larger realm of truly private immoralities immune from government interference than does George. The practical difference between the two positions is minor.

George negotiated the transition from observant Catholic upbringing to mature adult faith without serious mishap. Well read in the western philosophical tradition, he has been influenced significantly by the thought of Augustine and Aquinas. The great bulk of his writings swing free of the finer

[13] Paul Wachter, "A Mind on the Right," *Swarthmore College Bulletin*, January 2009.

points of faith, however, and of the specifically Catholic tradition of social and political reflection inaugurated by Leo XIII in 1891 with his encyclical letter on the new industrial order, *Rerum novarum*. Nevertheless, George is master of these reflections, and occasionally his writings focus on these matters.[14]

George began teaching at Princeton in 1985, even before completing his doctoral degree. He received tenure in 1994, and in 1999 was named McCormick Professor of Jurisprudence. Early in his teaching career he came into regular contact with Richard John Neuhaus, then a Lutheran pastor and public intellectual, but later a Catholic priest and founder of *First Things*. Neuhaus became not only his treasured friend and collaborator, but also something of an inspiration. George came to share and to develop in his own work Neuhaus's solid commitment to the basic rightness and, as a world historical matter, the novelty and importance of the American experiment in ordered liberty. Neuhaus and George both interpreted that experiment along common Madisonian and Tocquevillian lines: *Madisonian* in the way described at the end of the Introduction to this chapter; "Tocquevillian" for its conviction that religion, churches, and the family supply the essential civil-society structural supports for the Madisonian experiment to succeed.

George, like Neuhaus, has been both highly enterprising and savvy, if not cunning, in his approach to political engagement. Like Neuhaus, he has been a master builder of religious coalitions rooted in matters of deep principle, and not just as marriages of convenience for the duration of the culture wars. George has even extended Neuhaus's admirable work of bringing Christians and Jews together in common cause for the common good of America. George served, for instance, as Chair of the United States Commission on International Religious Freedom. He has also regularly engaged publicly (in joint presentations, conferences, paired commentaries) with interlocutors from across the spectrum of religious allies and adversaries, perhaps most famously in his teaching and lecturing with the celebrated African-American academic, Cornell West. During the years-long public American debate about same-sex civil marriage, he collaborated extensively with leading members of the LDS church, and with Muslims such as Shaykh Hamza Yusuf, who is perhaps America's most influential Islamic public intellectual.

14 See, e.g., his many writings on the Second Vatican Council's document on religious freedom, *Dignitatis humanae* (DH), and these two papers (written with the author) on the social teachings of Pope John Paul II: "Pope John Paul II," in *The Teachings of Modern Christianity*, ed. John Witte and Frank S. Alexander (New York: Columbia University Press, 2006), 220–257; "Pope John Paul II," in *Christianity and Family Law: An Introduction*, ed. John Witte and Gary S. Hauk (Cambridge: Cambridge University Press, 2017), 363–380.

Indeed, many of George's signal practical contributions to American law have been in defense of marriage and the family. He was, for example, a co-author of the proposed Federal Marriage Amendment, which during the first administration of George W. Bush attracted very widespread political and religious support (though never sufficient backing to bring it to a Congressional vote). He also helped to found and subsequently chaired the National Organization for Marriage, perhaps the leading activist organization in our nation's continuing legal argument about the meaning, nature, and benefits of marriage.

In the summer of 2000, George founded the James Madison Program in American Ideals and Institutions at Princeton. He remains this academic study center's director. The Program provides fellowship positions and research support for a select group of scholars each year, all of whom are required to live in Princeton and to meet regularly with their colleagues, so forming what has become a large and tight-knit community. George is also the Herbert W. Vaughan Fellow of the Witherspoon Institute (which he co-founded with Luis Tellez), an off-campus independent research center, dedicated to the study and promotion of the moral foundations of free, democratic societies. Both the Madison Program and the Witherspoon Institute have become models for initiatives on or near other major campuses.

George is also an award-winning teacher, whose courses on Civil Liberties and Constitutional Interpretation are wildly popular among students. His trademarks in the classroom are an engaging but challenging manner of presentation, and a scrupulous respect for all reasoned points of view.

II

For more than two decades George has been conspicuously in the forefront of national debate on a host of fundamental moral issues and the law. Much of the attention drawn to him has been scholarly. And a great deal of it has been negative; that is to say, concerned to refute George's arguments for limiting civil recognition of marriage to unions of a man and a woman, for example, or for greater legal regulation of immoral sexual acts. Sometimes these critics glibly associate George's positions with his Catholicism, as if George were somehow repackaging sectarian commitments. But none of his adversaries on these issues has so far explored, in a suitably careful way, the interplay of faith and reason in George's thought.

George has many scholarly supporters, and even admirers. Yet none of them has undertaken the task of critically identifying the influence of Christianity upon George's jurisprudential thought. One reason for this is that unlike most other jurists profiled in this volume, George is still actively engaged in intellectual work. His *oeuvre* is not complete; *post-mortem* or global analyses are yet impossible. Graduate students and young professors are just beginning to treat the "thought" of Robert George as a distinct subject matter.

It is nonetheless true that whatever could be said today of the influence of Christianity on George's work could just as well be said later. He is a mature scholar whose work has rested for decades upon the same philosophical and theological foundations. George's work is transparent. It is rigorously analytical. What you see is pretty much what there is. He is not a candidate for revisionist treatment on the basis of a long-suppressed manuscript or lost letter. There are not in his work the kinds of riddles or obscurities or *lacunae* to which these missing links could supply answers. Creative academic reinterpretations of his thought would merely distort it.

The neglect of the Christian influences upon George's thought also owes to the fact that the central influence upon his jurisprudential work is unmistakably *philosophical*: the new classical theory of natural law pioneered by Grisez, and developed by him in partnership with John Finnis and the late Joseph M. Boyle, Jr.[15] In the preface to *Making Men Moral*, for example, George acknowledges his "massive intellectual debt to Germain Grisez, whose work in fundamental moral theory I have drawn upon heavily in developing my central arguments."[16] Finnis's pathbreaking *Natural Law and Natural Rights* (*NLNR*) came out a year before George matriculated at Oxford. Its deployment of the new classical theory revivified a moribund tradition of natural law jurisprudence, and it has been an invaluable foundation of George's own work in jurisprudence.

Scholarly investigation of the influence of Christianity upon this whole new classical theory, and thus effectively of a foundational element of George's thought, is plentiful. One strand of this criticism is that the new theory is a poor

15 The new classical natural law theory was launched by Grisez in his 1965 essay in *The American Journal of Jurisprudence* (then *The Natural Law Forum*), "The First Principle of Practical Reason: A Commentary on the *Summa theologiae*, I–II, Q. 94, A2." Joseph Boyle was a doctoral student of Grisez's, who enriched the theory with deep Thomistic learning and logical rigor (Boyle died in late September 2016). Finnis came to appreciate Grisez's extraordinary work as early as the publication of Grisez's 1965 book, *Contraception and the Natural Law* (Milwaukee: Bruce Publishing). They began working together several years later. Finnis's remarkably disciplined but creative reading of texts and his analytical acumen especially contributed to the three men's common work. Perhaps the most important of their jointly authored publications is *Nuclear Deterrence: Morality and Realism* (Oxford: Clarendon Press, 1987), a sustained argument against America's nuclear targeting strategy, which these men criticized as inescapably involving an intention to kill enemy non-combatants in violation of the common morality.

16 *MMM*, xi.

interpretation, or even adaptation, of Aquinas's thought. Russell Hittinger's early work is one prominent example.[17] This point can be put aside here for two reasons: although Grisez, Finnis, and Boyle often defend their work as Thomistic (in my view, successfully), they mean finally for it to stand on its own cogency. In any event, George has devoted little of his energy to the interpretive question.

The more relevant criticism of the new classical theory (and thus implicitly of Robert George) is that it is *insufficiently* theological, that it is *too* autonomous of revelation and of authoritative Church teaching; in short, that the influence of Christianity is *too* attenuated.[18] The italicized evaluative words indicate several distinct sub-lines of criticism, and this chapter is not the place to rehearse or refute them all. The most important particular criticism is that, when all is said and done, the new theorists fail to provide the cogent philosophical explanations and defenses of the truth of those moral norms contained in the Decalogue and taught by the whole Jewish-Christian tradition down through the ages, especially the exception-less prohibitions on adultery, killing the innocent, lying, and the like. My judgment is that these criticisms founder. The more important point in this context is how this whole controversy sheds light (if it does) on the relationship between George's own Christian convictions and his jurisprudential thought.

So: it is important to note that a faithful Catholic could accept the truth of traditional moral norms on the basis of religious teaching, namely, the witness of Scripture and the authority exercised by the Church's teachers. George no doubt does so. But George would add that it is *reasonable* for a conscientious person to conclude, in light of all the relevant evidence, that these religious sources teach authentically, that they bear sufficient indicia of truth-telling and divine inspiration to warrant faith in them. So, the truth of traditional moral teaching does *not* depend upon the success of the new classical theory. If that body of work had never been conceived, it would still be reasonable to hold that, if the Church teaches a norm to be true, there is a sufficient reason to believe that it is so.

The new classical project is not, however, an apologetic, as if its province was to rationalize the faith. The new theory might function in that manner. But its principal aim is to bring the foundations of morality into view, and to illumine how human persons can reliably know, without reliance upon faith,

17 Russell Hittinger, *A Critique of the New Natural Law Theory* (Notre Dame: Notre Dame University Press 1987).

18 Benedict M. Ashley, O.P., in a generally sympathetic review of Grisez's moral theology, expressed reservations about his use of Scripture and suggested an alternative in "The Scriptural Basis of Grisez's Revision of Moral Theology," in Robert George, ed., *Natural Law and Moral Inquiry* (Washington, DC: Georgetown University Press, 1998), 36–49.

that inherited moral teaching is, in fact, true. This undertaking bears many fruits. It can be an effective prolegomenon to faith. It can reassure the faithful that what they believe is reasonable, that they are not fideists. Most important, a successful philosophical grounding of the objective character and truth of traditional morality is a pearl of great price for anyone seeking to found democracy and freedom, not in the sandy shoals of moral skepticism and subjectivism, but in the solid ground of critical reason.

Indeed, and as we shall see in Part IV, George's greatest accomplishment has been to synthesize his own pioneering work on the concept of public morality with the new classical theory, to produce and defend concrete answers to what the law of our pluralistic democracy should be on controversial questions in bioethics, family law, abortion, religious freedom and other basic civil liberties, and the public regulation of non-marital sexual activity more generally. This body of work – which could be called an *applied public morality* – is unique, pathbreaking, and formidable. It is why Robert George is among the leading Christian intellectuals of our era.

III

The direct influence of the *information content* of Christian revelation upon George's jurisprudential work is modest. Truths unknowable to reason but which are part of the deposit of faith rarely play a unique and indispensable role in his arguments about what our laws and public policy should be. Put differently, what one needs to know about genuine human well-being in society can very largely be known by unaided reason. And genuine human well-being in society is the subject matter of George's jurisprudential thought.

It is nonetheless important to note that revealed moral truths (such as those of the Ten Commandments) confirm and reinforce natural reason's grasp of them. The fact that many, if not most, people in America who hold these truths hold them as religious deliverances, and not as the conclusions of philosophical argument, is a vital piece of information for any social theorist, George included.

The indirect influence of Christianity upon George's jurisprudential thought is, on the other hand, great. The whole of Christianity – the entire edifice of truths, conceived as an accurate description of the cosmos – functions for George as a set of global coordinates, bounding the space in which the public life in our democracy opens up as a realm of reason. George's Christian worldview also works as a complex architectural support for his reasoned contributions to that public life.

In short: Robert George's understanding of Christianity makes possible his philosophical jurisprudence. Let me explain, in seven parts.

One part is already apparent. It is George's understanding of *Romans* 2:15: "The demands of the law are written in their hearts, while their conscience also bears witness."[19] Scripture attests that revealed moral truths are also available to unaided reason. They can be – and are – known without the benefit of revelation. These truths are foundations of just co-existence in a political community.

Religious attestation to these truths of morality is nonetheless supremely valuable to a political community. Revelation makes them known to some people, confirms them for others, and gives everyone who cleaves to them an additional strong reason to keep them: doing so pleases God and cements friendship with Him.

A second part is George's understanding of the opening lines of *Romans* 13: "[T]here is no authority except from God, and those that exist have been established by God." George holds with nearly the whole Christian tradition that here the Apostle asserts the basic compatibility of human government with the transcendent majesty of Our Lord. Government is morally legitimate; it is part of God's plan for humankind. So far considered, however, *Romans* does not exclude the most overtly theological forms of government,[20] and so does not (so far) establish the relative independence of jurisprudence from revealed content.

George's position is that government is divinely sanctioned – and thus morally legitimate – because it is necessary (or at least highly advantageous) to genuine human well-being. Governments are to be judged according to critical moral criteria, namely, the common good of the political society, especially including the government's respect for human rights. Further recourse to revelation to gauge the justice of government actions is not needed.

Third, human persons are, and must be treated as, self-constituting beings. From the opening sentence of his first book (*Making Men Moral*) George has maintained that neither political society nor the law can *make* people morally good. Only persons can "make" themselves good, by doing the right thing for the right reason. George has also shown – persuasively, in my view – how good laws can *help* persons to make themselves good. At the heart of his grasp of law

19 All quotations from Scripture herein are from the *New American Bible* (1991).

20 These would be: theonomy (direct rule by the Word of God; think perhaps of the Israelites in the desert), theocracy (rule by clerics or religious leaders; think of Iran), or some conception of human government as delegated divine authority (think of the divine right of kings).

is his view of it as a vital, but secondary, aid to human flourishing. Persons do not flourish by raw instinct, or by imitation. They thrive by and through their morally significant free choices.

This deliberating, choosing, and freely acting person is the center of social and political life. The law is *for* the person, not the other way around. To put the point bluntly: civil society is subsidiary to the freely-choosing person, who emerges, then, as the connecting point between the heavenly and earthly cities. Political society and its governance are great and in some respects God-like. But in the end they are instrumental to persons' attempts to constitute themselves as worthy of the heavenly Kingdom. The polity and its law can be well understood without adverting to divine things, save that they must be understood in relation to the person's full, authentic flourishing. And *that* includes his or her relationship to transcendent realities.

Fourth, the premium on self-constitution is at its apogee when it comes to religion. George has argued throughout his career that the central defect in Aquinas's brand of perfectionism was his commitment to legislating faith. "Aquinas makes the first principle of politics a matter of religious belief."[21] This view assumes the propriety of legislating morals "precisely in so far as they are accepted on religious authority and are the means to an end (i.e. heavenly beatitude) that religious faith puts forward but reason by itself cannot identify."[22]

George steadily maintains that the nature of religion is such that its value "simply cannot be realized or well served by coercive imposition. Any attempt by government to coerce religious faith and practice, even *true* religious faith and practice, will be futile at best, and is likely to impair people's participation in the good of religion."[23] "Communion with God, if God exists, is like communion with other human beings in its *reflexivity*; it is not communion unless it represents a free self-giving."[24]

Religious liberty may thus be securely grounded in the true nature of religion, and not in the revealed or authoritative doctrines of any particular religion. Even so, one can see from a glance at the Gospels that Jesus sought to coerce no one's faith.[25] Again, revelation confirms and elaborates what reason can at least dimly grasp.

21 *MMM*, 41.
22 Ibid.
23 Ibid., 220.
24 Ibid., 221.
25 George's position on religious liberty and the subtle interplay of reason and revelation is captured in a key passage from DH: "the right to religious freedom has its foundation in the

The ground of religious liberty, and corresponding limits upon government action, includes too a natural theological element. As the Second Vatican Council put it (in a passage which George endorses), those "acts whereby men in private and in public and out of a sense of personal conviction direct their lives to God transcend by their very nature the order of terrestrial and temporal affairs . . . . [I]t would clearly transgress the limits set to [the government's] power were it to presume to command or inhibit acts that are religious."[26] Here as well reason points to what the Christian tradition has, following Augustine, taken to be human beings' simultaneous belonging to two cities, one of God and the other of Man.

Fifth, here in accord with Aquinas, George recognizes the substantial *indeterminacy* of moral principles and basic moral norms. The human law-maker typically faces a considerable range of morally permissible ways to apply and specify the moral norm against, say, theft. The moral truth that stealing is wrong (and contrary to the Commandments) does not itself settle how to treat cheating among siblings, or whether public authority ought to treat bank fraud more or less severely than bank robbery, or how the many variations among thefts (forcible stealing, extortion, embezzlement) should be treated by the criminal law. Much less does the moral truth (or the Commandment) settle how anyone accused of criminal theft should be adjudicated guilty or not, and if adjudicated guilty, how that person should be punished.

This whole matter of what Aquinas called *determinatio* reflects the necessity of free authoritative choice in governing a body politic. The subject matter of jurisprudential thought – chiefly, a political society's civil law – is largely a matter of contingency: the choices these rulers have, in fact, made settle what that law shall be. The positive law of a civil society is thus autonomous from the natural law, in that it is not deducible or even inferable from it. The natural moral law is nonetheless finally essential to the intelligibility, and obligatoriness, of the positive law.

Sixth, this paramountcy of positive law extends all the way to constitutional matters, and thus to the basic charter of civil society. George argues in several of his writings that the natural law does not itself settle how much authority – if any – a particular branch of a government should have to give legal effect to norms of justice. A particular written constitution might vest a nation's highest court with considerable final authority to determine (for example) how to balance the competing interests of the community in security from terror

very dignity of the human person as this dignity is known through the revealed word of God and by reason itself." DH, 2.

[26] DH, 4.

attack and privacy of information about individuals. Another constitution might withhold this authority from courts, and instead vest it in the legislature or in administrative personnel answerable to legislators, not to judges. A third might lodge final decision-making on these matters in the executive branch, perhaps on the view that these officials are best informed about national security dangers. And a fourth might disaggregate this authority, and distribute tranches of it to each branch.

George's basic position is that none of these jurisdictional schemes is uniquely required by justice. Each is, or in certain circumstances could be, just. As a general matter the constitutional scheme ordained in the fundamental law – whatever that scheme happens to be – is controlling. It settles matters of government power. People, including important government officials, are morally obliged to adhere to it.

Finally, every Christian must be alert to avoid contradictions between revealed truths and what reasoned argument leads one to believe to be true. In the end, truth is one; there can be no contradiction between what God has revealed and what in fact there is. This tension is sometimes unavoidable and it can be painful. But it must be borne. The scholar working in jurisprudence is no exception to this rule.

George's jurisprudence rarely implicates in any direct way the datum of a truth of faith. But if we broaden our view to consider the relevance of the metaphysical constitution of the universe implicit in revelation, we can see more points of contact. For example: discussions of criminal law today often traffic in implicit denials of free choice. So does any jurisprudential school of thought which rests upon a deterministic account of how human persons operate. Reason is capable of rebutting these deformations. Christianity most certainly excludes all forms of determinism and materialism; the spiritual (non-material) reality of free choice alone disproves both. Christianity makes little sense unless humans can exercise free choice.

It is not a matter here of introducing the content of revealed truth – say, the Incarnation or the Resurrection of the Body – into political matters. It is rather that revealed truths are *true* accounts of what there really is. When Christians recite the Creed, they affirm belief in the human person as a union of soul and body, such that after the Last Judgment each human person is reconstituted *as* an embodied spirit. Any form of body-self dualism would therefore undermine the faith of Christians, who could no longer understand the dignity of bodiliness, and who would find it difficult to take seriously many aspects of faith – Jesus in the Eucharist, the virgin birth, resurrection of the body, original sin, and so on.

The truth that we are embodied spirits can be grasped by unaided reason. But Christian revelation makes plain that truth and provides additional reasons of the highest order for defending that truth, in season and out of season. George has made especially effective strategic use of the Christian view of the human person. He has argued brilliantly on the strength of this truth for the sanctity of life from fertilization until natural death.[27] His work on marriage as the one-flesh union of the spouses does as well. This work is all the more important because, as George argues often, marriage is the core principle of all sexual morality.[28]

IV

George was blessed to have at hand, when he began his academic career, a powerfully illuminating framework of moral analysis. He was fortunate, too, to be taught (formally or informally) by the framework's master craftsmen, Germain Grisez and John Finnis. Even so, George's achievement has been nearly monumental. His greatest work has been to deploy that framework to reconceptualize the moral foundations of civil liberties in a pluralistic society, such as our own.

Over the last three decades George has convincingly shown how guarantees of liberty and equality for everyone; religious freedom for all; and government respect for privacy and the fundamental truth that each person must be the author of his or her own life, are solidly grounded in metaphysical and moral truth. He has also shown how these truths stand not only at the bottom of our constitutional and legal structure of civil liberties, justifying them. He has demonstrated how the truth can, and must, serve as a continuing monitor of our liberties, lest they devolve into license and indulgence. George's work enables believers in the common morality of Christians and Jews to conscientiously support our constitutional arrangements and liberties, even as he provides them with the intellectual resources needed to fruitfully criticize contemporary aberrations.

We have already considered one half of the heart of George's reconceptualization of civil liberties: the truth that law is for freely choosing persons. Persons are not valuable just insofar as they contribute to the fulfillment of some government five- or fifty-year program. Persons are not raw human

[27] See especially George's books: *Body-Self Dualism in Contemporary Ethics and Politics* (with P. Lee) (New York: Cambridge University Press, 2008) and *Embryo: A Defense of Human Life* (with C. Tollefsen) (New York: Doubleday, 2008).

[28] See especially *Conjugal Union: What Marriage Is* (with P. Lee) (New York: Cambridge University Press, 2014).

matter to be molded according to the master designs of social engineers. Persons are not on (or off) the right track insofar as their outward behavior conforms to some ideal template. Sound civil law usually concerns itself with justice between and among persons, and this justice is mostly a matter of doing what is required. Civil law is, in other words, largely indifferent to persons' motives and the reasons why they do what they do. Nonetheless, persons are morally obliged to be good, to perfect themselves. They do so when they do the right thing for the right reason. And sound civil law can and should *help* persons to be good.

The other half comprises objectively true moral norms. We shall in this part explore just two aspects of George's founding of civil liberties upon the truth about human well-being. The first involves his reconstruction of the famed Hart-Devlin exchange more than half a century ago, on the basic justice – or injustice – of morals laws.[29] George demonstrated that such laws are justifiable, though *not* by Devlin's "conservative" defense of them. The second aspect is less focused but just as important. It is George's showing of how a proper understanding of true human flourishing grounds respect for the very large (but not unlimited) range of life choices and styles which persons choose for themselves. This is Robert George's exposition of "pluralistic perfectionism."

As to the first: In 1957, a blue-ribbon commission headed by Sir John Wolfenden recommended to the British parliament that it decriminalize private homosexual behavior between consenting adults. What became known as the "Wolfenden Report" ignited the most celebrated jurisprudential debate of the twentieth century, a series of scholarly exchanges between Oxford legal philosopher H. L. A. Hart and High Court Judge Patrick Devlin. The Report's specific proposal about sodomy rested upon a controversial and sweeping claim that "it is not the duty of the law to concern itself with immorality as such."[30]

Lord Devlin attacked head-on the commission's central argument that "there must remain a realm of private morality and immorality which is, in brief and crude terms, not the law's business."[31] Devlin maintained instead that "there can be no theoretical limits to legislation against immorality."[32] He shared the traditional belief that no functioning polity worth its name could be just an aggregation of individuals sharing space. People constituting a political

[29] *MMM*, 48–50.

[30] This account of George's treatment of the Hart-Devlin debate is taken from Chapter 2 of *MMM*.

[31] *The Wolfenden Report, para.* 61, as quoted in *MMM*, 49.

[32] Patrick Devlin, *The Enforcement of Morals*, as quoted in *MMM*, 49.

community are more than a mere crowd. They share something substantial about the meaning of the good life. "For society is not something that is kept together physically; it is held by the invisible bonds of common thought."[33] Devlin joined this descriptive claim to a normative moral claim, namely, that society is justified, as a means of self-preservation, in enforcing its morality, whatever it happens to be, because social cohesion around moral norms is integral to societal self-preservation.

H. L. A. Hart said little directly in favor of the Wolfenden Report's reasoning. But he attacked Devlin's position, arguing that societies routinely survive changes in the basic moral views of their members. It is absurd to suppose, Hart concluded, that when such a change occurs, we must say one society has disintegrated and been succeeded by another.

"[W]e can safely assume, however," George wrote, "that by 'society' Devlin meant, above all, a state of affairs in which individuals identify their own interests with those of others to whom they understand and experience themselves as integrally related by virtue of common commitments and beliefs."[34] If so, morals laws, as Devlin understood them, really do protect something of great value, namely, that integral relatedness we call community or civic friendship. Thus, Devlin's position, as George interprets it, survives Hart's criticisms.

Against Devlin, George maintained that the genuine immorality of an act is a necessary (but not alone sufficient) condition for the legitimacy of its legal prohibition on moral grounds. George conceded that "social cohesion" is a valuable thing and that it may (partly) justify morals laws if the morality it enforces is true; but, George concluded, the truth of a moral norm is a necessary, though itself insufficient, condition for its legal enforcement.

George has long maintained that morals laws are not excluded by any global principle of justice. He wrote in *MMM* that "[i]t is impossible to say in abstraction from a detailed understanding of the circumstances obtaining in a political community whether particular acts reasonably judged to be immoral ought or ought not to be prohibited by the laws of that community."[35] Those "circumstances" include further consideration of relevant moral norms, such as fairness and the overall common good of society, as well as contingent facts about that society, such as whether law enforcement resources would be better expended on more serious crimes; whether non-

33 Devlin, *Enforcement*, as quoted in *MMM*, 63.

34 Ibid., 70.

35 *MMM*, 190.

criminal means of discouraging the vice are available; and whether there is a popular moral consensus in favor of stricter regulation.

In some circumstances persons also enjoy effective civil protection of acts wrong in themselves, a right which is grounded in legitimate aspects of overall well-being. George explains: "The right to privacy, as traditionally understood, is not the substantive right to be legally free to perform certain 'private' acts, the immorality of those acts notwithstanding. It is, rather, the essentially procedural right to be free from governmental and other intrusions into one's home or office or other premises, or into one's files, papers, or other records, unless the government can justify invading private space or reviewing private information by providing powerful reasons."[36]

As to the second: George argued in *MMM* that Aristotle's cardinal error was his monistic perfectionism. According to the philosopher, there is one supremely valuable form of life that is the standard for everyone. George's diagnosis of the fundamental mistake in Aristotle's thought opens up into the foundation of the new classical theory, particularly its identification of many distinct aspects of flourishing, or what the theorists call "basic goods."[37] And, as George writes in the last chapter of *MMM*, readers persuaded by his arguments against the liberal prohibition of morals laws "may fear that a political theory which allows any room for coercive government action to uphold public morals will perforce validate too broad an exercise of coercion."[38]

These diverse and incommensurable goods ground George's invaluable account of "pluralistic perfectionism." Aristotle, George writes, failed to supply anything like an adequate account of why and how there is one uniquely superior form of life, towards which all persons should strive (if they could), and by which metric all would be judged. The great philosopher "plainly failed to allow room in his ethical and political theory for the diversity of irreducible human goods which, considered as providing basic reasons for action and options for choice, are the bases for a vast range of valuable, but mutually incompatible choices, commitments, and plans and ways of life."[39]

In the final chapter of *MMM*, George sketches how "pluralistic perfectionism" is not only compatible with important civil liberties but also how it provides the most excellent reasons for respecting and protecting them. The most important example is religious liberty. We have already considered

36 Ibid., 221.

37 One succinct account of this aspect of the new classical theory is chapters 3–5 of Finnis's *Natural Law and Natural Rights*.

38 *MMM*, 189.

39 Ibid., 38.

George's argument that religious freedom is best grounded in the nature of religion as a voluntary choice to accept the truth of some propositions and to enter into communion with God. Freedom of speech, George also argues, is best grounded in the need for communication among persons, which is "well-nigh indispensable to co-operation; and co-operation is vital to the realization of human goods."[40] In light of the fact that "government officials often have bad motives for restricting" even "valuable forms of speech,"[41] a broadly inclusive definition of protected speech, including some speech which by itself is valueless, is reasonable. Freedom of the press is a "species" of freedom of speech. Government should respect and protect it for the same reasons it respects and protects freedom of speech generally.

V

Civil liberties of speech, press, religion, and the like are today usually grounded in some kind of moral relativism or subjectivism. This common claim usually goes something like this: "Of course persons should be free to pursue what Christians and others might regard as a degraded lifestyle, for who is to judge what is vicious and what is virtuous? Why suppose that any such moral judgments are anything more than emotional reactions to acts which some view as offensive? Our Constitution must be read to prevent conservative believers from imposing their morality upon sexual minorities."

George supplies foundations in moral truth for all of our valuable civil liberties. This ground is neither "their" morality nor "ours." It is a matter of true morality, which is neither "conservative" nor "liberal." George's signal achievement is to synthesize these objective norms with the truth that we must be free to choose in order to flourish. In other words: one might say that the key to understanding what counts as human well-being is to see that it is neither truth nor freedom all the way down. And all together Robert George has supplied a robust defense of freedom under law.

40 Ibid., 195.
41 Ibid., 198.

Index